60

FARRAR
STRAUS
GIROUX

ANNE FISHBEIN

Tom Lutz

DOING NOTHING

Tom Lutz is the author of *Crying: The Natural and Cultural History of Tears*, which *The Washington Post* called "a tour de force of erudition." His other books include *American Nervousness, 1903: An Anecdotal History* and *Cosmopolitan Vistas: American Regionalism and Literary Value*. He lives in Los Angeles.

ALSO BY TOM LUTZ

American Nervousness, 1903: An Anecdotal History
Crying: The Natural and Cultural History of Tears
Cosmopolitan Vistas: American Regionalism and Literary Value

DOING NOTHING

DOING NOTHING

A HISTORY OF LOAFERS, LOUNGERS, SLACKERS,

AND BUMS IN AMERICA

Tom Lutz

FARRAR, STRAUS AND GIROUX

NEW YORK

Farrar, Straus and Giroux
19 Union Square West, New York 10003

Copyright © 2006 by Tom Lutz
All rights reserved
Distributed in Canada by Douglas & McIntyre Ltd.
Printed in the United States of America
Published in 2006 by Farrar, Straus and Giroux
First paperback edition, 2007

The Library of Congress has cataloged the hardcover edition as follows:
Lutz, Tom.
    Doing nothing : a history of loafers, loungers, slackers and bums in
America / Tom Lutz.— 1st ed.
        p.   cm.
    Includes bibliographical references.
    ISBN-13: 978-0-86547-650-9 (hardcover : alk. paper)
    ISBN-10: 0-86547-650-0 (hardcover : alk. paper)
    1. Slackers—United States—History.   2. Laziness—United States—
History.   I. Title.

BJ1498.L88 2006
174—dc22
                                                               2005027230

Paperback ISBN-13: 978-0-86547-737-7
Paperback ISBN-10: 0-86547-737-X

Designed by Debbie Glasserman

www.fsgbooks.com

1   3   5   7   9   10   8   6   4   2

TO MY WRITING PARTNERS,
CODY AND LAURIE,
AND IN MEMORIAM
KEN CMIEL

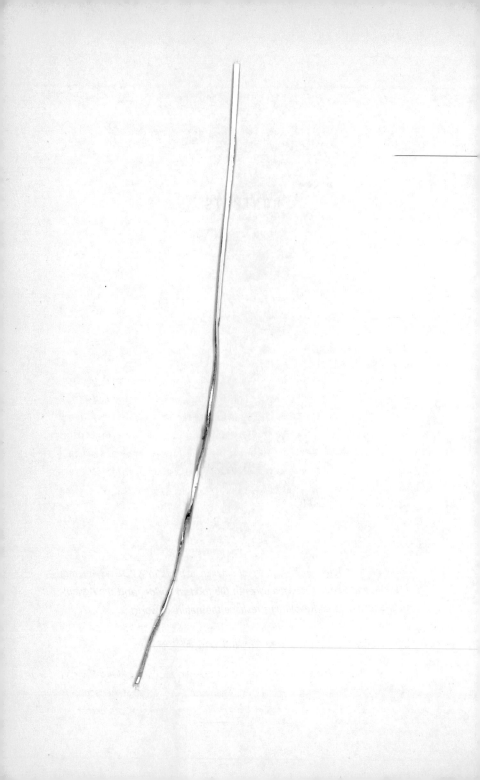

CONTENTS

ACKNOWLEDGMENTS

Paul Mandelbaum and Laurie Winer were ideal readers for the whole and are okay poker players. Leo Braudy, Ken Cmiel, Jay Fliegelman, and Rob Latham helped materially and, I don't know what you call it—spiritually, I guess. Jeffrey Charis-Carlson, Corey Creekmur, Kathleen Diffley, Loren Glass, Cody Lutz, Steve Molton, Angie Nepodal, Laura Rigal, Sean Scanlan, Harry Stecopoulos, Erica Still, Jeffrey Swenson, and Keith Wilhite read large chunks of it, and I thank them for their comments. On the way out the door, thank you to Brooks Landon and Ed Folsom. Melanie Jackson, thank you for everything, and Lorin Stein, you're no slacker, far from it. Jesse and Yarrow: you're my favorite daughters, and I love the way you work.

DOING NOTHING

I

CODY ON THE COUCH

In which the author confronts his son's laziness—and remembers his own, past and present—with comments on welfare queens, workfare, and preemployment testing—the emotional nature of the work ethic—work in the ancient world—Tocqueville, Thoreau, and Whitman on work in America and the trouble with fathers—slacker movies—academic work and other questionable labors—answers to "What makes good work good?" and "What did Jesus do?"—hippies and other dropouts—and the Way of the Slacker.

> "Every man is, or hopes to be, an Idler."
>
> —SAMUEL JOHNSON, *THE IDLER*, APRIL 15, 1758

I began this book shortly after my son, Cody, at the age of eighteen, moved from his mother's house into mine. His plan was to take a year or two off before beginning college, and he had come to Los Angeles with uncertain plans. His older sister had moved out a couple years earlier and had a fairly glamorous Hollywood job, and he thought maybe he could get a foot in that door or, perhaps, end up in a hot new band and become a big (alternative) rock star. Either way, he was coming west, the young man, and I looked forward to having him in the house full-time. For a decade he had lived with me only during summers and vacations, and although ours was by all measures a very good relationship, neither of us knew whether we would feel the same

ratio of success and failure, the same levels of satisfaction and dissatisfaction with each other, if we lived together all of the time. We were
both excited (if a little apprehensive) about this new chapter in our
lives. Whatever else, I was glad that I could give him a base from
which to chase a dream or two.

He knew I had taken time off before college myself. Finishing high
school in 1971 without the vaguest clue as to where my life was
headed, I was saved from the Vietnam draft by a high lottery number.
I spent most of the next decade wandering here and abroad, doing the
period's allotment of drugs (or maybe a little more), and working,
whenever necessary, at whatever presented itself. I spent time as a carpenter, line cook, factory hand, piano tuner, landscaper, gymnastics
instructor, day laborer and odd-jobber, lumberjack, kitchen manager
and caterer, farmhand, contractor, bartender, and musician. I read
Jack Kerouac early in this period and decided I would be a writer,
and so all of these jobs were instantly transformed into grist for that
mill. Kerouac suggested that literature's raw material could be one's
own simple, edgy life, and like many other boys in prolonged adolescence who came under his spell, I became convinced that my self-
absorption and confusion were worthy of commemoration in fiction.

And so I became a writer. Not really; that is, I wasn't actually writing anything, and wouldn't publish my first piece for many years, but
in my own often pot-, speed-, or acid-addled mind I had become a
writer. While hitchhiking around or riding the freight trains, I jotted
down a few desultory (and in retrospect mawkishly sentimental) journal entries, hoping that they would somehow become, without too
much work, novels—novels imbued with what I felt would be a delicious, Dean Moriarty–flavored, but updated, countercultural melancholy. And in the meantime, my search for a vocation, such as it was,
appeared to have ended happily. I was a writer, and my daily life was
effortless research. Every profound revelation I experienced after every
joint I smoked—that is if I could remember it—became part of my
stock-in-trade. I basked in this new sense of purpose and felt, vaguely,
that my place in the larger world was secure.

My escapades never did become novels, but even now, I may as
well sheepishly admit, I think of them as representing some kind of
achievement. Those years of itinerancy and odd-jobbing gave me
something I never could have had if I'd gone straight through college

and graduate school and into the life of teaching and writing I've been living for the last fifteen years. I'm glad to know how to sweat copper piping, wire a three-way switch, and bale hay, how to feed five hundred people lunch and use an oxyacetylene torch and a chain saw. I feel I know, in fact, what people mean when they talk about "the value of work." I loved the days spent rounding up cattle and moving them to fresh pasture in the Midwest, and the bizarre nights spent with those adventurous or oblivious people who pick up young freaks hitchhiking down the coast of California, or who befriend strangers they find wandering through the lonesome towns of the Great Plains. I'm grateful for the time I spent playing music in low-rent bar bands, glad that I rode the rails from Tennessee to California, from Denver to Pittsburgh, that I lived in a van on the Costa Brava, rode a motorbike through the hills of Montenegro, and choked on mosquito coils in a Thai beach hut.

And so I was pleased that Cody, instead of just following the crowd into college, was taking a more adventurous path. "Anyone can float along with the tide," my father used to say. "Even a dead dog can do it." In a classic case of parenting gone awry, my father said this hoping it would help me resist the peer pressure to drink, smoke cigarettes and pot, have premarital sex, and otherwise imitate Kerouac in the ever-swifter currents of the late 1960s. I adopted it as the moral under-pinning for my rejection of everything else he ever said.

∞

That was a different era, of course, and circa 1970 most people I knew considered rebelling against one's parents no more than a sign that one wasn't brain-dead. Times have changed, and Cody's desire to live with me in the year 2001 was no more exceptional than my mad flight from my parents thirty years earlier. So imagine my chagrin when, soon into our new life together, something that looked very much like a generation gap appeared. The first couple of days, when I came up from my basement study for a cup of coffee to see him lying on the couch and watching TV, I didn't think much of it. He had only just got here; tomorrow or the next day was soon enough to start respond-ing to the "Bassist Wanted" ads in the local rags and looking for a job. Eventually, though, I asked him, as he ate his cereal watching TV circa 11:00 a.m., what his plans for the day were, and he said, eyes to the screen, that he was going to finish getting his résumé together. Fine, I thought. Shouldn't take long: "I went to high school" would cover most of it. I'm going to the library, I told him, so my computer is free. I came back six or seven hours later. He was watching cartoons. He seemed slightly surprised by my question about his C.V. "Oh, yeah," he said. "It's almost ready for you to proofread for me."

This went on for days. I would come back from the library or a meeting, and he would be there, like an Edwardian neurasthenic, dourly contemplating the world around him from the comfort of a plush purple sofa. Had my son become a slacker? Was this the person he actually was? Hanging out in the summer or on weekends doing nothing was one thing, and obviously I had seen him do his share of that, but this wasn't the summer; this wasn't the weekend—this ain't no disco! Didn't the kid have any get-up-and-go? Life is short! Let's move it! The first Monday night, I asked if he wanted to come to the local club, where I played in the house band, and meet some musicians, since it was jam night. No, not really, he said, switching channels; maybe next week. The chances he would find simpatico musicians in my middle-aged blues scene were fairly slight, since his high school band had been heavy funk-metal-alternative. But it was *something* to do. You sure? Yeah, he said. Have fun. I'll see you tomorrow.

Of course, I thought as I drove to the bar, of course you'll see me tomorrow, because you'll be right there on the couch. I knew that I shouldn't be getting upset, that it was possible to see such lying about as part of a perfectly valid regenerative process, a kind of temporary moratorium as he adjusted to life after high school. He did, after all, have a lot of adjustments to make: to life in the big city after his adolescence in rural New England, without the community of friends and family he had left behind on the other coast, to a life without clear paths or plans, to life with his father. But at this moment I couldn't focus for very long on what his burdens might be. I couldn't focus because, I realized with a shock, I was too angry.

That was the biggest surprise. Having grown up dodging the sudden furies of my temperamental father, I began my career as a parent determined not to direct my own ready anger at my kids, and I had almost entirely succeeded. I could get fleetingly peeved, of course, in all the classic ways, at chores undone or other daily disappointments, but

I never indulged it, never blew up at them, never really boiled over. So I was shocked to learn that the sight of my son lying on the couch day after day made me furious.

It was a visceral, total reaction. The minute I walked in the door or came up from my office downstairs, my face flushed, my heart pumped up, my body flooded with adrenaline. I would turn around, go into the kitchen, and tap my fingers on the tile counter, or go back down to my office, sit down, cool down. My father's anger always seemed to propel him to action, sometimes violent action, but mine confused and stymied me. I couldn't seem to stop it from happening, didn't understand it, and just hoped I was hiding it fairly well.

Why this anger? So what if he was wasting time? One could argue that all of my time before college had been wasted—an argument my own father had in fact made—and by any measure I had, in fact, squandered an enormous amount of time. If anyone was able to understand my son's temporary incapacity, then, it should have been me. I kept telling myself that it was a different world then, more fat on the land, more utopia in the air, more second chances waiting in the wings, but however many times I said it, I couldn't convince myself that this was why I was so angry. When I had imagined Cody taking advantage of a year or two off before college, I always saw him doing something exciting, challenging, and worthwhile. He had recorded two CDs with his high school band, and L.A. was the perfect place to try his kind of music. One of his musical heroes, Flea, lived in our neighborhood; Beck was right around the corner; alternative music clubs like the Silverlake Lounge and Spaceland were down the street. He had shown a bit of a flair for narrative even in grade school and had done some playing around with a video camera, which was one reason he talked of following his older sister into the film world, a world in which his youth was an asset. He had always been an avid outdoorsman, fly-fishing, mountain biking, and camping even deep into the winter. This was California, damn it; opportunities for outdoor adventure were everywhere.

Confining his adventures to the couch was obviously not what I had in mind, but still, why did it make me so crazy? If he was stretched out on the sofa at the age of thirty-five, obviously I'd have a case, but the kid was only eighteen.

I started to write this book at least in part to understand my ire as I watched my son do what I had seen him (and myself) do many times before: he was doing nothing. In my forties, I necessarily had a more acute sense of the shortness of life, but why should he? He was still husbanding the proceeds of his summer job on an organic farm in Massachusetts, not hitting me up for spending money. He was the one at the classically hormonal age, so why were mine firing?

The answer, I began to sense, had to do with my own twisted relation to work, a pathology that I share with many people of both my own and my father's and my son's generations. I came of age during one famous generational rebellion against the work ethic, and Cody came of age during another. When he was an impressionable eleven and fourteen, the two films that helped define the slacker in the 1990s came out—Richard Linklater's *Slacker* (1991) and Kevin Smith's *Clerks* (1994). These films took as their informing ethos the idea that work was worthless, depressing, and unredemptive. Cody says that Kevin Smith's films, when he was growing up, seemed to him amateurish, and he can't remember even noticing that the work ethic was up for discussion. He watched *Slacker* with his older sister and got bored. But he was a fan of *Wayne's World* (1992), about a slacker who lives with his parents after he has graduated; and he and his sisters wore out a tape of *Ferris Bueller's Day Off* (1986), a high school slacker film that they could recite in its entirety. Cody thought at the time, he says, that "Ferris was the coolest."

These comedies also capture the anger that slacking provokes. The clerks' girlfriends get angry at them, their customers get angry at them, the other slackers get angry at them, they get angry at each other. Ferris's sister is furious with him, his parents perturbed, his best friend pissed off. The emotional history of slackerdom runs the gamut from the tragic to the farcical, but of all the feelings it evokes—pride, frustration, boredom, anxiety, hilarity—anger, I have come to find, is one of the most common.

∞

Anger at slackers, for instance, has fueled the assault on the welfare state these past dozen or so years. On one side is the fury at the "welfare queens," who, we've heard and read, are vampiric layabouts sucking the lifeblood out of honest, hardworking taxpayers. John Ashcroft, when he was senator from Missouri in 1995, gave a speech to the Heritage Foundation in which he told several horror stories, including this one about a five-month-old girl named Ariel Hill:

> She was born on Christmas Eve 1992 and killed in May of 1993. She lived with her twenty-two-year-old mother and father and four other siblings in a squalid one-bedroom apartment in public housing. The family's principal source of income was welfare. One day, her mother grew tired of her screaming, placed her in a sink, and burned her with hot water. She had not been fed in days. She died weighing less than seven pounds. When investigators examined the apartment they found a scrap of paper with each child's name on it and the dollar amount that they were worth on welfare. A life reduced to the dollar amount of a welfare check.

Now there is a story that could make a person angry—angry, for instance, at an economic system that can produce such tragedies, angered by the lack of education, opportunity, support, and community that might foster such dire deeds. This is not what made Ashcroft angry, however.

What made Ashcroft angry was that this woman, he believed, had babies simply to increase her welfare check, one of the classic myths that demagogues have tapped into over the last half century to foment protest against the welfare system. From George Wallace's attack on "welfare loafers" to Lester Maddox's claim that the Aid to Dependent Children program was "a reward for promiscuity" to Newt Gingrich's claim that the welfare state taught children "not to work, not to acquire property, not to learn to read and write and to wait around for that welfare check," the welfare recipient has been damned as just pure lazy. Entitlement programs, from this irate perspective, are over-entitlement programs. To take just one sample from the many Listservs and blogs that have had welfare cheats as their bugbear:

> Twenty or more years of welfare has proven it does not work. What works is work . . . hard work. So, get off the pitty pot and get a job, all you welfare loafers. Quit moaning and expecting me and others who do work to support you with our tax dollars. Earn your own damn money the hard way, just like I do. Get a job! I'm mad as hell!

This kind of anger was mobilized in the legislative battles at the state and federal level that brought in a host of "workfare" and "earnfare" programs, what Bill Clinton called the "end of welfare as we know it" in the 1990s.

Clinton used this last phrase to usher in what is most commonly referred to as the welfare reform legislation of 1996, the actual bill being the Personal Responsibility and Work Opportunity Reconciliation Act of 1996, a title that really does get at the heart of the matter: work, in America, is not simply an opportunity; it is our personal responsibility, perhaps our prime moral imperative. In the late 1970s people would get angry if anyone suggested that a woman at home with children was "not working." She was not getting paid, perhaps, but her work was never done, the feminists and the traditionalists agreed. By the 1990s the workfare debate suggested the opposite, that a woman at home with several young children, if she was on public assistance, was a cheat and a slacker, and she needed to get out of the house and work, even if it meant serving fast food, in order to have self-respect and be a proper role model for her kids. (The other side in this debate was, and is, angry at the lack of compassion, the lack of historical perspective, and the heartless political manipulation involved in dismantling the welfare system, a system that was built in response to the woeful poverty of the 1930s and expanded in the War on Poverty in the 1960s. Senator Daniel Patrick Moynihan called the 1996 act "the most brutal act of social policy since Reconstruction. Those involved will take this disgrace to their graves.")

Workfare, in which people are denied access to the "safety net" of social programs if they can't prove they work at a job, is a clear indication of how conflicted our beliefs about work are. We insist that everyone work, despite the latest study showing that workfare is bad for families—increasing adolescent crime and decreasing school performance—despite the fact that we know the jobs available to most people at the bottom of the economy will not provide a living wage, and despite the entrenched resistance (from the same political quarters) to raising the minimum wage. Most people, even many who push such legislation, suspect that these low-end jobs are not worth doing, much less vehicles for self-fulfillment or moral growth. The Generation X author most closely associated with the figure of the slacker, Douglas Coupland, calls them McJobs, and they are, for the population lucky enough not to have them, the prototypical signs of career failure. "Would you like fries with that?" is a punch line only when you don't work at Burger King. When, in the film *American Beauty* (1999), a middle-class man in a midlife crisis quits his white-collar job to work a fast-food drive-up window, he is by his own ac-count "happier," but we understand that his is in part a hyperbolic protest and in part an admission of defeat, as well as the hip film-maker's joke. Tending the automated French fryer has nothing to do with what we mean by work when we talk about the value of work. The workfare proponents and other anti-welfare forces would have us believe, however, that such a job represents virtuous activity when someone else, especially someone unrelated to them, does it. McJobs are much more likely to fuel than to defuse class rage, much more likely to teach people the futility than the value of work.

The "value of work" is, under some descriptions, a contradictory phrase. Work, as opposed to play or leisure or other activities, is pre-cisely that which is done not as an end, but as a means: we can play basketball, but if we are in the NBA, it is work; we can cultivate our gardens as a form of relaxation, but for the immigrant gardeners of Los Angeles, it is work. On both sides of these equations, the activity may be found pleasurable, and on both sides there is some inevitable pain or dissatisfaction. But even if professional gardeners or basketball play-ers love the activity, they don't necessarily love that part of it which is work. Framing any particular activity as a means, as a livelihood or ob-ligation, might enhance or might degrade it (think of the differences among labels like *professional artist*, *sex worker*, or *professional stu-dent*), but as John Locke said in 1706, "Labour for Labour's sake is against nature," or in Jeremy Bentham's words a century later, "taken in its proper sense, *love of labour* is a contradiction in terms." We can love the activity that brings in our paycheck, we may feel lucky that we get to play basketball for a living, but we love the game and the money, not the *work*.

In fact, when basketball or reading novels or traveling becomes work, it can involve a precipitous loss of pleasure. We all can under-stand that work might have its own pleasures, but that is a different matter. Take the case of Hollywood, where people work all the time, constantly, even though many don't seem to actually *work* more than a couple of months a year. The forced resignation of the president of

Portland Community College

the Writers Guild of America a couple years ago, after it was found that she had not produced enough work to be an active member of the guild (which requires one ninety-minute script every three years), is one piece of evidence for how intermittent Hollywood work can be. Chuck Slocum of the WGA says that in any given year, 50 percent of the writers in the guild get paid for their work. In Screen Actors Guild elections, 75 to 80 percent of the votes are cast by actors earning less than $2,000 a year, which is less than a week's work at SAG rates. Of course there is endless unpaid work that many of these people do. Screenwriters write and pitch for years without making a sale, and actors read, audition, and train, all off the books. Part of the work in Hollywood is going to see a lot of films, of course, and watching a lot of TV, and getting massaged and facialed and depilated and mudbathed and hotspringed and colonicized, and going to premieres and parties and lunches and dinners and breakfasts. This is especially true for those who have already made it, but even poor aspirants, every day going deeper into credit card debt, consider these important work activities. Most of it, of course, looks a lot like lounging or pampering or, in fact, doing nothing. Many will tell you grimly, though, that it feels like nothing but work.

Whenever we imagine a welfare mother or a workfare mother hearing such talk, we can understand the kind of anger that surrounds issues of work and leisure, even the smoldering envy we might associate with revolution. Just as often, though, it can seem the stuff of dark comedy. Imagine a workfare mother taking on a job as a nanny, not for a rich person, but for another workfare mother, and at the same time hiring her employer as a nanny for her own children at exactly the same rate she is getting paid, so that they both have child care except during their mutual half-hour commute by bus twice a day. They would both break even, except for the bus fare and the taxes each would pay, taxes that could support, oh, some corporate welfare scheme, say ethanol manufacture or, better, some Halliburton contract—and we can see that even in dire cases there is something potentially, if very darkly, farcical.

In relation to my son, I was failing to appreciate the ironies, but the more research I did into the history of slackers, the more it became apparent that the slacker was a deeply ironic figure. Despite the anger he or she can elicit in relatives or in political discourse, the slacker appears in print and on the screen sometimes as a countercultural hero, sometimes as a dangerous criminal, sometimes as a social pariah, but more often than not over the last 250 years—*Slacker* and *Clerks* are comedies, after all—the slacker has been a figure of fun, a character in a cultural farce. The anger and the comedy are two sides of the same unearned coin, as the famous comedy duos all knew—Abbott getting mad at Costello, Hardy getting mad at Laurel, Burns mad at Allen, Crosby mad at Hope, Martin mad at Lewis, often, of course, because they didn't do the work they were supposed to do.

∞

The slacker has been around only for the last two and a half centuries: he (and until recently it was always "he") is a fairly recent figure, and "slacker" is an even more recent word. "Slack" had been around since Old English variants, as a physical property of objects like ropes. And in the seventeenth century "slacken" became a common way to denote a relaxation of activity. By the nineteenth century, a "slack" could mean a slowing or lull in business. But 1898 is the earliest instance of "slacker" in anything like its modern sense—in the OED, when it began to replace some earlier epithets for people not pulling their loads. In 1909, in H. G. Wells's novel *The History of Mr. Polly*, we get a picture of the slacker that is very much like that of our own, except that Mr. Polly refuses to wear the badge proudly:

> He could not grasp what was wrong with him. He made enormous efforts to diagnose his case. Was he really just a "lazy slacker" who ought to "buck up"? He couldn't find it in him to believe it. He blamed his father a good deal—it is what fathers are for—in putting him to a trade he wasn't happy to follow, but he found it impossible to say what he ought to have followed.

It is no accident that Mr. Polly blamed his father, by the way, just as my anger was precisely because it was *my* son on the couch. Throughout the history of slackerhood, as we will see, fathers and sons have either worked out or failed to work out the conflicts at the center of the culture of work.

It wasn't until World War I that the word came into common usage, when it was used to mean someone who dodged military service.

(Not entirely coincidentally, "beat" and "deadbeat" were also first used, during the Civil War, as slang terms for deserter.) The popular magazines during the Great War were full of stories like "A Slacker with a Soul," and recruiting posters asked "Are You a Slacker? If Not, Enlist." Only in the late 1980s and early 1990s did "slacker" become what it is today, the widely used term for someone with a distaste for work, an identity that can be conferred or claimed, however ironically. Something very much like the slacker, however, has been around since the middle of the eighteenth century, when some young men proudly called themselves idlers and, later in the century, loungers. In the nineteenth century there were loafers. Like slacker, these names could be used as insults or adopted proudly as a protest against the way things were.

A disinclination to work is as old as work itself, as far as we can tell, certainly as old as any extant texts we have on the subject. But the slacker and his forebears, the loafer, lounger, and idler, are a bit different. Before the Industrial Revolution, the slacker as an identity, as a kind of person, did not exist. In ancient Greek, Roman, and Middle Eastern civilizations, work was by and large considered a curse, accorded dignity only to the extent that it made possible the *vita contemplativa*, the higher life of the mind. Labor had no honor in and of itself, and certainly no enthronement among the virtues. Hannah Arendt, who has written some of the most important philosophical ruminations on work, argues that when you think about the modern work ethic, "you are immediately aware that its most important feature . . . is its glorification of labor, surely the last thing any member of one of the classical communities, be it Rome or Greece, would have thought of as worthy of this position." Antipathy toward labor, we might even say, has been the norm since the beginning of time: in Genesis, when God expels Adam and Eve from Paradise, he does so with a host of curses, damning Eve to experience pain in childbirth and subjugation to her husband, and he damns both of them to a life of labor, saying, "In the sweat of thy face shalt thou eat bread." The necessity to work for survival is thus, in the Judeo-Christian tradition, the original curse, the punishment for the original sin. What distinguished gods from men in ancient Greek culture is that the gods were "remote from toil and misery," wrote Hesiod, who despaired that he could not live in the golden age but was cursed to live in his own fallen age of iron, never ceasing to toil "from day or night, in constant distress." Work, in classical culture, was the curse of mortals in a fallen world, the province of slaves, or punishment for decadence or debt. There was no work ethic as we know it, only forms of coercion. What the bondsman thought of his labor, what the servant thought of hers, we cannot know: they have left little record, owing to their own illiteracy and to the fact that the literate tended to find the experience of slaves and servants not worth consideration. For Aristotle, such workers are merely "human tools," some of which are sharper or more efficient than others. They can only do the work, as Plato suggests in *The Republic*, for which they are fit, while "citizens" are fit for higher things.

There are a few proverbs in the Old Testament against sloth and sluggardliness, but there, too, labor is primarily a blight and a bother, a necessity, and at best a duty. Work was never an occasion for establishing self-worth or self-love, never a source of pure satisfaction. Paul's epistles in the New Testament have, to our ears, a recognizably moralistic ring—"if any would not work, neither should he eat," he writes to the Thessalonians—and thousands of Sunday sermons have suggested that this represents a significant change from God's curse in Genesis, that Paul is the first spokesperson for the value of work. But Paul is still insisting on work as above all an obligation. The internalized work ethic counseled by later sermonizers would not appear until the Protestant Reformation. Until then, work remained compulsion, a way to avoid the devil's snares, or at best duty; it was primarily a diminishment rather than an expression of human being. Thus there could be no slackers in the modern sense—people whose identity involved their refusal to believe in the value of work—because everyone, in a way, was already against work. Everyone, we might say, was a slacker. Someone like Falstaff, in Shakespeare's *Henry IV*, might seem to have the kind of comic rejection of work we see among modern slackers, as we are introduced to him with a joke about his not needing to know what time it is. Purse-taking, he declares, making fun of the Puritan ethic, is his vocation, and " 't is no sin for a man to labor in his vocation." But Falstaff's sloth is a problem because it leads to sin, encouraging him to drunkenness and thievery: idleness is simply the devil's playground. His real problem is that he rejects the notion of honor, not that he doesn't work. The king, his companion in dissolution at the beginning of the plays, at the end gives Falstaff a "competency," ensuring that he doesn't have to work or steal. The king will give him more—not if he works, but if he exhibits "strength and quality," if he lives honorably. Falstaff's and the young prince's rebellion is against duty, not against work. Before work was widely considered a virtue, the idea of someone making an ironic, countercultural virtue of not working was almost unthinkable.

What we know about laziness in previous eras, and indeed what we know about the actual experience of work, is very slight. As Keith Thomas, editor of the *Oxford Book of Work* suggests, we know less about work over the long haul of human history than we know about almost any other essential human activity. Much of what we know about people's attitudes toward their daily lives in earlier periods is gleaned from literary sources, but until the nineteenth century, work was not considered a fit subject for literary representation. Even in Virgil's *Georgics* (29 B.C.E.), which catalog the tools and techniques of "the rustics" and provide advice about how to go about the work ("Be first to dig the ground up, first to clear / And burn the refuse-branches, first to house / Again your vine-poles, last to gather fruit"), plows are represented as digging into the earth without a plower, and the gods are given as much credit as the farmers. Part of Virgil's advice is to enjoy the long, workless winter and not overdo it in the growing season either: "Do thou praise / Broad acres, farm but few." What other small glimpses we get of working lives in literature before that time have little documentary value: we are safe in assuming that actual shepherds lived and loved, for instance, in some fashion other than that of the shepherds of most pastoral poetry.

Henry David Thoreau, himself one of the great mid-nineteenth-century loafers, wrote in an 1854 lecture:

> It is remarkable that there is little or nothing to be remembered written on the subject of getting a living; how to make getting a living not merely holiest and honorable, but altogether inviting and glorious; for if *getting* a living is not so, then living is not. One would think, from looking at literature, that this question had never disturbed a solitary individual's musings. Is it that men are too much disgusted with their experience to speak of it?

Thoreau is most famous, of course, for *Walden* (1854), in which he rails against working for a living and praises the study of nature, a study his neighbors mistake for idleness. Although, in *Walden*, Thoreau details the work he does hoeing beans and otherwise attempting to live a life of self-sufficiency, he writes very little about the other work he performed during his life. He reported to the secretary of his Harvard class in 1847 that he had many occupations: "I am a School master—a Private Tutor, a Surveyor—a Gardener, a Farmer—a Painter, I mean a House Painter, a Carpenter, a Mason, a Day-Laborer, a Pencil-Maker, a Glass-paper Maker, a Writer, and sometimes a Poetaster." He described very little of this in his prose. (He also, as it happens, lived on and off with his father for many years as an adult.)

Even what we have in the way of working-class autobiography, according to John Burnett, who has edited an anthology of such writings, has very little to say about work, almost as if "work . . . was not a central life-interest of the working classes." Worker-diarists were much more interested in transcribing their social and intimate lives than their work lives. Perhaps the lack of choice, the paucity of options made discussing work uninteresting, unremarkable. Perhaps these diarists had simply imbibed their culture's tradition of avoiding the description of work in prose. One has to assume that they had attitudes about it, and in fact, one has to assume that as the Pyramids arose from the Egyptian desert, many different attitudes were distributed among the stonecutters, that some were more and some less engaged by their work, some more and some less averse to the whole project. But there is no existing testimony on either side. By the nineteenth century we begin to get some direct talk, but even here a very incomplete picture emerges. Karl Marx, for instance, produces a lot of documentary evidence about working conditions in nineteenth-century factories but very little actual testimony from workers. We have some reports from parliamentary hearings, images from a few Victorian novelists and poets like Whitman, and we can assume many things—that the terrible conditions speak for themselves, for instance, and that the rise of "working men's federations" and later unions indicate widespread dissatisfaction with working life. But we also know that under the very worst conditions, under chattel slavery, for example, a wide range of attitudes about work is possible, not just because of hierarchies, such as the status of "house" versus "field" slaves in the American South, but within each of those groups as well. And we know that even under the most optimal conditions, in the cushiest niches of government, business, show business, or academia, for instance, different attitudes, different levels of satisfaction and dissatisfaction exist.

How people experience their work and how they talk about it may not be the same thing: just as the slave will censor any statement about work in front of an overseer, so, often, will elite workers. What we say to our coworkers about our work, especially coworkers we plan to rise above or are afraid of sinking below, can be very different from what we might say to our boss, to a prospective employer, to shareholders, or to outsiders, and different again from how we might bitch to a friend or a spouse. Each and every social situation elicits different ways of talking, rendering all testimony about work attitudes more or less unreliable. This is true for any number of areas—drug use or sex, for instance—where there are likely to be negative consequences for honesty: we have little historical documentation, and what we have is suspect.

Anti-work attitudes are unreliable for a more important reason as well. The famous or almost famous idlers, loafers, loungers, and slackers through history had to produce work about not working in order for us to know them. And many of them, it turns out, were closet workaholics or reformed slackers. Anything even approaching uncorrupted firsthand testimony is impossible to find. What we often get is something like my son's inexpressiveness on the matter or, rather, that gap between verbal and gestural expression that young people often find themselves living in. Are we just too lazy, at that age, to bother saying what we might mean? Or is the lack of distance we have on our own activity, and thus the misapprehension about what we are actually up to, that which enables our slacking and at the same time prohibits our articulation of it? At any rate, the testimony of slackers, like that of workers, is and always has been untrustworthy.

We need, then, to tease the meaning of slackerism out of its many disguises and lacunae, if meaning is there to be had. In the film *Slacker*, for instance, which helped cement the word's current meaning, characters represent a wide range of idle lifestyles and a wide range of articulateness, from the most arcane academic jargon-spewing to the monosyllabic. The characters discuss anarchism and nihilism, try to get by selling odd trinkets or playing in bands that don't rehearse, and consider the possibility that life is but a waking dream or the hallucination of aliens. They attack yuppies and the work ethic. As one character says, "Sure I live bad, but I don't have to work at it." Another, asked what he is up to, says he has a band rehearsal in four or five hours, and he's kind of getting ready for that. This is *the* definitive film on the slacker ethos at its height in the early 1990s, but it does not articulate a position on work, and it is not the product of a slacker—writer/director/producer Linklater, at forty-five, has his fifteenth movie in production. What can he really know of it? Real slackers would be, logically, too slack to write their own history. All we have, thus, is a set of images concocted by others, handed down to us in the form of Hogarth's etchings of *Industry and Idleness*, Charlie Chaplin's Little Tramp, Thoreau's self-portrait, Linklater's atmospheric portraits, Ashcroft's polemical cartoons. When I see my son on the couch, it is in the context of these representations of the slacker. He becomes one of these images for me. That, of course, is not really his fault at all.

∞

I was, as I say, far from appreciating such ironies while Cody was on the couch. Marxist cultural critics would have an easy explanation for my anger: they would say that my body was simply showing itself to be an unwitting agent of ideology, my anger literally an embodiment of mainstream cultural values. And they might be right. At least since Tocqueville, foreigners have noted the intensity of the American work ethic, and perhaps I was just mindlessly, bodily enforcing community standards. Tocqueville, after traveling through the states in 1831 and early 1832, congratulated Americans on the way freedom and equality encouraged people to be admirably productive, but he also noted two problems. He warned that the desire for physical gratification—the very desire, he argued, which fuels industriousness in the first place— can take the upper hand, luring people away from work and toward dissipation. And the American dedication to industriousness itself, he thought, might bring on a kind of moral and motivational exhaustion:

> The reproach I address to the principle of equality is not that it leads
> men away in the pursuit of forbidden enjoyments, but that it absorbs

> them wholly in quest of those which are allowed. By these means a
> kind of virtuous materialism may ultimately be established in the
> world, which would not corrupt, but enervate, the soul and noise-
> lessly unbend its springs of action.

Tocqueville thus anticipates Max Weber's critique, in *The Protestant
Ethic and the Spirit of Capitalism* (1905), of the lonely incarceration
people feel in a purely materialistic work ethic.

But can this be right? Surely I wanted more out of life for my son,
not less. I didn't want to enforce some kind of soul-deadening enervation on him. I wanted the opposite.

As did Tocqueville. His double fear—that the work ethic would fail
and that it would be too successful—is complemented by a double
fantasy of free work and free leisure; that is, he imagines America as a
land in which work is freely engaged and fairly remunerated and
which thereby makes possible a life of abundant leisure as well. He
suggests that the thirty-one congressional representatives from the
western states, had they "remained in Connecticut," would have remained common laborers rather than becoming the rich and distinguished gentlemen they are. Their freedom of movement and
opportunity resulted in their advancement and, he suggests, the
leisure that allows them to quit working and dabble in government.
Most rich people in America were once poor, he writes, and thus
"most of those who now enjoy leisure were absorbed in business during their youth." America, therefore, is not what makes this fantasy
possible, but a certain way of being in America; had the western legislators remained in Connecticut, they would not have found either
their true work or their leisure. They would have simply been workers,
stuck, unfree, uninspiring, and unleisured.

Work, in America, has always been thus: the stuff of fear and exuberance, of the highest calling and the lowest degradation. And not
working, doing nothing, has always been the same. In the 1580s
Arthur Barlowe wrote, about Roanoke Island, "The earth bringeth
forth all things in abundance, as in the first creation, without toil or labor"—one of many reports by Europeans suggesting that America was
Eden. Earlier, Columbus reported that all the gold one could want
was there for the picking up and that the islands of the Caribbean
were paradise. The colonizers soon found, of course, that gold needed

to be mined and that agricultural crops did not, in fact, spring unbidden out of the earth. The labor force needed to exploit the economic potential of the colonies was provided, by and large, through bondage: African and sometimes Indian slaves and European indentured servants. A census in 1708 in South Carolina, for instance, showed 3,960 free whites, 120 indentured whites, 4,100 African slaves, and 1,400 Indian slaves. Kingston, Rhode Island, in 1730 had 935 whites, a portion of whom were indentured, 333 African slaves, and 223 Indian slaves. By the time of the American Revolution, more than 60 percent of all European immigrants had arrived as indentured servants. These servants were treated as slaves: in 1756, Elizabeth Sprigs, indentured as a servant in Maryland, wrote to her family in London that she was "toiling Day and Night . . . and then tied up and whipp'd to that Degree that you'd not serve an Animal." Although indentures were for limited terms, after which the servant was free, roughly half of all indentured immigrants in the seventeenth and eighteenth centuries did not outlive their indentures.

A couple of decades after Tocqueville, the great self-proclaimed "loafer" Walt Whitman famously celebrated the hammering of the blacksmith and the scything of the harvester in thrilling, exuberant lines, at the same time singing the praises of loafing, lounging, and idling as the royal road to social and aesthetic pleasure and fulfillment. In "A Song for Occupations," Whitman writes, "In the labor of engines and trades and the labor of fields I find the developments, / And find the eternal meanings. / Workmen and Workwomen!" And then he produces one of his famous catalogs:

> House-building, measuring, sawing the boards,
> Blacksmithing, glass-blowing, nail-making, coopering, tin-roofing,
>   shingle-dressing,
> Ship-joining, dock-building, fish-curing, flagging of sidewalks by
>   flaggers,
> The pump, the pile-driver, the great derrick, the coal-kiln and
>   brickkiln,
> Coal-mines and all that is down there, the lamps in the darkness,
>   echoes, songs, what meditations, what vast native thoughts
>   looking through smutch'd faces,
> Iron-works, forge-fires in the mountains or by river-banks, men

around feeling the melt with huge crowbars, lumps of ore, the due combining of ore, limestone, coal,

The blast-furnace and the puddling-furnace, the loup-lump at the bottom of the melt at last, the rolling-mill, the stumpy bars of pig-iron, the strong clean-shaped trail for railroads,

Oil-works, silk-works, white-lead-works, the sugar-house, steam-saws, the great mills and factories,

Stone-cutting, shapely trimmings for facades or window or door-lintels, the mallet, the tooth-chisel, the jib to protect the thumb,

The calking-iron, the kettle of boiling vault-cement, and the fire under the kettle,

The cotton-bale, the stevedore's hook, the saw and buck of the sawyer, the mould of the moulder, the working-knife of the butcher, the ice-saw, and all the work with ice,

The work and tools of the rigger, grappler, sail-maker, block-maker,

Goods of gutta-percha, papier-maché, colors, brushes, brush-making, glazier's implements,

The veneer and glue-pot, the confectioner's ornaments, the decanter and glasses, the shears and flat-iron,

The awl and knee-strap, the pint measure and quart measure, the counter and stool, the writing-pen of quill or metal, the making of all sorts of edged tools,

The brewery, brewing, the malt, the vats, every thing that is done by brewers, wine-makers, vinegar-makers,

Leather-dressing, coach-making, boiler-making, rope-twisting, distilling, sign-painting, lime-burning, cotton-picking, electroplating, electrotyping, stereotyping,

Stave-machines, planing-machines, reaping-machines, ploughing-machines, thrashing-machines, steam wagons,

The cart of the carman, the omnibus, the ponderous dray,

Pyrotechny, letting off color'd fireworks at night, fancy figures and jets;

Beef on the butcher's stall, the slaughter-house of the butcher, the butcher in his killing-clothes,

The pens of live pork, the killing-hammer, the hog-hook, the scalder's tub, gutting, the cutter's cleaver, the packer's maul, and the plenteous winterwork of pork-packing,

> *Flour-works, grinding of wheat, rye, maize, rice, the barrels and the*
> *   half and quarter barrels, the loaded barges, the high piles on*
> *   wharves and levees,*
> *The men and the work of the men on ferries, railroads, coasters, fish-*
> *   boats, canals; . . .*
> *In them the development good—in them all themes, hints,*
> *   possibilities.*

An exhaustive and exhausting list, but one that, in its very excess, suggests the overemphasis on work that has been central to American culture since the beginning.

At least as often, however, Whitman extols *not* working. "I loafe and invite my soul," Whitman writes at the start of "Song of Myself": "I lean and loafe at my ease observing a spear of summer grass." At the beginning of his career, in a newspaper piece in 1840, he wrote "I have sometimes amused myself with picturing a nation of loafers . . . Only think of it! an entire loafer kingdom! Adam was a loafer, and so were all the philosophers." More than forty years later he described his book *Specimen Days* (1882) as "a mélange of loafing, looking, hobbling, sitting, traveling—a little thinking thrown in for salt, but very little." Whitman loved work, and Whitman loved loafing. Even though he obviously managed to accomplish an enormous amount of work in his life (he started working as an office boy at the age of eleven), his family was often enraged at his loafing, even at his writing about loafing. His father tried to get him to work on the family farm, but his son refused. Walter Whitman Sr., thought by some to be the model for the angry drunkard in Whitman's temperance novel, *Franklin Evans* (1842), died in 1855, perhaps enabling the launch of Whitman's poetic career; it was, at any rate, the year *Leaves of Grass* was first published.

My anger at my loafing son, however much it might have been directed by my own internalized work ethic, was also a desire that he experience some kind of Whitmanian loafing exuberance. The couch just seemed like inertia, not the kind of loafing to which one invites one's soul. I would have been happy to have him a penniless hardcore bass player, playing music I didn't really care for and losing money at it. I would have been happy to find him unemployed, huddled over a screenplay or filming a spear of summer grass. Or at least I told myself I would have been.

Whatever the mix of complex, contradictory motives driving me, my anger, like that of my father and Whitman's father, was evidence that our understanding of work, our relation to work, is always emotional. As the organizational psychologists and the cultural studies scholars tell us, the work ethic is not so much a set of ideas and beliefs as a description of what we *feel* about work, whether we think about the work ethic as such or not. And it is not just poets and fathers who feel these things strongly. The language of feelings saturates much of our talk about work—we love our job, we hate our job, we thank God for Fridays, we are blue on Mondays. We are proud of our work, happy with it, frustrated by it, excited or bored. Even the less obviously emotional attitudes, like satisfaction and fulfillment, are imbued with sentiment. The *feeling* of accomplishment is what we look for, even more than accomplishment itself. The work ethic, like any ethic considered analytically, can seem to be a kind of disembodied abstraction, an ethos rather than pathos. But the work ethic is something that, except when we are thinking about ideology or social policy, we feel. We experience the work ethic as a feeling.

This would explain both my son's depressive boredom on the couch and my anger as a response: work ethics result in complex emotions. Contemporary social scientists who attempt to assess people's work ethics use batteries of tests that essentially interview subjects about their feelings. One study isolated sixty-three "affective work competencies" that combine to make an individual's work ethic. "Affective work competency," besides being a classic form of social scientific tin-earism, doesn't quite get at the full range of what we might call the emotional life of work. Nor does the growing industry of "preemployment testing," which sells interview packages designed to suss out employees' work ethics, and which also assumes the emotional nature of the work ethic: "If you got credit for work someone else had done," such a test asks, "how would that make you feel?" Followed by similar questions: "If everyone stayed until five, and you got to go home at four, how would that make you feel?" The score on the test is based on whether the applicant has the right feelings about work-related situations. The assumption is that one's feelings about work *are* one's work ethic. Despite the obvious incentive to cheat, the test companies claim that they do a verifiable sorting job, that people's true feelings will out, and that those feelings will predict how diligently a worker will perform. And so it should perhaps be no surprise that when the work ethic is thwarted, ignored, resisted, or subverted, some-thing emerges that can look a lot like emotional illness, like neurosis, depression, neurasthenia, or an affective disorder.

From the slacker perspective, of course, the classic work ethic itself is a kind of emotional derangement, and loafing is the cure. The flip side of slacker melancholy is slacker glee, the delightful, entertaining insouciance of Chaplain's tramp, twirling his cane, whistling, be-mused. This is one reason the slacker can make us, when we aren't angry, unaccountably happy. Slackers represent an affront to our fun-damental beliefs about our lives and duties and thus can occasion everything from the church giggles to rage, from fear to exuberant de-light. We can feel attacked or ashamed, insulted or amused, repulsed or enticed.

∞

Philosophers have danced around the work ethic's emotional core, but never quite addressed it. Hannah Arendt, for instance, notes that all European and many other languages make a distinction between work and labor, that labor is associated with efforts of the whole body, while work is associated with efforts primarily of the hands, just as many of these languages also use "labor" to refer to the pains of child-birth. Arendt offers a third category, "action" (as in "political action"), which she clearly finds the most satisfying kind of effort. Labor is pain, "toil and trouble"; work can give an "inevitably brief spell of joy"; and she quotes Dante to the effect that "delight necessarily follows" action. Although hers is clearly set up as a simple set of analytic distinctions, she can make those distinctions only through reference to pain and satisfaction—in other words, to feelings.

Arendt's main argument, though, gets at the nub of the problem. Freedom from labor was once considered a necessary condition for art, science, philosophy, and politics, she writes, and it was understood that such activity was the province of a privileged few. The modern age's glorification of labor has resulted in what she calls a "laboring so-ciety," in which everyone, theoretically, has a job. Artists, presidents, ministers, priests, and philosophers think of themselves as doing jobs necessary to society, whereas in earlier eras philosophers and kings had not only a less mercenary, but a less instrumentalist view of their activity, and therefore a wider purview, a more capacious sense of their engagements. To reduce all human activity to a form of labor, Arendt suggests, is to belittle human creative possibility.

This, in fact, might hold another key to my anger at my son's apparent slackerhood. Perhaps I was feeling the kind of anger that results from shame—shame that maybe I had, after all, been duped. Maybe I had known better when I was my son's age, before I had become part of this laboring society and fully accepted my place in it. Maybe the artists and beachcombers and communards and dropouts were right, that life held more mystery, more possibility, more beauty than could be grasped from an existence dominated by narrowly conceived quotidian labors. What was I doing all wrapped up in my career? Wasn't I supposed to write a novel, after all? Did I trade that dream for a mess of potage?

Max Weber, coming at the problem from a different direction, felt that by the beginning of the twentieth century the work ethic had gone from enabling human activity to becoming an "iron cage." It is significant that Weber, having trouble finishing his famous book, found the inspiration for this final, dark understanding of the Protestant ethic only after visiting the United States, in 1904. "The Puritan wanted to work in a calling," Weber wrote upon returning home to Germany. "We are forced to." Perhaps my sneaking suspicion that I had been involuntarily imprisoned by the work ethic—and aren't we all capable of such a suspicion?—perhaps that suspicion, shame or no shame, just pissed me off. Weber, who nicknamed the "Protestant ethic," traces its origins in the writings of Luther, Calvin, Baxter, and other religious thinkers in the sixteenth and seventeenth centuries, and at the center of his reading is the notion of the "calling," a basic life task, a chosen field of endeavor ordained, according to Luther, et al., by God. What slackers sometimes lack, what my son seemed to lack, was precisely such a calling. And just as the slacker is a relatively recent cultural innovation, so is the notion of a calling: as Weber noted, it does not exist in antiquity or in Catholic theology, but is a product of the Protestant Reformation.

What was new in the Reformation's notion of the calling was that one's lifework became "the highest form which the moral activity of the individual could assume." And Calvin's wrinkle was to argue that, since salvation and damnation were preordained, the elect, the saved, would feel the call of God in their worldly lives and therefore would work successfully in their various callings. God's will, according to Calvin's writings and their elaboration after his death, was absolute, and nothing an individual might desire or do could change it. What necessarily follows is that those who were successful in their worldly endeavors were so through divine will, while those who were unsuccessful were clearly damned. In Weber's reading, Calvinism was a purely rational, unmystical, unmagical religion in which God was omnipotent and people were powerless. Some were bound for eternal bliss and some for eternal hellfire, their lives on earth logically demonstrating which group they belonged to: God backed the winners. "In its extreme inhumanity," Weber writes in one of his many bursts of near poetry, "this doctrine must above all have had one consequence for the life of a generation which surrendered to its magnificent consistency. That was a feeling of unprecedented inner loneliness." Such loneliness, Weber felt, not unlike lying on a couch, alone, day in and day out, was the fate of mankind in a rationally predetermined world, a world in which nothing one did could help solve the basic existential dilemmas or interrupt the unfolding of one's own ultimate fate. If one is to be so fundamentally alienated, the slacker has continually asked the culture over the last centuries, why not relax? Why bother? If whatever we do leads to the wasteland, why not just sit tight, do nothing?

∞

"My father always called me a useless article," Chris Davis tells me, driving through Bristol, England. "He said it in a rather nice way, of course." In the midst of my research I had come up to Bristol from London to meet Davis, and he picked me up at the train station in a tiny, beat-up old sedan that was perhaps once green. I had seen his posts on whywork.org and references to his very elaborate Web site, idletheory.com, in which he lays out his general theory of idleness, a theory that accounts for all phenomena in the universe—physical, biological, social—in terms of idling. He is a slight man, maybe 150 pounds, in jeans, a faded GALICIA T-shirt, and blue Windbreaker, topped by a well-worn blue canvas cap. His greenish-gray eyes are the only large things about him, and they beam out of a face that begins wide and tapers into not much of a chin. A slight sag here and there announces that he has perhaps passed fifty, but there isn't much evidence otherwise. He drives us to a pub, the George, just past the edge of town. "I spend an enormous amount of time in pubs just like this," he says. He doesn't lock the car, and given its sorry state, one can see the wisdom in not making that particular effort. The pub is surrounded by cornfields and stone walls, and except for the cars going past on the macadam, there isn't much trace of the last few hundred years.

Inside, we order a couple of pints and some lunch, which he is glad, he says, to let me buy. I make the mistake of ordering the hare, and all the old saws about British cooking waft through my head as I choke down the brown glop, liberally strewn with shattered bone. "I spend a fair amount of time just listening in at places like this," Davis says. "One thing you never hear people say is, 'Gee, I can't wait to get back to work.' They are all complaining about it." Davis has spent time as an architect and as a graduate student and university researcher, but now he gets by with a little freelance computer programming. This requires a small amount of very intense activity for a fairly short amount of time. "And then I just bunk off," he says. Working as an architect one day, he was extremely bored. He looked down at his watch, and it said 2:13. I'm going to be here for another three hours, he thought, and I don't want to do anything. He looked at his watch. It was still 2:13. He waited for what seemed a long time—still 2:13. He thought, I am so bored time has stopped. He quit. Now most of his time is his own. "I don't get up until eleven in the morning," he says. "And I don't feel guilty about it."

Davis was one of the early mainstays of whywork.org, where his essays on idleness are often referred to by those who take part in that site's ongoing Web forum. The two main organizers of whywork.org were D. J. Swanson, founder of CLAWS, an acronym for Creating Livable Alternatives to Wage Slavery, who lives in British Columbia, and Sarah Nelson, like Davis from Bristol and founder of something called the Leisure Party. I ask Davis if that is an actual political party. He laughs. "No. Nobody would ever be that energetic!" The whywork forum usually has a number of people on the verge of dropping out of wage slavery who are looking for advice from people who have already made the plunge. It doesn't really interest Davis that much. "CLAWS is practical," he says. "For people who don't like their jobs, their bosses. I don't have this problem." He is, instead, interested in theory.

"Idle theory" is at one level quite simple. "All living creatures have to work to stay alive. Some have to work harder than others. Those creatures that need do little work to stay alive are more likely to survive periods of difficulty than those that must work harder and longer." Evolution is thus based, Davis writes on his site, on the "survival of the idlest." This makes a kind of immediate sense. The more perfectly adapted to its environment, the less an organism would need to struggle. The organisms that are struggling are by definition having trouble with their environment. Human beings have, over their history, gradually struggled less. They have developed tools that speed up the work needed to fulfill basic needs for food, clothing, and shelter. A knife cuts faster than teeth; a bag or bucket carries more than hands can. This results in a net increase of idle time, time that people can spend in pursuits other than self-maintenance. "It is in this idle time that humans can do as they wish, rather than as they must, and they can think, talk, and play—i.e., act as free moral agents. In idle theory, humans are seen as part-time free moral agents, only free to the extent that they are idle." And idleness is therefore the base of all ethical systems as well. Why is it unethical to steal? Because it decreases the idle time of another, who must now replace that object with more work. Everything that increases idle time is ethically good; everything that decreases it is bad. "The meek shall inherit the earth" is one of the many biblical aphorisms in favor of idleness, Christ's "lilies of the field" speech another. Davis finds the prejudice toward idleness in systems of etiquette as well. If two people are walking through a narrow tunnel wide enough for only one, who backs out? The person closest to his entrance: the option requiring the least effort is the polite solution. Why do we give our seats on the bus to older people? It requires more effort for them to stand.

"We're still dominated by a small group of thinkers—Marx, Freud, Darwin," Davis tells me between chips. "Freud isn't what he was twenty-five years ago, but Darwin! I just love taking shots at Darwin." Why? "Because he sees nature as a war. This idea has permeated our whole society, and it's profoundly destructive, divisive, not just because it's racist—and he is racist—but because the culture is permeated by the idea that skirmishing for survival is natural. The idea is a menace! War is the opposite of everything I'm trying to get to." The biological sections of Davis's theory quickly exceed my ability to follow the mathematical models and cellular explanations, but the general point is clear enough: even at the most primitive level, organisms tend toward idleness. "Just as Freud brought sex to the fore, I'd like to make leisure, idleness, more important. The twentieth century was sex. I'd like the twenty-first to be leisure."

We have another pint. "It's very interesting to actually talk to someone about all this," he says. He had written a long essay on idleness at the university, but it wasn't written very well, he thinks; the couple of people who read it mistook it for a labor theory of value in the Marxian sense. One friend dismissed it with "you and your stupid ideas!" Davis used to wake up thinking he was crazy. After all, why should he have found this key if the world's most renowned thinkers hadn't, while other revered figures, like Darwin, held the opposite view? The more he looked, though, the more he was convinced, and the more he found support among other philosophers and scientists, such as Maupertuis, Leibniz, Euler, Fermat, and Feynman. "I'm a dreamer, and idle theory is the deepest dream I've ever had. It's my El Dorado, like a city I've discovered."

He wrote the main essays in a burst of activity and added essays on politics, aesthetics, economics, the fossil record, Java and Tetra computer simulations of the biological data, and much more. "Yes, you're right. For someone who believes in idle theory, I've been quite busy," he says, smiling. "The theory's like a tree. It grows up; it branches out a bit. It's always surprising me. There's always a new angle. I've had lots and lots of theories. This is my best one." He pushes away his empty plate and brings his pint glass front and center. "Why do you do it?" I ask. "Why don't you, as your theory urges, remain idle?" He looks at me kindly, as if I am perhaps a bit dim-witted. "This is my idleness. If a pot of money landed on me, I'd keep on with idle theory, because I think it's a great idea." One shouldn't confuse idleness with inactivity, he says. The fisherman (an example Davis uses in one of his posted essays) may look like he's idle as he sits, intent on his line, but at that moment he is constrained, not free. When he isn't fishing, he may go for a walk and look more active, but he is actually free to do anything at that moment and so is idle in evolutionary terms; his stationary fishing is active, his walking is a form of idleness, which he engages in for pleasure. The artist's model, sitting still, is theoretically active; the amateur sculptor chiseling away at a block of marble for pleasure is theoretically idle.

"And so it is all about pleasure, then?" I ask. Davis admits this is the least developed part of the theory. "In my imaginary little worlds, my models, I'm not concerned about whether they're happy. The fisherman: Does he enjoy fishing? Of course it is always better if one does." Davis takes a sip from his glass and ponders this. "Perhaps," he says tentatively, "like sex, there's an evolutionary advantage in making idleness pleasurable." He shrugs, thinks. I ask if he has tried to publish his ideas, and he laughs. "As science fiction?" he asks. "No. I can't imagine any publisher being interested." He works on his idle theory, he assures me, for the pure pleasure of it. "There's a kind of ecstasy in seeing things in a new way," he says.

What else does he do for pleasure? He answers in terms many in the long history of slackers, from Samuel Johnson to Jack Kerouac and beyond, would approve: "I spend massive amounts of time sitting in pubs like this."

∞

My students also spend massive amounts of time drinking, and they know something about work. Since I have been teaching at a large state university, most of my students work at service jobs to get by, on average twenty or more hours a week. In the unscientific but fairly intensive polling I've been conducting, they fall into two camps. About a quarter of them hate slackers: slackers in their own workplaces make them angry. In a very few cases, these angry anti-slackers can point to actual work they have had to do because coworkers weren't pulling their own weight—an extra bed to make for a hotel worker, an extra sandwich behind the counter—but much more common is just a galling sense of unfairness when another worker gets away with doing nothing. The students in this group also tend to get some satisfaction from their jobs, even if they feel the work itself is below them. Another quarter are unabashed, boastful slackers. They like to tell stories of the summer job they had that required thirty minutes of work a day, timed to a supervisor's visits. They chuckle as they describe a course in which they managed a B while showing up only three or four times during the semester, proud of their accomplishment. They have few positive work memories. The rest fall between these two poles, or more accurately, they identify at different times with each of the other groups. Not surprisingly, there is some correlation between attitudes toward work and a sense of the future—more of the anti-slackers know what kind of work they'd like to get after college than do the slackers. The anti-slackers may be apprehensive, but they are hopeful. The slackers, if not hopeless, have at least buried their hope deeper than their apprehension. The middle group, again, feels sometimes one way, sometimes the other.

The one film I can count on all my students having seen, in the same way one could count on all students having seen *Ferris Bueller's Day Off* a decade ago, is Mike Judge's *Office Space* (1999). A small film—it grossed only $10 million in its theatrical run—*Office Space* has continued to have strong VHS and DVD sales, so strong that the latest version of the DVD was being sold in large cardboard aisle displays at Best Buy checkout counters as late as 2003, a rare event for a four-year-old film. "More than a comedy," said eFilmCritic.com that year, "it is an anthem for the downtrodden cube-borgs everywhere, who have had the life and soul stomped out of them by an uncaring corporate entity." The film opens with three friends, all miserable at their jobs at a bland Everycorporation called Initech. The protagonist, Peter Gibbons (played by Ron Livingston), remembers his high school guidance counselor asking what he would do if he had a million dollars. The counselor suggested that if you knew what you would do without money constraints, then, like Thoreau or Chris Davis, you would know what you really thought worth doing. Peter remembers that he couldn't come up with anything. "Nothing?" a friend at work asks. Nothing. "I guess that's why I'm here" at Initech, Peter admits. His girlfriend wants him to be more ambitious and makes him go to an occupational hypnotherapist. The therapy session backfires because the therapist, who has asked Peter to relax, dies before he can snap Peter out of the trance. Peter remains relaxed.

So relaxed, in fact, that he takes the next day off. His girlfriend dumps him when he refuses to respond to her goading. He then has a conversation with his new love interest, Joanna (Jennifer Aniston):

PETER

I really don't like my job and I'm not going to go anymore.

JOANNA

You going to quit?

PETER

No, I'm just not going to go anymore.

JOANNA

Won't you get fired?

PETER

I don't know. I'm not going anymore.

JOANNA

Well how will you pay your bills?

PETER

I never really liked paying bills. I think I just won't do it anymore.

JOANNA

Well, what do you want to do?

PETER

I want to take you out to dinner, and then go back to my apartment and watch kung fu movies with you.

Peter doesn't entirely convince Joanna, who continues to take a commonsensical view of the matter. But he is full of evangelical verve and tries to convert his friends to his new view: "We don't have a lot of time on this earth. We weren't meant to spend it this way," he tells one. "Human beings were not meant to sit in little cubicles staring at computer screens all day, filling out useless forms, listening to eight different bosses drone on about mission statements."

The movie suggests that the main reason people feel incarcerated by their work is that it is inescapably boring, the tediousness compounded by any attempt to avoid it. When the newly relaxed Peter rambles back into the office in a Hawaiian shirt, a serene smile on his face, in order to dismantle his cubicle with a kind of Whitmanian exultation while strains of corny steel guitar luau music dominate the sound track, he is called in to talk to the outside management consultants who are reviewing the staff in preparation for downsizing. He shrugs and goes to talk to them. They ask Peter to describe an average day, and he explains that he always came in about fifteen minutes late, using the side door so no one noticed, and then spaced out for an hour or more: "I just stare at my desk, but it looks like I'm working. I do the same thing in the afternoon. In a given week I only do about fifteen minutes of real, actual work." The consultants seem both shocked and somewhat impressed, and ask him to continue. "The thing is, Bob, it's not that I'm lazy, it's that I just don't care," he says. "It's a problem of motivation. If I work my ass off and Initech ships a few more units, I don't see another dime." His only real motivation is to not be hassled by one of his bosses and to not lose his job. "But you know, Bob," he explains, "that'll only make someone work just hard enough not to get fired." The consultants decide he should be promoted.

Providing a counterpoint to Peter's gray-collar angst is Lawrence, his happy-go-lucky, mulleted, beer-drinking construction worker next-door neighbor, whose answer to the million-dollar question of what he really wants to do is, "Two chicks at the same time, dude!" He doesn't comprehend Peter's dilemma, feeling that work is work and not such a big deal. In the denouement, Peter takes a job with Lawrence, doing construction work in the open air, and completing the happy ending, he gets the girl. The film thus quite shamelessly recoups the work ethic, but this little forced coda is not what its fans love about it. Instead they respond to the fantasy of escaping soul-deadening career paths and gloryless futures, of being able, when the downsizing consultants say, "You've been missing a lot of work lately," to respond blithely and happily, "I wouldn't say I've been *missing* it, Bob!" *Office Space* is an anthem of this generation's infatuation with doing nothing, in the same way that *Walden* and *On the Road* were for earlier generations. It is the fantasy of avoiding the humdrum working life, of being Kerouac or Thoreau rather than a drab, dreary data puncher.

∞

Mihaly Csikszentmihalyi has been studying young people's work attitudes for decades now, and in one of his many sociological studies in the mid-1990s, a graduating senior told him that none of his friends knew what they wanted to do for a living:

> I mean they know they want to go to college and they know they're probably going to have to go to graduate school, but no one is really sure exactly where they're going to be and what they're going to be doing. They just talk about how they want to, you know, be friends and have barbecues.

This senior was, Csikszentmihalyi concluded, a "player" rather than a "worker." Out of roughly 900 students in the study, he identified 130 as players, based on the fact that they reported themselves as engaged in play more than 50 percent of the time. A slightly lower number were workers, engaged in work more than half the time. These groups at the two poles had more distinct attitudes toward work and play than the rest, as one would expect. The players were united in resenting the idea that they would, at some point in the near future, be forced to choose a conventional lifestyle of some sort. "My main goal in a personal career is not to have a nine-to-five job where I sit in an office and write or sit in an office and type or whatever," one told Csikszentmihalyi. "It's this, I get ill almost thinking about that. I want to get out and do things and meet people."

What the players really want, Csikszentmihalyi suggests, is to get the kind of satisfaction from work that they get from play, which for one reason or another—bad experiences in bad jobs, bad parental training and examples, bad curricula—they do not associate with work. One of the goals of education should be, he suggests, helping students associate productive labor with self-esteem and satisfaction. The way to do this, he thinks, is through recognizing what he calls "flow." Flow is the complete absorption in activity that is necessary to optimal experience: autotelic activity—activity that is its own end, like intense child's play, the "unconsciousness" of a basketball player who can't miss, or any complete fusion with one's work process. The workers in his study already, at some level, understood this. What the players get from play and what the workers get from work is the same thing, the satisfaction inherent in flow.

We can all recognize this, and Csikszentmihalyi admits that what he is describing was recognized by the early Taoists and many others since. When people say they love their work, they usually mean, in fact, that they can be totally, unself-consciously absorbed by it. My father-in-law has been in retail sales for some forty of his sixty working years, and the thing he hates the most is having no customers. At eighty-two he no longer feels a need to be the top salesman on the floor, striving after commissions; he just hates being bored, loves being engaged with customers, knows that he is having a good day when he looks up and sees that the time has flown. When I worked as a broiler cook in a steak house, I loved the busy times, when dozens of waiters clamored for their meals and every second counted, twirling on the greasy floor, tongs and steaks flying, not a spare millisecond anywhere. I wasn't truly "unconscious," because I remember feeling exhilarated, and I remember noticing that I felt that way. The absorption wasn't total, but it was close enough: it was, in Csikszentmihalyi's terms, flow.

Csikszentmihalyi's conclusions are more or less what one might guess—that high school curricula should be intellectually engaging, intrinsically motivating, oriented toward creativity, and clearly linked to future job options, and that parents should be more involved in students' lives. I spent enough time in my son's high school classrooms to know that the curriculum failed on all counts, but as Csikszentmihalyi suggests, some attitudes about work are already well formed by the time a student is in his or her teens. Still, even if Cody didn't get it from school very often, he knew flow. I had seen him practicing his bass; I had seen him fishing and tying flies; I had seen him deeply involved in all sorts of challenging, satisfying activity. He had, in fact, by his own reckoning, loved the fairly grueling work he did on the truck farm, and thus he knew about the satisfactions available from work. But none of this was helping him get his résumé typed up.

A number of other sociologists and psychologists have attempted to understand what makes good work good. Sociologist Eliot Freidson, for instance, argues that modern work has for too long been understood as alienating, that the Marxist and later critiques of work, however salient, have hindered sociologists from understanding its opposite, which he terms, somewhat unfortunately, "labors of love." Such unalienated labor, like artists who work assiduously at their art for no pay, should provide a model, Freidson thinks, for labor in general. This was Thoreau's point as well (and, it must be said, Marx's). Instead of alienated labor at his father's pencil factory, Thoreau would find good, solid, satisfying labor in hoeing his own beans and building his own room. The "quiet desperation" of men, he argued, is based in their obeisance to conventions, including the norms and routines that lead them to questionable labors for questionable ends. "If the engine whistles, let it whistle till it is hoarse for its pains. If the bell rings, why should we run? We will consider what kind of music they are like." Throw off the yoke, Thoreau counsels, and work only that bare minimum necessary. After all, he suggests, "one generation abandons the enterprises of another like stranded vessels," and so why should these students and sons know what it is they will do with their lives? Why should they be able to say what it is they might do, or how it will be different from what has been done before? Why should they even entertain our questions about it?

∞

Well, for one thing, because we know better. Thoreau should have known better, too. Rereading *Walden* in middle age above all impresses one with Thoreau's immaturity—by which I mean his willingness to believe the lies he tells himself. He built his cabin on the pond at the age of twenty-eight, but he didn't publish *Walden* until he was thirty-seven, at which point, one would have hoped, he was too old (and owed too much to the then fifty-one-year-old Ralph Waldo Emerson) to believe this kind of adolescent bravado: "The old have no very important advice to give the young, their own experience has been so partial, and their lives have been such miserable failures. I have yet to hear the first syllable of valuable or even earnest advice from my seniors," he writes, still including himself among the young, rather than the old failures, even though the average life expectancy in 1850 was thirty-eight. In his eulogy for Thoreau, Emerson said, "I cannot help counting it a fault in him that he had no ambition."

Why would Thoreau send that list of occupations to be published in his Harvard class notes? For the same reason I listed my own occupations: we are authorizing ourselves in some way. How better to demonstrate that we had something to say about work in general than by showing that we had worked not just at writing, that dubious labor of the intellectual sort, but at "real work" as well? Thoreau carefully

divides his occupations by their status, starting with schoolmaster, tutor, and surveyor and then to the various trades. He also fudges things.
He adds "Pencil-Maker" to the list of trades he followed, but in fact he
worked in his father's pencil business less as a tradesman than as an
engineer. He developed a way to use local low-quality graphite by mix-
ing it with clay to achieve sufficient hardness, redesigned the grinding
mill, and he even sometimes signed himself "Henry D. Thoreau,
Civil Engineer." But one assumes that Thoreau also felt compelled to
list his occupations because he didn't, at that point, have much of one.
His announcement of his unconventionally broad (for a Harvard graduate) experience in the world of work, his jeremiad against work, and
his unemployment are all part of the same slacker complex.

    In this Thoreau is like many writers, intellectuals, and profession-
als, all those whose work isn't of the more obvious, physical kind. I, for
one, see myself in completely contradictory ways: insufficiently socialized into good work habits and attitudes and, at the same time, overly
socialized, overly concerned with my work, my success, my status, my
accomplishments or lack thereof. I am convinced, and not without
good evidence, that I am astoundingly lazy. Although I have a few ambitions and I follow through on some of them, I don't work enough, I
don't persevere, I don't get enough done, I waste time. Surely I have
spent more hours playing Freecell on my computer than the average
person, or the country would have ground to a halt by now. I look at
the stupendously long shelf of books written by William Dean Howells or Henry James or Honoré de Balzac and think, Yes, by God, I
and my contemporary ilk are slugs. The Stephen Kings of this world
still manage a book a year or more, but most of the people I know who
are writers and professors produce roughly the same amount of work I
do, often less, making me think that maybe the academic life has become a haven for the lazy. I try to convince myself that some of the
time I spend entertaining myself is a *kind* of work. I'm a literature professor, and so reading novels is work, obviously, and given the importance of popular culture these days, even the airport thrillers and
mysteries are important for me to read. And I can't ignore the more
dominant forms of narrative in my own time, can I? So all those
movies, all that TV—work. It's important for me, professionally, not
just to be cognizant of but to *study* popular culture, and so I work to
stay current, watching *The Sopranos* and *Curb Your Enthusiasm* and

The Daily Show, going to see the latest Hollywood blockbusters (and of course the festival-anointed independents), reading *Harper's* and *The New Yorker* and *Vanity Fair*, surfing the reality shows and Tivo-ing Billy Wilder and Michael Curtiz films. Oh, and *Reno 911* (very interesting) and *Iron Chef* (fantastic) and *Arrested Development* and reruns of *The Rockford Files*. And of course March Madness and the NBA play-offs. Where would one draw the line? A lot of sitting on the couch is involved, as it turns out, but still, this is all a kind of work for me, isn't it?

And so my life of sloth blends imperceptibly into my pathological flip side, my workaholism, and this is the odd thing: I can just as easily argue and believe that I work, not too little, but entirely too much. My sense of my own laziness may simply be the perverse guilt engendered by a work ethic that digs its dominatrix heel into my back and rarely lets me up. I *do* seem to work all the time, and not just watching TV. I mean real work. Days and nights, weekends, writing, researching, preparing lectures, reviewing, editing. (It's 12:30 a.m. as I write this sentence, and I wrote my first sentence at 9:15 a.m.) I wake up in the middle of the night obsessing about things I haven't finished, or having a dream-state revelation that may or may not solve a major transition problem in a piece I'm struggling with. Sometimes I get up and write for an hour or two in the middle of the night. I hop out of bed feeling already behind, and caffeine keeps me going late. I edit my prose on the treadmill at my gym. I read articles in the professional journals *while* I'm editing film clips to show a class. Often when I'm not working, say driving in the car or trying to fall asleep with the caffeine jitters, I'm thinking about my work, anxious about it, preoccupied, worrying conceptual problems, jotting down notes, planning new forays. I never seem to stop or rest.

Everyone I know is in the same boat. We are all lazy imposters, and we are all workaholic slaves. We work way too hard and not nearly enough. What can this possibly mean? Is slackerism somehow as much a part of our lives at this point in history as our vaunted work ethic? Are the two simply two sides of the very same coin?

The feeling of being overworked is not a simple case of self- or mass delusion. My job as a professor is demanding, with endless meetings and dissertations to direct, books to review, journals to read, tenure cases to prepare, and books and articles to publish and peer-review, not to mention a little classroom teaching. My record isn't as impressive as some in my profession, but still, I am among the most "productive scholars," defined in terms of books and articles per year, in my perfectly respectable major research university department. Besides, I tell myself, and it's true, I work at other things as well. I raised three children (each with a somewhat idiosyncratic work ethic), and I've written and sold some nonacademic nonfiction. I've written some screenplays, some of which I've been paid for. I've continued to have a semiprofessional music career, performing in clubs or recording, at least once a week, for a long time more than a hundred gigs a year. I've done some serious home improvement, single-handedly producing additions, new kitchens, new baths. I paint and I write poetry with no intent of circulating either. Some of these are hobbies, of course, but again, where do we draw the line? Even if I count only that work for which I get paid, I still rack up much more than the twentieth-century standard of forty hours a week, even more than the 1990s professional standard of fifty hours.

This is the most common complaint of professionals these days. They wish there was a clearer demarcation between work and play. They wish they didn't have to work all the time. They yearn, at least theoretically, for a nine-to-five job that was simply over at the closing bell. The kind of job that meant one didn't bring work home, much less on vacation. Nobody wants to punch in, but we would all like to be able to punch out.

And still. None of the work, the quasi-work, or the semi-work I do seems to lessen my slacker guilt, if for no other reason than the simple fact that I *aspire* to be a complete slacker. The Joe Walsh line, "They say I'm lazy, but it takes all my time," runs through my head. I'm pretty sure that one of the main things that got me through my Ph.D. program was the promise of a breezy life of three-day workweeks, thirty weeks a year, a life in which I would never have to get up in the morning. Even after I saw that this clearly wasn't the way the academic world worked, the Platonic ideal of half banker's hours kept me going. It kept me plugging away through the seasonal shifts when fourteen-hour days turned into eighteen-hour days at the end of each semester. And yet I seriously don't know what I would do if I had to adjust to a nine-to-five job. I'm not sure I could do it.

In seeing my son on the couch, I suppose, I saw my ego, my alter ego, my alter alter ego, and on and on, in a hall of opposing mirrors. Bound to be upsetting, I suppose, especially now that I can no longer really indulge in the fantasy offered by *Office Space* or *Walden*, the fantasy of being free of the whole mess, of resolving these conflicted feelings and identities and pressures, of walking blithely through the woods listening to the sounds of the chickadee or an imaginary Hawaiian guitar, at peace with my own relation to work.

∞

When I was my son's age, though, I was deep in precisely that fantasy. I lived with some friends on a midwestern farm—we called it a commune, but before and after this time, kids just called it having housemates—in an idyllic setting, trying to live on nothing, with nothing, so I could do next to nothing. At least a mile in any direction from a neighbor, with a straight view to the deep Mississippi Valley two miles away, we could sit on the front porch of our ancient stone house and watch the mist roll down the river in the mornings. Living on the land so I wouldn't have to work, taking jobs I never planned on having for more than a few months, developing home-brewed versions of Buddhist antimaterialism and Marxist resentment, I worked hard to escape working. Little pleased me more than ending up on unemployment. Pot-smoking indolence was my métier.

Doing nothing, in those days, was a political and philosophical project. The hippie curriculum included a large dose of Eastern religious thought, as translated by westerners. Alan Watts, Baba Ram Dass, *The Tao of Physics*, Kerouac and Ginsberg, Aldous Huxley, *Autobiography of a Yogi*, and *The Tibetan Book of the Dead* were all standard fare on hippie bookshelves, along with Carlos Castaneda, *Stalking the Wild Asparagus*, and the *Whole Earth Catalog*. And one of the main lessons of these books was that striving, pushing, desperate grabbing at the brass ring—any and all ambitious desires—were worse than distractions; they were the very stuff that made nirvana impossible and were destroying the planet. One had to let go, drop out, be free; it wasn't just asceticism, not just a rejection of the material comforts and false promises of consumer culture, but a repudiation of desire itself. "What are you doing? Planning for the future?" Ram Dass asked in *Be Here Now* (1971). "Forget it baby, that's later. Now is now. Are you going to be here or not? It's as simple as that." Ram Dass had himself dropped out of the academic rat race, reinventing himself in a kind of midlife reincarnation, so that he was no longer Richard Alpert, Ph.D., professor of psychology at Harvard, but Baba Ram Dass, a quasi-Indian quasi-guru whose new job was, what, freelance philosopher? His dropping out made possible his philosophy, just as, he assured us, the less we desired, the more we would get (that sounds good, doesn't it?); the quieter we became, the more we would hear. "Resistance to the unpleasant situation," he wrote, on the authority of the *Tao Te Ching* and the Zen masters, "is the root of suffering." Not only should one not work toward a better life, one shouldn't even attempt to make marginal improvements to an obviously bad situation. Doing nothing, in this syncretic proto–New Age view of the world, was a sign of wisdom.

By doing nothing, we were purifying our consciousness of base desires, and this would someday, somehow—the programs were never quite worked out except cosmically—mean the progress of human being into its full promise. In the meantime, it was obvious enough that striving was destroying the world. All the great inventions—the internal combustion engine, electricity, air travel, air-conditioning—these were the gross despoilers of the planet. Television? Mind control. Medicine? Invasive, destructive god-playing: herbs and massage could do it all better. Every human attempt to improve the world ended in violence, pollution, tyranny, corruption. The will was always the will to power, and Nixon was the final proof that power was bad. Doing nothing, as the hermit saints and Chinese sages knew eons ago, was the highest good.

This perennial philosophy continues to find adherents. Steven Harrison, in *Doing Nothing: Coming to the End of the Spiritual Search* (1997), counsels his readers to "sit in a room for a week and do nothing . . . If we wish to approach our mind, the most direct way is to do nothing. If we want to go beyond our mind, do nothing." Véronique Vienne, in *The Art of Doing Nothing* (1998), says that to "cultivate the seeds of serenity" we should "follow in the footsteps of Thoreau," learn to ramble rather than walk purposefully, and thus "achieve a state of higher consciousness." Tom Hodgkinson's *How to Be Idle* (2005) is a straightforward advertisement for doing nothing and an excellent catalog of historical justifications for the same; Carl Honoré's *In Praise of Slowness* (2004) recommends a weekly "do nothing day"; Fred Luskin and Kenneth Pelletier's *Stress Free for Good* (2005) proselytizes for "zero-based thinking"; and Fred Gratzon's *The Lazy Way to Success: How to Do Nothing and Accomplish Everything* (2003) simply declares, "Hard work is a fraud."

As Gratzon's subtitle suggests, however, many of these books promise not just spiritual but worldly success if one follows their prescriptions. Karen Salmansohn's *How to Change Your Entire Life by Doing Absolutely Nothing* (2003) makes the argument explicitly: by learning to do nothing for five minute intervals several times a day, one has more "energy, power, clarity, and speed . . . like you've never experienced before!" Deepak Chopra, in *The Seven Spiritual Laws of Success: A Practical Guide to the Fulfillment of Your Dreams* (1995), too, promises more power and money through idleness than achievement. Desire, which in Buddhist thought is the origin of all suffering, is for Chopra precisely the thing that will give us the infinite power to fulfill our destiny; desire, he writes, has "infinite organizing power" when we surrender ourselves to the "dance of the universe." Doing nothing, for Chopra, is finally just another technique employed in the pursuit of success and gratification, a habit of the successful person, the answer to who is moving your cheese.

But me and my hippie pals, back on our semi-commune, we were much purer than that. We weren't slowing down just to speed up; we believed that success, as our corrupt society defined it, wasn't worth having. (Unless it was a certain kind of artistic success, one that wasn't too "commercial," like that of the Grateful Dead, for instance, who sold millions of albums but not tens of millions like the sellouts.) The only good that would ever come of our dropping out of the rat race had nothing to do with personal gain. Again we weren't clear on what the exact mechanism was for this, or how our inactivity would finally be responsible for it, but we knew that somehow it was helping to bring on the dawning of the Age of Aquarius, when universal higher consciousness, peace, and harmony would reign throughout the world. I'm not sure I ever entirely believed that, frankly, but I did believe that America's success was the cause of a global crisis, and that to take part in it was evil. Americans consumed the vast majority of the world's resources, used five times as much energy as the rest of the world, rained napalm on civilians to keep its rate of consumption possible, polluted aquifers everywhere, threatened the planet itself with nuclear annihilation. It was our moral responsibility not to partake. Aquarian renaissance or no, refusing to work in this huge, evil machine was a moral victory.

But. Nevertheless. I somehow ended up working all the time anyway. I couldn't afford to buy a camper top for the back of my beat-up Datsun pickup truck, so I built one from two-by-fours and plywood, with little windows and a hip roof, classic hippie-craftsman style: equal parts rustica, impracticality, whimsy, and numskullery. Working with technologically backward, used, and beat-up tools—the kind one can afford with minimal gainful employment—using the marginal skills of an accidental jack-of-all-trades, building the topper took weeks. It ended up so heavy that it immediately halved the truck's payload, and it required constant painting and caulking. The cedar-shake roof turned into a road hazard at high speeds and had to be redesigned and rebuilt. Getting it on and off the truck was a four-man job. It was, finally, a lot of work.

We didn't want to pay rent, so we took care of our landlord's cattle, did some plowing, harrowing, and haying, or whatever the season required, in exchange for rent. We grew the majority of our own food, of course, with a huge vegetable garden and elaborate canning and freezing and drying in the fall. We raised and kept chickens for eggs and meat, and sometimes some ducks and a hog or two. In the fall, I would take one of the horses and ride through the hills, collecting small, gnarled apples from the wild apple trees and bringing them home to press and jar up: gallons and gallons of cider that required perhaps only an hour's labor per gallon, maybe a little more. We cut our firewood with two-man bucksaws because it kept us out of the chain-saw-fossil-fuel-evil-empire-military-industrial complex. We spent every free minute sawing and splitting wood for heat, and just barely kept the house above freezing. We hauled logs to a local sawmill and worked with the rough, nasty boards to build sheds, beds, and shelves.

We also grew our own soybeans in those days. To make one's own tofu, hippie-style, requires the usual preparing of ground, plowing, rototilling, fertilizing, planting and cultivating, hacking out the weeds with a hoe, and then a long season of organically removing pests. This is followed by hand harvesting the plants and hauling them up to cull the beans. The culled beans need to be cleaned and sorted and then soaked, cooked, mashed, curdled, and pressed. The whole mishegaas comes, roughly, to about five or six hours of labor to produce a few pounds of the stuff. When you do the math, there is very little time left to eat it in.

I remember my father visiting once while I was culling beans; he was a corporate executive, baffled by my reversion to the peasant activities his family had escaped a few generations earlier. He also had a vegetable garden back home, thinking of it as the kind of reinvigorating relaxation Chopra and Salmansohn would applaud. But he found my back-to-the-land life a bit bewildering. I saw through his eyes that day, and saw how ridiculous our life looked. Here we were, spending the majority of every day in hard manual labor in order to provide the rudiments of food, clothing, and shelter. I couldn't explain to him exactly why it all made sense to us. We felt that our life was rich, and we weren't really wrong. Our food was fantastic. That apple cider was the best I have ever had, and thirty years later I can still almost taste it. We had free beer and wine because we made it ourselves; yes, it was horrible beer and worse wine, but that, in this case, wasn't the point. The pleasure of cross-country skiing out when a car couldn't make it the two miles to our mailbox and the nearest road, or eating, on homemade pasta, the tomatoes we had dried on racks in the sun—it was like being on vacation in Umbria, except for the hassles and the pipes freezing. Splitting logs in midwinter as the sun set, a cake of ice growing in my beard as my breath condensed and froze, I had what I have since learned was the kind of primitive, authentic experience that D. H. Lawrence (whom I hadn't yet read) complained had been stolen from modern man. And even if it meant I had to toil long hours every day, I got some delicious, fundamental pleasure from knowing that, like Thoreau (whom I also hadn't yet read), I only had to work at a paying job a few months a year to survive.

Like Thoreau, in fact, my quasi-communards and I were proud of both things—proud of all the work we did, how self-sufficient we were, how proficient in the traditional crafts and labors, and, at the same time, proud of our early, irregular retirement from the world of bourgeois employment. I had a sneaking suspicion that the unresolved contradictions wouldn't bear looking at too closely if I wanted to retain my sense of moral superiority, and so, again like Thoreau, I

was careful about what I decided to examine closely. I simply continued to rock back and forth, from primal worker to blissful slacker and
back again, hour by hour, day by youthfully endless day.

∞

And now, oddly, I find myself somehow still in the same wobbly boat.
I have to admit that I'm still stupidly proud of the fact that I rarely
have to "go to work": beyond a few hours of class and a few hours of
meetings, every other minute is fungible. I like it when people from
other walks of life say, "Wow, nice work!" And I am also proud of the
enormous amount of work I do. I enjoy telling people how diligently I
labor.

The work ethic, in fact, seems to demand not so much work as the
announcement of it. Ten o'clock at night on the phone with someone,
it isn't uncommon to hear, "What are you going to do now?" "Try to
get a little work in." It doesn't matter which end of the conversation
I'm on. "Me, too, I guess," the other one says. We may or may not
then go back to work. It isn't dishonesty; it's like a loyalty oath, a
pledge of allegiance. We are agreeing at such moments about what is
important, valuable, just as we do when we scoff at our work, berate its
impositions, whine about its fruitlessness, or castigate ourselves for our
own inveterate procrastinations. We all can feel overworked (under-
paid) and unappreciated, but we all at least occasionally fear we are
impostors, freeloaders, bums. Are we working hard? Hardly working?
Always the same jokes, the same bitching, the same confessions, the
same self-admonitions and self-advertisements.

This bifurcated relation to work has deep cultural roots. "Consider
the lilies of the field, how they grow," Jesus was said to have said—you
notice that though supposedly a carpenter, Jesus didn't seem to drive
very many nails—"they toil not, nor do they spin: and yet I say unto
you that even Solomon in all his glory was not arrayed like one of
these." The promise of toil-free divine beneficence seems to coexist
comfortably with the idea that Adam and Eve and we their progeny
are cursed with work for disobeying God and with the idea that idle
hands are the devil's playground, both of which, in the history of
Christian sermonizing, have gotten much more airtime than the lilies.
This doubleness is found everywhere, as when Paul, echoing Jesus on
the lilies, writes to the Corinthians that "God is able to provide you

with every blessing in abundance, so that you may always have enough of everything" before admonishing the Thessalonians, as I mentioned, to work or starve. It is this later letter that is quoted more often. "For we hear that some of you are living in idleness, mere busy-bodies, not doing any work," he continues. "Now such persons we command and exhort in the Lord Jesus Christ to do their work in quietness and to earn their own living." Long before the Protestant ethic described by Weber was developed, in other words, the cultural seeds of our current double vision were well ensconced.

When Weber wanted a document that expressed the spirit of modern industrial capitalism "in almost classical purity" to begin his discussion of the Protestant ethic, he turned to Benjamin Franklin's *Advice to a Young Tradesman* (1748) and the rest of his writings, including his *Autobiography*. Franklin's advice is not, Weber notes, a set of simple clues to shrewd business dealings; where another person might consider the poor handling of money as foolishness, Franklin thinks of it as a dereliction of duty. "It is not mere business astuteness, that sort of thing is common enough," Weber writes. "It is an ethos," an ethos Franklin proselytized in its purest form. Ever since Franklin, that ethos has been preached, usually to the converted, over and over again, from the pulpits of the nineteenth century to the business best-sellers of the twenty-first.

What Weber doesn't mention is that, also since the eighteenth century, a persistent, if smaller, counter-chorus of slackers has kept up a running commentary, a shadow culture advocating a kind of shirker ethic, responding directly and indirectly to Franklinian proscriptions and pomposity. If the self-made man pulling himself up by his own bootstraps is the typical American, the slacker is his necessary twin, a figure without whom American history is equally unthinkable. My relations to my father and to my son are very similar to those of many fathers and sons for the last two hundred years, as in many of the stories I am about to tell. They argue about work and not working, about what good work is and what it means. Throughout the historical variations, ideas of something like the slacker and something like the workaholic have been bandied about, and these images have continued to be at the center of what it means to be an American.

And not just American. In every country in the world, in our global age, there are slackers. This book focuses on the history of

Anglo-American loafing, with occasional forays onto the European continent, which makes sense, given the early entry of Europe and America into the industrial era, but everywhere, as groups have become part of the industrialized and postindustrial economy, they have retooled not just their workplaces but their work ethics as well. And alongside these processes, slacker subcultures have sprung up as energetically as the factories. In those places, like Germany or France, for instance, where industrialization was on largely the same schedule as in England, slackers arrived at roughly the same time. The founding German slacker is Werther, Goethe's hapless hero from *The Sorrows of Young Werther* (1774). Like Samuel Johnson and Benjamin Franklin, the subjects of the next chapter, and just a couple of decades later, Goethe was writing in response to the dawning of this new age, and his idle, dilettantish protagonist is both a remnant of a dying class system, full of resentment at his lost privilege, and a new kind of man, the Sturm und Drang harbinger of the Romantic movement. Werther was an enormously popular character who wrote a little, sketched a little, read poetry, and thought about his career only intermittently and impractically. Goethe later regretted having written in conscious sympathy with his protagonist, drawing on details of his own life: "Oh, how often I have cursed those foolish pages of mine which made my youthful sufferings public property!" At the end of the novel, Werther sits down at his desk in a blue waistcoat and yellow vest, an open book in front of him, and shoots himself. After the novel was published, there was a spate of such suicides, in which young men, some dressed in the same yellow and blue, shot themselves at desks with an emblematic open book in front of them, causing Goethe's novel to be briefly banned in Italy, Germany, and Denmark. It was perhaps Werther who prompted Goethe's contemporary Georg Christoph Lichtenberg to say, "The greater part of human misery is caused by indolence," but in any case, Goethe's book shows the power that slacker characters can have in a culture's imagination.

Before it took on its identity as the twentieth century's "worker's paradise," Russia was a bit slower in taking on the industrial order, so its first great slacker hero, the titular hero of Ivan Goncharov's *Oblomov* (1858), arrived some eighty years after Werther. Oblomov is a slacker on a grand scale. An upper-middle-class "superfluous man," Oblomov takes the novel's first 150 pages to rise and get dressed. After coming "within an ace of getting out of bed" several times, the narrator tells us bemusedly, "Half-past ten struck, and Oblomov gave himself a shake. 'What is the matter?' he said vexedly. 'In all conscience 'tis time that I were doing something! Would I could make up my mind to— to—.' " He calls his valet. He stays in bed. The novel is classic slacker comedy, except that it ends tragically, Oblomov eventually expiring from inaction, his inability to be motivated shown to be a disease.

This mixture of comedy and tragedy follows the slacker as he migrates with capital and industrial development. In India, where industrialization developed slightly later again, slacker characters appeared from the 1920s on—films with "loafer" in the title appeared in 1926, 1973, and 1996, for instance—and as economic and working life changed, generational battles about work and leisure found their way into literature, song, magazines, and now the Web, which given the rapid revisions of India's place in the world economy has provided fertile ground for slacker talk. S. Venkateswaran, a.k.a. Arvind, a.k.a. Bill, a.k.a. the Chennai Bill Gates, runs a Web site called vetty.com from Chennai (formerly Madras)—*vetty* meaning, in Tamil, "slacker." Venkateswaran himself is no slacker, and this points out an important aspect of slackerism's place in cultural change: "Really it's very hard to come up in life," Venkateswaran says on his biography page. "I think if you don't work your hardest, you will never succeed." He associates himself with slackers simply as a way to announce his up-to-dateness, to assert his postmodernity, his international Infobahn currency. This is not an identity in any standard sociological or psychological sense. Like his mess of nicknames, *vetty* is a reference to the social world, not to the self, and not even to that self's actual social world. *Vetty*, like slacker, is an identity, but not one that even most people attracted to it want to claim for themselves except ironically.

Throughout the developed world, such ironic slackerism is common. Corinne Maier's *Bonjour Paresse: The Art and the Importance of Doing the Least Possible in the Workplace* has been a bestseller in France since it was published in April 2004. It contains ten maxims, beginning with "You are a modern day slave" and ending with "Tell yourself that the absurd ideology underpinning this corporate bullshit cannot last forever." These are not really rules for conduct, though; they provide, like many slacker manifestos before them, a kind of satiric critique, not a recipe for success. Maier's bestseller is simply the latest in a long line of French slacker thought, from what Flaubert called "the marinade"—moratoriums from work in which one hangs out and waits for inspiration—to the recent spate of slacker films: *Ma Vie Sexuelle* (1996), *Nénette et Boni* (1996), *The Dream Life of Angels* (1998), *Time Out* (2001), *Tanguy* (2001), and *Osmose* (2004). High-culture critics like Roland Barthes defended idleness as well:

> Have you noticed that we always speak about the right to leisure time, but never about a right to idleness? I wonder moreover if here, in the modern Occident, if *not doing anything* really exists. Even those people who have a completely different, tougher, more alienated and laborious, life than my own don't do "nothing" when they're free. They always do something.

When he can suspend all of his normal activities, on a Sunday for instance, he is happy "because it is a day unfilled, a silent day when I can remain idle, that is, free. Because the saintly form of modern laziness is, at the end, freedom."

This notion of freedom remains central, from its darkest incarnation in the infamous ARBEIT MACHT FREI sign over the gates of Auschwitz to the semi-facetious "Manifesto for the Art of Doing Nothing" recently offered by the German artist Johannes Auer (a.k.a. Frieder Russman). Art, Auer writes, "is indifferent to the means of producing art. Art is concept. Art is doing nothing." Marcel Duchamp, Auer argues, did very little work in his lifetime yet is one of the most important artists of the twentieth century, and artists should take a clue and try to do nothing. Throughout the 250-year history of the industrial work ethic and its slacker double, these two proclamations—that work will set us free (often directed at the most unfree laborers) and that doing nothing frees our highest potentialities—have been heard around the globe.

An art student in Shanghai expressed to me what is the common view: everyone, now, as China's industries grow so rapidly, has to think about work. She searched for the right metaphor and said, "The cats play every day. We do, too. It's just that we, for some reason, need to ask why, and then we get depressed and don't want to work." The characters in Wei Hui's bestselling *Shanghai Baby* (2001), in their fairly absolute disinterest in work, are much like the characters in

Western slacker films and novels, and one twenty-year-old in Beijing told me that his parents were having an especially hard time adjusting to the newly industrialized, informationalized China. Both university agronomists, his parents had always been the kind of people "who kept a hot cup of tea on their desks," he said, a euphemism for not getting any work done. As Communist Party members, this had been for them a perfectly acceptable way of life. All of a sudden they were expected to accomplish things in exchange for receiving their salaries, and they were having trouble. Thirty years ago they had simply been smart and lucky. Now they were slackers.

Everywhere there are slackers, sometimes self-defined, sometimes, as in the case of this man's parents, defined by others. Sometimes they are guilt-laden, sometimes unrepentant, sometimes figures of tragedy, but more often figures of fun. This man smiled at the image of his parents' hot-tea cups—they represented a past that was both reviled and mourned, with a kind of wistful bemusement we often reserve for the young and the very old, those whose breaches of social mores are not only forgiven but somehow inspiring. Ah, to be outside the rat race! Werther, Oblomov, the phantom *vetty*, and the Chinese slacker parents are at once both cultural ideals and the opposite; they are available as figures of contemptuous dismissal, of condescending amusement, and of guilty longing.

∞

In contemporary America, mainstream culture is deeply infused with such slacker variations, from Seinfeldian shows about nothing to celebrity Buddhism, and from *South Park*'s loafer children to the election and reelection of a president with a well-noted distaste for diligence, a spotty employment record, and the most extensive vacation schedule of anyone who has ever held the office. We may consider successful, fulfilling work to be an absolute good, a necessary part of the fully lived life, but gleeful, ecstatic leisure, lying on a hammock without a care in the world and a little umbrella in our drink is an image of earthly paradise: the "life of Reilly," we call it, taking what was at one time an ethnic slur against the lazy Irish as a synonym of comfort and ease. "Now watch this drive," says the president on the golf course to the assembled media anxious to know his war plans. Just as the work ethic does, slackerdom provides images of the best and the worst our culture has to offer. Together they provide our defining pathologies, our manic, obsessive-compulsive, blood-pressure-aggravating workaholic syndromes on the one hand, and on the other, frivolous, lackadaisical denial or immobile, inactive depression.

The world of work is not simply constructed of feelings and attitudes, of course, but of material tasks and social relations. As I will try to show, slackers appear when that world is objectively changing. From the eighteenth century, when the slacker figure first appears as a response to the Industrial Revolution, to the recent slacker response to the Information Revolution, slackers make big news whenever the world of work undergoes serious structural change. The change from an economy of manual farming and manufacture to one of mechanized farming and factories in the eighteenth century, the change from a manufacturing economy to a service economy in the middle of the twentieth century, and the change in the 1980s from a world of paper to a world of bytes are in many ways very different, but they have had a number of comparable effects. The first time I read an article about young people no longer being able to expect to earn what their parents had, for instance, was when I was in my twenties. My children, now in their twenties, read virtually the same articles, with updated references. Of course these writings applied only to a portion of the population; immigrant workers had no such problem, and in most cases they could still count on outearning their parents. The "idlers" and "loungers" of the eighteenth century, however, whom I'll be discussing in the next chapter, faced an economic situation similar to that of myself and my children: their class status meant something different for their economic future than their parents' status had. Slackers tend to be from exactly that kind of group. Despite slurs about laziness in the lower classes, slackers are almost entirely drawn from the middle class or are on their way down to meet it.

The number of hours middle-class Americans work, which declined steadily from the turn of the century into the 1960s, began to rise again in the 1970s and has continued to rise through the present. Our "productivity," we heard then and we hear now from the same sources, has also increased, even though the studies conducted by industrial engineers and business school professors are unanimous in suggesting that longer hours make people, on average, less productive. Ever since Elton Mayo, the founder of industrial sociology, conducted the influential Hawthorne studies in the 1920s, people have studied the effect of people's daily working environment on their output and on their sense of satisfaction. Such studies have become more and more bleak, and the anecdotal evidence (as in a recent look at the number of Ivy League law school graduates who have "dropped out" of the law in recent years) also speaks to a massive dissatisfaction with even the most lucrative and prestigious work. Robert Reich, the former secretary of labor, argues in *The Future of Success* (2001) that people for the foreseeable future need to make a choice—they can have a good job or they can have a good life.

Slackers are precisely those who argue that the good life is better than the good job. We don't have to quit our jobs to feel the full force of that argument. The loafers, loungers, and bums who have, over the last two centuries, provided us with a sometimes earnest, sometimes parodic commentary have periodically helped reshape the culture of work in America. They have encouraged us to think of work, whether we are compensated financially or not, whether it fulfills our obligations or not, in terms that complement rather than compete with our sense of the life worth living, replacing duty and necessity with pleasure and satisfaction. The demand made by those who attack the work ethic is that we ask: Are the goals we are working toward worthy? Do we believe our own rationales? Does our work deliver the implied promise of our work ethic? Are we wasting our lives?

The anti–work ethic rhetoric of all slacker subcultures relies on the economic productivity of workers for its very being, of course, just as my son relied on the income that bought the couch he was on. Someone pays the bills, someone makes the film and sets the type, someone buys the book or the DVD, but that is hardly the point. What is important is not the utopian dream of a work-free world, but the cultural give-and-take such dreams engender. The slacker offers us a relaxed view of life from the couch or pool chair, or, in earlier eras, from the gentlemen's club, the open road, or the poolroom—a view that sees our striving and efforts stripped of the value we habitually imagine them having. In the same way that physicians and psychotherapists show us other ways to respond to disease, dysfunction, and injury, slacker subcultures have performed an important emotional function, expressing and adding to our culture's repertoire of feelings about work.

Those feelings have been, much more often than not, what are usually called negative emotions. My son reminded me of an Edwardian neurasthenic because many neurasthenics were, we could now say, slackers: medical opinion even then was divided on the question of whether all neurasthenics were, in fact, simply malingerers. And the eighteenth-century loungers, nineteenth-century loafers, 1920s lost expatriates, 1950s beatniks, and 1990s slackers often described themselves as indescribably bored, as depressed, as having "the vapors," as exhausted, as beat, as downtrodden. These feelings, I am going to argue, are appropriate because slackerism can also be a kind of mourning. Slacker subcultures are built out of a sense of loss, a loss of innocence, a loss of ideals, a loss of purpose. Sometimes they are mourning, explicitly or implicitly, a world destroyed by change, as the Lost Generation did the world destroyed by the Great War. At other times they have mourned a gentlemanly ideal destroyed by industrialism; in other words, they mourned for the life they had thought would be theirs: the life of aristocratic ease their parents had and they and their siblings would not be able to sustain. Sometimes, like Thoreau and hippie back-to-the-landers, slackers mourn a disappearing sense of self-determination. Sometimes they mourn the loss of meaningful work or, as is often the case, the passing of their own preadult lack of concern for the future. As a result, slacker subcultures can sometimes have strong reactionary strands, as in the case of elite slackers yearning for a level of privilege and prestige that only an outmoded class system could provide. But in most cases, as in that of the immediate post–World War II generation that came of age mourning the passing of a world in which heroism was still possible, slacker subcultures engage our sense of value precisely through that which they mourn. Thoreau, we feel, was right to object to the destruction of the New England forest by the textile industry; the Beats were right to decry the corporatization of everyday life.

Such protest was undoubtedly *not* my son's intention in sitting on the couch. Not all slacking is part of a subcultural movement. Sometimes it is just personal, or encouraged by life-cycle moments, like graduations, midlife crises, and the like. The dreams of freedom that sustain some kids through high school, for instance, or the vast possibilities that seem to wait after college—these are replaced by mundane facts, and we mourn their passing, which is one reason late adolescence is such a time of melancholia and nostalgia. Even then slacking can have its effect. When I stopped feeling enraged and took his feelings seriously, I had to acknowledge that indeed his generation faces a different world of possible and probable work than mine or any before it, that my work ethic was out-of-date, not something he could feel as his own. He needed to reinvent the work ethic for himself. In the meantime, he was simply an accidental slacker. He would have to reinvent what that meant as well.

Should I have been so worried about it? Probably not. As the Beats—who rediscovered in Buddhism a do-nothing philosophy—argued, doing nothing is far from easy. It is a discipline, a practice. "To do nothing is the most difficult thing in the world," Oscar Wilde wrote half a century before them, "the most difficult and the most intellectual." The Way of the Loafer is steep and hard. Sometimes one needs to hunker down and work to relieve the pressure. "I have achieved satori," the Zen monk said to his master in a famous koan. "Now what do I do?" "You could sweep the floor," the master replied. After doing nothing, doing something is the only next move. Besides, sometimes work, even for a slacker, just feels good, like a kind of relaxation.

So I shouldn't have worried so much. No one, except the dead, can do nothing forever.

II

THE IDLER AND HIS WORKS

In which the "Idler," the world's first slacker, appears in 1758 — Benjamin Franklin and Samuel Johnson usher in the modern world — and the Agricultural and Industrial Revolutions reshape the nature of work.

Benjamin Franklin had a bit of a problem with his father, too. The youngest son out of seventeen children, Benjamin was originally sent to grammar school to help prepare him for the ministry — "my Father intending," he wryly put it, "to devote me as the Tithe of his Sons to the Service of the Church." The schooling lasted only a year, however, because his father feared the expense of the necessary college education and was wary of the "mean Living many so educated were afterwards able to obtain." It is also possible his father already saw his son's ornery streak, what Franklin calls in his *Autobiography* his "disputatiousness," and therefore realized he was temperamentally unsuited to the pastor's life. Or he may have just wanted the extra hand. At any rate Franklin was brought back into the family chandlery business at the age of ten. He cut wick for candles, filled dipping molds, ran errands, worked in the shop, and hated it all. "I dislik'd the Trade and had a strong Inclination for the Sea," he wrote much later, and his father, having already lost one son to the seafaring life, fearfully took young Benjamin around to see carpenters, bricklayers, and metalworkers, hoping to find another trade that might interest him. Since

Benjamin had always loved books, they finally settled on the printing trade, and twelve-year-old Benjamin was apprenticed to his brother James for a period of nine years.

He took to the work at first, quickly developing "great proficiency in the Business," in his own words, and then he started writing for the publications he was printing, primarily his brother's newspaper. He began with poetry, his first topical ballad selling "wonderfully" well. But like many fathers of poets before and since, Franklin's was not enthused: "My Father discourag'd me, by ridiculing my performances, and telling me Verse-makers were generally Beggars; so I escaped being a Poet, most probably a very bad one." Franklin's father, Josiah, was, in fact, a transitional figure in a changing culture of parenting. "In no other period of our past," the historian Kenneth Lynn wrote (in 1976, around the time my father was confounded by my relation to soybeans), "can we find the top leaders of American society speaking as gratefully as these patriots did about the fathering they received." Older notions of patriarchal authority were being replaced, in the eighteenth century, by the kind of parental affection and direction that has since become the norm, a change from which the revolutionary generation was the first to benefit. Josiah Franklin still acted the patriarch, but in a muted fashion. He mocked Benjamin's poetry, but he didn't forbid it. He wasn't about to let young Benjamin make his own decisions, but he helped him change trades and apprenticed him to one Benjamin found agreeable. Josiah had had no such luxury himself, his own father apprenticing him to an older brother in the dyeing trade; there is no record he felt any loss when, moving to America, he dropped dyeing forever and became a soap and candle maker.

Franklin stopped writing poetry but began writing topical essays. He published his first pieces in the guise of an old woman named Silence Dogood, hiding his authorship even from his brother, who was already jealous of his younger brother's modest success as a poet. The essays enjoyed a burst of fame, and when his brother was jailed briefly for sedition, based on his own fiery editorials, Benjamin got to take over the printing business and newspaper, and he made a bit of a name for himself, as himself. Once his brother was released, Benjamin took the first opportunity that presented itself to skip out on his apprenticeship, running away to Philadelphia at the age of seventeen.

He claimed that his brother beat him, but perhaps more important, he wanted to be independent and enjoy the fruits of his own labor. In Philadelphia, "remote from the Eye and Advice of my Father," he writes, he was quickly successful enough that the provincial governor, Sir William Keith, suggested that Franklin set up his own printshop, sending him with a letter of recommendation back to his father to get additional capital. His father wouldn't back the venture, saying Benjamin was too young.

The text in which Franklin tells these stories, the *Autobiography*, was itself originally written as letters to Benjamin Franklin's own son, William, and although it records Franklin's rebellion against patriarchal authority, it spends much more time detailing the development of his work ethic. William was already forty when Benjamin began writing it, in 1771, and although they were close at that time, they would be estranged shortly: William remained a loyalist through the Revolution, and Benjamin never forgave him for "the part he acted against me in the late War." William by 1771 had been appointed royal governor of New Jersey, and when hostilities broke out, he went to England. Benjamin left almost nothing in his will for William, saying that if England had won the war, he would have had no fortune to distribute. Franklin's work ethic and his antipatriarchal rebellion against royal authority were part of the same package, his insistence on self-determination at the individual and social level. The men of the Revolution were prepared for breaking ties with their symbolic father in England, as the historian Jay Fliegelman has argued in further developing Lynn's argument about changing parental relations, because they had broken the ties of authority to their own fathers. The work ethic Franklin espoused in his Poor Richard epigrams and described in his autobiography was more than anything a program for making one's way in a world devoid of authority.

Not coincidentally, at exactly the same time that Benjamin Franklin was helping to invent the work ethic as we know it, Samuel Johnson was almost single-handedly inventing the slacker. Near contemporaries, they represent the poles of work philosophy at the dawn of the Industrial Revolution: Franklin the great exponent and exemplar of the virtues of regular, regulated work; Johnson the man who claimed not just that every man is or wants to be an idler, but that "even those who seem to differ most from us [idlers] are hastening to increase our fraternity; as peace is the end of war, so to be idle is the ultimate purpose of the busy." In a world where sons, starting at the age of ten or younger, simply did the jobs (or, higher up the hierarchy, moved into the positions) that their fathers picked for them, there were no slackers. The options made possible by modernity, the indecision prompted by the fact that there were decisions to be made, the welter of potential lives facing a young person in the modern world— these were necessary ingredients in the making of both proselytizers for the work ethic and slackers. If there is no choice, no alternative, if life is laid out in all its medieval inevitability, there may be a lot of work but no need to extol its virtues. There may be some idling here and there, but there are no Idlers.

Franklin was born in 1706, a scant three years earlier than Johnson, lived almost six years longer, until 1790, and had the more obviously active life. In the decade of the 1750s, for instance, Franklin conducted his famous electrical experiments, invented the lightning rod, published many scientific papers and his annual almanacs, established the first American fire insurance company, helped found Pennsylvania Hospital and what would become the University of Pennsylvania, was elected alderman and appointed deputy postmaster general for North America, negotiated treaties with the Ohio and Delaware Indians and the Iroquois confederation, drew and published the first American political cartoon, formed a militia and helped build frontier forts, and traveled to England as a representative of the Pennsylvania assembly. In the same decade, Johnson basically just wrote, but he wrote a lot—reams of poetry, some three hundred periodical essays, a novel, and, in an extraordinary feat, the first major dictionary of the English language.

On May 1, 1760, the two men met for the first and perhaps the only time, at a social gathering in London, Johnson's home turf. Johnson, no friend of revolutionaries, kept his distance and avoided conversation, but James Boswell, Johnson's famous biographer, found Franklin "all jollity and pleasantry." Johnson and Franklin were both classic Enlightenment figures in their different ways, rationalists and cynics, pragmatic and not prone to metaphysical speculation. They were born into a world that would change in unfathomable ways at an unprecedented pace, and the lives and writings of both men were equally marked by the political and cultural revolutions of their century. Although they took their stands and established their authorial and social personae on opposite sides of an enormous cultural divide, they shared much more than either would perhaps have liked to admit.

∞

In the 1750s in England and America, revolutions were under way, with more to come. The philosophical and scientific revolutions of the seventeenth century—the work of Galileo, Kepler, Newton, Hobbes, Locke, Pascal, Descartes, and Spinoza, for instance—were being vigorously extended in the eighteenth century by philosophers, mathematicians, and scientists such as Hutcheson, Hume, Berkeley, Leibniz, Voltaire, Diderot, Boerhaave, Taylor, Hoffmann, Linnaeus, Euler, and Bernoulli. The complex European wars of these years, along with each country's overseas adventures and skirmishes, re-arranged global power and trade and helped create the conditions for the French, American, and Industrial revolutions. Technological in-novations in manufacturing, transportation, printing, medicine, and agriculture changed the way people lived and worked. Franklin's and Johnson's writings registered these changes in their very different ways, interpreting, moralizing, satirizing.

Historians are agreed that the Agricultural Revolution of the eigh-teenth century was an important precondition for the Industrial Revo-lution that followed quickly on its heels. The standard story for many years had been that a band of heroic individuals—Jethro Tull, Lord Townshend, Arthur Young, Robert Bakewell, Thomas Coke, and Robert and Charles Colling—transformed agricultural life in En-gland from a peasant subsistence economy to a capitalist system so pro-ductive that it could feed the new millions in industrial cities with fewer total agricultural workers than in the past. Tull's seed drill, first introduced in 1701, not only improved the germination rate and thus harvest yields but also inaugurated a long line of machine inventions and improvements. Lord "Turnip" Townshend championed crop rota-tion featuring the turnip, a nitrogen-fixing plant that increases the yield of anything planted after it, as did Young, an agricultural innova-tor and proselytizer. Bakewell, Coke, and the Collings engaged in se-lective breeding, leading to heavier, hardier livestock.

Many recent histories have taken issue with this story, claiming that

Young was, in Eric Kerridge's words, "a mountebank, a charlatan and a scribbler" who was a failed farmer himself; that Coke, too, was better at self-promotion than agriculture; that Lord Townshend did not introduce turnips, which had in fact been grown on his family estate since he was a small boy; that Tull's was not, in fact, the first seed drill; that Bakewell's longhorn cattle were not a success; and that the basic ideas of crop rotation and selective breeding had simply been copied from the practices of Dutch innovators. The historians also disagree about whether the Agricultural Revolution happened in the first half of the century or in the second half and about whether or not the agricultural boom was primarily the result of new land (drained marshes, cleared woodlands, former pasture) being put into production. But however the history is told, the fact remains that enormous changes took place, resulting in more than doubling the average weight of sheep and cattle at Smithfield market from 1710 to 1795, a 50 percent increase in per-acre yields of wheat, and the successful feeding of the burgeoning population. As the British population tripled, from six million in 1750 to almost eighteen million a hundred years later, farm production by and large kept pace.

Jethro Tull's *The New Horse Houghing Husbandry: or, an Essay on the Principles of Tillage and Vegetation* (1731) calls attention, in its title, to one of the many innovations: instead of oxen, horses were, indeed, being used for houghing (hoeing, or cultivation) and other tasks, pulling newly designed cultivators, planters, and other machinery, and this was recognized as exciting and world-transformative. John Laurence's *A New System of Agriculture* (1726), Young's *A Course of Experimental Agriculture* (1770), and other reports helped spread the revolution across England and abroad. And these developments had obvious material effects on people's working lives. More horses, more machines, and more productivity all meant less human labor per pound of food. Up to 90 percent of the medieval population performed agricultural labor, but by 1750 in England, this had dropped to 53 percent, and by 1800 it would fall to 37 percent and stay on that steady decline: by 1850 only one-fifth, by 1910 only one-tenth of the workforce in England was in agriculture. Much of the rest of the workforce moved off the farms into towns and cities and found, or at least hoped to find, work in the industries and services of the new urban, proto-industrial world.

The causes of the Industrial Revolution, just like those of the Agricultural Revolution, are the subject of numerous debates, but its occurrence and basic timing are fairly clear. In 1721 what is often called the first textile factory appeared in England, and by the 1730s more and more workers were being hired in the textile industry. Thomas Lombe's machines for winding, spinning, and twisting silk in 1718 and John Kay's flying shuttle loom in 1733 revolutionized the making of cloth, and by the end of the century, after the introduction of James Hargreaves's "spinning jenny" in 1763, Richard Arkwright's "water frame" in 1769, Samuel Crompton's 1779 "spinning mule," and Eli Whitney's 1793 "cotton gin," the weaving process had been fully mechanized. The increased wool and cotton and flax produced by farmers brought down the prices of raw material, the technological advances made for lower production costs, and the displaced agricultural workers formed a large, cheap labor force. Advances in steel smelting in the 1730s and 1740s and, of course, the gradual development of the steam engine, from the steam pump of the early century to James Watt's engine in the late 1770s, set the stage for the huge industrial boom of the early nineteenth century in both England and the United States.

The most significant social change that accompanied these booms was the increase in population and that population's increased concentration in urban areas. London would grow from 650,000 to 960,000 between 1750 and 1800; Edinburgh would double from 50,000 to 100,000; Manchester would quadruple from 17,000 to 70,000. And the American colonies were growing even faster, owing to successive waves of immigration: there were roughly a quarter of a million colonists in 1700, a million by 1750, 2.5 million by 1775, and more than 5 million by 1800. Franklin's Philadelphia was a town of 2,000 in 1700 and would reach 25,000 by 1760 and 40,000 before the turn of the century; Boston had 6,500 residents in 1700, more than twice that by 1750, and 25,000 in 1800; New York started the century with 5,000 and ended it with more than 60,000.

The frenetic activity of Franklin on so many fronts—scientific, civic, political, military, cultural—was one exceptional man's response to these vast social changes, to new ways of working, to the new forms of knowledge and understanding being produced. Of course Franklin was helping to construct these new worldviews as well. His electrical experiments, for instance, which he reported to the Royal Society in London in 1750 and published as *Experiments and Observations on Electricity* the next year, introduced the terms "battery," "conductor," "condenser," "positive charge," and "negative charge" (and the + and − signs to represent them), and transformed the field. "Franklin's law of conservation of charge," claims Harvard historian of science I. Bernard Cohen, "must be considered to be of the same fundamental importance to physical science as Newton's law of conservation of momentum." And Carl Van Doren wrote, "He found electricity a curiosity and left it a science." Franklin's electrical experiments helped make the world what it would become.

Similarly, Johnson's dictionary was for words what Linnaeus's *Fundamenta Botanica* (1736) and *Philosophia Botanica* (1750) were for plants: an attempt to catalog and organize the full variety of them. Like Franklin's all-embracing curiosity, Johnson's literary and lexicographical work was a significant and comprehensive response to these social and technological changes. Attempts to catalog the universe, whether Linnaeus's ordering of plants or Johnson's of words, were fueled, like Franklin's electrical experiments, by an Enlightenment sense of the human capacity to comprehend and thus control the natural world. They helped codify a world in which traditional understandings and methods suddenly seemed insufficient. Franklin saw no reason to accept the frequent loss of barns and houses to fires caused by lightning, and it was exactly this drive for human control over natural phenomena that led religious traditionalists to brand his lightning rod heretical. Johnson's *Idler* essays, too, overturned a long history of religious and secular attitudes toward work, giving birth to a seemingly endless line of loungers and loafers, who, excoriating their society and themselves, framed the debate about industry, idleness, and their meanings for centuries.

∞

When Franklin was a boy, his father frequently repeated a proverb of Solomon's to him: "Seest thou a Man diligent in his Calling," he reports his father quoting, "he shall stand before Kings, he shall not stand before mean Men." This quote from Proverbs (22:29) has been translated in different ways over the years. The *King James Version* (virtually all Bibles in English in America in the eighteenth century used the King James translation) reads "Seest thou a man diligent in his business?" To replace "business" with "calling" is to give the proverb a peculiarly Protestant religious dimension, one that, unlike his father, Franklin would presumably dismiss: in his many Poor Richard sayings and in his other writings he takes a much more secular view, as, in fact, does this Old Testament verse. From the crusty, no-nonsense rural woman, Silence Dogood, in his first published essays to Richard Saunders in the various editions of *Poor Richard's Almanack*, Franklin's various personae always had a secular slant. They reminded readers of the importance of being thrifty, swift, diligent, and skillful in one's work or business but never asked them to consider their "calling." Franklin, who was silent on very little, had virtually nothing to say about the relation of one's work to God's will, about whether one should choose work based on a divine calling, or about the relation of one's work to one's eternal reward. His father's understanding of work was no longer his own.

Around 1730, Franklin writes, he decided to try to work toward what he called "moral perfection." In order to do so, he kept track, in a notebook, of his practice of thirteen virtues: temperance, silence, order, resolution, frugality, industry, sincerity, justice, moderation, cleanliness, tranquillity, chastity, and humility. He also devised his famous daily schedule as the best way to insure many of these virtues— industry, order, moderation, and resolution:

	5–8	Rise, wash, and address Powerful Goodness; Contrive
The Morning Question, What Good shall I do this Day?		Day's Business and take the Resolution of the Day; prosecute the present Study; and breakfast?
	8–12	Work
	12–2	Read, or overlook my Accounts, and dine

2–6	Work

	6–9	Put Things in their
		Places, Supper, Music,
Evening Question,		or Diversion, or
What Good have I		Conversation,
done to day?		Examination of the
		Day.

10–4	Sleep

Like the *Rule of St. Benedict* (which also thought that "idleness is the enemy of the soul"), Franklin's schedule is divided between periods of work and periods of reading and reflection. But the schedule is free of any kind of religious activity except the most secular of expressions of fealty, addressing not God or even a higher power, but "Powerful Goodness" once in the morning.

It is Franklin who first said "Time is money," and this brief phrase frames the American understanding of work from then on. In *The Way to Wealth* (1758), Franklin strung together the various sayings from his almanacs in the mouth of a character (Father Abraham) quoted by his fictitious narrator Richard Saunders, or Poor Richard. In the middle comes this paragraph on time, work, and money:

> It would be thought a hard government that should tax its people one tenth part of their time, to be employed in its service. But idleness taxes many of us much more, if we reckon all that is spent in absolute sloth, or doing of nothing, with that which is spent in idle employments or amusements, that amount to nothing. Sloth, by bringing on diseases, absolutely shortens life. *Sloth, like rust, consumes faster than labor wears, while the used key is always bright*, as Poor Richard says. But *dost thou love life, then do not squander time, for that's the stuff life is made of*, as Poor Richard says. How much more than is necessary do we spend in sleep! forgetting that *the sleeping fox catches no poultry*, and that *there will be sleeping enough in the grave*, as Poor Richard says. If time be of all things the most precious, *wasting time* must be, as Poor Richard says, *the greatest*

prodigality, since, as he elsewhere tells us, *lost time is never found again*, and what we call *time-enough, always proves little enough*: let us then be up and be doing, and doing to the purpose; so by diligence shall we do more with less perplexity. *Sloth makes all things difficult, but industry all easy*, as Poor Richard says; and *he that riseth late, must trot all day, and shall scarce overtake his business at night*. While *laziness travels so slowly, that poverty soon overtakes him*, as we read in Poor Richard, who adds, *drive thy business, let not that drive thee*; and *early to bed, and early to rise, makes a man healthy, wealthy and wise.*

In Franklin's moral universe, "getting" (which means either the earning of money or the accumulation of stock) is always good, and "spending" (by which Franklin always means consumer spending) is always wasteful. One has only so much time in a life, and since work is the only way to "get" and "getting" is the goal, anything that doesn't lead to the making of money is a waste of time. Work is good not because it is a duty or calling, not because it provides necessities and luxuries, but because it is the prime means toward the goal of life itself. In fact, nothing but work, these adages argue, is worth doing.

Franklin, however, did not entirely believe the Poor Richard maxims himself, or he had, at any rate, an ironic relation to them. "Drive thy business, let not that drive thee" is the most obvious place where something like what would become the slacker critique of work is clearly acknowledged; but even the caution "lost time is never found again," can cut both ways, meaning either one should keep one's nose to the grindstone *or* not lose all one's time to grinding one's nose. Franklin, for instance, decided exactly this when he blackmailed his way out of his father's chandlery shop with threats of going to sea, again when he skipped out on his apprenticeship to his brother and hitched a ride to Philadelphia, and yet again when he retired, at the age of forty-two, in 1748. He wanted to lose no more time working. He turned over the printshop to his new partner, David Hall, had his portrait done in frilled silk sleeves, curly wig, and velvet coat, and moved into a much larger house at a tonier address. The accomplishments of the decade that followed, listed earlier, were all gentlemen's pursuits, all civic service and scientific and artistic recreations befitting his new station as a gentleman. At best these activities would produce profit only circuitously, and nothing in *The Way to Wealth* would explain the virtues involved. His time was no longer money; his money, in fact, had become time.

The Way to Wealth is a funny document. The fictional persona, Poor Richard, listens to the fictional Father Abraham, who speaks in a pastiche of the published sayings of Poor Richard. This double embedding allows Franklin to wink at the reader in a kind of mock modesty. Father Abraham is an old dodderer, a blowhard without an original thought in his head, and even Richard seems a bit worn down by what he calls Abraham's "harangue." Richard is tickled to hear himself so often quoted, but he admits that it "must have tired any one else." More important, the people who listened, he notes somewhat abashedly, "approved the doctrine; and immediately did the contrary." This kind of ironic distance Franklin has on his own dogma is evident in his daily life in Europe as well. He became notorious in London in the 1760s for his daily "airbath," which consisted of lying uncovered and naked on a bed for an hour, a practice he claimed was good for one's health. And when John Adams joined Franklin as part of the American delegation in Paris in 1778, Adams was appalled by his boss's work habits.

> I found out that the business of our commission would never be done unless I did it . . . The life of Dr. Franklin was a scene of continual dissipation . . . It was late when he breakfasted, and as soon as breakfast was over, a crowd of carriages came to his levee . . . some philosophers, academicians, and economists . . . but by far the greater part were women . . . He came home at all hours from nine to twelve o'clock at night.

Adams reports that Franklin kept his constant dinner invitations carefully noted in a pocket hornbook, and "it was the only thing in which he was punctual." One of Franklin's French friends wrote that though Franklin indeed did do his work, "there never was a more leisurely man." Adams was more blunt: "He is too old, too infirm, too indolent and dissipated to be sufficient for the Discharge of all important Duties." In September the Congress disagreed and brought Adams home, leaving Franklin as its sole representative in Paris, dismissing as well the other members of the delegation who had complained of Franklin's indolence.

In giving the impression of laziness, Franklin was breaking another of his own rules: he wrote that it was more important to appear busy than to be busy, the appearance of virtue, he felt, being at least as essential as virtue itself. "I cannot boast of much success in acquiring the *reality* of this virtue," he writes of his attempts to be humble during his quest for moral perfection, "but I had a good deal with regard to the *appearance* of it." When he was first setting up as a young printer, he could see that "the industry visible to our neighbors began to give us character and credit," and after he was successful, he continued to make a show of his own industry, careful "to avoid all appearances to the contrary," pushing rolls of paper to his shop in a wheelbarrow down a busy street and then allowing his workers to take over once he was in the door. Franklin's concern with the appearance of industry recalls the early computer games that had a button to push so a graph would appear if the boss was coming: it is a stratagem, a simple, almost comic ruse. The famous Franklinian work ethic is at its heart a bit of a sham.

∞

Samuel Johnson introduced the Idler to the world in 1758 (the same year as Franklin's *Way to Wealth*), and like Franklin, Johnson had a complicated relation to the appearance of industry. "It will be easily believed of the Idler," Johnson wrote as he introduced the character, "that if his title had required any search, he never would have found it." Of course the Idler didn't have to supply his own title; Johnson did it for him. In part because of seventeenth-century censorship and libel laws, it had become common practice for British essayists to write under pseudonyms, and Johnson was, like all British writers, heavily influenced by Joseph Addison and Richard Steele, whose pseudonymous essays in *The Tatler* (1709–11) and *The Spectator* (1711–14) were considered the best the early eighteenth century had to offer. Johnson's first major essay series in the early 1750s was published under the pseudonym the Rambler, a name that evokes a certain lackadaisical lassitude, but the Idler is one step closer to pure indolence. In the first issue of his new series, Johnson lays out the characteristics of his persona and, as it turns out, the outlines of the slacker. He suggests that idling is not a sin, but in fact the true desire of all: "Every man is, or wants to be, an Idler. There is perhaps no appellation by which a writer can better denote his kindred to the human species." He explains that idling allows one to appreciate life, while striving destroys that appreciation: "The Idler who habituates himself to be satisfied with what he can easily obtain, not only escapes labours which are often fruitless, but sometimes succeeds better than those who despise all that is within their reach, and think of every thing more valuable as it is harder to be acquired." The Idler solidly rejects Franklinian striving toward accumulation and achievement, rejects precisely that ethos at the center of the new industrial capitalism that is transforming social life.

The first *Idler* essay suggests that the new economic man, the man who applies himself diligently to self-improvement and self-advancement, is aberrant, that the Idler, in fact, is the natural man:

> It has been found hard to describe man by an adequate definition. Some philosophers have called him a reasonable animal; but others have considered reason as a quality of which many creatures partake. He has been termed likewise a laughing animal; but it is said that some men have never laughed. Perhaps man may be more properly called the idle animal; for there is no man who is not sometimes idle.

After this tongue-in-cheek philosophical excursus, he suggests that calling man the idle animal "is at least a definition from which none that shall find it in this paper can be excepted; for who can be more idle than the reader of the Idler?" The move from premise to comic insult is quick; it happens at the speed of comic timing. We have met the Idler, and he is us.

The joke is also, at least in part, that the self-appointed Idler is not so idle; he is writing while we are only reading. "That the Idler has some scheme, cannot be doubted, for to form schemes is the Idler's privilege," he writes, explaining that most idlers remain fairly quiet about their plans, knowing that their audience might remember former schemes that came to nothing. Nonetheless, "hope is not wholly to be cast away. The Idler, though sluggish, is yet alive, and may sometimes be stimulated to vigor and activity. He may descend into profoundness, or tower into sublimity; for the diligence of an Idler is rapid and impetuous, as ponderous bodies forced into velocity move with violence proportionate to their weight." The image of the Idler as everyman is followed by one of a huge, static blob "forced" into movement and then threatening everything in its path: self-deprecation and self-praise follow each other in quick loops. Johnson suggests, for instance, that one of the great advantages of being an idler is that it saves one from the poisonous envy of others: "The Idler has no rivals or enemies. The man of business forgets him; the man of enterprise despises him; and though such as tread the same track of life fall commonly into jealousy and discord, Idlers are always found to associate in peace; and he who is famed for doing nothing, is glad to meet another as idle as himself." The idler has no enemies for half a sentence; then the man of business despises him. The back and forth, the celebration and denigration of the idler: this doubleness will be the hallmark of the slacker for the rest of the figure's history.

Johnson was, famously, an untidy man. Even his often fawning biographer James Boswell was taken aback at their first meeting. He recorded in his journal that Johnson was "a man of most dreadful appearance . . . troubled with sore eyes, the palsy and the king's evil. He is very slovenly in his dress and speaks with a most uncouth voice." In the version Boswell published, the same basic picture comes through:

> He received me very courteously; but, it must be confessed, that his apartment, and furniture, and morning dress, were sufficiently uncouth. His brown suit of cloaths looked very rusty; he had on a little old shriveled unpowdered wig, which was too small for his head; his shirt-neck and knees of his breeches were loose; his black worsted stockings ill drawn up; and he had a pair of unbuckled shoes by way of slippers.

By all accounts, he was a huge, clumsy man, with smallpox scars and scrofula, tics and tremors; he was depressive, a grandstander, and, yes, sometimes publicly indolent. His appearance, as has been true of slackers since, is related to his indolence: only a lazy person wouldn't powder his wig, wouldn't clean up the rust and dust, wouldn't take the necessary pains to be couth.

The picture Boswell draws and the bemused celebration of indolence in *The Idler*, though, do not jibe very well with Johnson's own journal entries. There he regularly berates himself for his indolence and idleness. On April 24, 1764, for instance, some four years after the last *Idler* essay, he wrote, at three in the morning:

> My indolence, since my last reception at the Sacrament, has sunk into grosser sluggishness, and my dissipation spread into wider negligence. My thoughts have been crowded with sensuality; and except that from the beginning of this year I have in some measure forborn excess of strong drink, my appetites have predominated over my reason. A kind of strange oblivion has overspread me, so that I know not what has become of last year; and perceive that incidents and intelligence pass over me without leaving any impression . . . My purpose is from this time. To reject or expel sensual images, and idle thoughts. To provide some useful amusement for leisure time. To avoid idleness. To rise early. To study a proper portion of each day. To worship God diligently. To read Scriptures. To let no week pass without reading some part. To write down my observations.

He sounds like Franklin in his *Autobiography*, not some happy-go-lucky idler.

These are the words, in fact, of a melancholic. Johnson's father suffered from melancholia, as did Johnson and, on occasion, Boswell. Johnson was well acquainted with Robert Burton's *Anatomy of Melancholy* (1621), which identified idleness as a main cause of melancholy. According to Burton, "Idlenesse" was "the bane of body and minde, the chiefe author of all mischiefe, one of the seven deadly sins, and sole cause of this and many other maladies." When Johnson was seventy, he wrote to Boswell,

> The great direction which Burton has left to men disordered like you, is this, Be not solitary, be not idle: which I would thus modify;—if you are idle, be not solitary; if you are solitary, be not idle. There is a letter for you, from
> Your humble servant,
> SAM JOHNSON
> London, October 27, 1779.

In an earlier letter, he encouraged his friend Hester Maria Thrale to develop "an implacable impatience in doing nothing" because if the mind "learns to soothe itself with the opiate of musing idleness, if it can once be content with inactivity, all the time to come is in danger of being lost."

For a man beset by melancholic indolence, Johnson accomplished an enormous amount. His *Dictionary of the English Language* (1755), with its 40,000 definitions and 115,000 quotations, took nine years (and the help of six assistants), which he gleefully noted was significantly less than the fifty-five years and group of forty the French Academy needed to produce theirs. Before Johnson's *Dictionary*, the most extensive English dictionary had 3,000 entries, and his remained the standard until the publication of the *Oxford English Dictionary* a century and a half later. The *OED*, again by way of comparison, took a total of seventy years to complete and had scores of editors and contributors. Johnson also wrote critical biographies of fifty-two poets, wrote essays on (and edited) the complete plays of Shakespeare, and produced more than three hundred essays in the *Rambler* and *Idler* series, numerous poems, a novel (*Rasselas* [1759]) and other tales, prefaces, travel writing, sermons, satires, and parodies. He did voluminous political writing and reporting, kept diaries, and wrote countless letters. He was not, after all, a very good idler at all.

Despite such labors, however, Johnson was most often remembered as the Idler he represented. Thomas Percy, for instance, told Boswell that he remembered Johnson at Oxford "generally lounging at the College gate," keeping other students from their studies, "if not spiriting them up to rebellion against the College discipline." If nothing else, these reports of Johnson as a slacker are a testament to the persuasiveness of his prose. But they also suggest the potency of the slacker image that he helped invent. Johnson's Idler carries his deep ambivalence about work, his understanding of the degradations of the market and at the same time his obviously deep need to produce for that market, his practical acceptance *and* principled rejection of the claims of commerce, and his profound engagement with *and* aloof detachment from his own ambitions. Thus is the slacker born, and thus does he address his readers, themselves of at least two minds.

∞

Arguments about the pragmatic value of industriousness, such as Aesop's fable of the ant and the grasshopper, have been around for millennia. Harvest and store, or starve. But the work ethic that develops during the Industrial Revolution adds notions of nobility, character, pride, sinfulness, and virtue—in other words, internal qualities. The industrial work ethic is not just what we do, of course, but who we are, not just how we feel about our jobs but how we feel about ourselves. So, too, is the slacker ethic; to decide whether to work or be idle is a question not just of whether we do something or not, but of what kind of person we decide we are, or find ourselves to be.

Samuel Johnson, the busy idler, and Benjamin Franklin, the industrious dilettante, did for work what writers, and perhaps only writers and other artists, can do: they took the evolving understanding of their time, the understanding of what it meant to be a person living and working in the world, and created a series of crystallizing images. The complex images they concocted have remained so central to our understanding of work that hundreds of years later we still recognize them, still find them compelling, and still haven't resolved any of their internal contradictions. They continue to structure the debates about work, which is why those debates, however much they are constituted as a case of virtue pitted against vice, are also more clearly, from another angle, a case of ostentation pitted against irony, or earnestness against savoir faire. The genius of these two philosophers of work, one might even say, is their ability to hold these opposite attitudes in productive tension. Who is the more earnest, finally, or the most knowing? Who the more pompous, the more sophisticated? The first impulse is to see Franklin as the standard of sober pomposity, producing earnest recipes for moral perfection, and Johnson as the knowing ironist. But Franklin was also the air-bathing, flirtatious epicure, and Johnson a guilt- and angst-ridden moralist. How could we say who, finally, more fundamentally helped shape the work ethic we have inherited?

The standard answer, especially since Max Weber, has always been Franklin the schedule maker, but for what audience? What would the effect have been on my son, recumbent on the couch, had I read the central chapter of Franklin's autobiography to him? "It was about this time that I conceiv'd the bold and arduous Project of arriving at moral Perfection." Could he have any response to that but some variety of derisive laughter? On the other hand, what about Johnson?

> While a man, infatuated with the promises of greatness, wastes his
> hours and days in attendance and solicitation, the honest opportuni-
> ties of improving his condition pass by without his notice; he neg-
> lects to cultivate his own barren soil, because he expects every
> moment to be placed in regions of spontaneous fertility, and is sel-
> dom roused from his delusion but by the gripe of distress, which he
> cannot resist, and the sense of evils which cannot be remedied.

He might have jumped to agree that wasting "hours and days in attendance and solicitation" sounds like a bad idea. Yes, he might have
said, I, too, would like to cultivate . . . wait, my barren soil? The more
closely one attends to Johnson's idler prose, the more complicated
it becomes, the more it slips from compliment to insult, the more
deeply ironic it appears.

But then again, doesn't Franklin's statement cry out for an ironic
reading as well? Moral perfection? Could anybody possibly mean
that? Franklin, like Johnson, was known for his wit, and that wit leav-
ened many of his moral maxims. Take, for instance, Poor Richard's
second grindstone adage, that "a man may, if he knows not how to
save as he gets, keep his nose to the grindstone." When such statements have been repeated by civic leaders, politicians, and clerics, it
has always been with a noticeable diminishment of humor and a less
nuanced relationship between will and penury. Instead of "I am a
strong believer in luck and I find the harder I work the more I have of
it," which acknowledges the importance of luck while at the same
time undercutting its importance, we eventually get the kind of irony-
and subtlety-free politics that brought us the Personal Responsibility
and Work Opportunity Reconciliation Act of 1996. Franklin may be
the central framer of American ideas of work and responsibility, but
he was rarely as uninteresting, conceptually, as the faux moralism of
that bill's title. And he was not the humorless, secularized Puritan described by Max Weber, who claimed that Franklin crucially "gets
nothing out of his wealth for himself, except the irrational sense of
having done his job well." Franklin was also very concerned to get his
air baths, his long French salon afternoons, and his fancy late suppers.
His wit, his consistent recourse to irony—rather than what Weber
takes to be his Protestant work ethic—is what has made his writing
about work so resonant for so long.

The Idler and his diverse descendants were even more tied to forms of wit, sarcasm, satire, and ambiguity, and slacker prose is never without irony—sometimes ham-fisted, but often not only subtle but complex. The result is a series of pictures of idlers, loafers, loungers, and slackers that may seem, at one level, like a call for converts, like an invitation to identity. But those idlers were always, in fact, riven with self-doubt. The idler's opposite number, the ethical worker, may always have been driven, as Johnson suggested, by a leisure ethic, but the idler, like Johnson himself, has almost always been driven by a work ethic as well. The slacker has rarely been the advertisement for himself he advertises himself to be.

III

LOUNGERS, ROMANTICS,
AND RIP VAN WINKLE

In which the Lounger, the Idler's spiritual brother, appears toward the end of the eighteenth century—Meander, Abel Slug, Esq., and other icons of lounging have their say—and Rip Van Winkle sleeps through his career.

After Johnson's *Idler*, there was never a period when some version of that ironic persona was not featured in the magazines of England and America, just as there was never a time, after Benjamin Franklin, when one could not find printed instructions for getting ahead through diligence. At times, either party to this cultural conversation could veer toward earnestness, but much more often, especially for the idler side, some comedy has been part of the package. In the late eighteenth and early nineteenth century, there was an explosion of slacker narratives and characters, images of the culture's complex fear and exuberance about the profound industrial reformation of the world.

The Lounger, for instance, a magazine published in Edinburgh from 1785 to 1787, or some thirty years after Johnson's *Idler*, was almost hysterical in its desire to play out the figure. *The Lounger* was edited by Henry Mackenzie, at the time the leading man of Scottish letters and one of the foremost literary lights of the British Isles. An important member of the Scottish Enlightenment, he helped found the Royal Society of Edinburgh and was important in forwarding the

careers of Walter Scott—who dedicated *Waverley* (1814) to Mackenzie, "the Scottish Addison"—and Robert Burns. Mackenzie was born
in 1745, and so was a child when Franklin and Johnson, in middle
age, began to construct the industrial work ethic and the slacker ethic.
He became famous not for anything related to work, but as a writer of
sentimental novels, especially *The Man of Feeling* (1771), a tear-
soaked testament to male schmaltz. He was also successful in law and
government, working as an attorney for thirty-four years and then as
comptroller of taxes for Scotland for another thirty years until his
death at age eighty-six. Like Johnson, he was not the slacker he pre-
tended to be, and Scott was quite surprised when he met Mackenzie:
"We would suppose a retired, modest somewhat affected man with a
white handkerchief and a sigh ready for every sentiment. No such
thing. H.M. is alert as a contracting tailor's needle in every sort of
business—a politician and a sportsman." No slouch at home, either,
Mackenzie had fourteen children.

Mackenzie's *Lounger* was a hit not just in Edinburgh but in London and beyond, in the colonies and ex-colonies. It contained a variety of essays, some more clearly didactic than others, but most of them
difficult for readers now to comprehend. The introduction to the first
number of the magazine begins, "Nothing is perhaps so difficult as to
find out business proper for the idle; and though it may appear para-
doxical, yet I believe none have so much need of it as they," and the
paradoxes just keep piling up from there. Some people, the writer suggests, do nothing and then, out of boredom or shame, end up "dissipated without amusement, and intemperate without pleasure." These
idlers get what they deserve, both in terms of their own dissatisfaction
and their censure by others. "There is however a kind of men . . . who
hold a station of less destructive and more dignified indolence . . . idle
of conduct, but of active minds." This kind of man, of course, is the
lounger.

So far we are in Johnson's basic territory, with slightly more emphasis on the life of the mind. The eighteenth-century writers were accustomed by their classical educations to think of literary and learned
pursuits in terms of what Cicero called *otium cum dignitate*, leisure
with dignity, such *otium* (its opposite *negotium*, or business) being the
necessary condition for producing art and literature. Thus idlers and
loungers claimed that they, like Roman philosophers, simply wanted

more time for the higher pursuits, that they were devotees of contemplation rather than crude mammon. And Mackenzie claimed that the lounger has all sorts of other advantages as well. Unlike men in a particular profession, who necessarily spend most of their time with colleagues—doctors comporting with doctors, lawyers with lawyers—the lounger knows everyone. "He who is an idler without unsocial dispositions, finds occasional companions in all characters and professions," writes Mackenzie. The lounger is superior, not just in this but in all ways to his busy counterparts, and the British lounger superior to the loungers in other countries. In France and Italy, he notes, there are no direct synonyms for lounger, because the near-loungers are too busy: they "contrive to do nothing . . . with so much interest in their looks, and so much movement in their gestures" that they almost aren't loungers at all. As in Franklin's case, the appearance of one's relation to work is more important than the relation itself.

But then things get murkier as the author admits that he both liked and didn't like being called a lounger: "If at any time I felt the undignified sound of the name, yet I took credit with myself, on the other hand, for not deserving it. It flattered a secret pride, to be somewhat more than the world thought me." He is proud to be seen as a lounger, but proud of his "secret" work, proud to be a better lounger than the French or Italians (who don't deserve the title), and proud to not really deserve it himself, because he is writing—work that prima facie disqualifies him. He forgives himself for the disqualification immediately, however: "A Lounger of the sort I could wish to be thought, is one, who amidst a certain intercourse with mankind preserves a constant intimacy with himself; it is not therefore to be wondered at, if he should sometimes, if I may be allowed the expression, correspond with himself, and write down, if he can write at all, what he wishes this favorite companion more particularly to remark." This lounger's ironic distance on himself, his wit, is of more importance than his identity as an idler. What follows continues to add layers of irony. In explaining the lounger's need for intellectual company, he writes, "Even the perfect idler, like some other harmless and insignificant animals whom naturalists are acquainted with, though he can live on air, cannot subsist in vacuo," and the gag is in noting his own insignificance, after so many pages of self-praise and congratulation.

In the Letters to the Editor section, obviously fictional since it is the very first issue, we get a letter complaining about "female Loungers":

> I sincerely wish that many of my friends and visitors would follow your example, and learn to be idle without disturbing those who are obliged, from their situation, to be busy. I suffer daily so much from the intrusion of a set of female Loungers, (forgive me for using your title), that it has prompted me to address myself to you, in hopes that you will, in some of your future Essays, teach my unfortunately idle friends how to employ their tedious forenoons without obliging me to be as idle as themselves.

The letter is supposedly written by a woman who wants to be freed from "the heavy burden" and "fatigue of entertaining Lounging Ladies" who simply want to escape "their own . . . insipid company." But it is written by Mackenzie, obviously, who then, as the Lounger, graciously responds:

> That branch of our family of which she complains is so numerous, and so difficult to deal with, that I am afraid the attempts of any in-dividual for their better regulation or disposal would be fruitless . . . They are a sort of vagrants, or sturdy beggars, whom, like the others of the tribe, idleness sets afloat, to the disquiet of the industrious part of the community.

He suggests a "new bill for the improvement of Edinburgh" which "might provide a work-house for those fashionable mumpers." The workhouse would have different departments, for the making of nov-els, and "Enigmas," and "the fabrication of Scandal."

By now it has become less clear what side of what issues the magazine is on. Another letter announces plans for a *Biographia Loungeriana Scotica; or, The Lives of the most eminent Loungers of Scotland*, in two volumes, one on the "Strenuous Loungers," one on "Indolent Loungers." The fictional letter writer gives the example of "My late cousin, Sir Thomas Lounger of Loiterhall in Lingerdale," and of his own father, who "died of lethargy, with which he had been long afflicted." Mackenzie seems to be indulging in random humor here, for what is the point? Are the strenuous loungers the ones who are idle in conduct but have active minds, or are they the dissatisfied debauchers? Who is the target of all these jokes? The lounger living at Loiterhall or the idle reader of these idle jokes? Surely this can't all be Mackenzie's guilty conscience and surely not simply an elaborate display of wit. The Lounger is a satirical figure, and as such offers a critique, in this case one that goes in several directions at once, making fun of both industry and idleness, the drab future and the decadent past, while puncturing the delusions of both useful and useless citizens.

A further explanation is suggested by *The Lounger's Miscellany; or the Lucubrations of Abel Slug, Esq.*, a London fortnightly that started just as Mackenzie's died, and clearly modeled itself on *The Lounger*. Lasting for twenty issues in 1788 and early 1789, the eponymous Mr. Slug announces that he "dedicate[s] these pages to the peculiar use and service of loungers, . . . those who place their *summum bonum* in oscitancy [*sic*] of mind, vacancy of ideas, and a general and studied negligence. Instead, therefore, of complimenting the lounger on his industry, I shall rather commend the vigour of his indolence." This is fun, too, perhaps, but there is always a question of how much fun of this sort anyone would really want to have. Of more interest is the definition of the lounger that is offered, also in the introductory issue:

> THE LOUNGERS are a remnant of the Epicurean sect; their pleasure comes in the absence of pain, and their business in having nothing to do. The life of a Lounger may perhaps with more propriety be likened to a dream, than that of other mortals; from which if he should by any mischance be awakened, as he walks through the world in his sleep, like Caliban in the Tempest, "he cries to dream again." Thus he may be said to live perpetually in that state in which the heroes of the golden age died, "as if overcome with sleep;" his days passing away in torpid inactivity, a state of existence which cannot properly be called animal or vegetable, like the retirement of a tortoise, or a swallow's winter.

The self-deprecation is very much like that of Johnson's Idler or Mackenzie's Lounger, if slightly more colorful and animalistic. But the Epicurean tag takes something that had been in the background of Johnson and Mackenzie and pulls it front and center. Abel Slug, Esq., finds leisure important because it is necessary to pleasure, Epicurean pleasure.

Lounger profligacy is different from the desperate grasping for pleasure of the run-of-the-mill bourgeois, Slug suggests. The "doctrine of Epicurus," he declares, "seems well calculated to form that ornament of the human species, an unruffled sensualist, a debauchee without passions." This will become a larger and larger part of the slacker image over the years: the slacker has time to stop and smell the roses, so the slacker knows which roses smell best. The slacker— the slackers will argue in various ways from this time on—is the most up-to-date, the most fully informed, the most enlightened consumer. And as Mackenzie suggested, the slacker is the best person to make the cultural products, like ironic slacker manifestos and novels, which others looking for pleasure should consume.

This makes a certain kind of sense. Since getting and spending are the two basic economic activities, arguments about one imply arguments about the other. Just as Franklin's dicta included imprecations against idleness and against wasteful spending, so the idlers and loungers of the late eighteenth and early nineteenth centuries railed against work regimentation and parsimoniousness. If the work ethic suggests that slackers lead useless lives of pure consumption, the slackers suggest that work is the contemptible half of the equation, that work is a kind of idling over the unworthy part of human existence. Life is made good and whole not by getting, which after all only makes sense as preparatory, the slackers suggest, but by spending. The obvious, oppressive logic of Franklin's work philosophy—don't spend, just keep getting—was countered by the completely impossible logic of the slacker: don't get, spend.

∞

The British Isles exported these writings to America, where they were quite popular and sprouted new imitators, following upon a long and much more literal history of sending idlers across the Atlantic. In 1609, the Virginia Company, eager for more agricultural workers, told the City of London that they would be glad to take the swarms of idlers off their hands if the City would contribute to the costs of their transportation. In 1619, a year more famous for the arrival of the first twenty Africans in Virginia, James I wrote to Sir Thomas Smyth, the treasurer of the Virginia Company:

> Whereas our Court hath of late been troubled by divers idle young people, who though they have been twise punished still continue to followe the same havuing noe employment; we have noe other course to cleer our Court from them have thought fitt to send them unto you desiring you att the next opportunitie to send them away to Virginia and to take sure order that they may be sett to worke there, [otherwise] they will never be reclaimed from the idle life of vagabonds.

The Virginia Company, less sure that this was such a good deal, balked, but ended up taking half of the one hundred the court wanted. In 1618 and 1619, London courts also sent some two hundred orphans to the colonies so they wouldn't become an idle burden on the crown, arranging to have them apprenticed to various trades and shops. Although Francis Bacon warned against sending "scum" to the colonies, John Locke was one of many who thought vagrants should be sent to America, and John Donne thought it a good way to "sweep your streets, and wash your doors from idle persons."

When they arrived in the colonies, the vagrants and orphans tended to be immediately indentured along with most of the other immigrants. Of the roughly 130,000 British immigrants in the seventeenth century, 75 to 85 percent were indentured servants. On arriving in America, they found themselves subject to fairly strict laws against loitering. In 1633 the Massachusetts General Court attempted to fix wages low enough to require men to work longer hours, but they failed and instead simply decreed that "all workmen shall work the whole day" on threat of punishment. Whipping and fines were imposed for idleness in Plymouth Colony, Connecticut, and Rhode Island in the late seventeenth and early eighteenth centuries. Connecticut in 1750 had "An Act for Restraining, Correcting, Suppressing, and Punishing Rogues, Vagabonds, Common Beggars and other Lewd, Idle, dissolute, Profane, and Disorderly Persons, and for setting them to Work." The clergy did what it could to help, as well; Benjamin Colman, a minister in Boston, reminded his flock in 1717 that "all Nature is Industrious and every Creature about us diligent in their proper Work." Colman, John Cotton, Thomas Hooker, and Cotton Mather were, according to historian Paul Bernstein, "the last bastion of God-centered work values," and John Cotton preached that "cursed is he that doth the worke of the Lord negligently, and the work of the calling is the worke of the Lord." Cotton Mather is said to have remarked about the unemployed, "Let them starve."

Mather was an important influence on Franklin, at first through his writings and then through his scientific activities and his library, which he opened to Franklin as a young man. So it is no surprise that as Franklin secularized the work ethic, it retained many of the same basic values, such as the distinction between the deserving and undeserving poor, a distinction maintained by the majority of important thinkers, writers, and politicians in the colonies and early republic. Thomas Jefferson, Benjamin Rush, Richard Henry Lee, Samuel Adams, Henry Laurens, John Adams, Nathaniel Ames, John Pynchon, Samuel Johnson (the American Samuel Johnson, that is), Samuel Willard, John Brainerd, Benjamin Wadsworth, and John Winthrop all distinguished between what they called the "deserving poor" and "sturdy beggars," the latter being chronic, habitual malingerers. They believed that giving charity to loiterers only increased begging and never helped stem poverty. Boston built a workhouse in 1685 for those "who lived in idleness and tipplinge with great neglect of their callings." Almost a century later, in 1769, Boston commissioned and adopted a report on the condition of the poor that concluded that idleness is "the parent of all vices." Boston and Newport warned off vagrants in the 1720s and 1730s, and New York and Philadelphia made a concerted effort to drive off vagrants in the 1760s.

It should be noted that most of these attitudes come from the northern cities, and that the South began under a somewhat different dispensation. In Jamestown, for instance, John Smith proposed a work program in 1612 that featured a four-hour workday, leaving the rest of the day for "pastimes and merry exercise." In Spanish America, as one historian notes, "work did not redeem and had no value in itself. Manual work was servile. The superior man neither worked nor traded." And for certain observers at the time, the entire country was more relaxed than England. The Philadelphian John Dickinson, for instance, studying law in London from 1754 to 1756, found England to be a land of overpaced, turbulent "luxury and corruption." In letters to his parents, he wrote, "Notwithstanding all the diversions of England, I shall return to America with rapture . . . Tis rude, but it's innocent. Tis wild, but it's private. There life is a stream pure & unruffled, here an ocean briny & tempestuous. There we enjoy life, here we spend it."

Dickinson's complaint is the standard complaint against modernity, that it destroys one's relation to nature and to time. But whatever unruffled innocence Dickinson nostalgically remembered was quickly disappearing in America as well. Industrialization in the colonies meant that in America, as Franklin was reminding people, time was to be spent or saved rather than enjoyed. And by the end of the century, American versions of Johnson's and Mackenzie's ironic resistance to the new order appeared as well. One of the earliest was the "American Addison," Joseph Dennie, the man who more than any other established the lounger in America. Dennie was a child during the American Revolution, five years old in Boston during the Tea Party and six during the Battle of Lexington, where his parents moved that year. As a boy, he wrote poetry that he found so moving he would cry as he read it. His mother seemed to find it similarly moving and encouraged him, but his father, a prosperous merchant and importer of West Indian molasses, rum, hemp, and sugar, told him to stop. "In my boyhood," Dennie wrote when he was in his thirties, "I remember a parent would sometimes repeat lessons of economy as I sat on his knee, and then lift me in his arms, that I might look on Hogarth's plates of Industry and Idleness." Hogarth's series of etchings, from 1747, told the story of two London apprentices, Tom Idle, who is indolent, turns to a life of crime, and is finally executed for murder, and Frank Goodchild, who is diligent, marries the boss's daughter, and becomes lord mayor of London. It is an odd object lesson to be showing a knee-sitting–size boy, given the series' prostitutes in dishabille, and it is also very scanty on the work ethic itself, however fulsome on the rewards and punishments involved. Only the first of the twelve plates shows Goodchild at work, sitting at a loom, while Tom idles at his. The rest show either Tom Idle debauching or Goodchild reaping his rewards. Small wonder that Dennie was not successfully indoctrinated: "On youthful fancy," he wrote years later, "the picture was more impressed than the precept."

His father sent him to a commercial school when he was fifteen to learn bookkeeping, and at sixteen he began working as a clerk in a countinghouse. As Dennie's early-twentieth-century biographer politely put it, "A year's employment was enough to convince all concerned that Dennie's talents were not of the mercantile variety." He was sent to live with a minister in nearby Needham to prepare for Harvard, which he then entered in 1787. In his first letters home he recounted his typical Harvard Wednesday: up at 6:00; prayers and a recitation of Homer until 7:15; 7:30 breakfast; 10:00 a lecture on divinity; 11:00 a lecture on mechanics; 12:30 dinner; 3:00 a lecture on the planet Mercury; 4:00 recitation of the Greek Testament; 5:00 prayers; and then an evening spent preparing the next day's recitations. "This I think is quite sufficient employment for one day," he wrote, "but the three last days in the week we have very little to do." Although he would come to have many more complaints against Harvard, this was the last time he complained of having too little work.

∞

Dennie was recognized at Harvard as a promising student. Joseph Story remembered him as "the most talented, taking light literature as a standard" in his year, with a vivid imagination and great facility as a writer. "He might unquestionably have taken the highest rank in his class, for he had great happiness, both in writing and in elocution; but he was negligent in his studies, and not faithful to the genius with which nature had endowed him." Dennie remained a great reader (often "feasting all night upon some literary banquet"), but detested the rest of his study; mathematics, for instance, he considered "a barren speculative science that neither fills the brain nor ameliorates the heart." He went on in this half-disengaged manner for two years, but in his senior year he fell afoul of the authorities. The exact circumstances (i.e., how much drinking might have been involved) are not entirely clear, but otherwise the records of the college paint a plain picture of events:

It appeared that one of the Governors of the College having repaired to the room of Dennie and Welles [his roommate] in consequence of a disorder there, in the afternoon of the 30th of the last month, was treated by Dennie with great disrespect; that he remained covered in the presence of said Governor, until ordered to

take off his hat; that when spoken to he replied to him in an insolent
manner, that he positively refused to go with him to his chamber,
when ordered, and persisted in his neglect to do so.

For this open rebellion, Dennie was "degraded ten places in his class,"
a punishment that was announced in the chapel after morning
prayers.

Dennie, like many a young rebel before and since, reacted to this
chastisement by becoming more and more defiant and insolent,
egged on by his "lively coterie." A couple of months later, things came
to a head when Dennie read a speech by William Pitt to his fellow
students in chapel. Supposedly this was a simple declamation of an
important feat of oratory, but it was clear to everyone listening that
Dennie was referring, only slightly obliquely, to the "Governor of the
College" who had gotten him into such trouble. Pitt's speech (his famous reply to Horace Walpole, which, incidentally, had been
recorded by Samuel Johnson when he was a political reporter) begins:

> The atrocious crime of being a young man, which the honorable
> gentleman has, with such spirit and decency, charged upon me, I
> shall neither attempt to palliate nor deny, but content myself with
> wishing that I may be one of those whose follies may cease
> with their youth, and not of that number who are ignorant in spite
> of experience. Whether youth can be imputed to any man as a re-
> proach, I will not, sir, assume the province of determining; but surely
> age may become justly contemptible, if the opportunities which it
> brings have passed away without improvement, and vice appears to
> prevail when the passions have subsided. The wretch who, after hav-
> ing seen the consequences of a thousand errors, continues still to
> blunder, and whose age has only added obstinacy to stupidity, is
> surely the object of either abhorrence or contempt, and deserves not
> that his gray hairs should secure him from insult.

Dennie was suspended for six months.

Dennie may thus be said to have become the first truly American
slacker, one who like Johnson and Mackenzie was always ready to criticize the status quo, but one who, very unlike those otherwise quite
conservative Brits, was simply against any and all authority—an early

version of the Brando slacker character in *The Wild One* (1953), who, when asked what he's rebelling against, answers, "What've you got?" Remaining true to type, after being expelled, Dennie railed against the "race of Jackasses" that punished him, and against Harvard itself, "that sink of vice, that temple of dullness, that roost of owls." In the six months he spent away from the "solemn blockheads" on the Harvard faculty, he continued to read and wrote letters to his fellow students from Connecticut, arguing the relative merit of various writers. After a course of reading Hume, Beattie, Hobbes, and other philosophers, he writes that "time is wholly lost" if it is spent tackling the intricacies of their thought, and he adds metaphysics to the list of useless disciplines. "To cultivate this barren, unprofitable science is worse than wasting time, it is murdering time." He also wrote, with sober foreboding, about what he might do after graduation, which would happen as soon as he returned, filed a formal petition for reinstatement, and took a final examination that June. After what he called "these last acts of pigmy despotism" had been exercised, he left the college without attending commencement ceremonies, glad to be free of the "dark and hollow manoeuvres of a club of stupid pedants." Dennie, then, unlike the middle-aged Johnson or Mackenzie, begins his career as a spokesperson for idlers while a late adolescent, the age that in the next century would produce the most slackers, just as his rebellious, anti-authoritarian gloss would remain a central part of slacker identity.

Though he may sound like an irascible and pissy young fellow, there are many testimonials to Dennie's good company. He is described by friends as a brilliant conversationalist, witty, jovial, quick, and gay, "a charming companion." He decided to study law and spent some time in an attorney's office in New Hampshire, but when he was offered £200 a year (considered by his circle to be a fairly meager salary) to be a lay reader, a kind of unordained minister, at a church in Portsmouth, New Hampshire, he quickly agreed. "Convinced more & more every day of the brevity and uncertainty of life, I deem it madness to lose in unavailing sorrow and repinings a single hour," he wrote to a friend, and it was perhaps this carpe diem attitude, and perhaps his fondness for cigars and whist, that resulted in that contract not being renewed after six months. He went back to the law, opening a small office (he didn't want too much business) in Keene in 1794, where he proceeded to be at best a lousy lawyer. According to one of his contemporaries, he was much more interested in the occasional well-turned phrase in his law reading than in the arguments or precedents, and so all he could do in court was repeat some of those phrases, nicely shaped into a classically ornate oration, much to the amusement and sometimes admiration of his auditors but to the distress of his client.

He continued to practice law halfheartedly, to the tune of £90 a year or so, through the end of the decade, but after a spectacular oration, full of learned frills, in front of a judge with no classical education who humiliated him for it, he stayed away from courtroom appearances. He also began publishing periodical essays and eventually took a larger and larger part in the magazine world, including the editorship of the *Farmer's Weekly Museum*, where his salary of £110, combined with the intermittent income from his law office, brought him back to his marginal pay as a lay preacher. Two essay series—one called *The Farrago* (or mixed fodder), and the other, in response to complaints that the *Farrago* essays were too frivolous, *The Lay Preacher*—made him famous, giving him a wide reputation as an elegant stylist. His flourishes and flair were, in fact, well beyond the capacity of the average American periodical writer, many of whom, like Franklin and his brother, were printers first and only accidental writers. Some of Dennie's essays were on political topics (he was a staunch Federalist), but more often they took on cultural issues or ethical questions. *The Farrago* sometimes spoke in praise of idlers and sometimes wrote as their scourge, starting with his first essay, when he defends "desultory literature," such as that he produces, against charges of triviality. The indolent, he writes, need to be given moral lessons in a form they are not too indolent to tackle. Of course it would be better for them to read Locke and Bacon, but they are too lazy, they need *The Spectator*, *The Idler* and *The Farrago*. The essay, like *The Idler* and *The Lounger*, winks at its readers: we, the indolent.

Like Johnson and Mackenzie, Dennie took on slacker pseudonyms: Meander, Samuel Saunter, Charles Chameleon, and the American Lounger. Meander's journal is classic fictional slacker autobiography: "Did *nothing* very busily till four. Seized with a lethargic yawn, which lasted till seven." In "The Lounger's Diary" an unnamed slacker gets a full, Franklin-like daily schedule:

Sunday morning, half past nine. Yawned;—execrably sleepy

Ten. Read half your bill.—Headach[e].

Half past ten. Too cold for church.—Headach[e] increased by bell.—N.B. To change my apartment, that I may avoid that noise.

Eleven to Twelve. Took my chocolate.—Read half a page of Henrietta Harville . . .

Twelve. Terrace—not a soul.—On my return saw a cocked hat with man under it.

Half past one. Dinner.–No appetite . . .

Half past five. Sipped tea with Feather.—N.B. His silk stockings.—N.B. The pattern seen last winter in town.—N.B. Not to tell him till he has worn them.

Six to half past. Yawned and rou'd.

Half past to seven. Rou'd and yawned.

Seven to eight. Got vapours looking out Microcosm.

Eight to nine. Wrote my journal.—Buckled my shoe.

Nine to ten. Intolerable vapours.—N.B. vapours greatest bore in the universe . . .

Ten to half past. Lounged to Dapper's room.—Caught him reading Latin . . .

The morning headache may or may not be a hangover, and drinking (and in later years drugs) have often accompanied slacker lifestyles. Overconsumption in general, in fact, marks the slacker. The comments about fashion—and Dennie was known, especially as a young man, for his dandyism—also show that, like the British lounger, the American one is as interested in consumption as he is in lack of production. One's silk stockings should be this year's pattern, not last's, and the right cocked hat is so important it almost obliterates its owner.

The Lay Preacher was successful enough to spawn a series of imitators, including the *Occasional Preacher, Itinerant Preacher*, and *Gay Preacher*. The English traveler John Davis reported that Dennie's was the most widely read series in America in 1802. And indeed in a literary world still completely dominated by British writing, Dennie quickly became a standout among American authors, collaborating with one of the few others, Royall Tyler, whose 1787 play *The Contrast* was the first major American theatrical production. Other significant American authors of the time included Susanna Rowson, Philip Freneau, Joel Barlow and the other Connecticut Wits, and Charles Brockden Brown: small-time operators, at best, compared with Robert Burns, William Blake, Mary Wollstonecraft, Fanny Burney, Samuel Taylor Coleridge, William Wordsworth, and Sir Walter Scott shipping books from Great Britain. It was a tiny literary pond that Dennie was making a splash in.

And he could do it without working too hard. A former apprentice remembered that Dennie wrote with great rapidity but was more often than not late with his copy. Going to the building where Dennie both lived and had his law office, the apprentice would regularly "find him in bed at a late hour in the morning . . . His *copy* was often given out in small portions, a paragraph or two at a time; sometimes it was written in the printing-office, while the compositor was waiting to put it in type." The apprentice, known as "the printer's devil," would sometimes interrupt Dennie in a game of cards, and Dennie would simply "ask some one *to play his hand for him while he could give the devil his due*." Dennie was the central figure at Crafts Tavern, which was "the resort of a *coterie* of wags, wits, and literati," according to one of them. "Wine drinking, late suppers, card playing, joke cracking, and the like formed the programme for frequent meetings," he remembered. "And the 'wee hours of the morning' were the only acknowledged signals for breaking up."

Dennie's fame led to new opportunities, as did his political writing. In the heated politics of the new republic, the Federalists believed that the Democrats would be like the French revolutionaries and have the blood of the upper class running in the streets, while the Democrats believed that the Federalists were secretly trying to give the country back to England and restore monarchial rule. Dennie's political satires and highly partisan filler pieces, promoting Federalist policies and politicians and viciously attacking their Democratic rivals, were appreciated by Federalist leaders, and in 1799 he moved to Philadelphia, still the national capital, to become the editor of the partisan *Gazette of the United States* and a private secretary to Timothy Pickering, then secretary of state. His job was a political plum, but Dennie wrote to his parents that it was no sinecure. Extremely demanding, he said, the job required six hours a day minimum, and often extra hours and evenings, calling on all his personal and literary skills. Still, when President John Adams replaced Pickering with John Marshall in May of 1800, Pickering's letter of recommendation to Marshall suggested otherwise: "I cannot, because I ought not, to conceal from you, that Mr. Dennie's habits and literary turn—I should rather say, his insatiable appetite for knowledge, useful as well as ornamental, render his service as a clerk less productive than the labours of many dull men." Dennie's appointment was not renewed.

In the *Gazette*, and his new magazine, *The Port Folio*, which began in 1801, Dennie continued to combine literary essays with political pieces. *The Port Folio* was advertised as a magazine in the style of Johnson's *Rambler* and Mackenzie's *Lounger*, and the first issue was written almost entirely by Dennie and John Quincy Adams. Adams, like his father a Federalist, would be elected to the Senate the next year and to the presidency in 1824, but his pieces for Dennie were not particularly partisan. His contributions to the first issue were a verse translation of Juvenal and the first installment of *Journal of a Tour Through Silesia*, a travelogue with observations on European politics and culture. With the election of Thomas Jefferson in 1800, Federalists like Dennie and the Adamses were sure that the country would go to pieces as the democratic rabble took over. Jefferson was no better than Robespierre, they thought, or at least said, and *The Port Folio* was decidedly and proudly reactionary, as signaled by the name of its pseudonymous editor, Oliver Oldschool, Esq. When Jefferson invited Thomas Paine to return to America, Dennie fired away:

> If, during the present season of national abasement, folly, and vice, any portent could surprise, sober men would be utterly confounded . . . that the loathsome Thomas Paine, a drunken atheist, and the scavenger of faction, is invited to return in a national ship, to America, by the first magistrate of the people! . . . If that rebel rascal should come to preach from HIS bible to the populace, and if the hair-brain'd Fayette should vex us with HIS diplomacy, it would be time for every honest and insulted man of dignity to flee.

This level of vituperation was common, not just in Dennie's magazines, but across a political journalism that accused Jefferson of keeping a "Congo harem" and Hamilton of being a "whoremonger." Dennie was in fact once sued for libel, but he was acquitted.

Dennie's lounger guises sometimes conflict with his overt politics. As historian and critic Laura Rigal has noted, the proto-consumerist ideals that Dennie's loungers espouse are at odds with both the Federalists and the Democrats, and the various personae that Dennie adopts do not all cohere into a simple position. Indeed, if the lounger of "The Lounger's Diary" is without ambition, not so with Meander, who is simply constantly sidetracked. "Overslept myself, did not rise till nine," he writes, but quasi-apologetically. "Dressed, and went out, intending to go to the office; but as the morning was uncommonly beautiful, I recollected an aphorism of Dr. Cheyne's, that exercise should form part of a student's religion. Accordingly I rambled in the woods for two hours." Meander is very easily waylaid ("Rose at nine, looked abroad; and the atmosphere being dusky . . . felt unqualified for reading"), but he is waylaid from his career as a law student, unlike the more compleat lounger of the "Diary," who has no career, and no desire for one, or even to be caught reading Latin.

Like the political debates in which Dennie was involved, his slacker satires circle around the question of class and the changing nature of work. The other writing Dennie published did as well. John Quincy Adams's travels in Silesia, which were published serially in the first forty-five issues of *The Port Folio*, are acutely interested in work and production. Unlike the idle midcentury rambler of Johnson—or that more contemporary, romantic rambler in the Lake District, Wordsworth—Adams seeks out factories to examine. In Grünberg, Adams inspects the spinning and carding machines used in the production of cloth, as he had earlier inspected the machines of England. In Bunzlau he studies a pottery yard and marvels at the size of the pots they produced. Everywhere he is interested not just in the people and the culture but in the processes of manufacturing. He is, as Rigal notes, a member of the industrializing class, and he writes in a letter home that he would feel guilty about going on a rambling vacation if he didn't know that he was also doing useful work in sizing up manufacturing along the way.

Manufacturing was, of course, the wave of the future. Matthew Boulton's Birmingham jewelry, plating, and silverware shop, founded in 1762, is often taken to be the first modern factory (Boulton would become James Watt's partner in 1775), but the manufactory, a kind of cross between an older form of workshop and the modern factory, had already transformed work for many. And this transformation was seen by some as the way to alleviate all work-related ills. In Philadelphia as early as 1769, a nonprofit stock company was proposed to start a linen factory with the express intent of providing employment to the poor. The number of poor in and around Philadelphia was growing, the prospectus claimed, and "many of them, especially in Winter, are reduced to great Straits, and rendered burthensome to their Neighbours." This scheme was an attempt to shift that burden from the neighbors to the poor themselves, who would pay their own way by working the poorhouse factory. The answer to the growing poverty caused by industrialization was increased industrialization.

Across all the political divisions of American society at the dawn of the nineteenth century, manufacturing was essential to basic policy and personal decisions. A letter from Thomas Jefferson to James Monroe in 1801, for instance, takes great interest in Eli Whitney's gun manufacturing, noting that Whitney's cotton gin is already in wide use; since the gun locks have interchangeable parts, Jefferson writes, they would be easier to repair on the battlefield, thus an obvious advantage for the military. Virginia in 1798 began to build its own manufactory of arms, with production beginning in 1803, to supply the state militia with weapons. The state, the civic organizations, and the laborers all began to see the world through this new form of work.

In the context of these changes, Dennie's loungers can be seen as a throwback to an aristocratic way of life that was disappearing in industrializing, democratizing America. The Federalists, in their fear of and distaste for the people, necessarily ended up often siding with aristocrats, and the lounger can be seen, from this angle, as a kind of bulwark against the materialist, leveling, democratic tendencies of the time, as someone who exercises a connoisseurship of knowledge and taste in a world overrun by "drunken atheists." But Dennie also used aristocratic pretension as an insult. In 1804, for instance, Dennie's *Port Folio* printed what was purported to be a found copy of Jefferson's diary that had been dropped mistakenly by the Potomac, and part of the political satire is to make Jefferson look not like a man of the people, but like a lounging aristocrat:

Monday 8 o'clock, 20ᵗʰ February, 1804

> Left Sally [Hemings]—damn's bore, to rise early—but must seem
> industrious, nothing to do. Met Madison at breakfast—don't
> much like him . . .
>
> *10 o'clock.* Wrote half a page of my dissertation on cockroaches . . .

In Europe, aristocrats lost ground as the Industrial Revolution advanced, because their income was from the land. What the historian
Peter Stearns has called "the maneuverings of these beleaguered aristocrats trying to compensate for their economic anachronism" took
many forms, including literary expression. When Dennie wrote that
"a democracy is scarcely tolerable at any period of national history,"
he longed for a more oligarchic world, one less "radically contemptible and vicious" than he claimed all democracies were. But
Dennie was not really a displaced aristocrat; his father was a fairly successful businessman, albeit one who had stopped earning (owing to
early dementia) by the time Dennie was in college, and who settled
no inheritance on his son. Dennie complained that he didn't find the
"Cosmo de Medici" he had hoped would support his literary work in
Philadelphia, and he was never a Medici himself; he simply imagined
a world in which his "learned leisure" was magnificently supported.

However much Dennie and his loungers pined for an aristocratic
yesteryear, they also looked forward to a more fully individualized,
more open world of options for work and consumption. It is not a
coincidence that many of the slackers he described were studying
to become lawyers—getting ready, however slowly, to oversee the increasingly complex contracts of a more thoroughly divided (as in "division of labor") and at the same time more complexly integrated
working world. What Dennie most sincerely hoped was that the classical notion of *otium*—that leisure whose purpose is learning, art, and
contemplation—would continue to have its place in a world that,
as Franklin's writing suggested, had no time to waste. "The 'man of
understanding' is rarely to be seen," Dennie writes, however self-
servingly. "In a world of weak ones it is our duty, it will be for our interest, too, to yield favors to the wise and bread to men of
understanding." Dennie hoped for a society that would give the necessary bread to men like himself and his literary friends. He hoped that
the kind of work he found important, but which clearly could not

compete in the same arena as metalworking factories and enormous textile mills, would nonetheless have its value recognized.

Why, then, are Dennie's loungers so pointedly useless? The hourly schedules in the fictional lounger diaries, like Franklin's schedule, suggest that he, too, felt that time was of the essence. Time is the ultimate commodity in an industrial economy. Agricultural work is task-oriented rather than clock-oriented; at harvest, time is always too short, but when it is raining during planting season, or when the ground is frozen, time is not as precious. In a factory, the relation between time and production is much more constant, and the clock becomes the measure of work. As Marx argued in "The Working Day" in *Kapital*, a certain amount of time produces the worker's salary, in effect, and a certain amount produces the factory's costs and profits, and therefore the most basic business planning and operation requires attention to clock time. As industrialization progressed more rapidly in England than in America, the transformation to a culture of clock time rather than "sun time" happened more quickly; a British visitor to the States in 1820 noticed that people did not, as he had become accustomed to at home, tell time by a clock, but always answered in relation to the sun: "If you ask what time it is, it either wants so many hours of noon, or it is so much before, or so much after *sundown*."

Franklin's schedule is clearly an early embrace of clock time, and the lounger diaries might seem to be the opposite, deriding the very idea that one should live life according to the clock. In a society obsessed with material gain and thinking of time as money, the loungers seemed to flaunt a willful disregard for their own economic interest. But however much the British aristocracy was the model for Dennie and his friends, they had no interest in living on the land. One thing slackers have always insisted on is their own up-to-date understanding of the world they are rejecting. The loungers were very much creatures of industrial mercantilism, and their consumerist hedonism, whatever else it might have been, was exceedingly modern. In his magazines Dennie proselytizes for a way of life—including buying the latest fashions—that he at the same time condemns as frivolous and wasteful, skewering the very options he offers. He keeps an ironic, at times depressive distance, as if he is somewhat bored not just by his culture's addiction to effort but also by his own poses. His melancholy is assuaged only by the comedy he finds in his own depressed debility.

He then packages that humor and sells it, and ends up working assiduously, if intermittently, at spreading both the gospel of idleness and
the pleasures of consumption.

Franklin and the loungers together usher in the new order of industrialized mercantilism, however fitfully. Franklin's writings insist on
regularity of habits, perseverance, and efficiency, and much has been
written on the necessity of such virtues in the new economy of his day.
But the loungers' championing of consumption—as long as it is connoisseurship—and of wandering and meandering also suggest necessary virtues in the newly interdependent importing and exporting
world of the turn of that century. As Marx said, the bourgeoisie cannot
rest until it has wandered over the face of the entire globe, and the literary loafers' open wandering and pleasure-seeking would be as important to the new economy as Franklin's regimented stability and
self-denial. One of Dennie's disciples praised him after his death in
1812 because, "instead of turning the meanders of fancy into a regular
channel," he allowed them to be "perpetually roaming, in quest of
pleasure." Franklin himself, of course, traveled and consumed widely,
as did Adams, the industrial spy, and many a full- or part-time literary
lounger.

The loungers can, in fact, be seen as spurs to work, just as reading
the strenuous maxims of the Franklins of this world can make a person want to step right off the treadmill. And this would explain some
of the self-deprecatory humor: the result of reading the story of Meander or the Lounger would be just as likely, and indeed perhaps more
likely, to induce someone to give up a life of idleness than to adopt
one.

∞

Back in England, hard on the heels of the lounger magazines came
the poets of indolence, otherwise known as the Romantic poets, and
they at their best saw the issue of work and slacking from several sides
at once. Unlike the satirists and politically motivated writers like Dennie, they tended to take idleness both more seriously and more
broadly, interested in the melancholic, guilt-ridden depressive version
of the lounger *and* the happy-go-lucky, ultra-relaxed connoisseur.
William Wordsworth, for instance, had a classic slacker profile: taken
to wandering the countryside as a boy (his father died when he was

thirteen), he continued to prefer "rambling" to work or study, having "little interest," according to a biographer, "in either the intellectual or social life of the university" he attended. "He never opened a mathematical book" and "even his literary studies were pursued irregularly." When he was supposed to be studying for his examinations in 1790, he set off instead for a long walk through the Alps. He spent his patrimony on his degree (conferred without distinction) and couldn't decide on a career. He considered the army, the church, the law, and teaching, and he rejected them all, moving to London to do nothing. "The world is too much with us, late and soon," he wrote in 1807: "Getting and spending, we lay waste our powers." But until that time he had done very little getting and consequently very little spending. He lived on a £900 inheritance left by a dying friend and wrote poetry during days "spent in a round of strenuous idleness," as he put it in *The Prelude*. He finished that autobiographical poem in 1805, but continued to somewhat desultorily revise it; it was not published until after his death. As a "rambling school-boy," he writes, he used to imagine what life was like for the shepherd he sees. He describes him as "A freeman, wedded to his life of hope / And hazard, and hard labour interchanged / With that majestic indolence so dear / To native man." In other poems, too, he talks of "voluptuous indolence," "pleasing indolence," and "happy idleness." Nonetheless, elsewhere he describes the flip side: berating "tiresome indolence" and "dissolute idleness," suggesting that shepherds are spared "the tedium of fantastic idleness," and blaming his own melancholy on the "Enchanter indolence."

Lord Byron, too, had a double relation to idleness. His first collection of poetry was titled *Hours of Idleness* (1807), which he meant to be somewhat self-deprecating. As if he knew the poems were not very good (at least not many readers then or now have found them so), he excused them in his preface by saying that poetry wasn't really his "primary vocation." These are just things, he said, he wrote "to divert the dull moments of indisposition or the monotony of a vacant hour." Of the poets of his day, he was the most active in public life. In 1812 he took a seat in the House of Lords and was a diligent member, using his first speech to discuss labor issues. He took the side of workers, speaking against the death penalty for workers who sabotaged industrial machinery. He argued that "nothing but absolute want could have driven a large, and once honest and industrious, body of the people, into the commission of excesses so hazardous to themselves, their families, and the community." Byron famously died fighting on the Greek side in their war of independence from the Turks, and in the meantime he had been an indefatigable writer of poetry, drama, and letters. He, like Wordsworth, rejects Franklin's notion of work for accumulation's sake. In *Don Juan* (1819) he suggests that everyday business, in fact, in its very meaninglessness, can drive one to a life of lounging: "His morns he pass'd in business—which, dissected, / Was like all business a laborious nothing / That leads to lassitude, / . . . And on our sofas makes us lie dejected, / And talk in tender horrors of our loathing / All kinds of toil . . ." But he is staunchly against "stagnant idleness" and has nothing but contempt for the "sauntering coxcombs" that "creep / To lounge and lucubrate, to prate and peep."

John Keats was described by a fellow student at his university as "an idle, loafing fellow, always writing poetry," the description capturing both his idleness and his industry. Sometimes his approach to indolence seems unambiguous, especially out of context. "Poesy!—no,—she has not a joy,— / At least for me,—so sweet as drowsy noons, / And evenings steep'd in honied indolence" he writes in his "Ode on Indolence" (1819). He knew Mackenzie's Lounger, whom he mentions in his letters, and he could play that part on occasion, as when, in a letter to his friend Charles Wentworth Dilke, he claims to have gotten over his "darling lounging habits a little," but says, "I will not make my diligence an excuse for not writing to you sooner—because I consider idleness a much better plea." Still, much more often he recognized such playfulness as the pose it was. To his brother he wrote, "If I had teeth of pearl and breath of lilies I should call it languor—but as I am I must call it laziness." Or, as when he writes to John Hamilton Reynolds of what he calls "delicious diligent Indolence!" he remains aware that what makes idle time precious is the work it makes possible—it is *otium*, not indolence that he values.

Like Wordsworth, Keats tended to see the pros and cons of lounging. "He who saddens / At thought of idleness cannot be idle," he wrote in a poem in a letter to Reynolds, "And he's awake who thinks himself asleep." In the sonnet "The Human Seasons" he takes idleness to be one of the "four seasons in the mind of man," neither more nor less than the other three. He takes idleness to be an autumnlike attitude, while spring is "lusty." In summer he dreams of similar desires, and winter is "pale misfeature." What distinguishes idleness is its lack of affect, "contented . . . to let fair things / Pass by unheeded." In "Ode on Indolence," he writes a tragic, more complex version of Mackenzie's Lounger. The speaker of the lyric is visited by three figures—Love, Ambition, and Poesy—that both inspire and haunt him with a sense of his own inadequacy. Why do they come? he asks.

> Was it a silent deep-disguised plot
> To steal away, and leave without a task
> My idle days? Ripe was the drowsy hour;
> The blissful cloud of summer-indolence
> Benumb'd my eyes; my pulse grew less and less;
> Pain had no sting, and pleasure's wreath no flower:
> O, why did ye not melt, and leave my sense
> Unhaunted quite of all but—nothingness?

Pain has no sting, but he is haunted by nothingness, a kind of Johnsonian idler without the fun. To friend Sarah Jeffrey the same year he wrote that he had been idle lately in part because of "an abatement of my own love of fame," and so the visitation by Ambition makes sense. A lack of ambition leads to idleness, but Keats goes further and suggests that ambition itself is a problem: "Poor Ambition! it springs / From a man's little heart's short fever-fit." To be "dieted with praise," he continues, is to be "a pet lamb in a sentimental farce!"

These three poets were interested, as this last poem suggests, in the place of poetry in the industrializing world, and so their invocations of indolence, like Johnson's and Mackenzie's, are written in opposition to the new gospel of industrial work. That gospel was being preached all across the West. In 1807 Napoleon Bonaparte rebuffed the church when it asked for a law against working on Sundays, saying, "The shortcoming of the French is not working too much . . . The more my people work, the fewer vices they will have." A French encyclopedia warned that "the result of a natural propensity of many beings to dispose of their lives in . . . doing nothing" fills "the asylums of opulence as invariably as the poor fill the convents, cloisters, and *hopitaux.*" And it went on to condemn the literary loungers who "find in laziness a consolation for their needs, to the point that they sometimes pass up eating, as do the Negro, the Bedouin, and the Spaniard, rather than working." The industrialized world worked, the "uncivilized" world didn't, and the inadequately civilized parts of France didn't work enough. Karl August von Hardenberg, the Prussian statesman whom Napoleon despised so much that he required his resignation from the cabinet as part of the Treaty of Tilsit in 1807, was in agreement on this issue. He argued that free trade removed "all the cushions of laziness." During the Industrial Revolution and ever since, the more the general cultural agreement seemed to be in favor of industriousness, the more the poets and other artists returned to the figure of the slacker.

∞

The best-known American literary take on temperance, industry, dalliance, and consumption from this period is Washington Irving's character Rip Van Winkle, who appears the same year as Keats's "Ode on Indolence" and Byron's Don Juan. Washington Irving was a disciple of Dennie's; he met Dennie in Philadelphia in 1807, and Launcelot Langstaff, one of Irving's early authorial personae, is based on him. A later alias, Jonathan Oldstyle, is a direct homage to Dennie's Oliver Oldschool. The story of Rip Van Winkle is told in the Sketch-Book of Geoffrey Crayon, Gent. (1819), and Geoffrey Crayon is, as the title announces, a gentleman, unlike Rip himself. The story is supposedly not written but found by Crayon, the original writer being one Diedrich Knickerbocker, a more raucous, bawdy, and earthy narrator than the gentlemanly Crayon, and one who is telling the story of a man, Winkle, even farther down the social ladder. Rip Van Winkle wakes up to a new world after having napped through its noisy birth. He has no capital and no profession. He should be a workingman, but he can't seem to get himself to work.

Rip is not completely averse to work itself; he was always willing to help a neighbor, even in the roughest tasks, or to run errands for the women of his village. Though his wife chides him constantly for his "idleness," the narrator points out that Rip could work at hunting or fishing all day long, without even the encouragement of a nibble. "The great error in Rip's composition was," simply, "an insuperable aversion to all kinds of profitable labor." He is the anti-Franklin. He takes to the woods, hunting for squirrels, whenever his wife becomes too shrewish, and one day, lying down to rest, he believes he hears a voice calling his name. A short, square man in clothes from some other century asks for help carrying a keg of liquor down the mountain, help that Rip, of course, gives. He spends an evening watching a crew of similarly dressed strangers drink and play ninepins, and he drinks a flagon or two himself before passing out. When he wakes, he returns to his village and finds it full of people he has never seen, and even more surprising, he discovers that his beard has grown a foot longer. The villagers ask him if he is a Federalist or a Democrat, and Rip has no idea. He has apparently fallen asleep for twenty years, during which time the American Revolution has passed, his wife has died, and his children have grown and married. Many a henpecked husband, the narrator concludes, wishes he could have a sip of Rip Van Winkle's flagon.

The story is a fantasy of escape, of course, and when Rip finds out that his wife is dead, he is glad to have taken so long to come home. Irving, in his *Tour of the Prairies* (1835), is often very smart about the difference between Indian reality and Indian myth—the Indian of poetry is no more real than the shepherd of poetry, he says—but he nonetheless loves to think about "the glorious independence of man in a savage state." He sees a young man and purrs:

> This youth, with his rifle, his blanket, and his horse, was ready at a moment's warning to rove the world; he carried all his worldly effects with him, and in the absence of artificial wants, possessed the great secret of personal freedom. We of society are slaves, not so much to others as to ourselves.

Rip Van Winkle is a comic version of this same dream of total freedom. Rip, too, has no "artificial wants"; he is one of those who "take the world easy, eat white bread or brown . . . If left to himself, he would have whistled life away in perfect contentment." Still, his wife's admonitions make it impossible for him to enjoy either the work he does do or the work he doesn't, and it is only when he escapes, and accidentally sleeps the last twenty years of his working life away, that he finds the peace he craves. When he returns to the village, he is old enough that his married daughter takes him in, and his conflicted relation to work ends.

If the story is a fantasy of escaping the new world of "profitable labor," it is also a cautionary tale about losing one's best years in avoiding it. The end of the story is far from a complete victory. There is some sense that Rip doesn't himself understand what has happened to him, and as the townspeople treat him like a harmless old man whose testimony on the matter isn't particularly important, we see that he has avoided not only work but significance: the only memory he retains of the major part of his adult life is a game of ninepins. The world is changing fast, the story warns, so fast that if one doesn't work at it, one gets left behind; to live life without working, as the loafers suggest, may be to lose life altogether. The slacker hero, as I've argued, can make one want, more than anything, to do something, maybe even to get to work. Rip Van Winkle, like many a slacker since, is the man we want to be—one who escapes the nagging nuisances of everyday life and is loved by dogs and children—and the man we want to avoid being. Slackers represent our fondest fantasies and our deepest fears.

IV

LOAFERS, COMMUNISTS, DRINKERS, AND BOHEMIANS

In which the Romantic hero, the loafer, and other odd variants in the early nineteenth century make their appearance—Karl Marx's son-in-law thinks the old man works too much—workers like to leave for a drink at the bar several times a day—the campaign for shorter hours starts to make headway—Herman Melville loafs in the South Seas—Bartleby the Scrivener "prefers not to"—and Bohemia arrives in America.

Karl Marx didn't have a son, but he had a son-in-law. Paul Lafargue, who married Marx's daughter Laura, was born in 1842 in Santiago, Cuba, the son of a planter, with African–West Indian, French, Jewish, and Carib Indian grandparents. When he met Laura Marx, in the 1860s, he was a dashing young man with a great shock of dark hair, a sweeping mustache, and an easy smile. He had moved with his family to France as a boy and as a young man became a follower of the anarchist Pierre-Joseph Proudhon. He met Marx when he traveled to London in 1864 for the First International, the historic first convention of the International Workingmen's Association.

His future father-in-law was not, at first, particularly impressed. Lafargue had come as the representative of the Mutualistes, a radical French Proudhonist group. Proudhon, who was most famous for the phrase "Property is theft!" might seem to be a natural ally of Marx's, but they fought each other's ideas in print, Marx accusing Proudhon of utopianism and other perceived sins. Lafargue defended Proudhon at first, but came to side more and more with Marxian socialism. After having made that inauspicious first impression, Lafargue gradually became Marx's confidant, though the two men continued to have a somewhat contentious relationship. In 1866, with Lafargue's courtship of Laura in full swing, Karl took to calling him "*il amoroso*." In a letter to Engels, Marx calls him "Monsieur Lafargue, my medical Creole" (he was in medical school at the time) and complains of "the outbursts of feeling these Creoles are subject to." He even claims that Laura has "a slight fear that the *jeune homme* [he was twenty-five] might do away with himself, etc." The two men became closer, however, and after Lafargue married Laura, he occasionally worked as Marx's secretary until Marx died, in 1883.

Soon after his father-in-law's death, Lafargue published his brief (his writings were always brief) reminiscences:

> I was only the scribe to whom he dictated, but that gave me the op-portunity of observing his manner of thinking and writing. Work was easy for him, and at the same time difficult. Easy because his mind found no difficulty in embracing the relevant facts and considera-tions in their completeness. But that very completeness made the exposition of his ideas a matter of long and arduous work.

According to Lafargue, Marx rose at eight, read the papers, and then worked until two or three the next morning, occasionally the whole night through. He stopped only for meals and an occasional walk for exercise. He also exercised by pacing in his study, where he wore a path in the floorboards. He had "a passion for work," Lafargue remem-bered in 1890. "He was so absorbed in it that he often forgot his meals. He had often to be called several times before he came down to the dining-room and hardly had eaten the last mouthful when he was back in his study."

Work was, in fact, Marx's enduring obsession. The earliest known writing of Marx's is an essay, "Reflections of a Young Man on the Choice of a Profession," written for a school assignment when he was seventeen. Written in Latin, it argues that only working for the good of all, rather than for personal gain, will bring happiness. The young Marx derides the idea of a personal calling, which he sees as a religious delusion. He points out that for most people, the "choice of profession" is severely limited by material factors: by the facts of their upbringing, their social world, and their natural capacities—a version of his idea that people "make their own history," as he wrote later, "but not in circumstances of their own choosing." Marx grew up near the Ruhr Valley, which by 1835, when he wrote this first essay, had been furiously industrializing for two decades, and the essay points to an important ingredient in the making of the modern slacker. In preindustrial Europe the "choice of profession" was not a problem for the vast majority of people, who simply continued doing the agricultural work their parents had done. In the upper classes choice was rarely an issue, either, since primogeniture was the common practice even where (as in England starting in 1540) it was no longer legally required: the first son inherited the estate, and the second son traditionally went into the military, the third to the clergy. Choice was only an issue, then, for the small but growing middle class, and it is precisely choice itself, the problems surrounding the choice of profession, that becomes increasingly central to middle-class thinking about work and thereby central to individuals who find themselves resisting the work ethic through the rest of the nineteenth and twentieth centuries.

Perhaps surprisingly, Marx's classmates thought of him as a joker and prankster, one who became popular as a writer of poetic lampoons aimed at his schoolyard enemies. One of his earliest poems, however, wasn't a lampoon; it was very earnest and written to his father, who told Karl that he simply couldn't understand it. (One can sympathize—here is a taste: "In bounds self-perceived, the Eternal / Silent moves, reflectively, / Until holy Thought primordial / Dons Forms, Words of Poetry.") The relationship between father and son, as seen in the letters between them, was pleasantly intimate, with just a bit of scolding and a bit of withholding here and there, but quite a lot of honest discussion, both personal and cultural. In a letter Karl wrote while a graduate student in philosophy in Berlin (where he had repaired after some trouble involving a duel in Bonn) he confided in his father about the "vexations" he experienced trying to complete his work, and his various procrastinations, such as hunting with his landlord and going "into town," there wanting "to embrace every streetcorner loafer."

In Bonn he had been president of the Tavern Club, which is just what it sounds like, a drinking organization, but once in Berlin he didn't wallow too long in his doubts about his future. He was committed to "work for humanity," which Lafargue later claimed was "one of his favorite sayings." Although his radical writings presented some difficulty when he tried to land his first job, he got one (not as a professor, as he'd hoped, but on a new opposition newspaper), and he worked diligently as an editor, political journalist, organizer, and writer from then on. He expected others to work, as well. Although the conditions for child laborers were currently deplorable, he told the First International, "I think every child above the age of nine ought to be employed in productive labor a portion of its time." He remained true to this ethic of productivity until the end: Marx died while working at his desk on March 14, 1883, at the age of sixty-four.

Lafargue was considerably less enamored of work. The year his father-in-law died, when Lafargue must have felt freed from a certain kind of scrutiny, he published one of the greatest screeds against work ever written, *The Right to Be Lazy* (1883). In this forty-page pamphlet he proposed a legal prohibition against working more than three hours a day. The anti-work ethic has a longer and nobler history than the work ethic, Lafargue wrote. The Greeks detested work and praised laziness, and it didn't start with them. Herodotus, he notes, couldn't decide where they might have received the idea, since all earlier cultures—the Egyptians, Thracians, Scythians, Persians, and Lydians—shared the same repugnance when it came to labor. Christ promoted laziness in his "lilies of the field" speech, according to Lafargue, and "bearded, stern Jehovah gave his followers the supreme example of ideal laziness—after six days' work, he rested for eternity."

Although there is a certain amount of arch humor in the book, he also engages in sober polemic. Like Friedrich Engels's *The Condition of the Working Class in England* (1845), *The Right to Be Lazy* relies on descriptions of working conditions and child labor in factories from government reports and other sources in order to highlight the debilitating nature of industrial labor. He quotes, for example, from L. R. Villermé's report on textile manufacture in Alsace in 1840:

> At Mulhouse in Dornach, work began at five o'clock in the morning and ended at eight o'clock in the evening, summer and winter. It was a sight to watch them arrive each morning into the city and de-

part each evening. Among them were a multitude of women, pale, often walking bare-footed through the mud, and who for lack of umbrellas when the rain or snow fell, wore their aprons or skirts turned up over their heads. There was a still larger number of young children, equally dirty, equally pale, covered with rags, greasy from the machine oil which drops on them while they work. They were better protected from the rain because their clothes shed water; but unlike the women just mentioned, they did not carry their day's provisions in a basket, but they carried in their hands or hid under their clothing as best they might, the morsel of bread which must serve them as food until time for them to return home.

Lafargue pleads with workers not to be complicit in their own oppression by believing in the ethical value of labor. The work ethic that arose with industrialism, he writes, is nothing but a ruse to get the proletariat to agree to its own degradation. Paint pictures, play music, philosophize, and versify, he counsels, not as work, not as commerce, but joyfully. In a better world, this is exactly what people would do after at most a two- or three-hour working day. Mechanization, he writes, has made possible the dream of the ancients to have a world not dominated by work. Machines produce hundreds of times what a worker can by hand, and so societies require only a tiny percentage of the workers' hours needed just decades earlier to accomplish the same tasks. In America, he notes, machines have become central to every aspect of agriculture, from weeding to churning butter. "Why?" he asks.

Because the free and lazy American prefers a thousand deaths to the bovine life of the French peasant. Plowing, which is so painful and warps the spine so well in glorious France, is, in the American West, an agreeable open-air pastime that is done while sitting, nonchalantly smoking a pipe.

One doubts American farmers would agree with this characterization of their labor, but such hyperbole comes quite naturally and regularly to Lafargue. "All individual and social misery," he concludes, "is born of the passion for work."

Lafargue himself never fell for what he called this "strange madness." He studied medicine briefly before coming under the sway of Proudhon, but he was not a very diligent student. He finished his medical degree after meeting Marx (hence "my medical Creole") but never qualified to practice. He tried starting many different businesses, all of which failed. As one biographer put it, he "never really got a grasp on the art of making a living." He received a small inheritance when his father died, in 1870, and this, coupled with handouts from Engels and to a lesser extent Marx when he was alive, allowed him to avoid regular wage labor. He served as a member of the International's general council and as its representative in Spain, spent a year in prison for sedition, helped found the French Workers Party, and wrote a variety of pamphlets for the cause. He continued writing sporadically throughout his life, publishing short tracts like *The Religion of Capital* (1887), *The Evolution of Property from Savagery to Civilization* (1891), and occasional pieces in socialist magazines, but he made very little money from his work. He and Laura Marx Lafargue committed suicide together in 1911. Their gardener found them, fully dressed, sitting in two armchairs, dead, with this note on the table between them:

> Healthy in body and mind, we are enjoying our lives before pitiless old age which has been depriving us of the pleasures and joys one after another, and which has been stripping us of our physical and mental powers, paralyses our energy and breaks our will, making us a burden to ourselves and to others. For some years we had promised ourselves not to live beyond 70, and we fixed the exact year for our departure from life. I prepared the method for the execution of our resolution. It was a hypodermic of cyanide acid.

He went on to say that they both felt "the supreme joy of being certain that in the near future the cause for which we devoted forty-five years will triumph."

Marx, Engels, Lafargue, and Proudhon (who began life, like Franklin, as a printer's apprentice) devoted their lives to the issues surrounding work in their industrializing society. Of the four, only Lafargue adopted an anti-work stance, and only he wrote with any kind of sustained irony. Marx in his early philosophical writings had a utopian vision of all people working not just at trades and manufacturing, but as poets and painters and musicians as well; still, he described this as unalienated labor, not as freedom from labor. Marx could be quite witty, especially when he was wielding an insult, but after his high school lampoons, comedy was never again his forte. Proudhon's pamphlet *The Utility of the Celebration of Sunday* (1839) recommends that instead of a "discussion of work and wages, organization and industry," it is time for a study of "a law which would have at its basis a theory of rest," but he said this in dead, sober earnest and never really performed such a study himself. Although an emphatic, animated writer, he never produced a funny line. *The Right to Be Lazy*, on the other hand, has a true slacker's investment in the satirical, humorous send-up of the era's pieties. And, perhaps most significantly, it suggests that avoiding work is not simply a choice one might want to make, but a fundamental human right, even responsibility.

∞

Marx and Lafargue were describing an industrial workplace that had been transformed over the previous century in indelible ways. The main images we now have of those changes are of the "dark, satanic mills" from the literature of the time (the phrase is William Blake's): a picture of brutal, unending, murderous, soot-blackened labors stretching from early childhood to early grave. Descriptions by Dickens and other novelists; the parliamentary investigations in the 1830s; Engels's famous description of working conditions in London, Birmingham, and Manchester in 1845; Upton Sinclair's brutalized slaughterhouse workers in *The Jungle* in 1906; and Lewis Hine's now-famous photographs of child labor a few years later—these indictments of working conditions have left a clear impression of factory misery and exploitation. The British Parliament's Sadler Committee in 1831, for instance, interviewed workers and got almost the same story from all: a factory life that began at the age of six or eight, started at five in the morning and ran until nine at night with forty minutes off for lunch, and featured regular beatings or "strappings" for lateness and other misdemeanors or errors. The massacres of striking workers, the machine maiming, the illnesses caused by breathing dust and waste, the children denied childhoods, the soul-crushing monotony—these are a necessary and accurate part of our general understanding of factory labor in the nineteenth century.

The transformation from the work world of the preindustrial era to that of water- and steam-powered factories happened slowly and incompletely over the century, however, spawning many different forms of compromise, refusal, and opposition. Workers were loath to accept the new, excessively regimented work schedule that factories attempted to impose. The preindustrial world of agricultural and artisan labor was structured by what historian E. P. Thompson calls "alternate bouts of intense labor and of idleness wherever men were in control of their working lives." This was in part due to the still irregular nature of transportation and the market and in part due to the nature of agricultural work, which was seasonal, interrupted by rain, forced into hyperactivity by the threat of rain, and determined by other uncontrollable natural processes. The force of long cultural habit ensured that the change from such discontinuous tasks to the regularized labor of the factory never went particularly smoothly. Workers did not easily hand over control of their working lives.

Around the time that Lafargue was developing his ideas about laziness and being chagrined by his father-in-law's daily industry, a New York cigar manufacturer grumbled that his cigar makers could never be counted on to do a straight shift's labor. They would "come down to the shop in the morning, roll a few cigars," he complained to the *New York Herald* in 1877, "and then go to a beer saloon and play pinocio [*sic*] or some other game." The workers would return when they pleased, roll a few more cigars, and then revisit the saloon, all told "working probably two or three hours a day," or exactly the amount of time Lafargue thought should be legislated. Cigar makers in Milwaukee went on strike in 1882, in fact, simply to preserve their right to leave the shop at any time without their foreman's permission.

In this the cigar workers were typical American manufacturing laborers, refusing to submit to the kind of steady work habits Franklin recommended and industrial economics encouraged and attempted to impose. Throughout the century, industrialists protested against what they saw as the laziness and recalcitrance of their workers. "Monday," one manufacturer claimed, was always "given up to debauchery" and recovery from the weekend's drinking. Saturday, payday, often resulted in the visit of a brewery wagon to the factory and the beginning of three days of said debauchery. The resulting nominal four-day workweek also saw its share of drinking. Daily breaks for "dramming" were common, with workers coming and going from the workplace as they pleased. An English cabinetmaker in 1846 wrote home that his American coworkers would frequently indulge in "a simultaneous cessation of work . . . as if by tacit agreement," and an apprentice would be sent out for "wine, brandy, biscuits, and cheese." Daily breaks were common for meals, snacks, drink, and reading the newspaper aloud to fellow workers. Workers came and left for the day at different times as well, for various personal reasons.

Although the English cabinetmaker was surprised by the laxity of his American peers, other immigrant British laborers brought their irregular work schedule with them to America. The potters in Trenton, New Jersey, mainly immigrants from Staffordshire, would, after "bursts of great activity," simply quit working for several days at a time, and their workdays were often, by twentieth-century standards, riddled with breaks. An owner of a New Jersey iron manufactory made the following notations in his diary over the course of a week:

> All hands drunk.
> Jacob Ventling hunting.
> Molders all agree to quit work and went to the beach.
> Peter Cox very drunk.
> Edward Rutter off a-drinking.

At the shipyards, the same tendency to stop working at irregular intervals and drink was the rule. One ship's carpenter at midcentury described a daily round of breaks for cakes and candy at least every two hours, a whiskey-soaked lunch, and regular trips to the "convenient grog-shops." Although some never went drinking, he said, others "sailed out pretty regularly ten times a day on the average" for whiskey. Management attempts to stop such midday drinking breaks were routinely met with strikes and sometimes resulted in riots.

Over the course of the century, the unorganized, quasi-spontaneous work stoppages these men described were accompanied by more organized attempts to unite the workers—if not the workers of the world, then those of specific factories or trades. Working people fought against what they saw as the evils of industrialism in many different ways, perhaps most dramatically seen in the Luddites' smashing of "frames," or powered looms. The Luddites were textile workers who were convinced in the 1810s that the new frames were replacing them, which they undoubtedly were, in that they enabled many fewer workers to produce the same amount of cloth. In the middle of the night, roving bands of Luddites would attack several mills, destroying the expensive new machinery and thereby inducing terror in the propertied classes. Historian Eric Hobsbawm has called it "collective bargaining by riot." By 1812 the destruction of factory equipment was widespread enough that Parliament passed the Frame Breaking Act, which allowed courts to impose the death penalty for industrial sabotage. This is the act that occasioned Lord Byron's speech.

Although industrial sabotage like that of the Luddites was less common in the United States, workers' strikes, such as those at the Lowell mills in 1834 and 1836, became more and more common, despite attempts to suppress them with violence and imprisonment. As early as 1806, American strikers were charged with criminal conspiracy for organizing "turn outs," and it wasn't until Massachusetts supreme court chief justice Lemuel Shaw's 1840 ruling in *Commonwealth v. Hunt* that workers were given the legal right to organize and strike. Unionism thereafter grew in America and reached one peak just before the panic of 1873; the depression that followed caused major inroads against union support, just as depressions had after the panics of 1821 and 1837. But by the 1880s, union activity was again on the rise, and at the peak of strike activity in that decade, as many as a million and a half workers took part in 1,500 strikes a year: unions, workingmen's parties, and worker cooperatives of various kinds were gradually becoming a significant force in the workplace. In England, the Chartists, the Luddites, trade clubs, friendly societies, and trade unions—and in France, Prussia, Bavaria, Saxony, and elsewhere, trade unions and various socialist and revolutionary factions—organized groups of workers for communal action. Usually this took the form of strikes, which had some effect on working conditions, some success in gaining concessions, and at the very least were successful in publicizing workers' grievances.

Nothing the unionists could do, however, could finally stop the industrial transformation of workers' lives. The standard practices of speeding up and stretching out (that is, speeding up the machines and increasing the number of machines each worker tended), along with the premium system, in which overseers were given bonuses for increased production, meant that workers were continually being pushed toward the breaking point. Between 1836 and 1850 in Lowell, for instance, the number of machines increased by 150 percent, while the number of workers increased by only 50 percent. The increasingly frenetic pace and accompanying fatigue led to a steady increase in worker injuries and deaths through the century. In 1881 alone, thirty thousand railroad workers are said to have been killed or injured on the job. Between 1907 and 1916, fully 25 percent of the recent immigrants employed in the Carnegie South Works had been injured or killed. Paul Fussell has argued that the true class system in America has always had one important divide: those who risk injury and death in their work versus those who do not. By 1911, labor activists Frank Bohn and Bill Haywood could claim that "in the United States 750,000 workers are killed and wounded in the shops and mines and on the railroads every year."

The strikes themselves were sometimes fatal, as well. Two New York tailors were killed by police dispersing a crowd of strikers in 1850, initiating a long line of deaths in what amounted to open class warfare. In the railroad strikes of 1877, at least ninety people were killed, and during the sugar strike in Louisiana in 1887, at least thirty workers, many of them former slaves, died in what one historian has called a "reign of terror." Between 1877 and 1910, U.S. troops were called in to break more than 500 strikes, and armed deputies and detectives fought strikers in many others: 25,000 men were deputized by U.S. Steel during the 1919 steel strike alone. In the last century and a half, some 700 workers were killed in America in strike-related attacks. During the 1890s, two workers were killed and 140 injured for every 100,000 workers who went out on strike; during the same period in France, by way of comparison, there were no deaths and three injuries per 100,000 strikers. In two years from 1902 to 1904, injuries rose to a rate of more than 1,000 per 100,000, or 300 times the French rate, and 198 strikers were killed. The United States has had the bloodiest labor battles in history.

And labor was the loser. Nineteenth-century employers, despite all of the strikes and agitation, succeeded in disciplining and regularizing work habits. Workers never again, even during the dot-com playroom heyday of the 1990s, approached the workday freedom of the early-nineteenth-century factory workers who could saunter out for a glass of rum whenever they felt like it. In May of 1835, workers in many different trades throughout the Northeast and as far west as Cincinnati struck for the right "to dispose of our time in such quantities as we deem and believe most conducive to our happiness." But over the course of the century, the main labor initiatives had less to do with control of workers' time during the workday than with limiting the number of required hours. The latter started as a movement for the ten-hour day, followed by the eight-hour movement, and finally, the shorter-lived six-hour movement. Carpenters in Philadelphia went on strike as early as 1791 for a ten-hour day, and carpenters in Boston struck for a ten-hour day in 1825. In the 1820s and 1830s, in fact, the quest for more leisure time was one of the central galvanizing desires that led workers to organize; and early on, sights were set beyond the ten-hour day. A several-weeks-long 1836 Philadelphia Navy Yard strike led to a ten-hour schedule there, but a labor paper in 1836 also declared, "We have no desire to perpetuate the ten-hour system, for we believe that eight hours' daily labor is more than enough for any man to perform." In 1840, President Martin Van Buren ordered a ten-hour day for all federal workers, in a pattern that would follow with the eight-hour day: federal and state governments shortened hours ahead of any actual legislation.

Through the 1880s, the right to do nothing was at the center of agitation for shorter hours. Eight Hour Leagues sprang up around the country, and the following became their semiofficial song:

> We mean to make things over, we are tired of toil for naught,
> With but bare enough to live upon, and never an hour for thought;
> We want to feel the sunshine, and we want to smell the flowers,
> We are sure that God has will'd it, and we mean to have eight hours.
> We're summoning our forces from the shipyard, shop and mill.
>> CHORUS:
>> Eight hours for work, eight hours for rest, eight hours for what
>>   we will!
>> Eight hours for work, eight hours for rest, eight hours for what
>>   we will!

Another verse even more directly invokes Christ's "lilies of the field":

The beasts that graze the hillside, and the birds that wander free,
In the life that God has meted, have a better life than we.

The eight-hour movement at first seemed to be a success. In 1865 Boston declared an eight-hour day for all city workers, followed within a few years by New York, Chicago, Detroit, San Francisco, and other cities. The federal government followed suit in 1868, and a year later President Ulysses S. Grant issued a proclamation that no reduction of wages could accompany the institution of shorter hours. In 1872, a hundred thousand tradesmen in New York City struck for an eight-hour day and won. In San Francisco, some twenty-five trade-based Eight Hour Leagues were formed among shipbuilders, plasterers, bricklayers, hod carriers, stonecutters, lathers, riggers, gas fitters, plumbers, house carpenters, and painters. Employers countered by firing workers and replacing them with new immigrants, but sometimes they simply acquiesced when enough skilled labor was not otherwise available. Some employers in San Francisco banded together to form a Ten-Hour League Society to protect against the eight-hour system, which they argued was "ruinous to the capital and enterprise of the city and the state." But in 1868 a statewide eight-hour law was passed. In many of the most populous states the eight-hour day seemed secure.

These reductions, though, were far from permanent. The industrial depressions of the 1870s, the ever-enlarging pool of unorganized, cheap immigrant labor, and continued resistance by business meant a return to ten-hour days for most trades by the end of the decade. Agitation for shorter hours reached another peak during the strike for an eight-hour day at McCormick Harvesting Machine in Chicago, starting on May Day in 1886. On May 3, in one of the best-known stories of labor violence in America, two workers were killed by police as they attempted to break up a confrontation between strikebreakers and striking workers at McCormick's South Side reaper factory. The following day the infamous Haymarket Riot began as a peaceful demonstration against the police brutality of the day before; a pipe bomb, probably detonated by police, perhaps by workers, killed seven policemen, and police firing into the crowd killed four protesters. Eight unionists were put on trial, all of whom were professed anarchists. Seven were convicted and four hanged, all on scant evidence. The panicked public reaction and the desertion from radical labor ranks of many workers after this event slowed the acceptance of the eight-hour day for almost another half century. Federally mandated eight-hour legislation for all (or almost all) workers wasn't passed until 1938.

The rationale for the shorter workday, which had always been based on a worker's right to leisure, gradually came to include the argument that shorter hours offered a way to cut the unemployment rate. John Maynard Keynes, for instance, argued in the 1930s for a three-hour day in order to maximize employment during the Depression. In 1930, Kellogg's plants in Battle Creek, Michigan, replaced their three eight-hour shifts with four six-hour shifts in order to keep more workers employed, and the plant ran that way until the early 1940s, when war production again increased demand. After the war, some workers continued on a six-hour shift, but gradually workers voted, department by department, often under pressure, to return to eight-hour days. The last of Kellogg's six-hour workers were pressured, by a combination of threats and incentives, into eight-hour schedules in 1985.

The main trade-off in the century before the Great Depression, according to historian Benjamin Hunnicutt, had always been between the desire of employers for longer workdays and the desire of workers for free time—with the increase of "free time" almost universally seen by workers as possible and desirable, as the natural result of economic progress. When Ralph Chaplin, of the International Workers of the World, called for a general strike in 1933, he argued that no worker should have to toil longer than two and three-quarters or three hours a day; for Chaplin the goal was to stop the exploitation of workers and starve the capitalist class, but a side benefit was the reduction of hours itself, what he called "THE revolutionary demand." Stopping to "smell the flowers" was not just a labor goal but one shared by many economists, such as John Stuart Mill, who had argued (before Lafargue had) that continued gains in productivity would require, eventually, less and less work from each laborer. The result would be "sufficient leisure, both physical and mental," Mill hoped, "to cultivate freely the graces of life." Access to *otium* would be democratized.

Fictional utopias had long called for shorter working days, and often for the same reasons. Thomas More's original *Utopia* (1516) featured a six-hour day, while Edward Bellamy's *Looking Backward:*

2000–1887 (1888), William Dean Howells's *A Traveler from Altruria* (1894), and Jerome K. Jerome's "The New Utopia" (1891) all favored the three-hour day. *Looking Backward* was, after *Uncle Tom's Cabin*, the bestselling American novel of the nineteenth century, and in it Bellamy depicts a utopia based on universal labor conscription, in which men and women work from the age of twenty-one until they turn forty-five, with women given time off for pregnancy and infant care. Workers pick the kind of work they want to do, and the more arduous the task, the fewer hours per week required:

> The principle is that no man's work ought to be, on the whole, harder for him than any other man's for him, the workers themselves to be the judges. There are no limits to the application of this rule. If any particular occupation is in itself so arduous or so oppressive that, in order to induce volunteers, the day's work in it had to be reduced to ten minutes, it would be done.

In Howells's utopia, social inequality is also corrected through minimizing the hours in the working day. When the narrator of *A Traveler from Altruria* first meets an Altrurian, he recognizes him because of the sense of leisure he radiates:

> I had not the least trouble in identifying him, he was so unlike all the Americans who dismounted from the train with him, and who all looked hot, worried and anxious. He was a man no longer young, but in what we call the heyday of life, when our own people are so absorbed in making provision for the future that they may be said not to live in the present at all. This Altrurian's whole countenance, and especially his quiet, gentle eyes, expressed a vast contemporaneity, with bounds of leisure removed to the end of time; or, at least, this was the effect of something in them which I am obliged to report in rather fantastic terms.

Like Paul Lafargue and the IWW, Howells assumed that equality meant spreading the workload evenly across society, and that doing so would reduce the average workday to three hours. The twelve-hour, ten-hour, or eight-hour day had only been necessary to support a leisure class that did not work. In Howells's, Bellamy's, and Jerome's utopias, the right to be lazy, like the responsibility to work, would be shared across the entire society. Utopia was a three-hour day. Universal slackerdom would be the final fruit of modernity.

But in the twentieth century, rising consumerism and the effect of the Depression (in which unemployment was seen as a tragedy rather than an opportunity) spelled the demise of shorter-hour agitation. The Kellogg workers, writes Hunnicutt, made their decisions to return to longer hours for a complicated set of reasons, not all of which were strictly based on their own economic self-interest. Workingmen's sense of lost privilege in a social world in which work was losing its ideological value, he suggests, was a factor; hence the sentiments he found among the male workers in Battle Creek that increased leisure time was for "sissies" and "girls." The Depression also encouraged people to perceive all unemployment as a hindrance to economic progress. Instead of seeing shorter hours as the result of economic progress, people began to think of "full-time work," which meant forty or more hours a week, as the true motor of economic growth, and economic growth as the ultimate goal. The failure of the Kellogg plan is one indication that these other worker understandings and desires began to trump shorter hours, and Hunnicutt sees this as a cultural tragedy, which prompts him to make an argument about the work ethic not unlike Lafargue's:

> The traditional working-class remedy for the ills of industrialization, the "progressive reduction of the hours of labor," has been nearly lost to the language. Now the dominion of work stands virtually unchallenged and seemingly impregnable. The job resembles a secular religion, promising personal identity, salvation, purpose and direction, community, and a way for those who believe truly and simply in "hard work" to make sense out of the confusion of life. The few who still doubt that work is life's center are condemned as heretics, and time outside work and consumption, without "entertainment" and technology's toys, is a new wilderness.

The slacker has always been such a heretic, and the kind of emotions slackers elicit vary based on the emoter's own relation to work and his or her historical moment. Shorter hours, even if the work is drudgery, can be either a blessing or a curse. The voice crying in the wilderness for no hours at all can seem aggravatingly unrealistic, amusingly reasonable, pointedly exaggerated, maddeningly obtuse, or heroically progressive. One's emotional reaction to such a voice is always conditioned by the largest historical forces and the smallest personal accidents.

∞

Like Paul Lafargue, Herman Melville had a famous father-in-law—Chief Justice Lemuel Shaw. And, again like Lafargue, at least in part in reaction to his father-in-law's prodigious productivity, Melville wrote one of the most significant paeans to slackerdom ever produced. Shaw had authored the first charter for the city of Boston in 1822 and had a very successful law practice, bringing in some $15,000 a year during the 1820s and 1830s. He then served as chief justice of the Massachusetts Supreme Court for thirty years, writing more than twenty volumes' worth of decisions, including, as I mentioned, *Commonwealth v. Hunt*, which established the American worker's right to organize, and influential decisions on segregation, negligence, and police power. Melville himself was interested in less strenuous work arrangements. His father, Allan, thought Melville did not work hard enough in school: "Without being a bright Scholar, he maintains a respectable standing, and would proceed further, if he could be induced to study more." And a certain lack of diligence seemed to stay with him. Years later, Melville's wife would admonish him each day "to be an industrious boy and not upset the inkstand."

Melville was born one year later than Marx, the year Irving published *Rip Van Winkle*, into a family that was reasonably well-off. But when Herman was just twelve, in 1830, the family fur and felt business collapsed, shortly after which his father died, leaving the family in considerable debt. Herman immediately began working, first as a clerk at the New York State Bank in Albany and then for a while on his uncle's farm in Pittsfield, followed by a stint as a bookkeeper in his brother's fur business back in Albany. He managed to obtain more schooling, a few months at a time, but he continued working at a variety of jobs before joining a ship's crew at the age of nineteen. He sailed to Liverpool and back and then spent part of a year on land, teaching and traveling down the Mississippi on a riverboat, before setting sail again in 1841, this time to the South Seas.

He left from New Bedford aboard a whaler, sailed around Cape Horn, and seven months later arrived in the Marquesas, a Polynesian island group roughly a thousand miles northeast of Tahiti. When he got there, he jumped ship and spent a month living with the local people on a small island before hitching a ride to Tahiti on an Australian whaler. He was promptly arrested and imprisoned in Tahiti as a mutineer. He managed to escape, however, and spent several months exploring Tahiti and nearby islands, working for a while on a potato farm. He then joined the crew of a Nantucket whaling ship and spent five months aboard before being discharged in Hawaii, where he desultorily took various odd jobs on land. After several months he joined the U.S. Navy and spent the next fourteen months on a frigate. He was away four years all told before he returned to Massachusetts and started to write novels based on his adventures.

The first of these was published in London as *Narrative of a Four Months' Residence Among the Natives of a Valley of the Marquesas Islands* (1846), and a month later in New York as *Typee: A Peep at Polynesian Life*. Highly autobiographical, the book is part ethnography and part novel, and it was reviewed in England (probably because of the title) as a somewhat unsuccessful quasi-scientific travel book, and more favorably in New York as a novel. Negative reviews came largely but not entirely from Christian publications, some of which objected to the author's very pointed critique of missionaries, while others objected to what they saw as the licentious titillation in his description of the local bare-breasted girls. Horace Greeley thought that *Typee* and Melville's other South Sea tales were "unmistakably defective if not positively diseased in moral tone, and will very fairly be condemned as dangerous reading for those of immature intellects and unsettled principles." Aided by such denunciations, the book was successful, and his publisher was happy to publish further seagoing tales by Melville.

Early in *Typee* the narrator paints a picture of shipboard ease, explaining Melville's desire (like the young Benjamin Franklin's) to escape landlubbing drudgery for the high seas. For twenty days after the rounding of the Horn, the trade winds pushed the ship toward the sperm whale's habitat in the islands:

> What a delightful, lazy, languid time we had whilst we were thus gliding along! There was nothing to be done; a circumstance that

happily suited our disinclination to do anything. We abandoned the
fore-peak altogether, and spreading an awning over the forecastle,
slept, ate, and lounged under it the live-long day. Everyone seemed
under the influence of a narcotic.

Even the officers had trouble staying upright, and reading was impossible: "take a book in your hand, and you were asleep in an instant." It
is all the narrator can do to shake off the "general languor" enough to
appreciate the beauty of the sea and sky.

But there are other problems aboard—the captain is tyrannical, the
meals scanty, the sick uncared for—and our narrator decides to hop
ship (as Melville did) in the Marquesas. Once there, he experiences
real lounging. He lives as his nonworking neighbors do, and this, perhaps as much as the scantily clad maidens, explains both the great appeal of the book and the outrage it engendered among conservative
critics. "Nothing can be more uniform and undiversified than the life
of the Typees," the narrator says. "One tranquil day of ease and happiness follows another in quiet succession." Fruit is simply plucked off
trees and eaten, and young women spend more time attending to their
hair than to any other task. "To many of them, indeed," the narrator remarks, "life is little else than an often interrupted and luxurious nap."
He likens the daily round of lunches and dinners around the village to
the life of a Western gentleman of leisure and feels that he has found
the perfect society. Every once in a while the men of the community
would come together to build a new hut, and "by the united, but easy,
even indolent, labors of all, the entire work was completed by sunset."
Women were even more sheltered from labor than the men. "Exempt
from toil," they spent their days swimming, adorning themselves, and
occasionally making mats or skirts, but even these minor labors seemed
like a form of recreation, like "those pleasant avocations which fill up
the elegant morning leisure of our fashionable ladies at home."

Throughout the novel the narrator's doubts about this relaxed way
of life pop up, sometimes explicitly and sometimes less so. At one
point, for instance, he describes the very old men of the village and
ends with this:

But the most remarkable peculiarity about them was the appearance
of their feet; the toes, like the radiating lines of the mariner's com-

pass, pointed to every quarter of the horizon. This was doubtless at-
tributable to the fact, that during nearly a hundred years of existence
the said toes never had been subjected to any artificial confinement,
and in their old age, being averse to close neighborhood, bid one another keep open order.

This is simply an amusing detail at one level, but it also shows, as Jay
Fliegelman pointed out to me many years ago, a certain amount of
anxiety about what pure freedom means. Splayed toes are not attractive. Too much freedom lets things loose that perhaps shouldn't be
loose. The free affections of the narrator's island paramour also begin
to seem too easy. Eventually the free, indolent life makes him anxious,
and feeling that he has become a prisoner, he decides to leave. He
flees, makes his way back to an international port, and, as Melville
did, signs up to be a working seaman again.

Typee and *Omoo*, which Melville published the next year, sold
quite well, being, as Walt Whitman said in his review of *Omoo* in the
Brooklyn Daily Eagle, "the most readable kind of reading" as well as
scandalous. Melville's writing soon became notoriously more difficult,
however, and sales for *Moby-Dick* (1851) and *Pierre* (1852) dropped
precipitously. *Typee* had sold almost 7,500 copies in the United States
in its first year. *Moby-Dick* would sell fewer than 2,500 copies in its
first two years and then only 25 copies a year for the next twenty years.
Eight months after publication, *Pierre* had sold only 283 copies.
Melville's future as a professional writer looked exceedingly bleak.

Melville had dedicated *Typee* to Lemuel Shaw, at that time a family
friend who had almost married Melville's aunt and who had helped
his mother financially after his father's death. A year after the publication of that first novel, Melville married Shaw's daughter, Elizabeth,
and Shaw then helped the couple get started with a gift of $2,000,
$1,000 of which built their first house and $1,000 of which was put
aside. This afforded Melville time to write and to slack. He wrote his
friend, the editor Evert Duyckinck, about life in his new home: "I
have been passing my time very pleasantly here. But chiefly in lounging on a sofa (a la the poet Gray) & reading Shakespeare." Shaw
would continue providing money, including $1,500 to finance
Melville's trip to Europe and the Middle East in 1856, and his wife
would inherit an income of $500 a year when Shaw died, in 1861.

Elizabeth also inherited sums from other relatives: more than $50,000 between 1880 and 1890, or five times what Melville ever earned from his writing.

While visiting one of his cousins in western Massachusetts in 1851, Melville had met Nathaniel Hawthorne, and that same week he wrote his famous review, "Hawthorne and His Mosses," one of the great literary love letters. He immediately decided to stay and, with another loan from his father-in-law, built a house nearby. The two men had a number of visits in the coming months, almost always urged by Melville. One famous letter, from Melville to Hawthorne, was written in April of that year. Melville had just read *The House of the Seven Gables*, published a month before, and he wrote his letter in the form of a book review, speaking of Hawthorne in the third person:

> There is a grand truth about Nathaniel Hawthorne. He says No! in thunder; but the Devil himself cannot make him say *yes*. For all men who say *yes*, lie; and all men who say *no*,—why, they are in the happy condition of judicious, unencumbered travelers in Europe; they cross the frontiers into Eternity with nothing but a carpet-bag.

Melville was at the same time completing *Moby-Dick*, which he would finish that September, his own treatise on travelers—injudicious, encumbered ones—and he dedicated the novel to Hawthorne, "In token of my admiration of his genius." But Hawthorne, always less interested in the relationship, left the Berkshires soon after for Concord, and it seems (we have only Melville's half of their correspondence in this year) that Hawthorne, who initially enjoyed Melville's company, grew wary, whether because of Melville's excessive ardor or for some other reason. Hawthorne's departure, along with the poor reception of *Moby-Dick*, is said to have kicked off Melville's first bout of depression, and he threw himself into writing his mad book *Pierre*.

At the same time, Hawthorne, in Concord, began writing *The Blithedale Romance*, in which critics have found allegories of his relationship with Melville, but which is also a novel based on the time he spent at Brook Farm, a Transcendentalist commune founded by a semi-successful minister named George Ripley, the journalist Charles Dana, Hawthorne, and several others. Originally intended as a commune where labor was more humanely apportioned, it began in 1841 with about fifteen members and lasted roughly six years. Ripley explained the group's basic philosophy in a letter to Ralph Waldo Emerson:

> Our objects, as you know, are to ensure a more natural union between intellectual and manual labor than now exists; to combine the thinker and the worker, as far as possible, in the same individual; to guarantee the highest mental freedom, by providing all with labor, adapted to their tastes and talents, and securing to them the fruits of their industry; to do away with the necessity of menial services, by opening the benefits of education and the profits of labor to all; and thus to prepare a society of liberal, intelligent, and cultivated persons, whose relations with each other would permit a more simple and wholesome life, than can now be led amidst the pressures of our competitive institutions.

The goal of having people choose only the work they felt inclined to do quickly proved impracticable. Somewhat less than a year later, elaborate methods of accounting for work hours replaced the free-for-all, and a ten-hour day in summer, eight hours in winter, became the norm.

Hawthorne's grandson Julian, in his 1884 biography of his famous grandfather, wrote that Brook Farm "seems to be intrinsically so barren of interest and edification, save only for the eminent names that were at first connected with it, that the present writer has pleasure in passing over it without further remark." The only advantage, his grandson thought, was that it taught Hawthorne how to plant corn and squash and gave him background for a later novel. In a biography of Hawthorne five years earlier, Henry James, too, had belittled the experiment:

> It would of course be easy to overrate the importance of this ingenious attempt of a few speculative persons to improve the outlook of mankind. The experiment came and went very rapidly and quietly, leaving very few traces behind it. It became simply a charming personal reminiscence for the small number of amiable enthusiasts who had had a hand in it. There were degrees of enthusiasm, and I suppose there were degrees of amiability; but a certain generous

brightness of hope and freshness of conviction pervaded the whole undertaking and rendered it, morally speaking, important to an extent of which any heed that the world in general ever gave to it is an insufficient measure. Of course it would be a great mistake to represent the episode of Brook Farm as directly related to the manners and morals of the New England world in general—and in especial to those of the prosperous, opulent, comfortable part of it. The thing was the experiment of a coterie—it was unusual, unfashionable, unsuccessful.

James manages a very intricate backhanded compliment—that their hope and conviction were more valuable than the little heed the world paid to it might suggest—and follows it by suggesting that the rest of New England shouldn't be tarred with the same brush. James finds it interesting that Hawthorne, a man with a "taste for old ideals, and loitering paces," should be attracted to the progressive communards, those "queer specimens of the reforming genus," and he begs off commenting on them or the other Transcendentalists, saying that except for Hawthorne, the only writer of the Transcendental generation of any importance was Emerson. Emerson insisted on radical individualism, or the opposite of communalism, counseling that (in James's words) "a man should await his call, his finding the thing to do which he should really believe in doing, and not be urged by the world's opinion to do simply the world's work." James suggests that while Hawthorne may have been strong enough to withstand the world's opinion, he was too "cold-blooded" to be part of the utopian dream; he was there only as a detached observer.

Cold-bloodedness doesn't explain Hawthorne's relation to the work of Brook Farm, however. By all reports, Hawthorne threw himself wholeheartedly into his agricultural labors at first, even though he had no previous farm experience and had never before encountered a pitchfork. In his letters in April and May he is proud of his labors and of his new muscles. "I have been chopping wood, and turning a grindstone all the forenoon," he wrote to his fiancée on April 22, 1841. "It is an endless surprise to me how much work there is to be done in the world; but, thank God, I am able to do my share of it,—and my ability increases daily. What a great, broad-shouldered, elephantine personage I shall become by and by!" But just a few months later he was

completely disillusioned, and his letters to his fiancée in August are
nothing but complaint:

> O, labor is the curse of the world, and nobody can meddle with it
> without becoming proportionably brutified! Dost thou think it a
> praiseworthy matter that I have spent five golden months in provid-
> ing food for cows and horses? Dearest, it is not so. Thank God, my
> soul is not buried beneath a dung heap.

Hawthorne, who had already done a stint as an inspector at the Boston
Custom House (a patronage job that left time for writing), came to
find Brook Farm a prison, and after only four months he was planning
his escape:

> And—joyful thought!—in little more than a fortnight I shall be free
> from my bondage,— . . . free to enjoy Nature,—free to think and
> feel! . . . Even my Custom-House experience was not such a thrall-
> dom and weariness; my mind and heart were free.

In *The Blithedale Romance*, the narrator comes to the same conclusion. The commune in that novel was based on the principles of
Charles Fourier, a French socialist who died in 1837. Fourier proposed a new form of society based on "phalansteries," communal
groups of 1,600 that would form the semiautonomous units of a new
world order. These communities would themselves be divided into
thirty-two choruses (sixteen male, sixteen female), each with its own
"pennants, plumes, and distinctive ornaments." Bees and beavers are
happy laborers, he argued, because they have a proper societal context
for their work. If industrial labor were to be completely reformed,
he predicted, there would be 37 million poets equal to Homer, 37
million mathematicians equal to Newton, and 37 million dramatists
equal to Molière (although "these are approximate estimates"), and
they would be evenly distributed among the phalansteries that would
constitute the society. The individuals in these groups would work
only at those tasks they wanted to work at; the natural distribution of
human types would take care of the rest.

The community in *The Blithedale Romance* begins with the highest
aspirations for the work they will do:

While our enterprise lay all in theory, we had pleased ourselves with delectable visions of the spiritualization of labor. It was to be our form of prayer and ceremonial of worship. Each stroke of the hoe was to uncover some aromatic root of wisdom, heretofore hidden from the sun. Pausing in the field, to let the wind exhale the moisture from our foreheads, we were to look upward, and catch glimpses into the far-off soul of truth.

Their well-laid plans come to naught. "The clods of earth, which we so constantly belabored and turned over and over, were never etherealized into thought. Our thoughts, on the contrary, were fast becoming cloddish. Our labor symbolized nothing, and left us mentally sluggish in the dusk of the evening." The experiment is for the narrator, as it was for Hawthorne, a failure.

In *The House of the Seven Gables*, written two years before *The Blithedale Romance*, Hawthorne described a character with a unique relationship to the world of work: Holgrave, although only twenty-two, has already had many jobs, as a schoolteacher, a schoolmaster, a salesman in a country store, the political editor of a newspaper, an itinerant peddler of cologne water and other essences, a dentist, a ship's officer, a public lecturer on mesmerism, and now a daguerreotypist. He had held each of these jobs "in an episodical way," the narrator tells us, and in many places, from the Midwest to Europe, including while in the latter a brief stay with a community of Fourierists. The narrator and the other characters in the book are amazed by Holgrave's breadth of experience and the lightness with which he approaches the question of a profession:

His present phase, as a daguerreotypist, was of no more importance in his own view, nor likely to be more permanent, than any of the preceding ones. It had been taken up with the careless alacrity of an adventurer, who had his bread to earn. It would be thrown aside as carelessly, whenever he should choose to earn his bread by some other equally digressive means.

This is comedic, of course, a fantasy of angst-free movement and choice, as if jobs were simply digressions, as if work were as lightly cast on and off as a phrase or an anecdote. Hawthorne's experiment with

Brook Farm is proof enough that he knew work to be much more fraught than that.

When Hawthorne moved to Concord, he met Thoreau, who, he said, "has repudiated all regular modes of getting a living, and seems inclined to lead a sort of Indian life among civilized men—an Indian life, I mean, as respects the absence of any systematic effort for a livelihood." Hawthorne found him at first physically ugly ("he is as ugly as sin, long-nosed, queer-mouthed, and with uncouth and somewhat rustic, although courteous manners") but sympathetic, with a true taste for literature. Thoreau did not grow on him; some months later he wrote to a friend that Thoreau "despises the world, and all that it has to offer, and, like other humorists, is an intolerable bore." Thoreau's experiment in living outside the mainstream was also, from Hawthorne's perspective, a failure. "He is not an agreeable person, and in his presence one feels ashamed of having any money, or a house to live in, or so much as two coats to wear, or having written a book that the public will read—his own mode of life being so unsparing a criticism on all other modes, such as the world approves." In the middle of Transcendental utopianism, Hawthorne remained apostate, keen to scrutinize and represent the slackers around him, but unwilling to see them without their warts and whininess, and disinclined to praise even their motives. Hawthorne could have chosen to write directly about the transformation of New England life by industrialization—the Lowell mills were internationally famous as representing the latest in technology and employee regulation and were just two towns away—but he chose instead to get at the issues sideways, to represent figures like Holgrave and the Brook Farmers, to examine the alternatives to the new order that slackers represented.

∞

The money inherited by Melville's wife did not pay the family bills in the 1850s, and as his writing income dried up, he needed a job. In 1866, at the age of forty-seven, he was granted one as an inspector at the New York Custom House for a salary of $1,000 a year. As in the case of Hawthorne's job, it was in part a sinecure, but his work as a deputy inspector consisted of a mind-numbing signing of forms, one for each ship processed. It has been described as a "grinding stint," although, as in Hawthorne's case, it was understood that Melville was an author and would have some time for writing. He continued to study poetry and poetics and write his own verse, often while at the Custom House, but he entirely stopped writing fiction. His failure to succeed as a professional author had induced his first crisis, in 1851, and the continuing decline of his literary reputation, his sullen, sole drinking, and his moody outbursts in the evenings all led him to depths of depression and social withdrawal. His wife finally felt compelled to consider the extremely uncommon solution of legal separation in 1867. That year, too, his son Malcolm committed suicide at the age of eighteen. Melville would spend almost twenty years working at this desk job, depressed and forgotten by his former public. Except for *Billy Budd*, written in his retirement, all of the texts we know—*Typee*, *Omoo*, *Redburn*, *White-Jacket*, *The Confidence Man*, *Israel Potter*, *The Piazza Tales*, *Mardi*, *Pierre*, and *Moby-Dick*—were published in just over ten years, to be followed by almost twenty-five years of quiet desperation, working at the landlubbingest end of ocean commerce.

Melville's most serious meditation on work and idleness comes fairly soon after the commercial disappointment of *Moby-Dick* and is set much closer to home than the seagoing tales: "Bartleby, the Scrivener" was published in 1853, a decade before Melville's own descent into depressive office habit, and then reprinted in *The Piazza Tales* (1856). Narrated by a middle-aged attorney with offices on Wall Street, it tells the story of Bartleby, a pallid, forlorn man who comes to work at the attorney's firm. It is a famously odd story, one that has kept literary critics hard at work theorizing and explicating ever since. The bare bones of the story are these: the narrator hires Bartleby to be a scrivener, or copyist. Bartleby at first does his work very diligently, in fact seems to do nothing but work, literally staying in the office day and night. He then gradually starts refusing to do the jobs asked of him. When asked to run an errand, he responds, "I would prefer not to." When asked to copy a letter, he again responds, "I would prefer not to." Eventually he won't work at all, and the narrator dismisses him. But Bartleby won't leave the office, saying, once again, "I would prefer not to." The narrator, unable to deal with Bartleby, moves out of the office himself, and the next tenant has him arrested. Bartleby, refusing to eat, or preferring not to, dies in prison.

The *New York Tribune* wrote that the stories in *Piazza Tales* were, like Melville's novels, excellent if perverse:

> [The stories] show something of the boldness of invention, bril-
> liancy of imagination, and quaintness of expression which usually
> mark his writings, with not a little of the apparent perversity and self-
> will, which serve as a foil to their various excellences. "Bartleby," the
> scrivener, is the most original story in the volume, and as a curious
> study of human nature, possesses unquestionable merit.

Other reviewers were most impressed by "strange and mysterious
things" (*New Bedford Daily Mercury*) and "a certain weirdness of conceit" (*Springfield, Massachusetts, Republican*) and found the story
"most painfully interesting" (*New York Knickerbocker*) and "sometimes
barely intelligible" (*London Athenaeum*). *The New York Times* thought
it would not help Melville's reputation, while the *United States
Democratic Review* thought that "the admirers of Edgar Poe will see,
or think they see, an imitation of his concentrated gloom in the wild,
weird tale, called 'Bartleby.' " Like many readers today, these reviewers felt the story's power but weren't sure what to make of it. Some recent critics have argued that the tale is about homosexuality, anorexia,
autism, or literary conventionality: whether or not we agree with such
interpretations, we can admit with the *New Bedford Daily Mercury* reviewer that the story "leaves some space for the *reader* to try his own
ingenuity upon,—some rests and intervals in the literary voyage."

Whatever else it is, "Bartleby, the Scrivener" is a tale about work,
and specifically work in the brave new world of Wall Street's capitalist
offices. There are two other copyists in the office when Bartleby arrives, Turkey and Nippers. Turkey is an excellent worker in the morning, but after going to dinner at noon and apparently having a few
drinks, he becomes completely irascible and incompetent. Nippers is
the opposite; although he doesn't drink, he has a "brandylike disposition" owing to a combination of severe indigestion and frustrated ambition. His indigestion is bad in the mornings, though, and seems to
be regularly settled by his noon meal; in the afternoon he is a very efficient and excellent copyist. The narrator/boss, frustrated by their off
times, is occasionally tempted to fire them, but he ultimately con-
cedes that between them they embody a workable arrangement. Since
Nippers's irritability lasts only until noon, and Turkey's "paroxysms"
begin only after, the narrator says, "I never had to do with their eccentricities at one time. Their fits relieved each other, like guards. When

Nippers's was on, Turkey's was off; and vice versa. This was a good natural arrangement, under the circumstances." Part of the story's humor lies in the narrator's self-deluding soft-selling of these eccentricities. From the point of view of a manager, his decisions are ludicrous, and when Bartleby gets odder and odder, eventually refusing to do any work at all, the narrator's inability to get rid of him is downright pathological. Unless, that is, we find something touching and humane about these managerial lapses, as if the attorney, despite his economic self-interest, were out of the goodness of his heart letting people determine their own work lives outside the regime of Franklinian, capitalist cost-benefit analysis.

Bartleby is not a workplace revolutionary. Although the story is published while strikes regularly hit the nation's factories, five years after *The Communist Manifesto* (and it is clearly in line with Marx's later writings on alienation), "Bartleby" has no direct mention of any of the various workers' movements of the time. The first few days Bartleby is in the office he seems an ideal, uncomplaining, diligent worker. He works "as if long famishing for something to copy," and the narrator's only grievance is that Bartleby doesn't seem "cheerful," but is instead silently, mechanically industrious. Bartleby is absolutely nonviolent and never makes a case for his own rights, much less his rights as a worker or as a part of any group. He has no sense of himself, apparently, as a social being, no desire to go out with the other workers for lunch or drinks—in fact, no desire to go out at all. He ends up living in the office and won't leave even when the narrator closes it down. Bartleby is not a revolutionary; he is inert. But this combination of initial diligence and later loafing helps establish an idea: the alienated worker is not someone inherently lazy; people do not become slackers because of their character but because of circumstance.

The first crisis occurs when the narrator asks Bartleby to compare copy—a task in which two or more people check their copies against an original that is read aloud. Bartleby simply replies, "I would prefer not to." The narrator is stunned. He decides that Bartleby must not have heard him, and repeats his request carefully.

> "I would prefer not to," said he.
> "Prefer not to," echoed I, rising in high excitement and crossing
> the room with a stride. "What do you mean? Are you moon-struck?

I want you to compare this sheet here—take it," and I thrust it to-
wards him.

"I would prefer not to," said he.

I looked at him steadfastly. His face was leanly composed; his
gray eyes dimly calm. Not a wrinkle of agitation rippled him.

The narrator is stymied, confounded. He is particularly bewildered by
Bartleby's serenity, his lack of emotion. Bartleby returns to his desk
and work, and the narrator uses a different scrivener for the task. A few
days later he needs four copies checked, which requires his whole
staff, including Bartleby. Again, Bartleby refuses, simply and civilly: "I
would prefer not to." Again confounded, the narrator finally asks,
why? Why won't you do it? " 'I would prefer not to,' he said, and gen-
tly disappeared." Nippers (in the morning) and Turkey (in the afternoon) were ready to "black his eyes for him," but the narrator forgives
Bartleby his "eccentricities," and indeed he feels proud of his own
benevolence; he is somehow doing Bartleby a service, since with his
odd refusals he wouldn't last long in any other law office.

The narrator is himself a bit of a loafer. "I am a man," he admits at
the outset, "who, from his youth upwards, has been filled with a profound conviction that the easiest way of life is the best." He is an "un-
ambitious" lawyer, he admits, who never litigates, never appears
before a jury or a judge, but "in the cool tranquility of a snug retreat,
do a snug business among rich men's bonds, and mortgages, and title
deeds." He also had for a while a politically appointed sinecure as
Master of Chancery ("not a very arduous office, but very pleasantly remunerative") until it was abolished by a new, less corrupt state constitution. Although he interprets his own disinclination to fire Bartleby
as charity, the story suggests it to be primarily an avoidance of the effort it might take. And his preference for the easy road undercuts any
moralistic condemnation of Bartleby he might otherwise indulge in.

It also helps explain why the narrator can't stop pushing Bartleby to
do things he knows he won't, as if—and he admits this to himself—he
"burned to be rebelled against." He harasses Bartleby as if he were du-
eling with his own guilty conscience. As a result, Bartleby's refusals
proliferate. The narrator asks Bartleby to go to the post office; Bartleby
prefers not to. He comes in on a Sunday and discovers that Bartleby is
in fact living in the office, but when he asks Bartleby why, and for par-

ticulars about his past, Bartleby prefers not to answer. Throughout these interchanges, there is a sense of foreboding and apprehension, suffused with absurdity and wry humor that the narrator seems completely unaware of. The narrator asks Bartleby if he would like help getting started in another line of work, offering a number of suggestions, but Bartleby rejects them all. Bartleby repeatedly claims, along with his preference not to engage in this or that work, that he doesn't really have anything against a particular job: the positions—a clerkship, bartending, even being a companion to a young man going to Europe—all have, Bartleby suggests, things he doesn't like, but he is not particular, really, they are all the same to him, he just prefers not to do any of them. The offer to be companion on a grand tour seems to be the clincher—what more relaxed, lounging profession could there be?—but still Bartleby demurs. "How would that suit you?" the narrator asks. "Not at all," replies Bartleby. "But I am not particular."

In the end, the narrator, unable to get anything from Bartleby but passive resistance, leaves the premises himself and finds other offices—again a comic response to the problem, filled, like the rest of the tale, with slapstick double takes. He later hears that the landlord has had Bartleby arrested for vagrancy and taken to the Tombs, and so he goes to visit and finds that Bartleby, who had lived on ginger nuts at the office, has ceased to eat anything at all. His passive resistance has become total, and he soon dies in the yard of the prison. "Ah Bartleby!" the narrator muses in the last sentences of the story. "Ah humanity!" Bartleby continues to resonate with readers because the fundamental conflict—between people who, whatever their own questionable relations to work, are perversely dedicated to making others work harder, and those who, for whatever nameable or unnameable reason, prefer not to—continues to animate debates between workfare and welfare proponents and detractors, between bosses and workers, between fathers and sons. Ah, humanity, indeed.

Men like Bartleby in America, that is, men who loiter, jobless and homeless, in the lobbies of buildings, have sometimes been sent to prison, as Melville's character was, but beginning in the 1820s they were also sent to workhouses. The Boston House of Industry, for instance, built in 1821, was meant to "repress the mischievous effects of that weak and listless sensibility, miscalled benevolence, which scat-

ters its bounty without discrimination," and to help encourage "industrious habits" in the poor. Unlike an almshouse, where maintenance
tasks might be assigned to inmates but which was otherwise supported
by city or state, the House of Industry was designed to be self-
supporting, through harnessing the labor of its own indigents. The
founders of the House of Industry distinguished among four causes of
poverty: old age, misfortune, infancy, and vice. Those too old or
young to work, they agreed, and those who were physically or mentally handicapped, deserved alms. But those who were poor through
their own vice (and who "constitute, here, and every where, by far the
greater part of the poor") needed to work for their keep. "Indolence,
intemperance, and sensuality are the greatest causes of pauperism in
this country," Josiah Quincy, soon to be Boston's mayor, wrote.
"Notwithstanding the imbecility induced by their habits and vices . . .
some of them fall little, and often not at all, short of the ability to perform, daily, the complete task of a day laborer." For such people, allowing them to live in an almshouse without working is "a perpetual
and very effectual encouragement to a thoughtless, dissipated and self-
indulgent course."

The problem with Bartleby is that he fits none of the categories: he
is not too old or too young. He is the opposite of intemperate and
seems to have no vices; he is neither thoughtless nor dissipated.
Bartleby is not, in fact, the kind of person the eighteenth and nineteenth centuries recognized as indolent, either lower- or upper-class
indolent. He seems instead to be another prototype of the modern
slacker, a young man who—is it on principle? or due to a lack of
desire?—decides that he shouldn't take part in the world of work,
and who, unlike the ironic loungers of the eighteenth century, does
so without self-deprecatory humor, in absolute, depressive earnest.
While the lounger luxuriates and snickers through his subversive refusal to become part of the middle-class world, Bartleby seems somehow condemned to refuse. Melville points up all the possible
explanations for Bartleby's refusal and shows that they don't quite explain it: maybe Bartleby is just lazy, but no, we see that he is, at least
sometimes, energetically diligent. Maybe he is mentally handicapped
and can't follow what the narrator is trying to say; but no, the narrator
is further aggravated by the considered attention Bartleby gives to the

narrator's requests before refusing to comply. Maybe he is a hothead; but no, he remains cool and calm throughout. Maybe he just hasn't found his true calling; but no, he isn't interested in any other options. Maybe he is a revolutionist, an anarchist, a socialist; but no, he is not that particular or motivated. Melville has put his finger on a central fact of slacker life: slackers may "prefer not to" not because they imagine a better option in the wings, not because they have a fully articulated critique at the ready of the capitalist or industrial or cultural imperatives to work, but just because nothing moves them to take part. Melville suggests that a culture's social values can sometimes lose their hold, allowing some people to resist what others find the irresistible social pressure to work. They simply prefer not to work because they prefer not to.

∞

Bartleby, in 1853, was found "wild" and "weird" by many readers, but his seeming rejection of bourgeois ethics, even unto death, was about to become more common. New York's Bohemia, in fact, has been said to have been inaugurated by a suicide craze in the 1850s, beginning with journalist William North, who drank prussic acid in 1854 and is credited, like other famous fictional and real plug-pullers—from Goethe's slacker Werther to grunge slacker Kurt Cobain—with starting a rash of suicides. The fad culminated with the novelist Henry W. Herbert (pen name Frank Forrester), who threw a dinner party on May 17, 1858, at the end of which he got up, stood in front of a large mirror, and shot himself through the heart: clearly a wilder and weirder end than Bartleby's anorexic fading away. Herbert is also often credited—not coincidentally—with introducing the modern sport of hunting to the print culture of the United States, arguing that it should be thought of as a leisure activity, not a means of procuring food. In other words, he advocated hunting as a way to do nothing rather than a way to do something. The Bohemians, like their French models, exalted *otium* and denigrated any striving after bourgeois success, attainment, propriety, or comfort.

Bohemians were closely related to "loafers." In *Two Years Before the Mast* in 1840, Richard Dana claims that the latter word is recently coined: "The men [in South America] appeared to be the laziest people upon the face of the earth; and indeed, there are no people to whom the newly invented Yankee word of 'loafer' is more applicable than to the Spanish Americans." The first entry for "loafing" in the *Oxford English Dictionary* is "living idly on other people, as defined in the American vocabulary," dated 1846, but Dickens used the word, always in quotes, in the 1830s and 1840s, and Charles Godfrey Leland, in *The English Gipsies and Their Language* (1873), claimed that the word first became popular among Gypsies in the 1830s and meant pilfering—"Where did you loaf that from?" is his example. The connection to Gypsies was important in England if not the United States. In 1857 Thomas Hughes described "a half-gipsey, poaching, loafing fellow" in *Tom Brown's Schooldays*. In the United States, the word had a less foreign feel; Harriet Beecher Stowe in 1850 simply says, "The men talked, and loafed, and read and smoked." And, of course, Whitman regularly identified himself as a loafer.

Whitman was also recognized as a Bohemian. French journalist and dramatist Félix Pyat is credited with introducing the term "Bohemian," also in the 1830s, also playing off a common French slang name for Gypsies. Like loafer, it quickly came to stand for a group of people distinguished primarily by their lack of money and lack of interest in work. In *A Prince of Bohemia* (1840), Honoré de Balzac has a character say, "This word 'boheme' is self-explanatory. Bohemia possesses nothing, yet contrives to exist on that nothing. Its religion is hope; its code, faith in itself; its income, in so far that it appears to have one, charity." The word became much more common after Henri Murger's *Scènes de la vie de Bohème* (1845–49), and the play by the same name produced in 1849. Murger's *Scènes* were romantic sketches of starving artists with unconventional love affairs, originally published in Parisian newspapers. The stories are best known now from musical versions, from Puccini's *La Bohème* (1896) through Jonathan Larson's *Rent* (1996). Murger's Bohemians, like Bohemians ever since, reject bourgeois success and propriety for a life of aesthetic and romantic pleasure. Unlike loafers, Bohemians are necessarily artists, or prospective artists—Murger claims that Homer, Molière, and Shakespeare were Bohemians. And as these musical versions suggest, Bohemians, unlike loafers, had an aura of tragedy. According to Alphonse de Calonne, in his 1852 work, *Voyage au pays de Bohème*, "The land of Bohemia is a sad country, bounded on the North by need, on the South by poverty, on the East by illusion, and on the West by the hospital. It is irrigated by two inexhaustible streams: imprudence and shame." Murger himself, his brief fame already passed, died poor in 1861 at the age of thirty-eight.

The New World Bohemians, when not at suicidal house parties, congregated at Pfaff's, a tavern in the basement of 653 Broadway, just north of Bleecker Street in Greenwich Village, modeled on the German rathskellers. Run by Charles Ignatius Pfaff, Pfaff's quickly became the unofficial center of American Bohemia, frequented by Walt Whitman, Ada Clare, Thomas Bailey Aldrich, Fitz-James O'Brien, Thomas Nast, Bayard Taylor, Fitz Hugh Ludlow, Louis Gottschalk, Adah Isaacs Menken, Artemus Ward, and, perhaps most significantly, Henry Clapp Jr. Having spent years in Paris, where he read Murger's *Scènes*, Clapp attempted to re-create Parisian Bohemia in New York. Sometimes called (even by himself) the Prince of Bohemia or the King of Bohemia, Clapp held court at Pfaff's and exerted great influence. "You will have to know something of Henry Clapp," Whitman told Horace Traubel, "if you want to know all about me."

Whitman had begun hanging out at Pfaff's after being fired from a Brooklyn newspaper in 1859, and he proceeded to spend what Whitman scholars Ed Folsom and Kenneth M. Price have called "a couple years of unemployed carousing." Clapp helped publicize Whitman's career in the paper he started, the *Saturday Press*, which by the late 1850s was more notorious than noted. The *Saturday Press* published a version of "Out of the Cradle Endlessly Rocking" and a couple dozen other Whitman poems and is often considered the first counterculture newspaper in the country. It is fitting, therefore, that the Bohemians at Pfaff's were against everything. They were against slavery, but also against what they saw as the stuffy moralizing of Boston abolitionists and the opportunism of politicians like Lincoln. They were, finally, against politics, arguing for a pure individualism and against all socialized restraints. Ada Clare, a writer, performer, and famous beauty, also known as the Queen of Bohemia and one of Whitman's closest friends at Pfaff's, stated that "a Bohemian is not, like the creature of society, a victim of rules and customs; he steps over them all with an easy, graceful, joyous unconsciousness."

The New York Times commented on the Greenwich Village Bohemian scene in 1858:

It would be better to cultivate a familiarity with any kind of coarse and honest art, or any sort of regular employment, than to fall into the company of Bohemians. They are seductive in their ways, and they hold the finest sentiments, and have a distinctive aversion of anything that is low or mean, or common or inelegant. Still, the Bohemian cannot be called a useful member of society, and it is not an encouraging sign for us that the tribe has become so numerous among us as to form a distinct and recognizable class that does not object to being called by that name.

William Dean Howells, too, was unenthusiastic about the group, or so he claimed later. As a young man, he had published poetry in the *Saturday Press* and imagined Pfaff's as a great literary center. The night he first actually went there, a trip he undertook as though it were a pilgrimage, he met and was impressed by Whitman. Otherwise he was not overwhelmed:

> I felt that as a contributor and at least a brevet Bohemian I ought not to go home without visiting the famous place, and witnessing if I could not share the revels of my comrades. As I neither drank beer nor smoked, my part in the carousal was limited to a German pancake, which I found they had very good at Pfaff's, and to listening to the whirling words of my commensals, at the long board spread for the Bohemians in a cavernous space under the pavement. There were writers for the "Saturday Press" and for Vanity Fair (a hopefully comic paper of that day), and some of the artists who drew for the illustrated periodicals. Nothing of their talk remains with me, but the impression remains that it was not so good talk as I had heard in Boston . . . I stayed hoping vainly for worse things till eleven o'clock, and then I rose and took my leave of a literary condition that had distinctly disappointed me. I do not say that it may not have been wickeder and wittier than I found it; I only report what I saw and heard in Bohemia on my first visit to New York, and I know that my acquaintance with it was not exhaustive.

Whitman disagreed. "There was as good talk around that table," he later said, "as took place anywhere in the world."

Henry Clapp, during his time in Paris, had also translated Charles

Fourier's *The Social Destiny of Man* (1857), one of the texts in which Fourier expounds on his theory that industrial labor is all tribulation and affliction and the society it has formed, one of false respectability and alienation. It's not clear how much of Fourier's other, considerably wackier theories Clapp actually believed, but he did maintain a belief that Bohemians should work only as they wanted to, live by their art, and spit on the gods of bourgeois propriety. Like Murger's characters, Clapp was always on the verge of dispossession. The *Saturday Press* in fact died twice, once in 1860 and again in 1866. In 1865 it was revived briefly, with the following announcement: "This paper was stopped in 1860 for want of means. It is now started again for the same reason."

One of Clapp's contributors to the revived *Saturday Press* was an unknown who published under the name of Mark Twain. Twain's very early story, "Jim Smiley and His Jumping Frog," which would later become "The Celebrated Jumping Frog of Calaveras County," introduced the first of the author's many unforgettable, underemployed semi-wastrels—a man so enamored of wagering that he bets on either side of any debate:

> Why, it never made no difference to him—he would bet on any-thing—the dangdest feller. Parson Walker's wife laid very sick, once, for a good while, and it seemed as if they warn't going to save her; but one morning he come in and Smiley asked him how she was, and he said she was considerable better—thank the Lord for his infinite mercy—and coming on so smart that with the blessing of Providence she'd get well yet—and Smiley, before he thought, says, "Well, I'll resk two-and-a-half that she don't, anyway."

Smiley was one of a long line of slackeresque characters that abound in Twain's tales: Tom Sawyer, who gets the other boys to paint his fence for him; Huck Finn's father, the drunk moocher; the backwoods thespian con artists the King and the Duke; arriviste Gilded Age politicians and racketeers; and assorted town layabouts and vagabonds like Injun Joe, the "half-breed loafer." Twain's one earlier story, published in a Boston comic paper when he was seventeen, is the story of a loafer and a dandy—two types who don't visibly work for a living—with the dandy getting the comeuppance: in an idle attempt to

impress two women, the dandy accosts the loafer, only to be humiliat-
ingly thrown into the river. These characters are two Western versions
of the slacker, but like Melville's sailors and copyists, they are culture
heroes of a very different stripe than the elite loungers of the previous
century. They are rougher, less aristocratic; they are drawn from the
new class of migrants set wandering the globe by the industrial economy. Twain showed a keen interest in class differences, whether alle-
gorized, as they are in *The Prince and the Pauper* (both of whom, by
the way, survive without working), or indirectly dramatized through
questions of race (*Pudd'nhead Wilson*), politics (*The Gilded Age*), or
history (*A Connecticut Yankee in King Arthur's Court*). Huck's famous
decision to light out for the territories before he can be civilized is a
desire to avoid the ethics and manners of the class above him, but it
follows directly on his declaration that he is done with the work of
telling his story: "There ain't nothing more to write about, and I am
rotten glad of it, because if I'd a knowed what a trouble it was to make
a book I wouldn't a tackled it, and ain't a-going to no more." One Bohemian step better than rejecting "civilization" and being an artist is
deciding that even writing literature is too much work.

In his late years Twain became famously bitter, with no more faith
in human community, at times, than Bartleby. Clapp's life, too, had a
Bartleby-like ending. He died, some ten years after Twain's piece was
published, as a pauper in the asylum on Blackwell's Island. But Bohemia lived on, and the general outlines of *la vie de Bohème* remained largely the same. Pfaff's was an isolated New York affair, but
by the 1920s Bohemia was everywhere, an aspect of life even in the
smallest cities in the country, a threat or refuge, depending on one's
stance, an object of desire or ridicule, but a fact of American life.
Years after his Greenwich Village days, Whitman visited Pfaff at his
new uptown restaurant and reminisced about the old crowd. "And
there Pfaff and I, sitting opposite each other at the little table, gave a
remembrance to them in a style they would have themselves fully
confirm'd, namely, big, brimming, fill'd-up champagne-glasses,
drain'd in abstracted silence, very leisurely, to the last drop."

V

NERVE CASES, SAUNTERERS, TRAMPS, AND *FLÂNEURS*

In which the doctors decide that overwork is a problem—Jerome K. Jerome takes a leisure trip up the Thames—the flâneur *and Saunterer make their bows—Oscar Wilde declares that doing nothing is the height of human achievement—the tramp becomes a hero and a social problem—and Theodore Dreiser flirts with failure but decides to work instead.*

Until the late nineteenth century, loafing, lounging, idling, and rambling had been the professional province of literary writers, legislators, and preachers. But starting in the 1860s, some new professions decided to have their say, chief among them the medical doctors and sociologists. George M. Beard, M.D., in analyzing what he saw as a high degree of "nervousness" among his patients, concluded that the pace of modern life, its noisiness and information overload, along with the wear and tear of overwork, were debilitating. Neurasthenia, the disease he invented to describe this debilitation, was not only often caused by overwork, it left its victims unable to work, and Beard proposed a number of cures.

Beard's favorite was cure by electricity. Since overwork ran down patients' batteries, the best a doctor could do for them was to zap them with some new energy. Beard used a "galvanizer," a large, imposing generator, and would have his patient strip to loosened underclothes. With one electrode placed under a foot, the other was placed between

Beard's hand and a wet sponge to increase conductivity, and Beard would then touch the patient over the entire body. Special attention was paid to affected areas, the head for headaches, the penis for impotence. The treatment would be repeated daily, or every other day, for months. The end was supposed to be the renewal of energy and vigor. For those who couldn't afford daily visits to the doctor to have their penis massaged with electrical current, stores and mail-order houses offered electric belts, complete with batteries and genital attachments, guaranteed to make "a new man."

S. Weir Mitchell, America's other main theorist of neurasthenia, offered a treatment more clearly related to overwork: the rest cure. Mitchell's version consisted of weeks and sometimes months of bed rest, during which the patient was allowed no activity whatsoever: no visits, no reading, no knitting, no writing. It was, we might say, a prescribed slacker regimen. The body would naturally, through a steady diet of milk and meat, regenerate its own energy, Mitchell argued, and then the patient could resume normal activities, including work. One historian has argued that neurasthenia was in fact "an inverted work ethic, an ethic of resistance to work or activity in all its forms," and clearly for some patients a resistance to work was enough to warrant a diagnosis of neurasthenia. Still, the diagnosis covered an enormous hodgepodge of symptoms and complaints, and varied from region to region and country to country. It was also applied differently to men and women. Men who couldn't or wouldn't work were often diagnosed as neurasthenic, for instance, but doctors gave the same diagnosis to women who *wanted* to work and study. Sometimes, even in these cases, physicians decided that their female patients were "malingerers," hiding behind their illness so as not to perform their duties as wives and mothers, and the suspicion always surrounded neurasthenic men as well.

Primarily, though, the accepted cause of neurasthenia for men was overwork. In Howells's A *Traveler from Altruria*, the narrator explains the American class system to the traveler: "Of course, you can have no conception of how hard our business men and our professional men work. I suppose there is nothing like it anywhere else in the world." The traveler, who comes from a land of three-hour workdays, is not impressed, and the narrator admits there are problems. "As I said before," he continues, "we are beginning to find that we cannot burn the candle at both ends and have it last long . . . There are frightful wrecks of men strewn all along the course of our prosperity, wrecks of mind and body." The insane asylums, he claims, are full of madmen who have broken under the strain of overwork, "and every country in Europe abounds in our dyspeptics" (dyspepsia one of the prime symptoms of neurasthenia). The traveler finds this all odd, which gives the narrator momentary pause. "I was rather proud of this terrible fact; there is no doubt but we Americans are proud of overworking ourselves; heaven knows why!"

Americans were proud of neurasthenia. It began as an upper-middle-class disease, since, the theory was, the more educated, refined, and civilized one was, the more sensitive one would be to the overwhelming pace of modern life, and thus the more it would wear one down. The simple people, with simple minds and simple needs, were no more likely to be deleteriously affected by modernity than they were to read Henry James or worry about the latest scientific discoveries. By the turn of the century, neurasthenia had spread through the international bourgeoisie as far as Kyoto, Calcutta, and St. Petersburg. By 1908, one physician, in his own *Confessions of a Neurasthenic*, said that the best thing about the disease was that it allowed one "to move in neurasthenic circles," and Dr. Beard happily proclaimed, "Not Greece, nor Rome, nor Spain, nor the Netherlands, in the days of their glory, possessed such maladies." Although it was often called the American disease, it became central to medical thinking in Europe and in Asia and had profound effects on the thinking of Max Weber, Émile Durkheim, Friedrich Nietzsche, Jean-Martin Charcot, Pierre Janet, and Sigmund Freud, among others. In the United States, everyone who was anyone had a touch of it: afflicted luminaries included Teddy Roosevelt, Henry James, William James, Samuel Clemens, William Dean Howells, Charlotte Perkins Gilman, Jane Addams, Theodore Dreiser, Emma Goldman, Henry Adams, Thomas Eakins, George Santayana, Josiah Royce, and Edith Wharton. When Freud set up shop among the well-to-do matrons of Vienna, he specialized in neurasthenic complaints, especially those for which no physical cause could be found.

Freud's "talking cure" assumed that for many neurasthenics, the problem and the solution were psychological. The electricity cure and the rest cure, on the other hand, assumed that the problem was physiological and that the psychological problems would disappear once the body was restored to its healthy state. Most doctors simply assumed that the disease covered such a wide range of symptoms and syndromes that neither a psychological nor a physiological explanation could adequately explain the full range of cases. Some people diagnosed as neurasthenics undoubtedly had what were at the time undiscovered viruses or other problems; some, again undoubtedly, would fit any number of current diagnoses: depression, anxiety, Epstein-Barr, chronic fatigue syndrome, post-traumatic stress disorder. And some patients, it seems clear in retrospect, whatever their real or imagined physical or psychological debilities, used the disease as a kind of moratorium from their lives. Charlotte Perkins Gilman, for instance, who would go on to become an important feminist writer and economist, was diagnosed as a neurasthenic after the birth of her child. Today she would probably be seen as having postpartum depression, but that had yet to be invented: the doctor diagnosed neurasthenia and prescribed a classic Weir Mitchell rest cure. Although she later wrote critically of the rest cure, she remained convinced that the disease was real and that the separation from her husband and child were necessary to her recovery. The rest cure drove her mad with restlessness and a desire for work; when she emerged from it, she left her husband for a life of work and political activism. For Gilman, and for many other women and men, the rest cure, by removing them from their everyday life and work, was the first step to making a new life. Leaving their duties behind for a spell of doing nothing began as therapy and ended as transformation.

It is no accident, then, that most patients with neurasthenia were fairly young men—and often men whose work lives or careers were unsatisfying—or fairly young women whose married life (or the very prospect of a married life) was unsatisfactory. The medically sanctioned period of pure slackerhood gave them the time and a legitimate excuse to change their lives, which often meant deciding on a new career. William James, the philosopher, had a neurasthenic breakdown when he was deciding what postgraduate field to study. He picked medicine, began working toward a medical degree, had another neurasthenic breakdown, and became a psychologist. Theodore Roosevelt, in another common pattern, had a breakdown when his political career suffered a setback. He was sent out west for a rough-riding exercise cure for his neurasthenia after losing an election in New York, and he came back reinvigorated and ready to run another campaign. His "time off" seems to have allowed him time to mourn his loss and rethink his relation to his work; instead of the leisure-class, aristocratic clothes he wore in his losing campaign, Roosevelt started to affect the hardworking "roughrider" image for which he is famous.

Later, Roosevelt helped institutionalize a space for legitimized slacking in his expansion of the National Park System. John Muir, who assisted him in that project, wrote in 1902 that "the tendency nowadays to wander"—or, we might say, ramble or saunter—"in wilderness is delightful to see. Thousands of tired, nerve-shaken, over-civilized people are beginning to find that going to the mountains is going home." These "retreats" from the pressures of civilization functioned as cures for the nervous debility suffered by modern overwork, he argued. Muir believed that nature could teach one, as Thoreau suggested, how to loaf. And loafing was good for what ailed.

One British writer who knew idleness and knew doctors was Robert Louis Stevenson. Stevenson was born in Edinburgh in 1850 and was a sickly, frequently bedridden child, often spending his days being read to by a nurse. At the University of Edinburgh in the late 1860s and early 1870s he was known as an "indifferent" student, with more interest in the local Bohemia than in academic work. He started to wear a wide-brimmed hat, a cravat, and so much velvet that his nickname became Velvet Jacket. He decided that he was going to be a writer, but his father insisted he go to law school, which he did, again diffidently, getting a law degree he rarely used. He and his father also had a falling-out over religion, leading the younger Stevenson to feel that he was a "damned curse" on his family. Told to head south for his health, Stevenson took up the aimless wandering that characterized his adult life, and on which he based his best writing. *An Inland Voyage* (1878) and *Travels with a Donkey in the Cévennes* (1879), both about wandering around in France, and *The Silverado Squatters* (1883), about his first trip to America, in 1879, during which he ended up extremely ill and under the care of doctors in San Francisco, established him as a professional rambler and writer in the 1870s. Back home, probably with tuberculosis (although never diagnosed as such), he was largely confined to bed again in the 1880s, when he wrote his most famous works: *Treasure Island* (1883), *Kidnapped* (1886), *The Strange Case of*

Dr. Jekyll and Mr. Hyde (1886), and *The Black Arrow* (1888). After this he set sail for Hawaii and Polynesia. He died just a few years later in Samoa from a cerebral hemorrhage.

In 1877, Stevenson published "An Apology for Idlers," one of the more straightforward, serious defenses of idling ever written. Idleness, he insisted, "does not consist in doing nothing, but in doing a great deal not recognized in the dogmatic formularies of the ruling class." He understood that idlers made non-idlers angry—"It is admitted that the presence of people who refuse to enter the handicap race for six-penny pieces, is at once an insult and a disenchantment for those who do"—but the idler himself is much more open-minded. "He who has looked on at the childish satisfaction of other people in their hobbies, will regard his own with only a very ironical indulgence. He will not be heard among the dogmatists." Stevenson admits that there are perfectly good arguments in favor of diligence, but he finds that these have no bearing on the value of slacking: "To state one argument is not necessarily to be deaf to all others, and that a man has written a book of travels in Montenegro, is no reason why he should never have been to Richmond." Besides, the idler learns all sorts of things, often "some really useful art; to play the fiddle, to know a good cigar, or to speak with ease and opportunity to all varieties of men." Extreme busyness, he thought, demonstrated a lack of real vitality, while idling shows not just a "catholic appetite" but a "strong sense of personal identity." And he seconds the doctors' assessment of overwork: "As if a man's soul were not too small to begin with," he writes, the overwork-ers "have dwarfed and narrowed theirs by a life of all work and no play; until they are at forty, with a listless attention, a mind vacant of all material of amusement, and not one thought to rub against an-other." Work destroys enjoyment and health. The busy man "sows hurry and reaps indigestion; he puts a vast deal of activity out to inter-est, and receives a large sum of nervous derangement in return."

William James's "The Gospel of Relaxation" (1899), written some twenty years later, is more balanced, and suggests that it is neither work itself nor leisure itself that cause the problems of nervous exhaus-tion so common in America. Instead, James believed, it is our attitude toward work. "The need of feeling responsible the livelong day has been preached long enough in our New England," he writes. "Long enough exclusively, at any rate." The Protestant work ethic had been so thoroughly drilled into us, James thought, that we worked fitfully and convulsively, as if our life depended on it, as if we were constantly not just getting our job done but saving our own souls. He suggests that people read Annie Payson Call, a magazine writer who had published *Power Through Repose* (1891) and articles on "Working Restfully." Nonetheless, he criticizes the medical practice of sending people abroad "to rest their nerves" when they break down from overwork, as he and his brother Henry James had been:

> I suspect that neither the nature nor the amount of our work is accountable for the frequency and severity of our breakdowns, but that their cause lies rather in those absurd feelings of hurry and having no time, in that breathlessness and tension, that anxiety of feature and that solicitude for results, that lack of inner harmony and ease, in short, by which with us the work is so apt to be accompanied, and from which a European who should do the same work would nine times out of ten be free. These perfectly wanton and unnecessary tricks of inner attitude and outer manner in us, caught from the social atmosphere, kept up by tradition, and idealized by many as the admirable way of life, are the last straws that break the American camel's back, the final overflowers of our measure of wear and tear and fatigue.

The answer is not to work less, but to work restfully. James's piece, in its evenhanded view, was a harbinger of things to come.

∞

Jerome K. Jerome wrote one of the bestselling books of the nineteenth century about the kind of rejuvenating, curative trip into nature recommended by Muir, Roosevelt, and some physicians. Jerome was born in 1859 in Staffordshire, where his father was a preacher and a failed farmer who had invested what was left of the family funds in the local coal and iron industries. The family lived a fashionable, comfortable life in a fashionable, comfortable house until the businesses, like the farm, failed miserably, bankrupting his father and wiping out his mother's inheritance. The family moved around frequently until they ended up where failures of the day ended up, in the East End of London. His father died when he was twelve, shortly after which Jerome began working. His mother died when he was fifteen, and he was on his own. He worked as a railway clerk at Euston Station and started moonlighting as a journalist and actor. Gradually the stage career took over, and during these years, he later claimed, he played every role in Hamlet except Ophelia.

The stage career prospered enough to allow him to quit his railway job and tour as an actor. After three years on the road, however, he tired of the life and returned to London, thirty shillings to his name. He proceeded to "sleep rough" (sleep outdoors)—unless the weather was bad, when he would get a room for ninepence—and scrounge for work. He began writing penny-a-line reports of police actions, coroners' inquests, and criminal trials. He also took work with a firm of commission agents, as a teacher, and as a solicitor's clerk (like Bartleby), writing on the side. Within a few years he published his first book, a series of humorous sketches based in part on his time as an actor, and he kept regularly producing essays, stories, and plays. Several of the plays were produced in the late 1880s, along with a collection of his essays, *The Idle Thoughts of an Idle Fellow*, published in 1886. In this book he claims to be a long-practiced expert on idleness:

> [My teacher] used to say he never knew a boy who could do less work in more time; and I remember my poor grandmother once incidentally observing, in the course of an instruction upon the use of the Prayer-book, that it was highly improbable that I should ever do much that I ought not to do, but that she felt convinced beyond a doubt that I should leave undone pretty well everything that I ought to do.

He feels, in fact, that idling is his strong point, and that while there are plenty of lazy people, plenty of slowpokes, there are very few true idlers. When he was a neurasthenic young man, a physician prescribed a rest cure, which he embraced as four weeks of dolce far niente at the beach. But like Gilman, he was strictly forbidden, in the Weir Mitchell style, to read or do anything. He found he was bored silly and couldn't wait to get back to his real life. "It is impossible to enjoy idling thoroughly," he concluded, "unless one has plenty of work to do." True idling has to be irresponsible. "There is no fun in doing nothing when you have nothing to do. Wasting time is merely an occupation then, and a most exhausting one. Idleness, like kisses, to be sweet must be stolen."

In 1889, Jerome published *Three Men in a Boat*, a novel that was a bestselling sensation and allowed him to do nothing but write for a living for the rest of his life. It tells the story with "hopeless and incurable veracity," he assures us, of a boating trip up the Thames with two friends and a dog. They were sitting around Jerome's flat, he tells us, talking about how bad they were—"bad from a medical point of view," that is—and what they should do about it. His friends George and Harris think perhaps they are neurasthenic, but "J.," as he calls himself, suspects he has liver problems. "I knew it was my liver because I had just been reading a patent liver-pill circular, in which were detailed the various symptoms by which a man could tell when his liver was out of order. I had them all." On the other hand, as he notes, he never read a patent medicine circular that didn't describe symptoms he was sure he had. The telling thing about liver disease, however, according to the circular, was that the prime symptom was "a general disinclination to work of any kind." And, in line with what the American doctors were arguing, the three men decide that their illnesses, even if they weren't entirely sure of the diagnoses, all had the same cause. "What it was that was actually wrong with us, we none of us could be sure of; but the unanimous opinion was that it—whatever it was—had been brought on by overwork."

And so, like Weir Mitchell, they decide that what they need is rest, and plenty of it, the specific prescription a boating trip on the Thames. Once the main commercial thoroughfare of the country, constantly clogged with barge traffic, the Thames had changed in the previous decades. Railroads had become the main carriers of freight after midcentury, and as barges all but disappeared, the river was becoming a leisure playground for Londoners. Boating was in fact the latest craze; in 1888 there were 8,000 registered boats on the river, and a year later 12,000, even as commercial traffic continued to decline. Some of these were steam powered, but most were not, and Jerome and his friends were staunchly anti-steam. Since they would be rowing, then, the trip was going to require some work, and right from the beginning there were fights about who should do what. Jerome, for starters, is quite proud of his abilities as a packer, and he thinks the others have no skill at it whatsoever ("when George is hanged, Harris will be the worst packer in this world") and declares that he should be in charge of it. The others agree, and sit down to pipes and brandy.

> This was hardly what I intended. What I had meant, of course, was that I should boss the job, and that Harris and George should potter about under my directions, I pushing them aside every now and then with, "Oh, you—!" "Here, let me do it." "There you are, simple enough!"—really teaching them, as you might say. Their taking it the way they did irritated me. There is nothing does irritate me more than seeing other people sitting about doing nothing when I'm working.

He assures us he never does that himself. Whenever he sees someone working when he is sitting around, it makes him hop and try to superintend. "It is my energetic nature," he confesses. "I can't help it."

Late in the book, the three have yet another argument about whose turn it is to row, and this sends him into a reverie about work:

> It always does seem to me that I am doing more work than I should do. It is not that I object to the work, mind you; I like work: it fascinates me. I can sit and look at it for hours. I love to keep it by me: the idea of getting rid of it nearly breaks my heart . . . Why some of the work I have by me now has been in my possession for years and years, and there isn't a finger-mark on it. I take great pride in my work; I take it down now and then and dust it. No man keeps his work in a better state of preservation than I do.
>
> But, though I crave for work, I like to be fair. I do not ask for more than my proper share.

He acknowledges that of course, everyone feels the same way, that everyone feels that they are doing more than their share. George, for instance, is convinced that there have never been "such a couple of lazy skulks" as Harris and Jerome, and Harris is convinced that he has never, in fact, seen George do a lick of work. "I've done more than old J., anyhow," George retorts, to which Harris responds, "Well, you couldn't very well have done less."

Such comedy about work remained Jerome's stock-in-trade, result-

ing in similar passages in his other novels and plays and further comic
essay collections such as *The Second Thoughts of an Idle Fellow* (1898)
and *Idle Ideas in 1905* (1905). During this same period, as the fortunes of turn-of-the-century industrialists accumulated, the upper
classes started to be called the leisure class. Thorstein Veblen did
more to popularize the notion of the leisure class than any other
writer, especially in his sardonic classic of political economy, *The Theory of the Leisure Class* (1899). Now perhaps most famous for having
coined the phrase "conspicuous consumption," Veblen argued that
much leisure-class activity, like weeklong boating excursions, had as a
primary goal the display of one's wealth—the longer the excursion,
the more obvious it was that one didn't need to be productive to survive. An enormous lawn, he argued, simply demonstrates that the
owner does not need the agricultural income that such land could
provide, and the acquiring of fluency in a dead language at a university proves not only that one doesn't need to work for a living, but also
that one doesn't even need to learn anything useful. A nonworking
wife and nonworking adolescent and postadolescent children are further proof of a man's wealth: he simply does not need their income.
Long larks on the Thames—except when they are grist for a popular
book about such larks—are the same.

Since many of the men in this new leisure class actually worked,
Veblen's "leisure class" was a bit of a misnomer. These men, who
might be called the working wealthy, did, nonetheless, support idle
wives and children, leisure-class dependents who didn't work at all.
These wives and children occupied themselves with leisure activities,
like boating on the Thames, golf, tennis, tourism, and partaking of
opera, art, and theater. After prolonged adolescences, the children
were faced with a decision. The decision for most of the daughters was
simply whom to marry, but the decision for the sons also included, as
the schoolboy Marx wrote, the "choice of a profession." This was complicated, in part because the leisure class, not surprisingly, had a
leisure ethic, not a work ethic. Jerome was born into the leisure class,
but he fell into the working class through his father's failures and
death. Jerome's comedy, in *Three Men and a Boat* and the *Idle
Thoughts* books, is compounded by leftover allegiance to leisure-class
values, by resentment of his exclusion from that class, and by a desire
to rejoin it, a complex Jerome's work shares with a lot of slacker com-

edy. The conspicuous leisure of these three overworked men who never work is a stab at elite men, even as it provides a fantasy of freedom from workaday concerns.

At the same time, Jerome and his friends see the rich as a different kind of people from themselves. They hate snobs. They hate the large steam-powered yachts and their over-entitled bullying of the smaller craft. They feel a kinship with the "old river hands" who also find any excuse to let someone else row. Some reviewers of the book objected to what they saw as Jerome's use of "clerk's" slang and "vulgarity," both of which were, in fact, part of the book's appeal to its middling, as opposed to elite, audience. Like the loungers of the eighteenth century, Jerome's idlers are men who are neither of "the classes or the masses," as Howells put it. These are the men whose relation to work and leisure, whenever they weren't keeping it at a humorous distance, made them feel sick, the men who the doctors of neurasthenia catered to, and the men who wrote about work and leisure, the men who produced images of their own conflicted relations to work for popular consumption.

The clerks, the commission agents, the actors, the legal workers, the professional writers—the people holding the kinds of jobs that Jerome held—were becoming the middle class as we would know it in the twentieth century, and Jerome, as a kind of pioneer guide to this class, performed a comic version of their dissatisfaction with the work lives looming ahead of them, lives that would increasingly be described in terms of Bartleby-like alienation and purposelessness. Through laughing at their desire for more freedom and ease, he suggested, they might get through their working days dreaming of trailing their fingers in a lazy river, all the while feeling superior to the truly leisured and the working poor alike.

∞

Along with loungers and loafers that were its version of the idler, the nineteenth century had its own versions of the eighteenth-century rambler, as well: the French called them *flâneurs* from the 1840s on, and starting a couple decades later, the English and American version became known as saunterers. In an accelerating modern and modernizing world, the *flâneur*, like the idler, was in favor of slowing down, idly strolling through or loitering in the city streets, taking in the scene. According to Walter Benjamin, the twentieth-century German critic, it was considered "elegant" for Parisian *flâneurs* of the mid-1800s "to take turtles for a walk." For Charles Baudelaire, whom Benjamin thought of as the ideal *flâneur*, this pace allowed both increased perception and a kind of invisibility: "For the perfect *flâneur*," Baudelaire wrote, "it is an immense joy to set up home in the heart of the multitude, amid the ebb and flow, . . . to see the world, to be at the center of the world, yet to remain hidden from the world." Walter Benjamin further romanticized this romantic notion and, like many champions of slacker ideals, claimed for *flâneurisme* both peace and excitement, both slowing down and quickening. The *flâneur* is marked by "irresolution," he writes, and yet,

> an intoxication comes over the man who walks long and aimlessly through the streets. With each step, the walk takes on greater momentum; even weaker grow the temptations of shops, of bistros, of smiling women, even more irresistible the magnetism of the next street corner, of a distant mass of foliage, of a street name.

This "intoxication," this invigorating, exhilarating sense of imbibing the fullness, the totality of experience, is, as it was for the eighteenth-century cosmopolitan loungers, a fringe benefit of being invisible to the world, a side effect of doing nothing. Baudelaire writes that the idler has the world as his oyster: "As *flâneur* he has omnipresence at his disposal, as a gambler omnipotence, and as a student, omniscience." The *flâneur* is the idler as God.

According to the earliest French commentators, intellectual curiosity was the key difference between the *flâneur* and common men. The normal bourgeois man will see an object in a shopwindow, Louis Huart wrote in 1841, quickly appraise it, and move on. The *flâneur*, on the other hand, will wonder about where the object came from, what kind of factory made it, what kind of raw materials went into it, where they came from; the object causes "a hundred types of reflections which the other spectator did not even suspect; it gave him the opportunity for a long voyage in the imaginary world, that brilliant world, the best and above all, the fairest of all possible worlds." That same year, Auguste de Lacroix went so far as to argue that the *flâneur* was like a scientist, one whose observations led him "to unknown con-

nections, to unperceived insights, to an entirely new world of ideas, reflections and sentiments, which suddenly gush forth . . . like a hidden
spring under the probe of the geologist." *Le Flâneur*, a magazine
launched in Paris in 1848, claimed to be written by *flâneurs* for
flâneurs. Feeling the pressure of the mass movements and workers'
movements of 1848, the magazine took a somewhat stronger view of
the *flâneur*'s observations:

> To go out strolling, these days, while puffing one's tobacco, while
> dreaming of evening pleasures, seems a century behind the times.
> We are not the sort to refuse all knowledge of the customs of another
> age; but, in our strolling, let us not forget our rights and our obliga-
> tions as citizens. The times are necessitous; they demand all our
> attention, all day long.

The magazine failed in its first year, perhaps because it didn't embrace adequately enough the requirement to do nothing, perhaps
because it did.

Like the *flâneur*, the Anglo-American saunterer required extraordinary powers of observation and a corresponding sense of superior appreciation. Thoreau wrote, "I have met with but one or two persons in
the course of my life who understood the art of Walking, that is, of taking walks,—who had a genius, so to speak, for sauntering." In fact,
many claimed that kind of genius for themselves: the saunterer appeared regularly from the 1860s on. Leigh Hunt published *A Saunter
Through the West End* in 1861. Charles Dudley Warner, Samuel
Clemens's coauthor, published a collection of his *Saunterings* in
1872. A book on "sauntering" through the resorts in Nebraska,
Dakota, Wyoming, Colorado, and Utah was published in 1879, and
there were many others in the years that followed, including *Saunterings in New England* (1883), "South-Coast Saunterings in England"
(1870), "A Saunter in Belgium" (1885), and "A Sauntering in Spain"
(1906). If the *flâneur* was a man of endless curiosity and attention, the
saunterer was something a little less. Sauntering, whether in Istanbul,
China, Maine, or Utah, was less strenuous even than traveling or tour-
ing, less committed, lazier. Sauntering in much of this talk is simply,
again like *flâneurisme*, a linguistic nod to a certain cultural style, as
when surfing morphs into Web surfing and channel surfing, a way to

give an old-fashioned ramble the feel of something more up-to-date. The saunterer was, in fact, an updated version of the Johnsonian rambler and the Wordsworthian walker, a man (again, almost always a man) who had the time and sensitivity to make something quasi-artistic out of the purely mundane, someone who could turn doing nothing into something worth doing.

Like the idler and the rambler, the saunterer also became an authorial pseudonym. *Town Topics*, a high-society magazine, for instance, named its weekly gossip column "Saunterings," signed by "The Saunterer." According to this Saunterer, there were two prime motives for existence: "money-making and festal enjoyments." His job was to report on the latter. The Saunterer visited clubs, restaurants, theaters, balls, and parties, congratulated the "best of the best" for their social accomplishments, and kept an eye on high society's miscreants, like "bicycle Godivas," with their improper clothing, and what he termed "tango pirates" who hung around dance halls. Unlike the best idlers and loungers, he didn't have a sense of humor. Society women, he said in a typically preachy tone, "should be clean, virtuous, stately women, free of all the taints and blemishes that are acquired from ordinary contact with the workaday world." He declaimed that New York high society was "the flower of civilization" and so "must be studied by anyone that has any interest in the human race." By 1920, even the Saunterer knew he was getting a bit stale, but he kept it up. "I know I shall be thought a horrible example of that ugly period dubbed Victorian, but I utter the criticism"—in this case, against the threat to civilization of society women taking part in amateur theatricals—"in all sincerity and with the kindliest of feelings, for everyone must realize that a line must be drawn somewhere, that some conventionalities must be observed in society or the whole fabric falls to tatters."

Much of the Saunterer's criticism and finger-wagging, then, had to do not with classic slacker issues, but with the leisure activities of the rich. Learning to ride a bicycle gave instructors unconscionable opportunity to put their arms around the waists of women and girls, and dancing instructors of course were Satan multiply incarnate. Riding in the park, theatergoing (with its displays of female flesh), restaurants with wine, sports instruction—everywhere the new emphasis on public and semiprivate leisure activities caused consternation to those, like the Saunterer, concerned (personally or professionally) with morality, particularly sexual morality, and specifically the sexual morality of women. Toward the end of this period Walter Lippmann would declare that "the whole revolution in sexual morals turns upon the fact that the external control of the chastity of women is becoming impossible," and these leisure activities have helped destroy that external control. For Lippmann the move from the front porch to the backseat, as he pithily put it, was a prime arena for the battle between modernity and tradition, and the wholesale abandonment of tradition was from his perspective unwise and unreasonable.

This level of analysis was beyond the Saunterer, and besides, the moral crusade against illicit sexual contact was not really his mission. The Saunterer was not, in fact, a leisured man who went to the parties and the parks like the class he reported on. He was a worker, a journalist on his beat. His pose as a moralist was primarily a device that allowed him the latitude to present titillating copy. The display of leisure that Veblen described as necessary to the status enhancement of the rich was this professional writer's material, without which he would have little to report. Though he might condemn the new pastimes of the newly christened leisure class, the last thing he would have desired was an end to them. Once again, in other words, we have in the Saunterer a professional slacker who turns out not to be one, a pretender, once again, to the workless life he describes. To pretend to be a slacker is simply one way to make a living as a writer.

Edgar Saltus, a self-proclaimed "idle dilettante," was at the center of high-class sauntering in Europe and America. Saltus claimed that he wrote his first book, *The Philosophy of Disenchantment*, "out of sheer laziness." He also proudly proclaimed it, in his opinion, "the gloomiest and worst book ever published," which may not be that much of an exaggeration. Although he claimed as his philosophic credo the phrase "I am, therefore I suffer," Saltus nonetheless thought that the novelist's job, in a neurasthenic world, was not just to entertain, but "to cure." One of Saltus's novels, *The Pace that Kills* (1889) has in its very title a warning against overwork and striving, and Saltus was clearly a wandering Bohemian. Like the eighteenth-century loungers, he studied law but never practiced it, electing instead to travel and write in a style of "leisurely skepticism and nonchalant preciosity." Harry Levin, a half century later, called Saltus's writing "a comic supplement to Veblen's *Theory of the Leisure Class*," in part be-

cause Saltus skewers the spa-going idlers of that class, the always traveling, never broadened elite, in novel after novel.

Saltus was often considered an American follower of Oscar Wilde,
but it is more correct to say that he was a fellow traveler. Saltus wrote,
in *Oscar Wilde: An Idler's Impression* (1917), a very unenthusiastic ap-
praisal of Wilde, saying that Wilde "was a third-rate poet who occasionally rose to the second class but not once to the first. Prose is more
difficult than verse and in it he is rather sloppy. In spite of which, or
perhaps precisely on that account, he called himself lord of language.
Well, why not, if he wanted to?" He recounts his meeting with Wilde
during Wilde's famous tour of the United States in 1882: "It was at
Delmonico's, shortly after he told our local Customs that he had nothing to declare but his genius, that I first met him. He was dressed like
a mountebank." He had long hair, knee breeches, and "all the mountebank trappings." When they met again in London shortly thereafter,
according to Saltus,

> in appearance and mode of life [Wilde] had become entirely con-
> ventional . . . He was married, he was a father, and in his house in
> Tite Street he seemed a bit bourgeois. Of that he may have been
> conscious. I remember one of his children running and calling at
> him, "My good Papa!" and I remember Wilde patting the boy and
> saying: "Don't call me that, it sounds so respectable."

But Saltus's final impression on that trip, as they sat in a restaurant
and Wilde recited some of his work, was even less flattering: "Before
me was a fat pauper, florid and overdressed, who, in the voice of an
immortal, was reading the fantasies of the damned."

The two men, so firmly linked in literary history as exemplars of the
idle love of beauty, as exalters of style over substance, did not, at least
from Saltus's perspective, agree on much except that Wilde was a brilliant conversationalist. Of the two, Wilde certainly more effectively
embraced the idle life. According to a friend, he never wanted "to do
anything" and was "at his best when he is lying on the sofa thinking."
He detested all sports, he said, except dominoes. In 1890 Wilde published a dramatic essay titled "The True Function and Value of Criticism: With Some Remarks on the Importance of Doing Nothing," in
which he elevated idleness to the level of a first principle. Rendered in

Socratic dialogue, the piece uses Ernest as an interlocutor and Gilbert
as the sage:

GILBERT

*Let me say to you now that to do nothing at all is the most difficult
thing in the world, the most difficult and the most intellectual.* To
Plato, with his passion for wisdom, this was the noblest form of energy. To Aristotle, with his passion for knowledge, this was the noblest form of energy also. It was to this that the passion for holiness
led the saint and the mystic of medieval days.

ERNEST

We exist, then, to do nothing?

GILBERT

It is to do nothing that the elect exist. Action is limited and relative.
Unlimited and absolute is the vision of him who sits at ease and
watches, who walks in loneliness and dreams.

As he was writing this and sketching the "languid" and "languorous"
Henry Wotton in *The Picture of Dorian Gray* (1891), he was, in fact,
quite busy. In 1891 he published four books and a long political essay
("The Soul of Man Under Socialism," in which he imagines a society
devoid of the compulsion to work) and wrote *Lady Windemere's Fan*
and the major part of *Salomé*. At this point in his life, his biographer
Richard Ellman suggests, "languor was the mask of industry." Still, his
periods of industry were few and short. His complete works come to
only twelve hundred pages, or roughly two years in the work life of
Henry James or William Dean Howells. "To win back my youth, there
is nothing I wouldn't do," he has one of his characters explain, "except
take exercise, get up early, or be a useful member of the community."

Although Wilde is in part in dead earnest in championing indolence, he is also obviously aware of the fun to be had in turning cultural values on their head, in much the same way that the
eighteenth-century loungers were. As in the case of his green otter-fur
overcoat and velvet knee breeches, he appreciated the effect and rev-
eled in defying expectations. The humor of declaring one's allegiance
to doing nothing was, whatever other point was being made, worth the

effort, as it were. He claimed that he detested work, that he only wrote and took on speaking engagements because this gave him the freedom to do nothing. His famous American lecture tour was financed in part as an advertisement for the New York production of Gilbert and Sullivan's *Patience*, a satire on aestheticism and aesthetes, and he seemed to understand that the lectures were far less important than his dandified presence itself. He took the lectures so lightly, in fact, that on the eve of his departure he hadn't begun writing them. When his ship docked in New York, he still hadn't gotten very far. The talk he finally produced was largely borrowed from the ideas of Walter Pater and concluded in as bald a statement of his assigned theme, aestheticism, as possible: "We spend our days looking for the secret of life. The secret of life is art." After he saw that his first lecture was being printed in the papers verbatim before he arrived in new towns, he realized he couldn't pretend to be speaking off the cuff, and he wrote a couple more, equally desultory.

If the writing of the lectures was not much work, the travel and performance involved was: he lectured 140 times while crisscrossing the country from New York to San Francisco, back to New York, up to Montreal and Quebec, west to Ontario, back to Boston and New York, down to Texas, and back through the South into New England once more and the Maritime Provinces. The writing and delivering of the lectures, in other words, remained well below the utopian ideal of three hours' work a day, but the travel and socializing involved—dinners, teas, and receptions with important citizens and literary figures in each city—meant a fairly hectic schedule. Wilde was remarkably open to reading other people's unpublished work and remarkably generous in his comments, and so he often had the poetry of the local hostesses to deal with as well. In *An Ideal Husband* (1895), a play written a decade later, he claims largely but not entirely facetiously that socializing is a lot of work: Lord Caversham calls his son a "good-for-nothing" idler, and Mabel Chiltern defends him: "How can you say such a thing? Why, he rides in the Row at ten o'clock in the morning, goes to the Opera three times a week, changes his clothes at least five times a day, and dines out every night of the season. You don't call that leading an idle life, do you?"

But for all his aristocratic wit and pretension, Wilde also famously felt at home with the miners he visited deep in a shaft in Leadville,

Colorado, where he had a ceremonial dinner with the men. The meal, he reported, was simple: "The first course was whiskey, the second whiskey, the third whiskey, all the courses were whiskey, but still they called it supper." He made many jokes about the miners, claiming that in the saloon a sign hung over the piano saying PLEASE DON'T SHOOT THE PIANIST; HE IS DOING HIS BEST. Wilde claimed he "was struck with this recognition of the fact that bad art merits the penalty of death, and I felt that in this remote city, where the aesthetic application of the revolver was clearly established in the case of music, my apostolic task would be much simplified, as indeed it was." But he was also struck by the difficulty of the miners' lives. He later wrote, in "The Soul of Man Under Socialism" (1891), that all manual labor— and at one point he singles out coal mining—should be done by machines. He agreed with the Greeks that society needed slaves in order to have art and culture, but he thought that modern society was fast coming to the point where those slaves could be mechanical rather than human:

> A great deal of nonsense is being written and talked nowadays about the dignity of manual labor. There is nothing necessarily dignified about manual labor at all, and most of it is absolutely degrading. It is mentally and morally injurious to man to do anything in which he does not find pleasure, and many forms of labor are quite pleasureless activities, and should be regarded as such. To sweep a slushy crossing for eight hours on a day when the east wind is blowing is a disgusting occupation. To sweep it with mental, moral, or physical dignity seems to me to be impossible. To sweep it with joy would be appalling. Man is made for something better than disturbing dirt. All work of that kind should be done by a machine.

Once machines do the work, we will see that "enjoying cultivated leisure," not work, is "the aim of man."

Most of the time, Wilde was much more flippant about work and leisure, as in the plays. When asked in Omaha about his plans for the future, he laughingly lit a cigarette, relaxed in his chair, and said, "Well, I'm a very ambitious young man. I want to do everything in the world. I cannot conceive of anything I don't want to do." That announcement, while seemingly the opposite of the desire to do nothing, is, in fact, of a piece: the announced desire to do nothing and the announced desire to do everything are both comic takes on the requirement that one do one's bourgeois bit, that one follow a calling, that one "do his part." Wilde's first enactment of this desire to do everything was to follow his nine-month lecture tour with a two-and-a-half-month vacation in New York and then several months of further vacation on the Continent. Saltus represents him as working intermittently hard early in life ("St. George, I believe, fought a dragon with a spear . . . But Wilde fought poverty, which is perhaps more brutal, with a pen. The fight, if indolent, was protracted"), but Saltus isn't the best source. He is writing after the scandals that sent Wilde to prison, and he makes a point of disapproving. Wilde was clearly capable of writing about work and leisure seriously, and clearly capable of writing about them facetiously. He was, after all, a man who wanted to do everything and who wanted to do nothing.

∞

Meanwhile, the working class had sprouted its own version of the saunterer—the tramp. Although it may seem somewhat obscene to conflate the belletristic idlings of Wilde and Saltus with down-and-out, often homeless wanderers, the tramp became, in this same period, another symbol of resistance to the workaday status quo. Whatever the reality of the tramp's position, once he became a fixture in American culture, he provided the same kind of analysis and criticism as the loafers and loungers had before. Real tramps, like real slackers, were transformed by journalists, novelists, illustrators, and filmmakers into cultural types, figures of fear and fun.

Vagrancy was criminalized very early in the American colonies, but the Industrial Revolution created larger and larger groups of economic migrants, and they have been called by a series of names: gypsies, tramps, hobos, bums, go-abouts, the homeless, and, by one hobo turned sociologist, the "nomad proletariat." Nels Anderson, born in a Chicago tenement in 1889, left home as a teen and rode the freight trains from town to town, doing occasional panhandling and occasional work, as a dirt mover, horse driver, or farmhand. He begged at back doors for food and was thrown off trains by rail-yard dicks. Eventually, though, he started going to school, graduated from Brigham Young University, and made his way back to Chicago (on a freight train) and into the sociology department at the University of Chicago. His book *The Hobo* (1923) was the first in Chicago's Sociological Series, a series of monographs that would put the Chicago School of Sociology (with such professors as Albion Small, Robert Park, Ernest Burgess, and Ellsworth Faris) on the international intellectual map. *The Hobo* was the first serious sociological study of homelessness, the first social-scientific study of out-of-work men.

Anderson was aided in his study by Ben Reitman, M.D., who also began life as an itinerant laborer and later became a physician and social reformer. Reitman, who is perhaps most famous for having been Emma Goldman's consort, claimed that there were three main categories of wandering men: tramps, hobos, and bums:

> A tramp is a man who doesn't work, who apparently doesn't want to work, who lives without working and who is constantly traveling. A hobo is a non-skilled, non-employed laborer without money, looking for work. A bum is a man who hangs around a low class saloon and begs or earns a few pennies a day in order to obtain drink. He is usually an inebriate.

Elsewhere, Reitman supplied a more pithy description of these types of the homeless: "The hobo works and wanders, the tramp dreams and wanders, and the bum drinks and wanders." Anderson preferred to describe the hobo as a migratory casual worker, the tramp as a migratory nonworker, and the bum as a nonmigratory nonworker. To these he added the nonmigratory casual worker and the seasonal worker.

Anderson interviewed thousands of tramps and hobos and concluded that there were six reasons men took to the road: unemployment, "industrial inadequacy," pathology, life crises, racial discrimination, and wanderlust. Unemployment is the most obvious, and can be due to systematic or idiosyncratic reasons, an economic depression, or a run-in with a supervisor. Industrial inadequacy might be the result of mental or physical handicaps, some of which might in turn be caused by injuries sustained on the job. The two main pathologies that resulted in migrancy, Anderson concluded, were congenital problems like "feeble mindedness" and what Anderson called "egocentricity, which leads to the conflict of the person with constituted authority in industry, society, and government." Racial or ethnic discrimination can force someone to look for work elsewhere, of course, and finally, wanderlust: the desire for new experiences, for novel excitements, the desire to see the world. The loafers, loungers, idlers, ramblers, and saunterers we have met so far, when they haven't simply been adopting a writerly pose, were people Anderson would say chose the role from some version of egocentricity or wanderlust. They have not been, as in the case of most of the tramps, hobos, and bums Anderson interviewed, forced into the role by chronic unemployment or underemployment. But like the loafers and loungers, tramps, hobos, and bums quickly became images in the popular imagination of freer, more authentic alternatives to the workaday world.

The larger the industrial economy grew, the more prevalent tramps and hobos became. The Panic of 1873 threw some three million people out of work and sent many of them on the road looking for new opportunities. At the same time, the rail system in the country had become so extensive (the golden spike linking the eastern and western systems was driven in 1869) that men could hop freights and move anywhere in the country quickly and for no money. As a result, people in communities around the country started to perceive what was most often called the "tramp problem." "There is no problem in social science that is just now more pressing than what to do with the great and increasing army of mendicants," *The New York Times* declared in 1875, "who from their mode of life have gained the name of 'tramp.' " Walt Whitman in 1879 found in the tramp problem an immense national failure:

> If the United States, like the countries of the Old World, are also to grow vast crops of poor, desperate, dissatisfied, nomadic, miserably-waged populations, such as we see looming upon us of late years— steadily, even if slowly, eating into them like a cancer of lungs or stomach—then our republican experiment, notwithstanding all its surface-successes, is at heart an unhealthy failure.

Whitman blamed capital for not living up to its side of the social contract, but more often editorials and articles, like William H. Brewer's "What Shall We Do with the Tramps?" in *The New Englander* in 1878, lambasted the laziness and shiftlessness of tramps and warned against the threat they posed to law, order, and community morals. Many writers in the 1870s blamed the Civil War and the bad habits developed by soldiers. "The reckless free life of the army," wrote Lee O. Harris in *The Man Who Tramps: A Story of To-day* (1878), "had given them a taste for wandering and a distaste for every species of labor . . . Once having tasted the fountain of indolence" they "lost all wish to labor." Francis Wayland, speaking at the 1877 meetings of the American Social Science Association, had a stronger argument: "Our great standing army of professional tramps," he claimed, is "at war with society and all social institutions."

Even a social reformer like Henry George found the tramp army frightening. In *Social Problems* (1883), he claims that "this terrible phenomenon, the tramp" was "more menacing to the Republic than . . . hostile armies or fleets bent on destruction." And then, in a final flourish, he declares that "country roadsides are nursing the barbarians who may be to the new what Hun and Vandal were to the old." Indeed, the labor journals of the day, although they were interested in arguing, like Whitman, that the real villain was not the indolent tramp, but the heartless capitalist, mouthed some of the same fears. The *Journal of United Labor* and the *National Labor Tribune* made it clear that they thought it unfair to assume that, as the *Tribune* put it, "society is a criminal and the tramps are its victims." But they also made a distinction between two kinds of tramps: "the honest laborer in misfortune, and the idle, improvident, vicious vagrant." The *Iron Molders' Journal* distinguished between the "hard-fisted mechanic or laborer to whom work would be a blessing" and "bummers." The *Workingman's Advocate* saw a difference between tramps who were "honest and industrious men" and "scamps who are prowling about the country, refusing to work, but neglecting no opportunity to steal and commit other crimes."

Whatever the explanations offered or distinctions made, the perceived threat represented by tramps resulted in legislation. Illinois passed one of the first "Tramp Laws" in 1874, and New Jersey did so in 1876, in part because of the increased migrancy caused by the 1873 Panic. In 1879 New York and Delaware passed their laws in response to the railroad strike of 1877, and by 1886 nineteen states had rewritten their tramp laws at least once. New York's was revised again after the depression of 1884. This later version was responsible for the arrest of 2,110 tramps in 1891, and 4,716 during the depression year of 1894; in that year 40 percent of all arrests in New York were for tramping or vagrancy. As this all suggests, the laws were, from the start, unconscionably broad. The Illinois law outlawed "idle and dissolute persons who went about and begged, runaways, pilferers, drunkards, night-walkers, lewd people, wanton and lascivious persons, railers and brawlers, persons without a calling or profession, visitors of tippling houses and houses of ill-fame, and wanderers." This kind of legislation often gave police enormous discretionary latitude.

One side effect of criminalizing unemployment (as well as backdoor criminalizing of labor organizing, tramp laws often being used to arrest union delegates) is that it made people more hesitant to walk off their jobs in protest. The Populist Kansas governor L. D. Lewelling drew one set of obvious conclusions. Although the Kansas legislature had strengthened its tramp laws in 1889, in 1893 the governor sent a circular to all the police chiefs in Kansas suggesting they be lenient in enforcing it:

> The right to go freely from place to place in search of employment, or even in obedience of a mere whim, is part of that personal liberty guaranteed by the Constitution of the United States to every human being on American soil. If voluntary idleness is not forbidden; if a Diogenes prefer poverty; if a Columbus choose hunger and the discovery of a new race, rather than seek personal comfort by engaging in "some legitimate business," I am aware of no power in the legislature or in the city councils to deny him the right to seek happiness in his own way, so long as he harms no other, rich or poor; but let simple poverty cease to be a crime.

Editorialists in Kansas and across the country reacted to Lewelling's circular by claiming that the governor was "consorting with anarchists and Communists" and making Kansas a haven for tramps everywhere.

Similar arguments were taking place in Britain during this period. An 1834 Poor Law Amendment Act made workhouse space available for anyone who needed it, but attempted to end any assistance to beggars outside the workhouse. In the 1870s a Crusade Against Outrelief tried to enforce these provisions in England and Wales. Norman Pearson, who wrote on ethical, religious, and social issues, took the congenital view:

> It is to be feared that the confirmed loafer and habitual vagrant are seldom capable of being reformed. It is a mistake to suppose that the typical pauper is merely an ordinary person who has fallen into distress through adverse circumstances. As a rule he is not an ordinary person, but one who is constitutionally a pauper, a pauper in his blood and bones. He is made of inferior material, and therefore cannot be improved up to the level of the ordinary person.

This kind of thinking, however foreign from our own sense of human possibility, had the counterintuitive effect of helping push through a series of British reforms in the first decade of the twentieth century. Since the "confirmed loafer" is congenitally doomed and cannot improve himself, something must be done to help him, and thus laws providing free meals and medical attention for poor children, weekly pensions for persons over seventy, and national medical and unemployment insurance were passed between 1904 and 1911.

By the 1910s, Charlie Chaplin's character, the Little Tramp, became the dominant image of tramping. Chaplin's character was his own version of what was already something of a stock character in vaudeville (such as W. C. Fields's tramp juggler) and in newspaper and magazine cartoons. *Happy Hooligan*, a cartoon strip about an Irish tramp, ran from 1900 to 1932, and before Happy, Tom Browne's strip *Weary Willie and Tired Tim* (starting in 1896) and numerous individual cartoons in *Puck* and *Life* had made the tramp a figure sometimes of comic derision and sometimes subversion, sometimes both—Happy is constantly doing good deeds that nobody believes he did; he is judged by his rags instead of his deeds. Happy has two brothers, also tramps: Gloomy Gus (yes, that's where it comes from), who doesn't have Happy's bright outlook on life; and Lord Montmorency, who has delusions of nobility. In one strip, the three brothers visit the House of Lords in London. A woman drops her muff from the visitors' balcony and it lodges on a light fixture. Happy leans over to get it, held by the ankles by his brothers. Guards think this is disrespectful, and they punch the brothers, who drop Happy onto the head of the speaker on the floor. The three are hauled off to the Tower of London. The brothers are regularly abused by rich children, policemen, and society people, and still the strips are rarely simple morality tales about class prejudice. Happy, Gus, and Montmorency are woefully dull-witted and are hard-pressed to ever think more than a frame ahead.

Chaplin, in *My Autobiography*, said that from the beginning he saw his own character as "many-sided, a tramp, a gentleman, a poet, a dreamer, a lonely fellow, always hopeful of romance and adventure." He could pass, comically, for a polo player, a duke, or a preacher, but he was also "not above picking up cigarette butts or robbing a baby of its candy." The Little Tramp also often provided fairly direct criticism of the class system. In *The Idle Class* (1921), for instance, Chaplin plays two roles, one as the Little Tramp and the other as a wealthy alcoholic, as if embodying what the *Journal of the Knights of Labor* argued about millionaires and tramps: they were, the *Journal* editorialized in 1893, "dregs and scum from the same social fermentation." The two men look so much alike (Chaplin playing both roles of course) that even the wealthy man's wife can't tell the difference. The wife, in fact, prefers the tramp—he is sweet, he isn't drunk or jaded— and the audience is supposed to prefer the tramp as well. The fairly obvious moral of the story is that nothing separates the two men but the luck of their birth. They are equally idle, but the Little Tramp is not, as the tramp laws would have one think, the inebriate. The rich man is. Chaplin's tramp, like Governor Lewelling's, is a dreamer and an honest seeker of happiness, not an anarchist threat to the social order. Chaplin's vagabond slacker is an image, in fact, of a better way to live. He skewers bourgeois pretension, and part of the fun is always to see how the Tramp manages to live the good life with no means. The romantic freedom that the Little Tramp represents may be no closer to any person's actual reality than is the threat of criminality run rampant, but it serves as a reminder that the agreed-upon goods and values of society always threaten to ensnare and foil happiness as much as they enable its pursuit.

∞

Several American writers spent time as actual tramps, and they helped pave the way for Chaplin's character. Jacob Riis, who would become

America's first famous photojournalist, began his life in America "on the tramp." Born in Denmark as the fourth of fifteen children, he worked as a carpenter until the age of twenty-one and then came to America through Ellis Island. He spent several years on the road looking for work. His autobiographical writings show an alternating pride and disgust over his life in these years, as he manages to get by, to get enough work, to better himself, to see the country, and to learn a series of trades. In 1873 he began to get work as a journalist and in the 1880s as a photographer, and in 1890 he published *How the Other Half Lives*, a photo-essay on the underprivileged of New York. Although it occasionally indulged in fearmongering, melodramatically representing verminous immigrants and lowlifes, *How the Other Half Lives* proffered a classic muckraking, reformist argument for better living conditions for the poor, one that had some policy ramifications, helping to institute regulations that improved tenement housing, for instance.

Riis was glad to tell the story of his tramping years as a stage in his rags-to-riches autobiography, but other writing tramps kept their tramp identity as their authorial persona and sold themselves as tramps. Like Riis, Josiah Flynt started his adult life as a tramp. His success as a journalist came quickly. After only eight months on the road, Flynt returned to New York and began publishing his stories of the tramp life in the country's top magazines. Collected as *Tramping with Tramps* in 1899, these essays roundly rejected the view of tramps as parasitic criminals. "On the contrary," he wrote, "they are above their environment, and are often gifted with talents which would enable them to do well in any class, could they be only brought to realize its responsibilities and to take advantage of its opportunities." Flynt thus continued in the vein of Riis to both scold and justify the "other half," but Riis by the time he was writing about the poor presented himself as bourgeois; Flynt liked to be thought of as an exceptional person among the exceptional people who were tramps. Like Riis, Flynt can be seen as an important proto-sociologist, describing the mores and folkways of these groups. In his 1897 survey, *Sexual Inversion*, for instance, Havelock Ellis included as an appendix an essay by Flynt on "situational homosexuality" among tramps. At the turn of the century, Flynt was the reigning expert on the tramp.

He was soon replaced, however, by Jack London. London dedicated his tramp memoir, *The Road*, to Flynt, declaring that Flynt was "The Real Thing, Blowed in the Glass." London hopped his first freight at sixteen, briefly joined the western wing of Coxey's Army, was jailed as a tramp in Buffalo at eighteen, and served thirty days in the Erie County Penitentiary. From the start, London considered himself above rather than below his environment, detesting the "stifling, shut-in air" and "petty routine" of the average job, and thus it is no accident that by the 1920s he was widely reported to be the most popular author among tramps and hobos. In a characteristic moment in *Martin Eden* (1909), a character extols the beauty of the road: "I never knew what it was to live till I hit hoboin'," he tells the protagonist. "I'm thirty pounds heavier, an' feel tiptop all the time. Why I was worked to skin an' bone in them old days! Hoboin' sure agrees with me." London managed to avoid stifling jobs not by going on the tramp, but by writing books that sold well, books that were successful in part because of London's romanticizing of what he called "the call of the road." Still, he, more than Flynt or Riis, had an economic understanding of the tramp's life, as expressed in one of his better-known speeches:

> What would happen tomorrow if one hundred thousand tramps should become suddenly inspired with an overmastering desire for work? It is a fair question. "Go to work" is preached to the tramp every day of his life. The judge on the bench, the pedestrian in the street, the housewife at the kitchen door, all unite in advising him to go to work. So what would happen tomorrow if one hundred thousand tramps acted upon this advice and strenuously and indomitably sought work? Why, by the end of the week one hundred thousand workers, their places taken by the tramps, would receive their time and be "hitting the road" for a job.

He understands the tramp as a member of the "surplus labor army" that capitalists need, the scapegoat for the economy's sins. "The 'road' is one of the safety-valves through which the waste of the social organism is given off," he said in a speech in 1905. "And BEING GIVEN OFF constitutes the negative function of the tramp."

This double attitude—the tramp as industrial refuse, the tramp as romantic hero—was common throughout the tramp literature of the turn of the century, just as it had been through the history of slacker figures. William Aspinwall, for instance, whose letters to reporter John McCook in the late 1890s were published in the *Independent* in 1901, referred to himself as a "Gentleman of the Road" and took great pride in his independence. While he complained of the tramp laws and the disrespect and privations he suffered, he nonetheless held on to a Whitmanesque view of his freedom: "I think if some of you Proffessors [*sic*], students, etc., would live more of a nomadic life and feel the enjoyment of the fresh air more and take more good wholesome exercise and live a more rough and tumble life," he wrote, "you would enjoy health and live longer." He also has a revolutionary bent, suggesting that "a half million Nomadic helthy [*sic*] tough Ho-Bos in America," if they were "organized equipped [*sic*] and disciplined . . . would make the grandest army that ever shouldered a gun and would be invincible." Aspinwall argues that his condition and that of the other tramps is something that society should remedy: "The general government should enact some laws to furnish all idle men work of some kind." Without such intervention, he writes, firmly hitting the fear button, "America will go back to the uncivilized state worse than the savage Indians before Columbus discovered this country."

What confounded some sociologists in the early twentieth century was the fact that many of the tramps and hobos they interviewed did not want to leave the life of the itinerant laborer for something more stable. Seventy percent of one researcher's sample had "no desire to escape from the life of the 'floater.'" Another remarked, "It seems that when a laborer has earned a sum which road tradition has fixed as affluence, he quits." For many of these researchers, the problem of the tramp was a problem of personal "maladjustment." For others, like Jack London or Nels Anderson, "Hobohemia" is primarily an economic fact, a series of temporary migrations that "bring the job-seeking man and the man-seeking job together," or that fail to do so.

But the general audience for stories by Flynt, Aspinwall, and London were interested in neither economics nor psychopathology. The fondness Americans have always had for characters like Chaplin's Little Tramp—or Martin Eden's friend, who puts on weight while on the bum—their attraction to the romance of the open road, depends on attention to the tramp's freedom, not the tramp's need. The tramp, when he is more a classic slacker than a tragic figure, is someone who has neither the desire to work nor the obvious needs that keep actual workers working and real tramps tramping. And thus Aspinwall, like Riis and Flynt, alternates between two views of tramping, between boasting and flagellating himself. Despite Aspinwall's paean to the rough-and-tumble life, he is, finally, not a slacker but a self-hating tramp, and he thinks that tramping should be eliminated through government programs; for this he is willing to incite fear. The audience for the tramp was based in part on readers' continued appetite for slackers, which continued to be large, and in part on their appetite for fear, which is always enormous.

∞

Theodore Dreiser almost became a tramp. He was eleven years old and already working when Oscar Wilde made his American tour, and was just beginning his writing career as Wilde's was in its final decline. In some ways there is no greater contrast in the history of literature—the elevation of style in Wilde is matched by a seeming ignorance of style in Dreiser, and wit is certainly the last attribute with which Dreiser would be credited. If Saltus felt sorry for Wilde's constrained beginnings, imagine his take on Dreiser's, whose father was an immigrant textile worker turned factory owner turned (after a ruinous mill fire) sporadically employed religious fanatic and factory hand. Dreiser and his nine siblings were "reared in superstition, fanaticism, ignorance, poverty, and humiliation," according to his biographer W. A. Swanberg, and Dreiser himself said he never knew "a man more obsessed" than his father "by a religious belief." Although the elder Dreiser had been an ambitious young man, after he lost all his money and more in the mill fire, he never again worked steadily toward worldly goals. Still, when Theodore's older brother Rome took to drinking whiskey and hanging out in front of the Terre Haute House, their town's grandest establishment, pretending to have just eaten there, his father was furious. "Loafers!" he would yell in a heavy German accent. "Idle, good-for-nothings!"

Dreiser himself had an overweening desire for worldly success. He was always willing to work, though not always capable of the tasks he took on. At the age of fifteen he got a job weeding onions, and an hour into it, after he complained about his muscles aching and the repulsiveness of the work, the farmer sent him packing with fifty cents' severance pay. Through his teens he was fired often, not for lack of effort so much as lack of ability, or a kind of distracted misapplication. Still, he was so desirous of success that he often lied about his current position. When, just before he was sixteen, he landed a job as a dishwasher at a restaurant in Chicago, for instance, he told his sisters he was a clerk in a haberdasher's shop. His self-aggrandizements in turn fueled his own continuing dissatisfaction. He was fired from a hardware store for announcing that the work was below him, and he was hired as an assistant in an artist's studio, perhaps because the artist was making time with Dreiser's sister Theresa. The artist was a fan of Walt Whitman's (this was 1887), and Dreiser was so excited to talk to him about literature at all hours that the artist couldn't stand it, fired him, and hired his brother instead. Dreiser then took a job at a rail yard, but he found the work too nerve-racking and quit. About to be fired from his next hardware job, he begged to be kept on and was, briefly.

Always a bit of a befuddled dreamer, he often worked hard but ineffectually, and he was saved from what seemed to be his fate by a former teacher, who paid for a year at the University of Illinois. After that he worked as a real estate salesman and as a bill collector. While collecting bills, he lied to a girl that he was a newspaper reporter and, thus goaded into the possibility, actually applied for a position on the *Chicago Daily Globe*. He was hired, and so, at the age of twenty-one, he somewhat accidentally started on his road as a writer.

Throughout his twenties Dreiser worked assiduously at his own success as a journalist, and he concentrated, whenever he could, on producing profiles of very successful men. "Those who interested me most," Dreiser wrote in his autobiography, "were bankers, millionaires, artists, executives, leaders, the real rulers of the world." He profiled the new millionaires like Philip D. Armour the meat-packer, Marshall Field the department-store king, Robert Lincoln, president of the Pullman Company, and Alexander Revell the furniture magnate. Some of these pieces were published in *Success Magazine*, which, as the title suggests, revered financial achievement and was dedicated, as the masthead announced, to "Education, Enterprise, Enthusiasm, Energy, Economy, Self-respect, Self-reliance, Self-help, Self-culture, Self-control, Work, Sagacity, Honesty, Truth, and Courage." Dreiser became, in fact, very successful at representing success. At the age of twenty-one he had been ecstatic to land a job earning fourteen dollars a week (although he did embezzle some funds from that job and was fired); only eight years later he had surpassed his wildest ambitions and was publishing up to fifty articles a year, for which the best outlets paid as much as two hundred dollars a piece. In 1900 he achieved what he considered the pinnacle, with the publication of his first novel, *Sister Carrie*.

On his way to that success, though, he lost job after job and doubted himself regularly, experiencing bouts of neurasthenia (as did, so it happens, Orison Swett Marden, the editor of *Success*). In 1903, after some career setbacks, he had a particularly severe relapse and sought medical treatment. He was depressed, insomniac, and constipated. He had indigestion, headaches, and rashes. He separated from his wife and found he simply could not write:

> I should say here that mine was a serious case of neurasthenia—or of nervous prostration. It had begun with the conclusion of a novel I had written three years before and which exhausted me greatly. It was enhanced by various physical indiscretions which it will serve no purpose to enumerate here and the general stress and worry incident to earning a living, as well as moving into a neighborhood entirely unsuited to my nature . . . the wretchedness of the poverty and the sight of the gloomy Blackwell's Island on which were housed the sick, the criminal and the insane of the city had a most depressing effect on me.

As if the ghost of Bartleby hovered over his comfortable life, Dreiser couldn't stop thinking about prison just when he should have been feeling successful. He had come close to his goal of becoming one of the "bankers, millionaires, [and] artists" who ran the world. His bid for artistic status, and thus membership in the leisure class, had been *Sister Carrie*, but it was rejected as salacious, copies pulled from bookstore shelves in fear of obscenity charges before it had a chance of success. In his neurasthenic state, he couldn't keep his journalistic career going, and his hundredfold increase in income of the past decade had been reversed, with no artistic success to make up for it. Preferring not to work at anything but art, sinking back into the poverty he came from, he found himself unable to climb back up. He was a nervous wreck. The doctors agreed that he was neurasthenic, his system debilitated by too much brainwork.

By the 1910s, the idea that the pace of American life was destructive for the individual and the society had been adopted by other disciplines as well. Charles Horton Cooley, one of the founders of American sociology, argued that nothing good could come of the kind of frenetic race toward success that Dreiser and others like him ran, a race that made it impossible for them to produce valuable work:

> Haste and the superficiality and strain which attend upon it are widely and insidiously destructive of good work in our day. No other condition of mind or of society—not ignorance, poverty, oppression or hate—kills art as haste does. Almost any phase of life may be ennobled if there is only calm enough in which the brooding mind may do its perfect work upon it; but out of hurry nothing noble ever did or can emerge . . . But ours is, on the whole, a time of stress, of the habit of incomplete work; its products are unlovely and unrestful and such as the future will have no joy in.

Here an overstrenuous work ethic destroys not just the worker but the work as well. Dreiser himself felt that his journalism was of no lasting value, so he had turned to literature. When that failed, he was unsure where to turn for meaning in his life.

His brother sent him to a then-famous spa run by William Muldoon, a champion wrestler, for a six-week exercise cure. Muldoon was one of several physical fitness gurus who would become rich and famous during the last decades of the nineteenth century, preaching a gospel of strength and vitality through exercise. On the high-culture end of this phenomenon was Dudley Allen Sargent, a gymnast who traveled with a circus but grew tired of "the company of loafers" in 1869 and took a job at Bowdoin College as director of gymnastics. He eventually ended up at Harvard, where he instituted the physical education system that would hold sway for the next hundred years. Many, such as Bernarr Macfadden, the "father of physical culture," Eugen Sandow, a vaudeville strongman, and physical culture writers like Thomas Inch and Martin Burns argued that exercise not only made one stronger but reversed the deleterious effects of modern living that

Cooley and the doctors described. Muldoon's spa catered to the elite, its $35-a-week price beyond the means of most, including Dreiser. His successful songwriter brother paid the bill.

But although the exercise cure helped a little, it didn't really work, and Dreiser tried what was, at the time, an unusual variant: the work cure. He made himself take a job piling lumber for the railroad, returning to the manual labor he hadn't done since he was a boy. He would later write of his time on the railroad as hourly, weekly, yearly knowing no surcease, "its grim insistence unrequited by anything save the meager wages wherewith it is paid." In fact, Dreiser only worked on the railroad for all of three weeks, but that was enough. The combination of medical attention and tough, unremunerative manual labor ($1.75 for a ten-hour day) cured him, and he began writing again in December. Like many neurasthenics, he used time as a spa patient and then as a working patient as a moratorium that allowed him to reinvent himself. Instead of a failed novelist he was once again a man who had pulled himself up out of the working class to become a writer. He worked his way back into the graces of editors and after a while was once again a very successful journalist. He also, a bit later, with the reissue of *Sister Carrie* in 1907, became recognized as an important novelist. By the mid-1920s he made more than $100,000 a year from his literary writing, and he was short-listed for the Nobel Prize in 1930. From then until his death he never stopped working. He continued scrambling after money, setting up Hollywood adaptations of his work, hiring himself out as a pitchman, giving lectures, selling pieces and books. His only time spent as a slacker was that done under duress and under the cover of a recognized medical syndrome. And he was cured of that illness by work. In this, in 1903, he was a little ahead of his time.

VI

SPORTS, FLAPPERS, BABBITTS, AND BUMS

In which the slacker becomes the villain of World War I and the hero of modernist literature—more fathers and sons—work goes out of fashion for the poor and becomes fashionable for the rich—booms and busts—Americans are told they need to "Sweat or Die!"—The Great Gatsby shows how to reconcile Benjamin Franklin and Samuel Johnson in modern times—and Al Jolson sings "Hallelujah, I'm a Bum!"

In 1918, a year after the United States had entered the Great War in Europe, an article written for the *Scientific Monthly* by a research scientist outlined the various problems caused, during wartime, by common parasites. The biologist discusses the problems caused by lice, mites, and worms of various kinds, explaining how soldiers can be irritated, diseased, or even hospitalized because of them. They can sideline the cavalry's horses and render the quartermaster's livestock inedible. The scientist then ends with this:

> No discussion of wartime parasites would be complete without mention of the profiteer who fattens on the body politic, the alien enemy that invades our institutions and destroys our substance, the slacker who, like the hookworm, is nourished by our organism but fails to function in its defense or support.

The word "slacker" here means draft dodger. Although there had been occasional uses of the word before this to describe a lazy person in Britain and the United States, someone who wasn't pulling his share of the workload, magazines like *The Nation, The North American Review, Month, The New Republic, Punch, Theatre, Poetry,* and *New Statesman* all published pieces on the perils the slacker posed in the late 1910s, primarily in the slacker's guise as a draft evader. The United States entered World War I and instituted a military draft in 1917, causing some 24 million men to register in the next two years. Those few who didn't, or were suspected of not registering or using artifice to avoid service, were branded slackers.

Cartoons of men trying to fake disabilities were regular newspaper and magazine fare, and stories of slackers became common in magazine fiction and film, suggesting that some shirking of duty was widespread. Men who seemed fit and yet weren't called into the military were automatically suspected of being slackers. Champion boxer Jack Dempsey, for instance, was accused of being a slacker and arrested. It was four months into his trial before a navy officer came forward and said that Dempsey had tried to enlist and was rejected, but the paperwork had somehow been lost. Slackers became objects of an enormous vigilante-assisted federal campaign in 1917 and 1918, spearheaded by the still-new Justice Department's Bureau of Investigation, which would eventually be called the FBI. Already actively investigating left-wing organizations for "alien subversion," the Bureau took on the job of hunting down draft dodgers and did so with the help of the all-volunteer American Protective League. The APL, founded by A. M. Briggs, an advertising executive from Chicago, grew to 1,200 chapters and a membership of 250,000 at the height of the war, with the verbal and financial encouragement of the Bureau's special agent in charge, J. Edgar Hoover. Given official police badges that read AMERICAN PROTECTIVE LEAGUE, AUXILIARY TO THE U.S. DEPARTMENT OF JUSTICE, APL members were encouraged to hunt down and report "seditious and disloyal conversation" or any other evidence of radicalism. Given quasi-official status by the FBI, they actively arrested and brought to authorities people they suspected of being unpatriotic.

In May of 1917, the Bureau, working with thousands of APL members and local police, performed what were called the "Slacker Raids," rounding up anyone suspected of draft evasion, pro-German sentiments, pro-socialist views (the Bolshevik revolution of that year had people very worried), or rationing infractions. Like the antiradical Palmer Raids to come in 1919, directed by Attorney General Mitchell Palmer and his then-assistant J. Edgar Hoover, the Slacker Raids cast their net wide, and those at the helm were cavalier at best about constitutional protections. Of the 50,000 men taken into custody and jailed until they could furnish proof that they had registered for the draft, fewer than 50 were eventually arrested for draft violations. Some 5,000 of the "suspects" were inducted into the military, but a later congressional investigation established that these forced inductions were little more than a public relations campaign to make the raids appear more successful than they had been. Despite this lack of actual success, however, the raids were considered a public relations triumph, and four months later the Bureau and the APL organized another large series of raids, again arresting thousands.

The war encouraged, as wars often do, stricter enforcement of laws aimed at fringe groups, and this included not just recent immigrants, some of whom were assumed to have divided loyalties, but anyone who was critical of the war, the government, or the economic system. The Slacker Raids included, in fact, through Justice Department urging, coordinated searches of twenty-four Industrial Workers of the World headquarters in September 1917, in which the union's books, minutes, financial records, correspondence, and membership lists were seized along with anyone unlucky enough to be in the office. These men were given, in yet another obvious constitutional violation, not individual, but mass trials. The largest in U.S. history took place in Chicago, where more than a hundred IWW leaders were tried at once, with bleachers installed in the courtroom for the defendants. Judge Kenesaw Mountain Landis (who would a few years later become baseball commissioner in the wake of the Black Sox scandal) sentenced 15 of these men to twenty years in prison, 33 to ten years, and 35 to five years. Large trials of IWW organizers were held at the same time in Wichita, Kansas, where 27 of 34 labor organizers were convicted of sedition and sent to prison, and in Sacramento, California, where all 46 defendants were convicted and sentenced.

They were not convicted of avoiding the draft. They were prosecuted under the 1917 Espionage Act, a forerunner to our own Patriot Act and its broad revocation of rights. The act made it a crime to aid, abet, or counsel anyone to avoid service, and the IWW was staunchly against the war. An article in the IWW weekly *Solidarity*, in April 1917, explained why:

> A slacker is not a slave who refuses to slit throats or get his hide perforated for the master class. A "slacker" is one who is too cowardly or stupid to join with his fellow workers against the exploiters of labor—one who neglects the interests of himself, his wife and family and of his class in order to make efficient profit or cannon fodder out of his worthless carcass.

In 1917, Maryland and West Virginia, and in 1918 New York, New Jersey, Kentucky, and Massachusetts passed laws requiring all able-bodied men to be regularly employed for the duration of the war. Arizona passed a law forbidding the employment of or giving aid to anyone who was a deserter or a slacker. The point of these laws was less to maximize actual production (much less to contain actual threats to public safety) than to rally the populace around images of, as it was called at the time, "100% Americanism." The close perceived connection among hobos, socialists, unionists, and foreigners, along with a belief in the necessity of a concerted national "effort," helped suggest that ferreting out slackers and fighting labor leftists at home somehow constituted an aid to the soldiers fighting abroad.

Slackers became regular characters in plays, films, and fictions. Usually these featured draft-dodging protagonists who are reformed, through accident or love, and then take up their patriotic duty. The Hollywood slacker films were unabashedly propagandistic. *Mrs. Slacker* (1918) tells the story of a rich coward who marries his washerwoman in order to avoid the draft as a married man. She, however, finds out and leaves, saying she refuses to be a "Mrs. Slacker." She ends up fumbling onto a German plot to blow up the local reservoir and is captured by the spies; her husband finds her, saves her, and then, realizing the real danger the Germans pose, volunteers for the army with his wife beaming on. *The Slacker* (1917) is the same basic story, with a rich man marrying to avoid the draft. He, however, sees a German insult the American flag, and this is enough to rouse his patriotism from its slacker slumber and send him into the army. These were not sophisticated films. In *The Slacker's Heart* (1917), the plot is simply slacker loses girl, slacker makes a German kiss the flag, slacker gets girl. *The Claws of the Hun* (1918) and *Every Mother's Son* (1918) are somewhat more complex but come to the same conclusion: the slacker shapes up and ships out. A *Motion Picture News* editorial in 1917 claimed that "every individual at work in this industry wants to do his share," and alongside these anti-slacker films, the industry was busy producing anti-German films such as *To Hell with the Kaiser* (1918), *The Kaiser: The Beast of Berlin* (1918), and *The Prussian Cur* (1918). The editorial promised that "through slides, film leaders and trailers, posters, and newspaper publicity, [film studios] will spread that propaganda so necessary to the immediate mobilization of the country's great resources."

Mainstream magazines published many stories in the same vein, and like the filmmakers, editors took advice from the Committee on Public Information, the office created by President Wilson in 1917 to coordinate the government's propaganda efforts. Edward Bok, the immigrant editor of *Ladies' Home Journal*, made his position clear: "The *Ladies' Home Journal*," he wrote, "is not a 'slacker' magazine." This of course doesn't make entire sense if slacker means draft dodger, since a magazine can't be drafted. Nor were "ladies" being drafted. As people began to routinely extend the meaning of the word to include everyone not making an active war effort, the term began quickly to accrete its current connotations of laziness, antisocial lethargy, and lack of productivity. Businessmen unhappy with the slow pace of the U.S. Congress called it "our one big slacker" as early as 1919, and by 1921 this kind of use was widespread. When John D. Rockefeller described himself as a slacker in 1920, he and the interviewer put the word in quotes: "People persist in thinking that I was a tremendous worker, always at it early and late, summer and winter. The real truth is that I was what would now be called a 'slacker' after I reached my middle thirties." After 1920, the quotes disappeared, the draft-evasion sense drifted away (although it was revived briefly during World War II), and the word became a common replacement for lounger or loafer. By 1922, one journalist could feel safe (whether he should have or not) to drop the quotation marks while referring to Hamlet as a slacker.

∞

The war ended in 1919, and almost everyone in the 1920s agreed that it had changed everything. Ernest Hemingway, in *A Farewell to Arms*, in one of the best-known passages about the war, argues that it destroyed idealism itself, as his soldier-protagonist says:

> I was always embarrassed by the words sacred, glorious, and sacrifice and the expression in vain. We had heard them, sometimes standing in the rain almost out of earshot, so that only the shouted words came through, and had read them, on proclamations . . . now for a long time, and I had seen nothing sacred, and the things that were glorious had no glory and the sacrifices were like the stockyards at Chicago if nothing was done with the meat except to bury it. There were many words that you could not stand to hear . . . Abstract words such as glory, honor, courage, or hallow were obscene.

Hemingway was, famously, an eyewitness of what Leo Braudy has called the Great War's "world of blood, filth, and futility." The war shattered many people's faith in humanity, even many who never left home, and young writers often included the work ethic in the list of wartime casualties. John F. Carter, for instance, one of the first interpreters of what was being called "flaming youth"—the disillusioned, uncontrollable younger generation—published a piece titled " 'These Wild Young People' by One of Them," in *The Atlantic Monthly* in 1920. There he blames the war not just for the disenchantment of the young, but for their slacking. "We have seen the inherent beastliness of the human race revealed in an infernal apocalypse," he writes, and so "a great many of us, because they have taken away our apple-cheeked ideals, are seriously considering whether or not their game be worth our candle."

Ellen Welles Page, a young woman writing in *Outlook* in 1922, thought youthful disillusionment was the result of both the war and the comfortable advantages this generation had compared with previous generations:

> Most of us, under the present system of modern education, are further advanced and more thoroughly developed mentally, physically,

and vocationally than were our parents at our age . . . We have learned to take for granted conveniences, and many luxuries, which not so many years ago were as yet undreamed of. [But] the war tore away our spiritual foundations and challenged our faith. We are struggling to regain our equilibrium.

Such feelings of disruption and dislocation were very widespread, perhaps nowhere expressed as eloquently as in Warren G. Harding's presidential campaign slogan of 1920, in which he wistfully promised "A Return to Normalcy."

For some cultural critics, normalcy was not the cure, but the illness. The Harvard philosopher George Santayana, in his *Character and Opinion in the United States* (1920), complained about the pressure to conform in America: "You must wave, you must cheer, you must push with the irresistible crowd; otherwise you will feel like a traitor, a soulless outcast, a deserted ship high and dry on the shore." And at the center of the crowd's push was the belief in the value of work. "This national faith and morality are vague in idea, but inexorable in spirit; they are the gospel of work and the belief in progress. By them, in a country where all men are free, every man finds that what most matters has been settled beforehand." Santayana, imbued with the Greek sense of *otium*, the belief in the value of contemplation, finds America dominated by the machine and manic accumulation. What America needs, he thought, was to stop, retire, and think about what was really important.

King Vidor, one of the most interesting directors working during the silent film era, made an argument similar to Santayana's in *The Crowd* (1928), a film that, on the one hand, offers a simple morality tale about the importance of work and of distinguishing oneself from the crowd through achievement. But the film actually presents a fairly complicated disquisition on modern disillusionment. It is the story of a young office worker who has dreamed of really "being somebody" since he was a boy but who ends up getting fired for daydreaming about his future success in the advertising business instead of working at his clerk's job. The images of that job are disturbing, uncanny: the film opens with a now-famous, still-impressive tracking shot up the face of an enormous, characterless New York office building, starting at the ground. The building is a massive hive of indistinguishable comblike black windows, and the camera travels up, rolling by floor after identical floor. At one floor the camera turns and heads closer to the building, approaching until a single window fills the frame, and the camera seems to enter through it into a huge room, a room filled with row upon row of identical desks. The desks are in exact rows, each with an identical-looking man behind it, each sitting in the same position, writing in identical ledgers, elbows all at the same angles. The regularity is daunting, creepy. The image has become one of the classic representations of the industrial standardization of the clerical workplace, reprinted ever since. The camera closes in until we have a single man in the frame, our hero, and we see that instead of entering numbers in his ledger, he is actually doodling down advertising slogans on a scrap of paper that he shields from his overseer's sight.

As the clock ticks agonizingly slowly toward five o'clock, workers at various desks sneak surreptitious glances at it. When the bell rings, everyone hops up simultaneously. They all rush to an enormous washroom, where they queue up at a long line of identical, regularly placed sinks and wash their hands, all using the same motions— automatons. Unlike the miserable, robotlike workers in Fritz Lang's *Metropolis* (1927), though, these men seem happy enough; they slap each other on the back and make jokes. All the jokes, pointedly, are the same. In the front of the building, they exit, one after another. The first man out meets a woman who is waiting for him, and they go off arm in arm, smiling. The second meets another woman, smiling the same smile, and they go off arm in arm in exactly the same fashion. This is repeated until it, too, looks oppressive rather than sociable, dully routine rather than liberating. Even their personal lives, smiling as they are, are regularized and standardized, unchanging from man to man.

Our hero, however, is a different kind of guy. He's a bit Bohemian—he plays the ukulele, the hip youth instrument of the decade, and his bride's Victorian burgher family detests him—and he wants to enter the hippest and most modern of professions, advertising. But after his marriage, the kids arrive, and he is stuck in his boring job, copying numbers all day in even rows. Melodramatic tragedy ensues when his daughter is run over by a truck. He gets depressed, his ledger gets sloppy, and he loses his job. "The crowd laughs with you always," intertitles explain. "But it will cry with you only for a day." Our hero loses not only his job but his friends, his sense of hope, and the respect of his wife. He tries a series of other positions, like selling vacuum cleaners door to door, but has no success, in part because he feels he is meant for bigger and better things, that he is not just a cog. The houses he goes to are all the same, the women he tries to sell to are all the same, and he gets the same "no" at every door. "We do not know how big the crowd is, and what opposition it is," again the intertitles intone, "until we get out of step with it." His wife's family considers him a bum, and he gets more and more depressed. He almost commits suicide, but pulls himself off the ledge at the last moment and looks one last time for a job.

In the end, he gets hired to wear a sandwich board—advertising at last, but at its most degrading. Still, to be just an anonymous face in the crowd is good enough after his foray into jobless insecurity, and he returns to the bosom of his family, happy with the average life of an average man. This might seem to be a romance of socialization, in which the hero tries to live outside the norm only to be happily returned to it, except for the final images. In the last scene we watch the hero with his family at the theater, laughing: a classic happy ending, a family reunited. He turns to the man next to him, and they laugh and pat each other on the back. Everybody is happy. But when the camera pans back, we see more and more of his compatriots all laughing in much the same way. Further back we see dozens of people, all making the same gestures, laughing, bending forward at the waist, slapping their knees. The camera continues to pull back, and we see fifty, then a hundred, and then hundreds of people in the audience, all performing the same motions over and over. The specter of overstandardization rises again. Finally, our hero is lost in the sea of thousands of bodies lurching in laughter and pointing at what they see on the stage. The uncanny, squirming mass of bodies is frightening, standardization gone awry, individuality defeated, humans degraded into what almost appears, in the end, to be a mess of worms.

The hero, in his resistance to the standardizing forces around him, seems to embody Thorstein Veblen's idea that more than an aversion to labor, people have an "aversion to futility." Veblen had been arguing since the turn of the century that it was a theoretical error to think that people didn't want to work:

It is one of the commonplaces of the received economic theory that work is irksome. Many a discussion proceeds on this axiom that, so far as regards economic matters, men desire above all things to get the goods produced by labor and to avoid the labor by which the goods are produced. In a general way the common-sense opinion is well in accord with current theory on this head. According to the common-sense-ideal, the economic beatitude lies in an unrestrained consumption of goods, without work; whereas the perfect economic affliction is unremunerated labor. Man instinctively revolts at effort that goes to supply the means of life.

But this is simply untrue, Veblen argued. The "instinct of workmanship," the inherent desire of human beings to work toward the common good, was, he felt, *the* central economic fact. This instinct could be perverted into predatory behavior or exhausted or dulled by machine civilization, but it was nonetheless the essential basis of human action. The economic theories of his day assumed that people felt a natural revulsion from work, that avoiding work was a natural human attitude.

It is apparently among the moderately well-to-do, the half-idle classes, that such a revulsion chiefly has its way; leading now and again to fantastic, archaising cults and beliefs . . . a feeling of maladjustment and discomfort, that seeks a remedy in a "return to Nature" in one way or another; some sort of a return to "the simple life," which shall in some fashion afford an escape from the unending "grind" of living from day to day by the machine method and shall so put behind us for a season the burdensome futilities by help of which alone life can be carried on under the routine of the machine process.

Veblen argued that people should be revolted by industrial work, that it was perverse and incapable of fulfilling people's need to perform meaningful labor. Other economists had assumed that work was a curse, but Veblen found that work, in fact, was the only cure.

Carleton Parker, an economist at the University of Washington and a follower of Veblen's, expanded on Veblen's argument in the early 1920s:

This desire and talent that man has to mould material to fancied ends, be the material clay or pawns in diplomacy, explains much of human activity, while wages explain little. Prisoners have a horror of prison idleness. Clerks drift out of stereotyped office work, and the monotony of modern industrialism has created a new type of migratory worker. As James has said, "Constructiveness is a genuine and irresistible instinct in man as in bee or beaver." Man is then not naturally lazy, but innately industrious. Where laziness exists it is an artificial habit, inculcated by civilization. Man has a true quality sense in what he does: there is, then, a "dignity of labor," and it is the job and the industrial environment that produce the slacker, and not the laborer's willful disposition.

Being a slacker (which our hero in *The Crowd* is part of the time, strumming on his ukulele, refusing to go look for work) is a natural reaction to the apparent futility of industrial labor. Faced with the mindless, boring, repetitive, seemingly pointless labor of the clerk, people tend, like Bartleby, to prefer not to work. And, as in the case of Bartleby, the refusal is itself another kind of suicide.

∞

Some of the flaming youths were as eager to defend their relation to work as they were to explain their dissolution and slacking. John Carter says that F. Scott Fitzgerald is not entirely wrong in emphasizing the drinking, gambling, and promiscuity of the young (Fitzgerald had just published *This Side of Paradise*), but that this isn't yet the whole picture:

> Prohibition is put through to stop our drinking, and hasn't stopped it. [William Jennings] Bryan has plans to curtail our philanderings, and he won't do any good. A Draconian code is being hastily formulated at Washington and elsewhere, to prevent us from, by any chance, making any alteration in this present divinely constituted arrangement of things. The oldsters stand dramatically with fingers and toes and noses pressed against the bursting dykes. Let them! They won't do any good. They can shackle us down, and still expect us to repair their blunders, if they wish. But we shall not trouble ourselves very much about them any more. Why should we? What have

they done? They have made us work as they never had to work in all
their padded lives—but we'll have our cakes and ale for a' that.

The young, he claims, because of the problems bequeathed by their
elders, have to work harder than any previous generation. "All my
friends are working and working hard. Most of the girls I know are
working."

Work, in fact, is the great theme of this famous decade of flappers
and speakeasies. A time of wild economic swings, with boom and bust
cycles following each other rapidly, the decade saw periods of incredi-
ble growth and periods of total stagnation and deep unemployment.
The period is, of course, famous for its overall growth, its 64 percent
increase in industrial production being five and a half times the rate of
the decade before. And the other overall economic indicators—such
as a 500 percent increase in spending on recreational activities—all
point to a decade of unprecedented prosperity. But there were also severe economic downturns, in 1921, 1924, and 1927, so that the picture of large crowds of unemployed men fighting one another for the
chance of a day's work, the standard images from the Depression of
the 1930s, were already part of the American scene. In the middle of
The Crowd, the hero begs a man to let him in a long employment
line, pleading that he has a wife, a family. So do I, says the man, so do
most of us. As the business cycles turned, periods of opportunity were
followed by periods of enforced unemployment in rapid succession.

And the nature of work continued to change rapidly as well. Continued mechanization—as one business journal noted in 1923, "Machinery 'stays put.' It does not decide to go on strike . . . or take a job
in the next town"—was the main force at work. Assembly lines moved
four times faster in 1928 than in 1918, worker output per capita rose
20 percent just between 1923 and 1928, and from 1919 to 1929 the
number of industries that had electrified their production process rose
from 30 to 70 percent. Steel production rose by 50 percent in just five
years in the middle of the decade, and chemical and electrical equipment manufacturers increased production even more. All of this occurred with the total workforce holding steady at eight and a half
million workers, almost the same in 1929 as in 1919. This meant, as
the population of the country continued to grow, the surplus of workers continued to grow as well, the result of continued emigration from

farm country, where the tenfold increase in the use of tractors, for example, sent dispossessed workers to swell the unemployed in cities. The increased labor pool helped industries break unions across the country; to take just one example, the United Mine Workers saw its membership drop from 500,000 members to 84,000 over the decade. Total corporate profits rose some 50 percent in these years, but workers' salaries rose slightly less than 1 percent a year, another clear sign of a large surplus labor pool. There were fewer jobs per available worker, and the kinds of jobs available were changing as well. At the turn of the century, agriculture accounted for the largest number of workers (38 percent), followed by blue-collar jobs (36 percent), and then the white-collar segment, which remained a distant third (17 percent). By 1930 the agricultural sector dropped by almost half and the white-collar sector almost doubled. A larger percentage of the workforce was, for the first time, employed in white-collar and service jobs than in blue-collar or agricultural jobs.

And as the nature of work shifted from manual to nonmanual labor, the nonmanual workers like writers, intellectuals, educators, filmmakers, and journalists changed their tune. Instead of directing their arguments about the value of work to manual laborers, as they had in the past, they directed those arguments to their own class. Instead of prescribing rest for themselves, they prescribed it for the working class. And instead of praising idleness within their own group, they almost without exception praised industriousness.

In 1927, for example, the New York playwright and essayist Langdon Mitchell made a stab at explaining "our national disease" to get at the roots of "what is wrong with our America, with the life we lead." His father, S. Weir Mitchell, had concluded that modern life required forms of work and exertion unknown to previous generations, that nervous energy needed to be spent in so many ways that nervous bankruptcy was the increasingly common result, and that if overexertion and overwork were the culprits, rest and leisure were the cure. Thirty years later his son Langdon came to the opposite conclusion: the problem was not overwork, but too much leisure and its concomitant boredom. "Our leisure hours have no good meaning for us. We meet them as a man meets a dun or the shadow of death," Langdon Mitchell declared, extending the metaphor of bankruptcy. "Historical events have deprived the American of much that he should and once did possess . . . All he knows is that his life is empty, and he feels sad."

Salvation, the younger Mitchell argued, lay in art and culture. "We must, in short, look into our *civilization*," Mitchell stressed, into "the moral well-being that we try to embrace in the word *culture*." But more importantly, where his father diagnosed overwork, the younger Mitchell saw not enough work. Work, he thought, was the proper cure for ennui. There should be no rest, as his father thought there should be, for the weary. For the Mitchells and their class, leisure had gone from goal to problem, work from curse to therapy.

The Mitchells agree that the march of progress has got people feeling blue, but for Mitchell père the culprit is overcivilization, which broke people down and robbed them of the simpler relations to nature and one another that their less civilized ancestors knew. Where the father found too much civilization, Mitchell fils finds not enough. In an essay titled "What Is Needed," Langdon Mitchell comes up with a recipe for cure that repeats many of his father's precepts and much of his rhetoric, but again with twists: "Let me repeat and insist: cooking comes first. On that everything is based. No national culture is possible without it. No religion is safe without it. If the cooking is bad, the religion will get sick." Langdon Mitchell argued that good cooking meant a more refined sense of cuisine and a finer appreciation for the pleasures of food. His father, author of *Fat and Blood and How to Make Them* (1878), had also professed the importance of cooking. For him, however, this meant substituting the effete pleasures of fine food with the recuperative simplicity of a milk and beef broth diet.

S. Weir approved of what he called the "camp cure" of outdoors activity, because it was a temporary embrace of "the simple life," away from the excitements of the city, while his son praised open-air games "for the exhilaration they afford." S. Weir argued that only the healthy could withstand a passion for arts and fictions; his son recommended the excitement and stimulation of fiction and the other arts as cures for the sickness brought on by boredom. The father warned of the dangers of overwork while the son praised the happy workers of Whitman, the anonymous but ambitious farmers and tradesmen of America, and energetic, "self-made" politicians like Washington and Lincoln. In the space of a generation, excitement, absorption in work, passion, art, and culture had moved from being causes to being cures for our national maladies.

Any number of explanations might be offered for these reversals. The Great War had obvious impacts on American self-perception. Bureaucratic and industrial expansion and the standardization that accompanied it led to worries about whether authentic experience was still possible. The authorities recognized by earlier generations, especially the church and politicians, were losing their legitimacy. Langdon Mitchell's belief that art was a cure for inadequate civilization marks him as a quintessential modernist, a typical exponent of the idea that high culture was a necessary motor of progress. He is also typically modern in assuming that his father's Victorian culture had failed in that very task, seeing America and Europe not as the pinnacle of artistic achievement, but as timid and backward, as "an old bitch, gone in the teeth," in Ezra Pound's words, "a botched civilization." Victorian intellectuals and professionals asked what the impediments to the progress of civilization might be, and what threats individual backsliding and softening might pose to that progress. They had read their Plato and Gibbon, and they were aware that republics and empires could decline as well as rise. For the next generation, in the years after the Great War, the question seemed to be whether we had a real civilization at all, and if so, was any of it worth saving? Or was an entirely new art necessary?

The younger Mitchell answered yes, and it would be hard work. While Weir Mitchell saw his audience as an expanding leisure class, his son wrote for people he thought must, and should, work. "I am reminded as I write," his father had said in his dilatory style, "that what I say applies and must apply chiefly to the leisure class; but in others there is a good deal of manual labor done of necessity, and after all, the leisure class is one which is rapidly increasing in America, and which needs, especially among its new recruits, the very kind of advice I am now giving." Mitchell was sure overwork meant disease, but by his son's time the medical establishment itself had started to change its tune. Along the way, in the 1910s, many physicians seemed quite comfortable assuming that work was at one and the same time the prime cause of the disease *and* the prime cure. "In the civilization of our day no cause is more potent than overwork," the physician-authors of a standard 1912 *Handbook of Practical Treatment* declare, agreeing with earlier conclusions. Five pages later, they just as confidently proclaim: "Work, both mental and physical, is the best guarantee of health." Langdon Mitchell and most of his generation were squarely on this side, as his father had been on the other. "Class-war is engrained in the economic system," he admitted. "But irreconcilable differences of opinion are not the only cause of national ill-being . . . We all know the black dissatisfaction, the bitterness which gathers and festers in the Soul, when there is no outlet for its activities." Work is the cure for such blues, and brings "that joy which I shall forever insist is the birthright of every man."

∞

Benjamin Franklin may have been a great cheerleader for work, but one thing he never would have said is that work causes "joy." Whatever else work meant under the Franklinian work ethic, it was not fun or pleasurable. Throughout the 1910s and 1920s, though, many people worried precisely about how little joy was available from work. "Why Do They Work So Hard?" Robert S. and Helen Merrill Lynd asked in a chapter title in *Middletown* (1929), and they worried that "the amount of robust satisfaction" workers get from their jobs "seems, at best, to be slight" and "declining." A significant shift had clearly occurred. As Max Weber had warned, the Protestant work ethic had become an empty shell: "Stripped of its religious and ethical meaning," he wrote in 1905, the work ethic "tends to become associated with purely mundane passions, which often actually give it the character of sport." For Weber, this was a tragedy, a degradation, leaving people working without knowing why, striving without a real goal. But for many in the 1920s it meant the opposite. Langdon Mitchell finds in work not ethical meaning but gratification, delight. Work *should* be like sport.

The younger Mitchell was one voice in a general cross-class revolution against Victorian upper-class notions of work and leisure, a revolution that left the classes in largely the same economic relation to one another, but in which they might be said to have reversed ethics. In the 1920s, all of a sudden, everyone seemed to agree that the working class worked too hard and deserved more leisure, while the same voices suggested that the upper classes had too much leisure and not enough work. Felix Frankfurter, for instance, who would be appointed to the Supreme Court in 1939, was involved in a dispute over the eight-hour day in the 1920s with Elbert Gary, the chairman of the board of U.S. Steel, and Gary asked him how, in good faith, he could defend workers' right to shorter hours when he knew that both he, Gary, and Frankfurter himself regularly worked longer. Frankfurter rejoined, "Ah, . . . but think what interesting jobs you and I have." They found pleasure in their work, and they assumed that workers did not, that workers suffered from what Veblen suggested was the futility bred by their mind-numbing, machine-tending daily tasks.

As the work ethic switched classes, so, too, did neurasthenia. Fewer and fewer upper-class patients were diagnosed with the disease, and more and more working people—who had been theoretically exempt from the disease according to Dr. George Beard and the elder Mitchell—were diagnosed as having it. Physicians at the nation's veterans hospitals noted that there were no longer any professionals among the sufferers—a student now and then, or a teacher, but the rest were laborers, tradesmen, farmers. Some mental hygienists (a medical specialty that grew in response to the needs of the industrial workplace) argued that labor unrest was "psychopathological" and that blame could be placed not on inequity, but on faulty industrial engineering. Fatigue neuroses like neurasthenia were caused, they agreed with Veblen, because of the "monotony of occupation" forced on factory hands. Some argued that industrial insistence on efficiency required thinking, as one doctor put it, "what the man meant for the work, not what the work meant for the man. It is the latter question that has become the most important problem in the industrial world at the present time." We need to adjust men to jobs and jobs to men, another wrote. Victorian doctors had assumed that workers' melancholy and inefficiency were due to alcohol and agitation, but the new hygienists argued that "latent cravings" and "pent-up emotions" that found no outlet in work were responsible for both the alcohol and the agitation. In 1920 Abraham Myerson praised the latest book of the famous efficiency experts Frank and Lillian Gilbreth, *Fatigue Study*, because "the authors recognize some form of happiness as the aim of life and urge elimination of fatigue not only because fatigue hampers production, but because it hampers happiness." By the end of the 1920s, massive surveys, like the Hawthorne studies at Western Electric in Cicero, Illinois, attempted to make workers' jobs fit the ideal of middle-class work by asking laborers how they felt about their work.

Similar arguments were applied to the work of homemakers. The housewife suffered from an "occupational neurosis" because of the "oppressive monotony of her daily task"; what she needed, the experts agreed, was work that fostered and preserved her feelings of worth and dignity (this argument would be reprised some forty years later by Betty Friedan and others). The nation's manufacturers produced appliances and other products that promised to do exactly that, to reduce monotony and add dignity to her labor. "Bring a light touch to heavy work and the years will touch you lightly," promised Premier Duplex vacuum cleaners, and many appliance manufacturers insisted that women's real work was not the monotony of cleaning, but the more significant, ennobling calling of raising a family. Appliances could minimize the monotony and maximize the quality time spent with the kids.

Other ads and articles suggested that a woman's real job was to be the purchasing agent for the home. "A woman's virtue and excellence as a housewife do not in these days depend upon her skill in spinning and weaving," an article in *Ladies' Home Journal* in 1928 announced. "An entirely different task presents itself, more difficult and more complex, requiring an infinitely wider range of ability, and for those very reasons more interesting and inspiring." The fatigue caused by monotony could be alleviated by wise shopping—in part because, through shopping, one could procure the machines that would take over all drudgery, as per the utopian vision of Oscar Wilde and scores of others; in part because shopping, now a large part of women's work, had all the healthful benefits of any good work; and in part because housewives, in shopping for their families, were not just doing their job, they were making healthy families. The nature of the housewife's job was such that, adequately performed, it ensured a fully integrated relation between love and work, as well as a healthy economy. There was less and less need for a doctor in the house, not because machines and other products created leisure, but because machines allowed women to do what they were really good at, what has come in the meantime to be called "emotional work."

And middle-class men would become neurasthenic only if they didn't get enough work. Neurasthenia, in fact, could now be cured by the happiness, self-sufficiency, and dignity one could find only in one's work. And the blue-collar workers to whom neurasthenia had trickled down were busily being interviewed by efficiency experts armed with the latest psychologies in an attempt to find out how they might be happy with their work. The conclusion drawn from the Hawthorne studies was that how the worker felt toward his or her coworkers and how the worker thus felt about his or her actual tasks was more important than what had traditionally been seen as the top of the list of workers' desires: better wages, better physical work conditions, a shorter workweek. According to an editorial in the *Saturday Evening Post* in 1925, "In too many trades . . . work has become a means to an end, the price that is paid for big wages and the luxuries and recreations they make possible. But work should, in itself, be an end."

The comic reversal of this sentiment can be found in the Marx Brothers' *Cocoanuts*, which was a hit on Broadway in 1925 and a film in 1929. As in many of their shows, Chico and Harpo are unemployed flimflammers, while Groucho has a job, this time running a hotel in Florida. The staff of the hotel is in revolt, not having been paid in weeks, and Groucho says, "You don't want to be wage slaves, do you?" No, they all agree. "What makes you a wage slave? Wages!" And so he refuses to pay them. Groucho is also involved in one of the classic get-rich-quick schemes in American history, selling Florida swampland ("Who are you going to believe, me or your own eyes?") during the real estate bubble of the early twenties, proving himself to be a bigger con artist than the more obvious slacker candidates. A staple of the Marx Brothers' comedy—not just in *Cocoanuts*, but in *Monkey Business*, *Horse Feathers*, and *A Day at the Races* as well—was the enormous lengths they have to go to in order to get by without doing a proper job at anything, whether ineptly running a hotel, a college, a country, or a sanitarium for neurasthenics. They were always incredibly busy doing nothing.

But they were clowns. In "The Greatest Delusion in the World," written for the *American Magazine*, Dr. Frank Crane, a physician who wrote for popular magazines, announced that the biggest mistake a person could make was to think of work as an affliction. "The happiest people in the country are those that get up and go to work." The least happy people have breakfast brought to them in bed: "Happiness is a byproduct of work," he says, and so, no work, no happiness. Like Chaplin, he equated the nonworking rich and the nonworking poor: "The 'dangerous classes' are the idle endowed at the top, and the idle loafers at the bottom . . . The great mass of humanity is sound and sweet because it works. Work is better than play but we hate to admit it." Crane goes on to reach even greater heights of hyperbole, asserting that work is the greatest source of pleasure available on this earth:

> Work is the only means toward the one thing every healthy human being wants more than anything else in the world . . . This has been the happiest period of my life . . . because I love my work better than anything else on earth. I can think of no kind of play or vacation half so pleasant as this work . . . God bless it! For it is the immediate jewel of my soul . . . Even Heaven is a world of souls happy and blest because they are at work.

Leaving aside how Crane might know this last fact, any good slacker would find that these statements betray an extraordinary lack of imagination.

Hugh Wiley, writing in *The Saturday Evening Post* in 1920, was less ecstatic, but he ended with a fairly hyperbolic statement himself:

> The United States is now long on trouble and short on sweat. Most of the trouble will end when people of the United States realize that the cure is useful work . . . Work is the cure. It is the only cure . . . Work will buy life and happiness . . . There is no honest alternative. Sweat or die!

This is not supposed to be comic, though it is hard not to smile at it now. Sweat or die? On the other hand, Samuel G. Blythe's "Tapering Off on Work," from the same magazine in 1925, *is* supposed to be funny, but isn't. "I was a work addict," the piece begins, and it is one long conceit. Blythe's friends came and warned him to relax, he says, but he "was a habitual worker." A workaholic *avant la lettre*, he continues in this confessional mode of the alcoholic or drug addict: "Two or three days without work and I was nervous, fidgety, irritable, miserable. A week without work and I was a wreck. The stuff got me." Work, in the 1920s, was like a good drug—you had to be careful or you would simply want more and more of the stuff.

∞

The novels of the 1920s, that great decade of American literature, are obsessed with the question of work. Given the expatriate party people, the Algonquin Round Table drinkers, the Charleston-dancing speak-easy patrons, the high-living bootleggers and gangsters, the socialist-utopian leftists, and the flaming youth who were making the most news, one would expect that loafing, lounging, and slacking would find hearty support in the literature of the time. But the literary writers tended in the opposite direction, agreeing with the doctors and advice givers. The title character of Sinclair Lewis's *Babbitt* (1922) is a real estate agent who seems ridiculous for his shallow, pandering, booster pep talks, but his inability to find meaning in his life is tragic. Lewis contrasts him to the factory that "hummed like a million bees" and the synthetic-rubber researchers who had been working on a report for thirty-seven straight hours. Carol Kennicott, the hero of Lewis's *Main Street* (1920), wants to find "real work" but finds only tedium. Lewis wrote *Arrowsmith* (1925) to answer the criticism that he could produce only satire, that he was unable to construct a hero for modern times. Martin Arrowsmith is a man so obsessed with his work that he leaves his wife and child so that he can labor day and night in his lab. There he finds "the happiness of high taut insanity," the joy of working obsessively. It is supposed to be a happy ending, but it can be hard to see why: Arrowsmith is holed up in an oddly mythic, oddly surrealistic Thoreauvian laboratory in the Maine woods with his lab partner, who apparently does not have a single interest in life outside his work and never has. When Arrowsmith's wife asks him to come home to her and their son, he simply refuses. She tells him he's crazy: she is after all very rich and has built him a lab in their mansion; he readily agrees that she is right. "Oh, absolutely! And how I enjoy it!" he says to her. "We're insane, but we're not cranks!" Arrowsmith, exultant in his scientific overwork, has no use for normal human relations. He is not even sure that saving humanity from disease is a worthwhile project as he hunts for antibacterial and antiviral serums. He and his lab partner are devoted to an ideal that is indistinguishable from the work they do. Work is self-sufficient, an end in itself, an insanity that is its own cure, a pure pleasure.

In Sherwood Anderson's *Dark Laughter* (1925), his protagonist, a reporter, watches a butcher at work, fascinated by "the deft quick hands of the old meatcutter. They represented something to him. What was it? . . . Perhaps a way in which he would like to handle words." The "disease of life" that the reporter and the people he knows suffer from is alienation. Like T. S. Eliot's J. Alfred Prufrock, they are alienated from real experience. It comes, Anderson says, from "men getting away from their own hands." (An actual reporter, Clarence Pennoyer, the year before, had come to the same conclusion. After his first stint as a newsman, he had a nervous breakdown, and he was cured, as Dreiser was, by taking on manual labor. Loading and unloading trucks nine hours a day, he learned the pleasure of working, came to see that reporting was even more pleasurable, and went back to reporting.) William Faulkner's *Mosquitoes* (1927) features an artist who would rather work than go to parties or have sex. Anthony Patch in F. Scott Fitzgerald's *The Beautiful and the Damned* (1922) is damned by his lack of work: "I am essentially weak, he thought, I need work to do, work to do." Anderson's Hugh McVey in *Poor White* (1920) wanders the world looking for the right work. The protagonist of Edith Wharton's *Age of Innocence* (1920) forgoes love in the end for an ideal of working service. Carl Van Vechten condemns Hollywood in *Spider Boy* (1928) not because it is immoral, but because people there don't do any real work. Lewis's Dodsworth (*Dodsworth*, 1929) is completely dissatisfied when he is forced into retirement and completely rejuvenated when he finds new work.

Novels of every kind made similar arguments. Elinor Wylie's *Jennifer Lorn* (1923) is a critique of aristocratic leisure. Anzia Yezierska's *Bread Givers* (1925) has a heroine who, unlike the rest of her family, loves work; her evil, lazy father hates it. Harlem Renaissance authors as different as the staunch bourgeois Jessie Redmon Fauset and the avowed primitivist Claude McKay wrote novels populated by exemplary characters who love work and by faulty characters who try to get by without working. Not all work was created equal for these writers, and they all admitted that some work could be devoid of pleasure. Edna Ferber, Zona Gale, Ruth Suckow, and Edith Summers Kelley wrote of the soul-deadening, spirit-crushing monotony of women's unfulfilling, unpleasurable drudgery, while Dorothy Parker and Anita Loos wrote of the comic humiliations on all sides of those transactions in which women make a living because of their sex appeal rather than real work. Loos's Lorelei Lee, in *Gentlemen Prefer Blondes* (1925), is forever complaining about how fatiguing her life of finagling diamond tiaras is, a kind of backhanded compliment to real work, as is the original subtitle: *The Illuminating Diary of a Professional Lady.*

Work is a crucial element in Fitzgerald's *The Great Gatsby* (1925)—or rather its conspicuous near absence is. Because they don't work enough, the characters suffer from nervousness. Gatsby nervously drums his fingers. Nick Carraway, the narrator, describes himself as "restless." Daisy and Tom Buchanan anxiously flit about the world. Carraway works a little—he has gone into the bond business, but has done so while being supported by his father, and he seems to have plenty of time to cavort with the idle rich of East Egg. Gatsby, whose wealth is at first a mystery, and Meyer Wolfsheim, the gangster whose riches are slightly less mysterious in origin, siphon wealth without any normal work schedule or a conventional relation between effort and reward. The closest thing to a worker in Gatsby's social group is Jordan Baker, who is a professional golfer; she too seems never to train and rarely to compete.

The characters are, therefore, bored. "What will we do," asks Daisy, "this afternoon, and tomorrow and for the next thirty years?" Modern technology, servants, and money make life workless. "There was a machine in the kitchen," Carraway tells us in describing Gatsby's house, "which could extract the juice of two hundred oranges in half an hour if a little button was pressed two hundred times by a butler's thumb." The utopian's machines have taken over, leaving people (both Daisy and the butler) without meaningful work. After Gatsby is killed, his father comes to the funeral carrying Gatsby's childhood copy of *Hopalong Cassidy*. He opens it and shows Carraway the inside back cover, in which was written:

SCHEDULE

Rise from bed	6.00 A.M.
Dumbbell exercise and wall-scaling	6.15–6.30 A.M.
Study electricity, etc.	7.15–8.15 A.M.
Work	8.30–4.30 P.M.
Baseball and sports	4.30–5.00 P.M.
Practice elocution, poise and how to attain it	5.00–6.00 P.M.
Study needed inventions	7.00–9.00 P.M.

GENERAL RESOLVES

No wasting time at Shafters or [a name, indecipherable]

No more smokeing or chewing

Bath every other day

Read one improving book or magazine per week
Save $5.00 [crossed out] $3.00 per week
Be better to parents

Gatsby, the leisured gentleman, started out as Benjamin Franklin did, complete with the electricity, inventions, and admonitions toward moral perfection. "It just shows you," Gatsby's father says. "Jimmy was bound to get ahead. He always had some resolves like this or something."

The Great Gatsby is an unmistakably nostalgic novel, and what it is most nostalgic for is honest work. Fitzgerald himself later wrote that he had "an animosity toward the leisure class, not the conviction of a revolutionist, but the smoldering hatred of the peasant." The rich slackers Tom and Daisy spout nonsense and leave casualties in their wake. They have everything, the characters in this novel, all the money and things they should want—think of all Gatsby's beautiful shirts—and it brings them no pleasure. All around them, the novels, advice manuals, magazines, and films announce the answer loud and clear: work is the only lasting pleasure. The new professions, like bond sales, have nothing to recommend them, and the shenanigans of barbaric gangsters are obviously worse.

Hemingway made very similar arguments. His famous images of endless drunken parties and lounging café society, bookended by days and days of fishing and skiing, should not obscure the fact that Hemingway had a very strong work ethic. The slackers he described, however much they became models for pseudo-artists for decades to come, were actually objects of Hemingway's scorn. The Greenwich Village poseurs who invaded Paris in 1922 are scum, he wrote, scum that "has been skimmed off and deposited in large ladlesful on that section of Paris adjacent to the Café Rotonde," their main sin that they talk about art instead of working at it. "By talking about art," he wrote sarcastically, "they obtain the same satisfaction that the real artist does in his work. They have no time to work at anything else; they put in a full day at the Rotonde." Real artists do real work; pseudo-artists do pseudo-work. "What I had to do was work," he wrote later, in *The Green Hills of Africa*. "I did not care, particularly, how it all came out. I did not take my own life seriously any more, any one else's life, yes, but not mine. They all wanted something that I did not

want and I would get it without wanting it, if I worked." And Hemingway, even more than Fitzgerald, had a purely hedonistic view of why.
"To work was the only thing, it was the one thing that always made
you feel good."

∞

The hedonistic work ethic of the 1920s was accompanied by a faint
but audible (and equally hedonistic) slacker ethic. If Hemingway and
many other high-end writers and artists found in work the "one thing"
that would make them feel good, others continued to insist that life
"on the bum" was the only way to experience the joys of life. The
composer Ernest Block crowed, on moving to Santa Fe in the 1920s,
"Thanks be to God, I have found a place in America where men can
do nothing." Commissioner of Indian affairs John Collier claimed
that the "indolently industrious" Pueblos experienced the "fullness of
life through leisure." The painter Robert Henri argued that the option
"to work or not to work" is essential to nourishing the artistic sensibility, and Dorothy Parker quipped much more bluntly, "Work is the
province of cattle." Others helped sow the seeds of a widespread cultural confusion about work and slackerdom that would then frame the
growing unemployment of the 1930s. The Southern Agrarians, for instance, argued at the end of the decade both for pleasurable work and
for its cessation, in particular for a return to classical notions of *otium*.

The Agrarians, a group of writers, historians, sociologists, and other
academics based at Vanderbilt University in Nashville, thought that
the only way to recover a world in which labor was pleasurable was
through a full frontal attack on industrialism. Industrialism, they decided during the 1920s, was the prime cause of everything that was
wrong with America. Industrialism destroys everything but itself, and
this is not primarily, as we have grown accustomed to thinking, because industry is directly destroying the planet—annihilating the
ozone layer and melting the polar ice caps while polluting the water
we drink and air we breathe—but because of the way it makes us
work. "The first principle of a good labor is that it must be effective,
but the second principle is that it must be enjoyed," wrote the Agrarians in their manifesto, *I'll Take My Stand*, in 1930. "The act of labor
as one of the happy functions of human life has been in effect abandoned, and is practiced solely for its rewards." Since labor takes up

such an enormous part of any person's life, they declared, "it is a modest demand to ask that it may partake of happiness." Under industrialism, "labor becomes mercenary and servile," and things are so far gone, they thought, that people don't even complain about the work they do, even though it is "evidently brutalizing."

The Agrarians—foremost among them John Crowe Ransom, Robert Penn Warren, and Allen Tate—had a hedonistic work ethic like Hemingway's, but they disagreed with his belief that work was all one needed. Leisure, in the classical sense of free time for higher pursuits—philosophy, literature, art—was the only reasonable goal for individuals and for a society. The leisure that Americans partook of in the 1920s, they wrote, was of "dubious benefit," since it really was disguised consumption, not true leisure. "The kind of leisure provided by industrialism . . . helps nobody but merchants and manufacturers, who have taught us to use it in industriously consuming the products they make in great excess over the demand." We work frantically, and then we play frantically, and neither does us any good. "The furious pace of our work hours is carried over into our leisure hours, which are feverish and energetic. We live by the clock. Our days are a muddle of 'activities,' strenuously pursued. We do not have the free mind and easy temper that should characterize true leisure." We separate our lives into two parts, they wrote, one of which is mechanical, deadening labor and the other play "undertaken as nervous relief," and neither are "conducive to the harmonious life."

The Agrarians were college professors, many of them professors of literature, and one sometimes gets the sense that they protest too much. On the other end of the work hierarchy, people were also interested in throwing off mechanical labors, perhaps more straightforwardly. Down the road in Knoxville, Tennessee, a working-class kid named Harry McClintock had had some disagreements with his father, and in 1896, at the age of fourteen, he left home for good, heading out on a freight train. The next six years found him alternately on the bum and working civilian jobs in the Philippines during the Spanish-American War, in China during the Boxer Rebellion, and in South Africa during the Boer War. In 1903 or so he came back to the United States, having somewhere picked up the nickname Haywire Mac, and began working for the IWW in Spokane. When he was still a very young hobo, he sang folk songs and played the guitar, singing for handout suppers. He wrote new lyrics to old hymns, one he called "Hallelujah on the Bum." "There were only two or three verses at first," he said later, "but new ones practically wrote themselves. The junglestiffs liked the song and so did the saloon audiences, most of whom had hit the road at one time or another, and the rollicking, devil-may-care lilt of the thing appealed to them." He sang the song for soldiers in a Spanish-American War training camp, and they added new verses. After the war they took the song home with them to different regions of the country. The original lyrics are these:

> *Why don't you work like other folks do?*
> *How the hell can I work when there's no work to do?*
> > *CHORUS:*
> > *Hallelujah, I'm a bum,*
> > *Hallelujah, bum again,*
> > *Hallelujah, give us a handout*
> > *To revive us again.*
> *Oh, why don't you save all the money you earn?*
> *If I didn't eat, I'd have money to burn.*
> > *(CHORUS)*
> *Whenever I get all the money I earn,*
> *The boss will be broke, and to work he must turn.*
> > *(CHORUS)*
> *Oh, I like my boss, he's a good friend of mine,*
> *That's why I am starving out on the breadline.*
> > *(CHORUS)*
> *When springtime it comes, oh, won't we have fun;*
> *We'll throw off our jobs, and go on the bum.*

In the late 1920s a dozen different versions of the song were available as sheet music, and several recordings were made during the decade. McClintock recorded the song himself in 1926 and went to court to sue others for copyright infringement, managing, in the end, to establish his authorship.

McClintock's more famous song was also a hobo hymn, "Big Rock Candy Mountain," made famous again by Burl Ives in the 1950s and in the Coen brothers' *O Brother, Where Art Thou* in 2000. McClintock originally recorded it at the Hollywood Bowl in 1928.

One evening as the sun went down, and the jungle fires were burning,
Down the track came a hobo hiking, and he said, "Boys, I'm not
  turning
I'm headed for a land that's far away besides the crystal fountains
So come with me, we'll go and see The Big Rock Candy Mountains."

In the Big Rock Candy Mountains, the song continues, "handouts grow on bushes," the boxcars are always empty, and there are cigarette trees and lemonade springs. The song describes a hobo's paradise, where "all the cops have wooden legs, and the bulldogs all have rubber teeth and the hens lay soft-boiled eggs." The combination of freedom from work, freedom from harassment, and plentiful alcohol was specific to the hobo lifestyle, but it had obvious resonance to a wider audience:

In the Big Rock Candy Mountains you never change your socks,
And the little streams of alcohol come trickling down the rocks.
The brakemen have to tip their hats and the railway bulls are blind,
There's a lake of stew and of whiskey too,
You can paddle all around it in a big canoe.
    In the Big Rock Candy Mountains.
In the Big Rock Candy Mountains, the jails are made of tin.
And you can walk right out again, as soon as you are in.
There ain't no short-handled shovels, no axes, saws nor picks,
I'm bound to stay where you sleep all day,
Where they hung the jerk that invented work.
    In the Big Rock Candy Mountains.

McClintock was a classic slacker advocate. Called "the hardest-working bum on the West Coast," he continued to perform on the radio, recorded dozens of sides, worked as an actor (including in a couple of Gene Autry Westerns), and wrote a regular column for a national railroad magazine, all the while, from his mid-twenties on, working full-time as a brakeman. When he retired, he took a job with the Los Angeles Harbor Department, where he was when Burl Ives put his song back on the charts.

By the 1930s, riding the rails and sleeping rough were more common experiences as men were forced on the road to look for work, and songs like McClintock's had broader resonance. "Hallelujah, I'm a Bum" is at the center of a famously bad film from 1933 by the same name. Starring Al Jolson, with the rest of the music by Richard Rodgers and lyrics by Lorenz Hart, the film is a bit of Hollywood fluff, with Jolson working way too hard at being an amiable bum named Bumper (a name that deftly references his hitching free rides on the bumpers of cars, a bumper of Scotch, the bumpers of a billiard table, and the fact that he's a bum). Hart added some new lyrics to McClintock's song:

> *Hobo, you've no time to shirk, you're busy keeping far away from*
>   *work.*
> *The weather's getting fine. The coffee tastes like wine.*
> *You happy hobo, sing, "Hallelujah, I'm a bum again!"*

The new lyrics replace the real economic complaints of McClintock's version with irony ("busy keeping away from work") and replace obvious gripes with Tin Pan Alley pastoral ("the coffee tastes like wine"). The film also features a McClintock-like IWW socialist, named Egghead in deference to his big ideas, who hates slaving for the city (he picks up trash) and looks forward to a worker's revolution. He has a gospel of work, though, calling the bums like Jolson's character "parasites of parasites." You call yourself free, he tells Bumper, but you are a slave to cash just like the fat cats, living on handouts instead of your own labor: "Your socks and pants may have holes," he sings, "But you're plutocrats down to your souls."

Bumper, improbably beloved by everyone in his orbit, finally falls in love himself and decides to get a job. He wants to work at a bank, get promoted, "get promoted again," own his own bank, and give his love everything "she deserves." His African American friend Acorn wants no part—"Gotta shave every morning like a white-collah slave"—but he is Bumper's sidekick and quasi-valet, so if Bumper goes to work, then he has to go, too. The rest of the hobos put Bumper on trial for treason and find him guilty. When it all falls apart, the lover vanished and the jobs left behind, Acorn is overjoyed to be back on the bum again, and Bumper relaxes into his park bench with a smile.

The film was released in 1933, as men hit the rails and roads looking for work and the place of the hobo in American culture was changing dramatically. Ben Reitman's distinctions—that the hobo traveled looking for work, the tramp traveled without looking for work, and the bum neither traveled nor worked—broke down, in part because of the sheer number of men looking for work (on the road or at home) and not finding it. By the end of the decade, in serious works like Steinbeck's *The Grapes of Wrath* (1939) and comedies like Preston Sturges's *Sullivan's Travels* (1941), the relation between working and not working, and that between the haves and the have-nots, was stripped of whatever leftover Victorian morality was still there. Instead of blaming the poor for their plight or impugning their work ethic, people began to see poverty as an unintended consequence of economic life—a change in perspective that helped make the postwar welfare state possible. In the dire climate of Depression want, those who were working tended more often than not to feel lucky, while the unemployed 20 percent of the working population, without a paycheck and without a welfare system, stood in breadlines and battled for what few jobs were offered. Like the rest of the culture in the early 1930s, *Hallelujah, I'm a Bum* was simply confused about the way traditional bootstrap ambition, economic theory, dreams of wealth, class distinctions, leisure, and laziness translated into moral categories. Later in the decade, much of the confusion was replaced by despair.

Bing Crosby had had a hit with perhaps the classic song of a man on the bum, "Brother, Can You Spare a Dime?" in 1932. E. Y. "Yip" Harburg, who wrote the lyrics (for a musical that bombed before Crosby's recording), later said of the song's narrator that he isn't bitter: "He's bewildered. Here is a man who had built his faith and hope in this country . . . Then came the crash. Now he can't accept the fact that the bubble has burst. He still believes. He still has faith. He just doesn't understand what could have happened to make everything go so wrong":

> They used to tell me I was building a dream
> With peace and glory ahead—
> Why should I be standing in line, just waiting for bread?

The disillusionment has not turned to revolutionary anger or class resentment (despite the "they"), but it remains full of questions, bafflement. Another song from 1933, "Remember My Forgotten Man" (lyrics by Al Dubin), is sung by a woman who has lost her man first to the war and now to unemployed tramping:

> Remember my forgotten man, you had him cultivate the land;
> He walked behind the plow, the sweat fell from his brow,
> But look at him right now!

But again the upshot is unclear. The first lines simply state, "I don't know if he deserves sympathy, / Forget your sympathy, that's all right with me," even though the song is, in fact, pleading for sympathy. The song, by Harry Warren, was introduced in *Gold Diggers of 1933*, a huge Busby Berkeley musical, and the song ended as an upbeat, hopeful dance number, the chorus forming the National Recovery Administration eagle center stage. By the late 1930s, such spectacles were harder to pull off, and bums were more often represented as stoic victims than confused comic fantasies. Work and being on the bum, in the context of the worldwide Depression, were ethical puzzles, not the stuff of slacker comedy or pious prescription.

∞

Bertrand Russell, the British philosopher, mathematician, polymath, and activist, wrote a thoroughgoing critique of the industrial work ethic around the time of the Jolson film. "Like most of my generation, I was brought up on the saying 'Satan finds some mischief still for idle hands to do,'" he recounted in "In Praise of Idleness," first published in *Harper's Magazine* in October of 1932. "Being a highly virtuous child, I believed all that I was told, and acquired a conscience that has kept me working hard down to the present moment." But despite this training he could not escape, he had, in recent years, re-formed his understanding of work. "I think that there is far too much work done in the world, that immense harm is caused by the belief that work is virtuous, and that what needs to be preached in modern industrial countries is quite different from what always has been preached." He hoped for "a great propaganda campaign" that would inaugurate an era of increased idleness. "I hope that, after reading the following pages, the leaders of the YMCA will start a campaign to induce good young men to do nothing. If so, I shall not have lived in vain."

This sounds like another lounger or loafer satire, but Russell has a different goal. Leisure used to be the province of the upper classes, he argues, but now, thanks to modern industry, the right to leisure can be distributed evenly to everyone. The work ethic was the cumulative effect of years of forcing powerless peasants to produce more than they needed to support the idle warriors and priests above them. "The concept of people's duty to work, speaking historically, has been a means used by the holders of power to induce others to live for the interest of their masters rather than their own." Now, since the introduction of machines in productive processes, everything people want can be produced by wage earners working four hours a day, Russell claims, thus repeating the recommendation of John Smith for Jamestown in 1612 and coming in an hour longer than Paul Lafargue in 1883. "Only a foolish asceticism makes us continue to insist on work in excessive quantities now that the need no longer exists."

Russell himself did so much work that it took him four volumes of autobiography just to describe it. His *Collected Papers* come to some thirty-four volumes, and when "In Praise of Idleness" came out, he had published twenty-two books in as many years, while working as a professor, founding an elementary school based on his educational theories, lecturing in China for a year on philosophy, running for public office, giving radio addresses, and working as an activist for peace, social democracy, women's rights, and other causes. He encouraged the original slackers—the draft dodgers—during World War I and was fined, fired from his academic post, and finally imprisoned for antiwar protests. His activism remained pronounced enough that he was again dismissed from his professorship at City College, New York, in 1940, after being deemed "morally unfit" to teach by a New York court. He was arrested the last time and sent to prison for organizing a large peace demonstration in London in 1961, when he was eighty-nine years old. He published another half dozen books after that.

Russell's argument was that the kind of activities he was engaged in—writing, public argument, reading, political action—were activities of a different order than the chores that survival required, and that they were the right of all:

> In a world where no one is compelled to work more than four hours a day, every person possessed of scientific curiosity will be able to indulge it, and every painter will be able to paint without starving,

however excellent his pictures may be. Young writers will not be obligated to draw attention to themselves by sensational potboilers, with a view to acquiring the economic independence needed for monumental works, for which, when the time at last comes, they will have lost the taste and the capacity. Men who, in their professional work, have become interested in some phase of economics or government, will be able to develop their ideas without the academic detachment that makes the work of university economists often seem lacking in reality. Medical men will have time to learn about the progress of medicine, teachers will not be exasperatedly struggling to teach by routine methods things that they learned in their youth, which may, in the interval, have been proved untrue.

The goal was not, as in Lafargue's case, the right to be lazy, but the right to be active. Russell wanted not to redistribute wealth but to redistribute leisure and, thereby, the ability of all to practice any and all of the arts and intellectual pursuits and to enjoy any and all of the games and entertainments the culture has to offer:

> Leisure is essential to civilization, and in former times leisure for the few was only rendered possible by the labors of the many. Their labors were valuable, not because work is good, but because leisure is good. And with modern labor-saving techniques it would be possible to distribute leisure justly without injury to civilization.

The rich have always been "shocked," Russell writes, by the idea that the poor should have leisure, arguing that they would turn to drink and dissipation. In the nineteenth century, men worked fifteen hours a day, children worked twelve, and anyone who suggested things should be arranged otherwise was considered a meddlesome busybody. Allowing working-class people leisure time, the rich thought, encouraged the adults to drink and the young to mischief.

But leisure is degraded for the poor, says Russell, only because they work too much. With less work, leisure will be appropriately used:

> Since men will not be tired in their spare time, they will not demand only such amusements as are passive and vapid. At least one percent will probably devote the time not spent in professional work

in pursuits of some public importance, and, since they will not depend upon these pursuits for their livelihood, their originality will
be unhampered. But it is not only in these exceptional cases that the
advantages of leisure will appear . . . Good nature is, of all moral
qualities, the one that the world needs most, and good nature is the
result of ease and security, not a life of arduous struggle and hard
work.

Russell wanted not a Marxist revolution, but a rational one. He was
not a fan of the Soviet experience; he visited Russia in the 1920s and
was unimpressed. The work ethic that evolved with capitalist industry
simply needed to be reined in:

Let us, for a moment, consider the ethics of work frankly, without
superstition. Every human being, of necessity, consumes, in the
course of his life, a certain amount of the produce of human labor.
Assuming as we may that labor is on the whole disagreeable, it is unjust that a man should consume more than he produces. Of course,
he may provide services rather than commodities, like a medical
man, for example; but he should provide something in return for his
board and lodging. To this extent, the duty of work must be acknowledged, but to this extent only.

Just as the rediscovery of the pleasures of work by the middle class in
the 1920s was an effect of the roller-coaster booms and busts of that
decade, Russell's view of necessarily disagreeable labor and of egalitar-
ian economic principles as the basis of an ethics of work became
much more common in the 1930s.

The middle-class recuperation of work in the 1920s included an
understanding that valuable work was voluntary. Labor enforced
through poverty, mindless factory work, farm labor for workers with no
other choices: these were never what the proponents of pleasurable
work had in mind. By the 1930s, as jobs disappeared in the global Depression, easy distinctions between classes and kinds of work were van-
ishing along with confidence in the ability of people to make their
own choices. Not surprisingly, then, the culture of the late 1930s presents a complicated picture of the various attitudes toward work and
doing nothing. The drawings, paintings, and photographs of the 1930s

reflect this mix of cultural options, from Hugo Gellert's Soviet-poster-style, heavily muscled heroic workers in overalls, sledgehammers in hand, to the gothic mixtures of glory and degradation in Thomas Hart Benton's work. Many artists represented dispossessed characters, as in the paintings of Mabel Dwight, Reginald Marsh, and Eli Jacobi and the photography of Walker Evans and Dorothea Lange. Film, too, registered the flux. Charlie Chaplin's *Modern Times* (1936) was, like its insistence on not using sound for dialogue, a bit of a throwback, a recapitulation of ideas from the 1920s that were obviously still somewhat current, ideas about alienated factory workers dominated by their own machines. In contrast, in the film version of *The Grapes of Wrath* (1940), as in the book, the plight of the jobless makes work a simple good, and the right-thinking people are those who want the dignity of labor.

Images of degraded labor and degraded leisure were also still abundant. As in *The Crowd* or *Metropolis*, Chaplin's picture of the work world in *Modern Times* shows industrial work as an oppressive, deadening force, the machinery itself a cruel master. The image of the Little Tramp, older, sadder, and dressed in a worker's overalls rather than his tramp's glad rags, is poignant, as if the character's moment, like silent film itself, was a historical artifact. The fear of mechanization—as in the famous scene in which Chaplin is sucked in by the gears of the machine—is less of a pressing issue in the 1930s than it was in the 1920s. By the 1930s, many like Russell again saw the machine as a source of liberation rather than oppression. Slacker characters were often unsympathetic, quasi-aristocratic characters in the late 1930s and early 1940s, the classic version being Monty in James M. Cain's *Mildred Pierce* (novel 1941, film 1945). Mildred asks the handsome Monty what he does. "I loaf." She looks aghast. "In a decorative and highly charming manner," he adds. "Is that all?" she asks. "With me," he says, "loafing is a science." After this humorous opening, Monty turns out to be a complete heel, and Mildred's work ethic is meant to be heroic if a bit monomaniacal.

There is also a more interesting take on work and slacking emerging at the same time. George Cukor's romantic comedy *Holiday* (1938) and Frank Capra's *You Can't Take It with You* (1938) look forward to the postwar world of the Beat Generation and the sociological critique of Organization Men, and like Russell, they keep alive the notion of satisfying work that is entirely outside the wage system, a dream of throwing off the base idiocies of work as we know it. They insisted, along with Veblen, than not all work was created equal, that not all labor could satisfy the human desire for meaningful work. In *Holiday*, Cary Grant outrages his prospective father-in-law by deciding not to join his new family's financial firm. Grant plays, as he was himself, a working-class boy who has already made good and who, because he has been financially successful and because he hasn't grown up in the Establishment, can think for himself, decide for himself how he wants to spend the next few years. Instead of going to work for his father-in-law, he wants to go on an indefinite holiday. "I've been working since I was ten," he explains. "I want to find out why I'm working. The answer can't be just to pay bills or pile up more money. Even if you do, the government's going to take most of it." His fiancée is under the sway of her father and finds his refusal to continue getting richer perverse.

If she won't have him, though, as the blues songs are fond of saying, then her sister will. The sister, played by Katharine Hepburn, is a freethinker herself, and she applauds his Thoreauvian moratorium. "The world's changing out there," he tells her as she gazes at him admiringly. "There's a lot of exciting ideas running around. Some of them may be right and some of them may be cockeyed, but they're affecting all our lives. I want to know how I stand, where I fit in the picture. I can't find the answer sitting behind a desk." Yes, she says, although as an heiress without a career, it doesn't apply to her directly; yes.

This, as opposed to *Modern Times*, is something new under the sun. The idea that the world is changing and that this requires a thoughtful person to stop working may have been part of earlier slackers' motivation, but it certainly was never so consciously articulated. In the following scene, Grant's character, Johnny, tries to explain it to his father-in-law.

JOHNNY

I don't want too much money.

FATHER-IN-LAW
(astounded)

Too much money?

JOHNNY

Well, more than I need to live by. You see, it's always been my idea
to make a few thousands early in the game and then quit for as long
as they last and try to find out who I am and what goes on and what
about, now, when I'm young and I feel good all the time. Well, I'm
sure Julie understands what I'm getting at, don't you, Julie?

JULIE
(unhappy)

I'm not sure I do, Johnny.

FATHER-IN-LAW

You want to occupy yourself otherwise, is that it?

JOHNNY

Please don't make me feel guilty about it, sir. Even if it turns out to
be one of those fool ideas that people dream about and then go flat
on, even if I find I've had enough of it in three months, still I want
it. I've got a feeling if I let this chance go by, there'll never be another one for me, so I don't think anyone will mind if I have a go at
it, will they, Julie?

But of course Julie does mind. She doesn't need the money—in fact,
the family first suspects that Johnny is interested in her for her
money—but she wants him working and earning it just the same.

"I want to save part of my life for myself," Johnny explains. "It's got
to be part of the young part, you know: retire young, work old. Come
back when I know what I'm working for." Johnny doesn't invent this
quasi–anti-work ethic alone. He is mentored in his countercultural
ways by a couple of Bohemian college professors. They never spout
any anti-work rhetoric, they just approve of Johnny's decision, and
they are very uncomfortable among the rich go-getters. They drink
Chianti from basketed bottles and have eccentric artist friends who
wear berets and have foreign accents. The film is based on Philip
Barry's 1928 play of the same name, and it was first made into a film
in 1930. In both these earlier versions Johnny's two friends are not serious intellectuals but Fitzgeraldesque partygoers, blasé boneheads
with no other real plans, ideals, or ideas. The professors in the 1938

version, on the other hand, feel that Johnny's quest is important, and they encourage him not because they want to play with him, but because they believe that it is the only good and right thing for him to do. Like Russell, they are countercultural intellectuals, critical of a system in which money rules and art and introspection suffer.

These countercultural characters were not alone. Frank Capra's *You Can't Take It with You* from the same year (based on a Kaufman and Hart play on Broadway two years earlier) is the story of "crazy" old Grandpa Vanderhof (Lionel Barrymore) who opens his house to artists and inventors, a place where "everybody does just what they want to do." In explaining it to his daughter's prospective father-in-law, a successful businessman, Vanderhof uses a different argument from the one in *Holiday*: "I used to be just like you, and then one morning when I was going up in the elevator, it struck me that I wasn't having any fun, so I came right down and I never went back. That was thirty-five years ago." The 1920s hedonistic defense of work is here used to argue against having a job. If it isn't enjoyable, just don't do it. The result is a houseful of people making art, practicing dance, building rockets in the basement, and inventing ingenious products. Doing nothing was not an option, but the rejection of work for hire was nearly total. Jack Kerouac was sixteen when *Holiday* and *You Can't Take It with You* came out, and William Burroughs was already twenty-four. The stage was clearly set for the Beat Generation. Vanderhof's inmates and Johnny's crew of intellectuals and artists would be called, in just a few short years, Beats and Angry Young Men—a group of countercultural types dedicated to art instead of work, to ideas instead of material comforts, to a principled hedonism rather than conventional success.

But first the war intervened. With the United States gearing up for and finally entering World War II in 1941, the epidemic of joblessness came to an end, and wartime patriotism, for a time, largely supplanted other ways of talking about the work ethic in the mainstream of American culture. Nonetheless, even during the war, slacker cultures (pachucos, lindy hoppers, proto-Beats like those in *You Can't Take It with You* and *Holiday*, and Russellian pacifists) provided a counterpoint to the new patriotic work ethic. Don Tosti had a million-selling hit with "Pachuco Boogie"—a phenomenal feat for a regional Spanish-language record—followed by "Wine-O-Boogie" and "El Tirili (The Reefer Man)," celebrating a work-free dance- and drug-filled lifestyle in a Mexican American youth subculture that in fact continued to experience high rates of unemployment. Chester Himes, in *If He Hollers Let Him Go* (1945) and *Lonely Crusade* (1947), made it clear that the traditional work ethic was no match for rampant racism in the shipyards of southern California. Malcolm X, in the early forties, lived a life of drug-dealing crime and established himself in Harlem as a successful man completely outside conventional work ideologies. The Beat Generation's inaugural meeting of Ginsberg, Kerouac, Burroughs, and Herbert Huncke took place in New York in 1944, and that year Kerouac and Burroughs collaborated on a novel, *And the Hippos Were Boiled in Their Tanks*. The work ethic was losing its grip, and the slacker rebels were looking for a cause. The postwar world was already under serious reconstruction.

VII

BEATS, NONCONFORMISTS, PLAYBOYS, AND DELINQUENTS

In which new generations of the disaffected reinvent the slacker wheel as the world of work changes once again—Jack Kerouac and his dad have a falling out—the Man in the Gray Flannel Suit gets ahead and feels bad—Organization Man, white-collar workers, and other conformist losers—and women try on the flight from commitment.

Jack Kerouac's father was regularly disappointed. A printer in Lowell, Massachusetts, he loved watching his son play football in high school—the younger Kerouac had been his school's star running back and had been scouted by several universities—and hoped to watch him repeat his great success at Boston University. Against his father's wishes, Jack chose Columbia over Boston and left for New York. He spent a year at Horace Mann in New York preparing for Columbia and playing football with some success, but when he joined the Columbia team the next year, he and his father were both put out by how little he got to play. Then he broke his leg in a game and spent a couple of months in a cast, lounging in the training room, smoking a pipe, and reading literature. He came to think of the broken leg as a fortunate accident and relished the role of retired hero.

He went back to Columbia for his second year, and when it was again clear that he wouldn't be a starter on the team, he walked out. It was 1941, and many of his classmates were quitting school to enlist.

Kerouac instead aimlessly returned to his parents' new apartment in New Haven, where they had moved—his father's alcoholism led to many moves, as many as twenty in twenty years. Jack decided to return home, he wrote later, because of a profound realization he had after an intense daydream. In the daydream, he becomes a big football star in college and, after being the hero of the Rose Bowl, goes on to play professional ball for the New York Giants. At the same time, he becomes a famous author, feted about town and celebrated as "the greatest writer who ever lived," *and* is recruited as a professional boxer, becoming heavyweight champion of the world. He snaps to from this daydream realizing that his ambitions were ridiculously overblown, juvenile, and unreachable; they were, he realized, simply vanity. "It just didn't matter what I did, anytime, anywhere, with anyone," he concluded with a kind of reverse adolescent grandiosity.

This is, throughout the century, a standard narrative for slackers: because exceptional accomplishment looks unlikely, no achievement seems worthwhile. Doing nothing, many slackers have decided, is preferable to doing something, but nothing special. In telling the story of this period of his life in *Vanity of Duluoz* (1968), Kerouac asks himself, "Did I come into this world through the womb of my mother the earth just so I could talk and write just like everybody else?" He is convinced that, like the protagonist of *The Crowd* fifteen years earlier, he has some special task and some exceptional recognition awaiting him in the world. At the same time, he "suddenly realizes" that "we were all crazy and had nothing to work for except the next meal and the next good sleep." The rejection of striving is brought on, paradoxically, by an almost maniacal belief in his (possible) future achievements.

Kerouac believed that his decision to quit Columbia, he wrote in *Vanity of Duluoz*, was "the most important decision of my life so far." He hops on a bus and heads south, in a literary pilgrimage to Thomas Wolfe's hometown. "What I was doing was telling everybody to go jump in the big fat ocean of their own folly. I was telling myself to go jump in the big fat ocean of my own folly. What a bath!" He feels cleansed, free, and happy. But he runs out of money by the time he gets to Washington and has to turn around and head back to his parents in New Haven. His father is "mad as hell" about his decision, and when Kerouac quits a job after a single morning, his father tells him to leave:

> It's not that we don't want you in the house, but I have to walk a mile to that printing plant every morning, your mother remember was wiping tables at the Waldorf Cafeteria in New Haven last week while you were supposed to be making the football team. Here we whack along in the same pickle as ever. Why don't you people ever do right?

Kerouac leaves, saying to his father, "I'll show you." "Show me what you little punk?" "I'll show you that I'm going to become a great writer."

He moves into his own apartment in Hartford and works briefly pumping gas, feeling, he later wrote, like "a character in a Burgess Meredith movie," until he is fired. At night he writes short stories at his kitchen table, looking out a window at a brick wall that reminds him of "Bartleby the Scrivener." His parents return to Lowell, and he follows, landing a job writing for the *Lowell Sun* as a sportswriter, and his father is now extremely proud. Kerouac drops his belief in the futility of everyday achievement and revels in "whipping out my college sports coat and pants and regaining ye old necktie glamour at the desk in the bright morning of men and business things." But he also likes the job, he writes, because the work takes him only three hours a day, and the rest of the time he can sneak work on his novel. (In that novel—the unpublished *The Sea Is My Brother*—he describes himself as "one of Earth's biggest slothards.") One day even this abbreviated schedule seems too oppressive, and instead of going to interview a high school baseball coach, he goes home instead. "I just sat in my room and stared at the wall and fluffed off and said 'Ah hell, shuck, I'm not going anywhere to interview nobody.' They called, I didn't answer the phone. I just stayed home and stared at the wall." He and his father fight about it, and Kerouac has nothing to say in his own defense. He leaves on a bus to go south again.

In Washington, another friend helps him get short-lived jobs as a construction laborer and soda jerk. His construction job, as a sheet-metal journeyman's helper, proves to be very easy, as the worker drinks and often leaves work very early, after which Kerouac sleeps in a culvert. He wanders around the jobsite doing nothing and then goes into town, drinking gin and sightseeing in his work clothes. He quits and takes a lunch counter job, which he also quits to once again head back to Lowell. Once there in 1942, against his father's wishes, he joins the navy (complete with photographs, fingerprints, and signed contracts), has quite a few drinks, and later the same day joins the coast guard, has a few more drinks, and then immediately goes to the National Maritime Union Hall, where he begs for a seaman's job. He ships out that week on the SS *Dorchester* (he later said the job was "a sort of holiday" in which he imagined himself to be Melville), telling his father he would be home late, not to wait up.

That was early in the spring. He didn't return until October. When he came home, he reenrolled at Columbia, again joined the football team, again wasn't used in the first game, and again quit. His father came to plead with the coach, but Kerouac's football career was over, and shortly thereafter so was his college career. Too restless to stay at Columbia, he enlisted a second time in the navy, this time actually showing up for basic training. Not surprisingly, he hated military discipline, and one morning, only a month into his training, he simply threw his rifle on the ground during a routine drill, walked off the field, and went to the base library to read a book. He was taken for observation to a navy psychiatric ward. When a psychiatrist asked him who he thought he was, Kerouac answered, "I'm only old Sam Johnson." He meant, he later explained, that he was an independent thinker and an artistic idler. He was discharged after six months with an "indifferent character." He was twenty-one years old. His father decided that he was a worthless freeloader.

In 1944, back from his aborted military career, he met Lucien Carr, William Burroughs, and Allen Ginsberg, and the Beat movement was more or less born. When he was jailed as a material witness in the murder of David Kammerer by Lucien Carr (another story, but part of standard Beat lore) on August 14, 1944, his father refused to bail him out, telling him he could go to hell. A woman named Edie Parker, a friend of Ginsberg's, did bail him out and then married Kerouac the next week. He moved with her to Michigan, where her family was, and took a job as a ball-bearing inspector. But the job and the marriage lasted only a few months. Carr was sent to prison, and Kerouac signed up for another stint as an able-bodied seaman in the merchant marine. Before the ship even left port, though, he changed his mind and jumped ship. Now—his marriage, his military career, his college days, and his career as a sailor all burned bridges—Kerouac moved into Ginsberg's dorm room at Columbia and began writing his first to-be-published novel, *The Town and the City* (1950)—at least in part to justify himself to his father. It is a hardly veiled autobiographical story leading up to his arrest. The college eventually kicked Jack out, after which he moved into Burroughs's apartment on Riverside Drive. When Burroughs was arrested on drug charges, Kerouac was homeless again and moved back home with his parents. In 1946 his father died at the age of fifty-seven. Kerouac was twenty-five.

It was at this time that Neal Cassady arrived on the scene. Memorialized as Dean Moriarty in *On the Road* (1957) and later as himself in Tom Wolfe's *Electric Kool-Aid Acid Test* (1968), the legendarily handsome and charismatic Cassady had grown up in the hobo jungles of the West, riding freight trains and living on the streets. He convinced Kerouac to take his first cross-country hitchhiking trip in 1947, and Kerouac spent the next few years bouncing around the country, often with Cassady, to New Orleans, San Francisco, Mexico City, Denver, and back to Mexico, with occasional spates of writing back at his sister's house in North Carolina or at his mother's in Ozone Park, New York. He wrote about these travels in what would become *On the Road*, around the time *The Town and the City* was published to good reviews but poor sales. Kerouac brought his famous first draft of *On the Road*, typed on a 250-foot-long roll of paper, to his editor, Robert Giroux. When Giroux, who had spent what he considered an inordinate amount of time excising bloated passages from *The Town and the City*, started to talk to Kerouac about revisions, Kerouac walked out in a huff.

He was developing, at that time, the perfect slacker theory of composition. He would later draft his principles as "Essentials of Spontaneous Prose," in which he recommended thinking of literary language as an "undisturbed flow from the mind," with no revisions, preferably written in a state of semi-trance, "without consciousness." Writing thus produced, with no censor, no craft, no editing either during or after, was the essence, he argued, of literary expression. "Never afterthink to 'improve' or defray impressions, as, the best writing is always the most painful personal wrung-out tossed from cradle warm protective mind-tap from yourself the song of yourself." The prose in "Essentials of Spontaneous Prose" is itself not a great advertisement for the method, since the result seems raw and not entirely thought through:

> Not "selectivity" of expression but following free deviation (association) of mind into limitless blow-on-subject seas of thought, swimming in sea of English with no discipline other than rhythms of rhetorical exhalation and expostulated statement, like a fist coming down on a table with each complete utterance, bang! (the space dash)—Blow as deep as you want—write as deeply, fish as far down as you want, satisfy yourself first, then reader cannot fail to receive telepathic shock and meaning-excitement by same laws operating in his own human mind . . . No pause to think of proper word but the infantile pileup of scatological buildup words till satisfaction is gained, which will turn out to be a great appending rhythm to a thought and be in accordance with Great Law of timing.

Kerouac did do extensive revisions of *On the Road* before it was finally published seven years later, but he denied it, claiming that it was a single three-week, Benzedrine-fueled "undisturbed flow." And for the rest of his writing career he became more adamant about publishing unedited prose, with disastrous results. He claimed that Malcolm Cowley ruined *On the Road* with his editing, and that after Cowley edited *The Dharma Bums* (1958), Kerouac reinstated all his original wording and punctuation. By that time he was famous, reading on *The Steve Allen Show*, writing about the Beat Generation for *Playboy*, and his editors were not allowed to touch his prose. From then on he stuck to his refusal to revise or craft his fiction. Much of it is virtually unreadable by any but die-hard fans, an "infantile pileup of scatological buildup," to use his own description. He became a victim of his own press releases, turning into the unpolished, unedited, unrevised primitive he bragged he was.

In the years between the publication of his first two books, between the ages of twenty-seven and thirty-five, Kerouac worked briefly at odd jobs, with a stint alongside Cassady as a brakeman on the Southern Pacific in San Jose and a summer spent as a fire lookout on Desolation Peak in Washington's Cascade Mountains. He continued traveling—including a trip to Morocco, where Burroughs had moved—living hand to mouth and occasionally returning home, writing twelve manuscripts but publishing none of them.

During this time he met Gary Snyder, who furthered his interest in Buddhism and whom he described as the character Japhy Ryder in *The Dharma Bums*. Snyder was studying Eastern philosophy at Berkeley, and he encouraged Kerouac to think about his distaste for contemporary American middle-class society in religious and millennial terms. Here is Snyder's fictional stand-in holding forth:

> "I've been reading Whitman, know what he says, *Cheer up slaves, and horrify foreign despots*, he means that's the attitude for the Bard, the Zen Lunacy bard of old desert paths, see the whole thing is a world full of rucksack wanderers, Dharma Bums refusing to subscribe to the general demand that they consume production and therefore have to work for the privilege of consuming, all the crap they didn't really want anyway such as refrigerators, TV sets, cars, at least new fancy cars, certain hair oils and deodorants and general junk you finally always see a week later in the garbage anyway, all of them imprisoned in a system of work, produce, consume, work, produce, consume, I see a rucksack revolution thousands or even millions of young Americans wandering around with rucksacks . . ."

This becomes, from then on, Kerouac's basic understanding.

He finds the value of this countercultural philosophy to be proved by the fact that some of the hobos he meets already believe something similar, and further proved by the fact that some of the working people he meets are unhappy precisely because they don't have such a philosophy. He meets a hobo in the freight yard in Los Angeles, for instance, an ex-marine from Paterson, New Jersey, who explains why he bums. "That's all there is to it, that's what I like to do," the hobo explains. "I'd rather hop freights around the country and cook my food out of tin cans over wood fires, than be rich and have a home or work. I'm satisfied." A truck driver picks him up hitchhiking, and when Kerouac cooks him a steak over a campfire, the driver is astounded by how good it is. "Where'd you *learn* to do all these funny things?" the truck driver asks. "And you know I say funny but there's sumpthin so durned sensible about 'em. Here I am killin myself drivin this rig back and forth across from Ohio to L.A. and I make more money than you ever had in your whole life as a hobo, but you're the one who enjoys life and not only that but you do it without workin or a whole lot of money. Now who's smart, you or me?" The wish-fulfillment fantasy elements of this are clear enough, as are the inaccuracies—the idea that Kerouac was just a kind of hobo tourist, or that he didn't work, for instance.

When Kerouac was thirty-two, Snyder suggested to him that what he really wanted was to retire to a hut like Thoreau's, to his own Walden Pond. Kerouac agreed, and sleeping sometimes in the woods and sometimes on his sister's back porch in North Carolina, he reread *Walden* and spent his day meditating among the trees behind his sister's house. Though he is conscious that his brother-in-law is "sick and tired" of him "hanging around not working," he is proud of his lazy version of Thoreauvian meditation. "What do you do in those woods?" the good old boys at the general store in town would ask him. "Oh I just go in there to study." Aren't you a little old to be a student? "Well I just go in there sometimes and just sleep." This of course is said in part to goad them, but he also notices that they do a lot of nothing themselves, hanging around the general store, "rambling around the fields all day looking for something to do, so their wives would think they were real busy hardworking men." Kerouac thinks that they, too, "secretly wanted to go sleep in the woods, or just sit and do nothing in the woods, like I wasn't ashamed to do." Kerouac got drunk one night with one of these old men and explained that he meditated on the eternal dharma among the trees. "He really rather understood and said he would like to try that if he had time, or if he could get up enough nerve, and had a little rueful envy in his voice."

This is not, in fact, as Kerouac is aware, the kind of Buddhism Snyder himself practiced. "Why do you sit on your ass all day?" the Snyder character asks him in *Dharma Bums*. "I practice do-nothing," Kerouac answers, feeling it is an appropriately Zen answer. But the energetic Snyder responds, "My Buddhism is activity." Later he asks Kerouac, "Why do you sit around all day?" and Kerouac answers, "I am the Buddha known as The Quitter." Kerouac is embarrassed by his own inactivity, and he respects Snyder's greater knowledge and his greater energy. His recognition of his own guilty conscience, his own rationalizing, is clear at these moments. But at other times he revels in his rebellious rejection of the striving around him. "Dharma" is the essence, the truth of life, and he was convinced at such times that to be a bum was the only way to experience the truth, to be a bum was to reject the desires that drove the rest of the society, and to reject desire was the golden path to Buddhist enlightenment. In 1954 Kerouac wrote to Ginsberg that he had reached "the state you reach when you stop everything and stop your mind and you actually with your eyes closed see a kind of eternal multiswarm of electrical Power of some kind ululating in place of just pitiful objects and forms of objects." Through Snyder, Kerouac got his job working as a fire lookout, living at the top of a mountain, meditating, and taking two-hour naps, his only work to scan the horizon for smoke and occasionally sweep the floor of his shack. He comes to feel that in doing nothing on Desolation Mountain, he has "learned all."

The decade after *On the Road* saw the publication, in rapid succession, of the other books in the ongoing saga of his life. In the three years from 1958 to 1960 Kerouac published a total of six new books. He had become an instant celebrity, was interviewed in all the major newspapers and magazines, made his famous television appearances, and started to live the myth of his own life in a new way. Just as his theory of spontaneous prose, when he started to really believe in it, destroyed his writing, so the myth of the life he had written, once his public started to believe it, overwhelmed his actual existence. He drank more and more, and his tendency to alcoholic depression increased. He got a gig playing at the Village Vanguard, reading his work to jazz accompaniment, but he was often too drunk to perform, and it is said one night he actually vomited into the piano. He stopped writing and thought of himself as being like Melville at the end of his life, forgotten by his public, even though he was not yet forty and the Beat Generation he defined was still big news. Attacked by John Updike, Robert Brustein, Kenneth Rexroth, and Truman Capote (it isn't writing, claimed Capote, "it's typing"), his sales falling off, Kerouac retreated into his mother's house, moved with her to Florida, wrote less and less, and spent more and more time drinking with his local cronies, his alcoholism now unchecked. By the age of forty-seven he was dead.

∞

However much Kerouac's version of the slacker owes to Thoreau, it was clear from the consternation and adulation Kerouac incited that he represented a significantly new version of the phenomenon. As his early and ignominious decline and death suggest, his was no genteel wink at his audience, and he was no quipster like Johnson, Dennie, Wilde, or Jerome. Instead, like Bertrand Russell, Melville, and Thoreau, he called for a complete break with conventional notions of propriety and success; unlike Russell and Thoreau, his was an individual, and individualistic, quest. Fitting for a world devastated by Auschwitz and Hiroshima, Kerouac brought the non-comedic, depressive, alienated aspects of the slacker figure to the fore. Not for nothing was his cohort sometimes called the Angry Young Men. Kerouac and the Beats were impelled by what they announced was an unfulfillable dream. And they were the first slackers to announce their dreams on television.

The common view of the fifties had it as a quiet decade in which conventionality reigned, with only the occasional oddball like Kerouac to provide a fringe. Even Barbara Ehrenreich, whose *The Hearts of Men* (1983) offers the most compelling description of conformity in the fifties, argued that the "macho defiance" of the Beats would only turn into a more productive revolt against the norms of the 1950s in later decades. But when we look at the talk about work and working (and not working) in the fifties, we can see Kerouac and the Beats as the tip of an enormous iceberg. At no previous period in human history, in fact, had conformity been so roundly, widely, and consistently assailed. The 1950s was *the* decade of anti-conformity.

At the beginning of the decade, bestselling books by social scientists—such as David Riesman's *The Lonely Crowd: A Study of the Changing American Character* (1950) and C. Wright Mills's *White Collar: The American Middle Classes* (1951)—took conformity to be a central social problem. Riesman criticized conformity among teenagers, in business corporations, among consumers, in popular culture, and even among Bohemians. Mills calls the average man a "standardized loser" who was a conformist by default: unprepared for the future, manipulated by the media, stuck within an alienating hierarchy, and unable to find satisfaction in work. The middle class was, for these analysts, stranded in anxious inaction, conventionality reigning by historical accident.

And the sociologists were joined by a large and loud chorus of other anti-conformist complaints: *Playboy* was launched in 1953 (the year of Alfred Kinsey's *Sexual Behavior in the Human Female*), attacking what Hugh Hefner called "Calvinist" prudery and propriety, and *Mad* magazine was founded in 1952 with the goal of mocking all conformist pretense. Martin Luther King Jr., Thurgood Marshall, Rosa Parks, James Baldwin, Ralph Ellison, Richard Wright, and thousands of others made complacency about race relations impossible, while Ralph Ellison's *Invisible Man* (1952) blasted the imprisoning conformity in every role available to African Americans, including the roles of radical and reformer. The films *Rebel Without a Cause* (1955) and *East of Eden* (1955) mocked conventional parenting. Elvis Presley threw his hips at the vestiges of Puritanism. *The Man in the Gray Flannel Suit* (novel 1955, film 1956) became a symbol of conformist loss. *Peyton Place* (novel 1956, film 1957), *Invasion of the Body Snatchers* (1956), and many other films and novels attacked suburban and small-town self-righteousness. In the comic strips of the decade, characters like Beetle Bailey and Dagwood Bumstead fell asleep at their desks and passively resisted their superiors. The right-wing writer Ayn Rand railed against the "grayness, the stale cynicism, the noncommittal cautiousness" of a "culturally bankrupt" America while left-wing Harvey Swados debunked "The Myth of the Happy Worker." *The Caine Mutiny* (novel 1951, film 1954) impugned conventional beliefs in military authority; *The King and I* (Broadway 1951, film 1956) assailed the vestiges of royal and patriarchal authority; Kingsley Amis's *Lucky Jim* (1954) and Vladimir Nabokov's *Pnin* (1957) lampooned academic authority. *On the Waterfront* (1954) attacked conventional beliefs in law and business. These and a host of other novels, plays, essays, and films suggested that to conform was to be complicit with corrupt forms of authority and/or a sucker, a dupe of manipulators or "phonies," as Holden Caulfield called them in *The Catcher in the Rye* (1951). Nelson Algren completed his manifesto on the nature of writing in 1953, in which he claimed that the writer needs to "perceive that the true shore lies against the tides of his own time. If he is not to betray himself he will have to move against that current." Algren called his essay *Nonconformity*.

Conformity was a problem, many agreed, precisely because it included working at a job. In 1955 a puzzled citizen asked one of America's most prominent spiritual advisers, "What should a person do who is unhappy and bored in his job after twenty years but who earns a nice salary and hasn't the nerve to leave?" Norman Vincent Peale, in his advice column in *Look*, responded that the trouble lies in conformist thinking: "The trouble here seems to be the tragedy of treadmill thoughts. This individual has gone stale, dull and dead in his thinking," Peale writes, right in tune with Kerouac. "He needs an intellectual rebirth." On the other end of the therapeutic spectrum, Fritz Perls and Ralph Hefferline agreed, as the subtitle of their *Gestalt Therapy: Excitement and Growth in the Human Personality* (1951) suggests. They, too, complained of "an unnecessarily tight adjustment to a dubiously valuable workaday society, regimented to pay its debts and duties." The problem is that "the average man . . . is too responsible, keeps meeting the time-clock, will not give in to sickness or fatigue, pays his bills before he is sure he has food, too narrowly minds his own business, does not take a risk."

John Clellon Holmes, writing about the young anticonventional hipsters for *The New York Times Magazine* in 1952, argued that the Beats and the squares suffered from the same problem:

> In the wildest hipster, making a mystique of bop, drugs and the night life, there is no desire to shatter the "square" society in which he lives, only to elude it. To get on a soapbox or write a manifesto would seem to him absurd . . . Equally, the young Republican, though often seeming to hold up Babbitt as his culture hero, is neither vulgar nor materialistic, as Babbitt was. He conforms because he believes it is socially practical, not necessarily virtuous. Both positions, however, are the result of more or less the same conviction—namely that the valueless abyss of modern life is unbearable.

Agreeing about the abyss, William H. Whyte, a writer for *Forbes* magazine, published *The Organization Man* a year before *On the Road*, and in it he provided a critique of conformity as thoroughgoing as that of the Beats. Like the Beats, when he sees suburban housing developments, he feels superior: "The sight of rank after rank of little boxes stretching off to infinity, one hardly distinguishable from the other, is weird," he writes. "If this is progress, God help us." Whyte counsels understanding: "One must be sympathetic too, after all, it is a step up in life for the people who live there, and one should not begrudge them the opiate of their TV; here, obviously, is a group of anonymous beings submerged in a system they do not understand." The conventionality of the masses should elicit our pity, not our disdain, Whyte thought.

But he has nothing but contempt, really, for the people he calls "organization men":

> This book is about the organization man. If the term is vague, it is because I can think of no other way to describe the people I am talking about. They are not the workers, nor are they the white-collar people in the usual, clerk sense of the word. These people only work for The Organization. The ones I am talking about belong to it as well. They are the ones of our middle class who have left home, spiritually as well as physically, to take the vows of organization life, and it is they who are the mind and soul of our great self-perpetuating institutions. Only a few are top managers or ever will be . . . But they are the dominant members of our society nonetheless. They have not joined together into a recognizable elite—our country does not stand still long enough for that—but it is from their ranks that are coming most of the first and second echelons of our leadership, and it is their values which will set the American temper.

The Organization Man, by conforming to what the corporation wants, becomes a soulless, uncreative automaton, a company man with no self-direction whatsoever. This was Riesman's point in *The Lonely Crowd*: the inner-directed individual of the nineteenth century, he wrote, had become the outer-directed postmodern, a being with no autonomy, swept along by the people around him, by the sluggish tides of culture.

Whyte and Mills both insisted that it was the kind of work people did that made conformity so common. Mills makes the argument with his usual gusto:

> When white-collar people get jobs, they sell not only their time and energy but their personalities as well. They sell by the week or

month their smiles and their kindly gestures, and they must practice
the prompt repression of resentment and aggression. For these intimate traits are of commercial relevance and required for the more
efficient and profitable distribution of goods and services. Here are
the new little Machiavellians, practicing their personable crafts for
hire and for the profit of others, according to rules laid down by
those above them . . . But if the work white-collar people do is not
connected with its resultant product, and if there is no intrinsic connection between work and the rest of their life, then they must accept their work as meaningless in itself, perform it with more or less
disgruntlement, and seek meanings elsewhere.

Daniel Bell, in *Work and Its Discontents* (1956), asked, "Why do people accept the harsh, monotonous, repetitive jobs that tie them to Ix-
ion's wheel?" It is because they have made "a devil's bargain" with
consumption, as Japhy Ryder/Gary Snyder said, and whatever restlessness results turns not into militancy, but to "escapist fantasies." What
is needed, Bell concluded, was more autonomy.

Novelists and many of their protagonists rejected conformity. In
Sloan Wilson's bestselling novel, *The Man in the Gray Flannel Suit*,
and the film based on it the next year, the soulless conformist got one
of his nicknames. As Catherine Jurca has written, Wilson's character
Tom Rath (the *w* is silent) is a "man for whom suburban-corporate existence is defined as endless suffering." As such, the character is the
new everyman, anguished, angry, and dissatisfied with his life of surface conformity, but he and the other literary characters of the decade
are, Jurca writes, "malcontents, not mindless conformists." John
Cheever was starting to write his tales about alienated, unhappy suburban white-collar types, and dozens of other novels and films told the
same story: like the Beats, they rejected the soul death of the nine-to-
five world. In John Keats's *The Crack in the Picture Window* (1956),
John and Mary Drone (the title and names a bit "on the nose") are
represented as part of a world so conformist that every day as the sun
goes down, "some five thousand automatic stoves were switched on
while some five thousand wives cooked dinner for five thousand returning husbands." In J. P. Marquand's *Sincerely, Willis Wayde* (1955),
the protagonist drops jobs and houses as quickly as possible, moving
on to the next. "You've got to keep on moving and growing," he ar-

gues, as Kerouac did. "That's the American way." In *It's Only Tempo-rary*, a Charles Mergendahl novel from 1950, the protagonists want only to move out of their town and jobs but tragically remain stuck in their "temporary jail." Norman Mailer argued in "The White Negro" (1957) that the young rebels, the "hipsters," know that the "quick death" of nuclear annihilation or the concentration camps was a ver-sion of the "slow death by conformity." The contrast is clear and stark for Mailer: "One is Hip or one is Square," he writes. "One is a rebel or one conforms," and to conform is to die. Work is a central issue: to work toward conventional success, to keep meeting the time clock is to be "trapped in the totalitarian tissues of American society, doomed willy-nilly to conform."

By the end of the decade, writers, editorialists, and academics con-tinued and widened the attack. Ehrenreich notes that the most popu-lar topic for graduation speeches in 1957 was "conformity." John Updike's *The Poorhouse Fair* (1959) and *Rabbit, Run* (1960) seethe against normalcy, conventionality, and work. In *The Affluent Society* (1958), John Kenneth Galbraith would introduce the phrase "conven-tional wisdom" as synonymous with wrongheadedness. Paul Good-man and Irving Howe attacked the Beats as conformists themselves, "a conformity *plus royaliste que le roi*" according to Goodman. Others reinterpreted the decade just past as one that was the opposite of con-formist. Daniel Bell's *The End of Ideology: On the Exhaustion of Polit-ical Ideas in the Fifties* (1960) announced that conformity had been abolished: "Against the 'traditional society,' in which people led the same dull, rote, often brutalized lives, . . . modern society, with its pos-sibilities for mobility, occupational choice, theater, books, and muse-ums, is more differentiated, variegated, and life-enhancing." Rather than a decade of complacency, it was one of "extraordinary change" and "anxiety," in which no one supports "conformity. Everyone is against it." (Bell, by the way, had taken to calling Princeton's Center for Advanced Study, where he prepared this book manuscript, "the Leisure of the Theory Class.") In either case, not conformity but the attack on conformity is what characterizes the decade, and work was the motor of compliance. The hallmark attempt to enforce conformity at the beginning of the decade was Senator Joseph McCarthy's House Un-American Activities hearings, although, as Ehrenreich has pointed out, the Communists were portrayed as the ultimate conformists, the destroyers of individualism. HUAC kept busy ferreting out those who would replace the current economic system, a system in which, as even Bell admitted, "work has lost its rationale." Rather than proving that the decade loved conformity, McCarthy's committee demonstrates how far the losing side in the cultural debate about conformity was prepared to go in the fight.

When City Lights bookstore was raided in 1956 and Allen Ginsberg's *Howl* (1956) was confiscated as obscene, the forces of conformity seemed momentarily in ascendance. But Judge Clayton Horn, in his decision that the poem was not obscene, called it "an indictment of those elements of modern society destructive of the best qualities of human nature." He wrote in his decision in 1957 that "such elements are predominantly identified as materialism, conformity, and the mechanization leading to war." *Howl* is, among other things, a screed against modern degradations, but it is also a defense of a way of life, a glorification of lounging nonconformity. The famous first line—"I saw the best minds of my generation destroyed by madness, starving hysterical naked"—begins a litany of descriptions of the "angelheaded hipsters" like himself, Kerouac, and their friends and fellow travelers. These hipsters take endless rides on the subway high on Benzedrine, pot, junk, peyote, and wine, and they can talk for seventy hours straight as they meander through New York's boroughs. They are the kind of people who "retired to Mexico to cultivate a habit, or Rocky Mount to tender Buddha or Tangiers to boys"; they are "the madman bum and angel beat in Time." The enemy of these hipsters is Moloch, the machinery, skyscrapers, armies, prisons, factories, and governments of the workaday world. Rejecting Moloch, the hipsters "lounged hungry and lonesome," wandering through towns and cities across the country in search of visions and ecstasy, and "threw their watches off the roof to cast their ballot for Eternity outside of Time." They are the "mad generation" whose heroic antics—like throwing potato salad at university lecturers on dadaism and crossing the continent in a car in seventy-two hours—are completely bound up with their rejection of the industrial workplace.

President Eisenhower in his famous valedictory military-industrial complex speech agreed with Judge Horn and Ginsberg, arguing that stifling, overlarge organizations and mechanized war were a central problem. And like the sociologists, Eisenhower bemoaned the passing of earlier kinds of work:

> Today, the solitary inventor, tinkering in his shop, has been over-shadowed by task forces of scientists in laboratories and testing fields. In the same fashion, the free university, historically the foun-tainhead of free ideas and scientific discovery, has experienced a rev-olution in the conduct of research. Partly because of the huge costs involved, a government contract becomes virtually a substitute for intellectual curiosity. For every old blackboard there are now hun-dreds of new electronic computers. The prospect of domination of the nation's scholars by Federal employment, project allocations, and the power of money is ever present and is gravely to be re-garded.

Eisenhower saw more clearly than the sociologists that big money and big power were alienating forces, not just the bureaucratic mind that they spawned. Like Ginsberg, he understood that each technological move—from conventional to nuclear bombs, from blackboards to computers—had implications for the way we understand industry it-self. Like Ginsberg, he saw in the current order the makings of apoca-lypse—in the power of money, of Moloch, the destruction of the American dream.

∞

Ehrenreich sees the nonconformism of the 1950s as a male revolt, the beginning of American men's "flight from commitment." Most men were earning a "family wage"—that is, enough money for their wives to stay home and raise kids and keep house. This led men to see their wives as economic burdens, Ehrenreich claims, and encouraged them to fly the coop. And the idea that conformism and nonconformism were primarily male problems was common at the time. Paul Good-man at the end of the decade wrote that the "problems of youth" he wanted to discuss "belong primarily, in our society, to boys: how to be useful and make something of oneself. A girl does not *have* to, she is not expected to make something of herself. Her career does not have to be self-justifying, for she will have children . . . Our 'youth troubles' are boys' troubles." Anthropologist Wini Breines has since collected stories, some in the form of interviews, some in the form of fiction or autobiography written by women who came of age in the 1950s, and she argues that the now-obvious sexism of such assumptions meant that for many women, the only possible form of rebellion was to imagine themselves in terms of the male rebels they found in fiction and film. Helped along by the androgyny of James Dean and the teen singing idols, young women imagined themselves as versions of the Beat male poets and movie rebels they admired.

But one of Breines's subjects, Joyce Johnson, who was a friend of Ginsberg and his lover Peter Orlovsky and was briefly Jack Kerouac's lover—in addition to being a novelist and memoirist in her own right—saw it otherwise. She writes in her autobiography of not simply imitating the male rebels but imagining herself part of the rebellion herself. She reports feeling the implied criticism, as a young college student in the early 1950s, of the latest media label for her cohort: the Silent Generation. She did not want to be silent, and she approached Beat Bohemianism as the one road to save her from the conformity she saw looming in her future. By 1953, when she was an undergraduate, the Beat Generation's influence was already wide and strong enough that her middle-aged creative-writing professor at Barnard accepted Kerouac's sense of the literary as his standard. "How many of you plan to become writers?" the professor asked his group of young women on the first day of class. When they finally all more or less tentatively—it was a creative writing class after all—raised their hands, he rebuked them. "Well, I'm sorry to see this," he said. "If you were really going to be writers, you wouldn't be taking this class. You couldn't even be enrolled in school. You'd be hopping freight trains, riding through America." For Johnson, the professor's pronouncement, although she saw that it was sexist, was also in line with her own belief in vocation, one common since the days of the Romantic poets: if one knew one's calling as a writer, one gave oneself up to it without hesitation. This was what she wanted for herself.

One night in 1956, she, Ginsberg, Orlovsky, Orlovsky's younger brother, and others went to see the new Federico Fellini film *I Vitelloni*, about young Italian males who live at home with their parents and do very little, if any, work. They spend their lives like an Old World version of Ginsberg's angel-headed hipsters, drinking, smoking cigarettes, and manically chasing women. Johnson doesn't comment on the film, except to say that Orlovsky's younger brother, fresh from San Francisco, mistook it for a film about the Beats in New York. The night some weeks later when she met Kerouac, he, like Fellini's over-grown boys, asked her to buy him dinner and then take him back to her apartment. He didn't have a home (except for his parents') or any money. He also had no plans to get a job. He wrote every day and had written a dozen manuscripts that would eventually get published in the next decade. But he didn't do anything like the work sociologists complained about. She did. Johnson worked as a secretary at a pub-lishing house and paid for the apartment, while he sat at home writing and dreaming of meeting up with William Burroughs in Tangier. Like the men in Ehrenreich's account, she earned the "family wage" that allowed him not to work.

Kerouac stayed from that first night until he got his advance check (for *The Subterraneans*) six weeks later; he immediately spent it on a ticket to Morocco and left. Johnson was writing her own novel when she wasn't at work, and she was living what was then still the very un-conventional life of a single woman in her own apartment. Despite the famous return of Rosie the Riveter to housework, some women re-mained in the lower echelons of the white-collar workforce, with all that entailed. One day Johnson's friend Elise was fired without expla-nation, a simple notice in her Friday pay envelope. Instead of accept-ing it, Elise went back in on Monday morning, sat at her old desk, and typed nonsense until someone came to give her a reason for her dis-missal. She felt, she told Johnson, like Bartleby. And like Bartleby, she was eventually removed by the police.

Elise, after she was fired, moved to San Francisco, and Johnson, now more alone, reflected on her own life. She spent time with an artist who, she realized, appealed to her for the same reason Kerouac and Ginsberg did: they loved the "heightened moment, intensity for its own sake." She, like the workers in the sociologists' accounts, felt the gray sameness of her work and wanted what the artists seemed to share. She resented the fact that these wild, untethered moments were "something [the men] apparently find only when they're with each other." She asked herself how Beat she could possibly be, holding down a steady job, and it didn't help when Kerouac told her, "If I had to go and apply for jobs like you, they'd have to drag me into Bellevue in two days. That's why I am and always will be a bum, a dharma bum, a rucksack wanderer." So one day she just quit, realizing she had enough saved to live on for an entire week. "To my delight," she writes, "at last I'd joined the ranks of the scufflers." Twenty-some years later, when she wrote her memoir of the period, she tried to explain what it was all about. "I think it was about the right to remain children," she wrote.

And although the Beat sense of play, of scuffling, was, among other things, undoubtedly somewhat childish, their belief in the power of play was widespread. It was not just the basis of Riesman's sociological utopia, but that of many other utopias, from Herbert Marcuse's to Hugh Hefner's. Marcuse argued in *Eros and Civilization* (1955) against the idea that "whatever satisfaction is possible necessitates *work*, more or less painful arrangements and undertakings for the procurement of the means for satisfying means." Marcuse suggests instead that we should be governed by the "play impulse," and he describes it in classic slacker terms: "The impulse does not aim at playing 'with' something; rather it is the play of life itself, beyond want and compulsion." He longed to see the "transformation of toil (labor) into play." Only by playing with our "potentialities," he suggests, can people be free. Play is unproductive and useless, and this is precisely why it can liberate us not just from work, but from repression and exploitation of all kinds. Hefner, as he elaborated his "Playboy Philosophy" in the 1950s, came to the same conclusion as Marcuse. "Hefner helped the world discover toys," *Playboy*'s longtime executive editor Arthur Kretchmer told Gay Talese. "He said, 'Play, it's okay to play.'" Johan Huizinga's *Homo Ludens: A Study of the Play Element in Culture* was published in America for the first time in 1950. Not coincidentally, the first advertisements appeared suggesting to consumers that since they work hard, they should also play hard, something that would from then on be a perennial marketing appeal.

This growing interest in notions of play from World War II through the 1960s coincided with the birth of the "teenager," a word coined in the mid-1940s. Young people, as in the 1920s, had some disposable income, and so a youth culture built on entertainment and fashion products began to surface and then fascinate the rest of the culture. "Youth culture" only makes sense, of course, in terms of nonconformity—it is the name for the art, entertainment, and activities that do not conform to adult expectations. Hence, as Thomas Hine in *The Rise and Fall of the American Teenager* (1999) and Rob Latham in *Consuming Youth* (2002), have argued, the teenager as a market segment (or youth as consumers) and the teenager as a social problem (or youth as nonproducers) are closely linked. The marketing to young people—whether in terms of such toys as Barbie dolls, Mattel six-shooters, Silly Putty, and Hula-Hoops, or in terms of films, TV, recordings, magazines, and books—became a central fact of economic life. The effects of these products on their buyers also became a new focus of concern. The "juvenile delinquent" that is largely the creation of the 1950s was explained by some in terms of what the delinquents didn't do, which was go to school or have a job, as well as in terms of what they did do, although that was often not so much an embrace of criminality as a dress style—the famous T-shirt and Levi's of Marlon Brando and James Dean, the hair à la Presley—and the consumption of popular culture, including the products of Brando, Dean, and Presley. The cause of delinquency, according to Fredric Wertham's influential, if ridiculous, *Seduction of the Innocent* (1954), was the very popular culture—especially, Wertham thought, the comic books—the consumption of which was also the main evidence of delinquency's power. Other commentators were quick to find the causes of delinquency in all realms of youth culture: *Blackboard Jungle* (1955), the hit film about juvenile delinquency, was said to promote it, as did much of the rest of film and television, as well as rock and roll.

The other main cause of delinquency was the absent father. The introductory scroll of *Blackboard Jungle* explained succinctly: "Father in the army. Mother in a defense plant. No home life . . . Gang leaders have taken the place of parents." *Rebel Without a Cause* famously blames all problems on weak or absent parents. The CEO in *The Man in the Gray Flannel Suit* has a "wild" daughter he hardly knows. But even in less dramatic families, the suburban father, spending extra hours at work, commuting an hour each way to his job, often traveling as part of his job, was necessarily home less than his own father had been. And this absence became one of the main explanations for his alienation from his children. The middle-class father's dedication to work, which made possible his children's increased consumption of "youth culture," was then circularly made responsible for those children's lack of traditional values, including the work ethic.

And then, finally, of course, the problem was the kids' lack of direction itself: the tagline to *The Delinquents* (1957), an early Robert Altman film, was "The kids that live today like there's no tomorrow!" The long dream of universal high school attendance had just been nearly realized, and this kept many students out of the workforce longer than any previous cohort. Problems of unemployment after the war, along with the changing nature of work in a deindustrializing, proto–information economy, kept some young people out of the workforce even longer. Teenage labor force participation fell steadily from 1945 to 1965. College attendance was on the rise. The nonworking young were increasing in number, and the fact that they were not working was a sign not only of the success of American culture—a vindication of the society that gave them such freedom and opportunity—but also a challenge to that same culture, an undermining of the very work values that had made their new lives possible. The problem was that all kids wanted to do was play.

Many of the sociologists simply couldn't blame them. C. Wright Mills argued that all labor in the middle of the twentieth century was alienated, and therefore all working people were estranged from their work. "Whatever satisfaction alienated men gain from work occurs within the framework of alienation," he wrote in *White Collar*. "Whatever satisfaction they gain from life occurs outside the boundaries of work; work and life are sharply split." Work meant nothing to the people doing it, he claimed, and gave them no sense of direction or pleasure. Leisure was almost as bad, consisting of frenzied mass amusements and escapes, even though it did, in the form of weekends and vacations, provide a contrast to work: "The weekend, having nothing in common with the working week, lifts men and women out of the gray level tone of everyday work life, and forms a standard with which the working life is contrasted." As such, leisure activities provide people with their basic identities and are major factors in forming their preferences. But Mills takes a very dark view of it all:

> The amusement of hollow people rests on their own hollowness and does not fill it up; it does not calm or relax them, as old middle-class

frolics and jollification might have done; it does not re-create their spontaneity in work, as in the craftsman model. Their leisure diverts them from the restless grind of their work by the absorbing grind of passive enjoyment of glamour and thrills. To modern man leisure is the way to spend money, work is the way to make it. When the two compete, leisure wins hands down.

And this, of course, is a hollow victory.

Mills himself tried to remain integrated, refusing to make a distinction, for instance, between what he wore at home and what he wore to work. In an era in which his colleagues at Columbia University worked in tweed jackets and ties, he rode his BMW motorcycle into campus and taught in work boots, khakis, and flannel shirts—never a white collar. It was a workman's rather than a professional's outfit and, in fact, a beatnik outfit, though Mills did not identify with them. He claimed, in fact, like Bartleby, to be a member of no group whatsoever, preferring to live alone and be alone: the loner as analyst of modern loneliness.

Riesman, on the other hand, was hopeful. Like Marcuse, he thought that in "play," rather than work, people had the greatest chance to break through the social and commercial barriers they had helped erect and to find some actual autonomy. Leisure was the only sphere in which the over-adapted automaton of modern industrial life might be able to reassert autonomy and individuality. He admits that he is much better at analyzing the obstacles to this after-work autonomy than he is at pointing out the path to its realization. But he remains convinced that people's best weapon against the forces of gray conformity lay in using their leisure time to discover their own true desires and aspirations.

"Few can quarrel with this idea" of play, Daniel Bell wrote a few years later, "perhaps because it is so amorphous." Bell notes that there has been a vast increase in leisure, the workweek dropping from seventy to forty hours a week between 1850 and 1950. And he commends the spread of amateurism in all sorts of fields. But this cannot, he argues, make up for unsatisfying work. If we are to have a more satisfying life, we need "a new appetite for work"—work that not only "feeds the body" but "sustains the spirit." He, too, though, runs into trouble providing a program to get there. If he was right to criticize the utopianism of Riesman's belief in play, he and many of his fellow sociologists nonetheless missed Riesman's more radical point that work, as it exists for the majority of people, is not a calling and can afford none of the justification and validation that one's "lifework" is supposed to provide. Only play, Riesman (and Marcuse and Hefner and Kerouac) suggested, could bring meaning; only *not working* made real life begin.

To the extent that issues of work, play, and delinquency remained more the province of boys than girls, it was because so many middle-class women, after their foray into the factory during the war, were in fact back in the home. Then as now, this was a trajectory that appealed to some and not to others. One woman who emphatically rejected that premise, and the only one who fully breached the Beats' gender barrier in the 1950s, was poet and writer Diane di Prima. In two retrospective accounts—*Memoirs of a Beatnik* (1969) and *Recollections of My Life as a Woman* (2001)—she describes her growing sense of herself as a writer, in the same terms that Ginsberg and Kerouac expounded: being a writer, a true writer, meant being "an outcast, outrider, and *explorer*," one who would sacrifice everything for art. Joyce Johnson envied the freight-hopping abandon of her male poet friends, but di Prima lived it. " 'Sacrifice everything' we would write on apartment walls," she remembers, and when she dropped out of college and got an apartment in Alphabet City and a very part-time clerk's job, she literally did become an outcast. "No woman lived alone in that world" of working-class immigrants "unless she was a whore," di Prima writes, and she suffered a daily gauntlet of condemnation from her neighbors and landladies. She nonetheless felt justified because she was an artist and "there was no higher calling than this." She quit the clerk's job and whittled her work schedule down to four or five hours a week (as an artist's model), spent months on end crashing on friends' couches, shared her low-rent apartments with as many people as was necessary to get minimal bills paid, and came "into poverty as into an inheritance." What she bought with this "dire poverty," she says, was the "luxury, the freedom to pass my days as I pleased, exploring, researching whatever came to mind, writing in front of ancient oils at the Metropolitan, walking Manhattan from end to end, talking everywhere to strangers." The poverty was simply "the terms of the deal I'd managed to cut," she said. "I thought myself lucky." Eventually she, too, joined the Beat cross-continental nomads and went back and forth to California before settling there in the 1960s. She, like the male Beats, saw that "it was only a step from the artist-as-outlaw to the outlaws themselves," and she spent time with bikers, junkies, burglars, and thieves. She spent her last dollars on live and recorded jazz.

Memoirs of a Beatnik was expressly pornographic—her editor at Olympia Press, Maurice Girodias, would send back her manuscripts with "MORE SEX" written across the top of the pages—and she obliged at length. It was essentially hackwork, written to support her move to San Francisco in the late 1960s, but she managed to keep her Beat proprieties and convictions intact. The book draws heavily on her own experiences as a teenager and young woman and expresses a young Bohemian girl's sense of freedom and adventure (especially sexual adventure) in the early 1950s, including her discovery of Ginsberg's *Howl* and subsequent meeting and orgies with Ginsberg, Kerouac, et al. Di Prima understood that the boys were the center of cultural and each other's attention, but she decided that they were nevertheless all in the same boat together. In *Recollections* she describes her conclusion:

> I realize that there truly was this determinedly male community of writers around me in the 50s. This thing I am constantly questioned about, as in: "How did you survive it? Where were the women?" There truly was this male cabal: self-satisfied, competitive, glorying in small acclaims . . .
>
> I saw these guys, myself and the others, as artists simply. All striving was for and of the Work, and I loved them for it . . . And seeing it thus made it possible for me to walk among these men mostly unhit-on, generally unscathed. Made it possible to walk the Dreamtime. Eternal world of the Poem . . .
>
> And I loved each of them. Love them still. Dear friends and companions of the holy art—the sacred task of pushing the container.

Notably, di Prima's sense of the poet's life is much more involved in notions of "work" and "striving" and "sacred tasks" than Kerouac's. And although she did spend some time living on handouts from sexual partners, she also supported various male hangers-on much of the time. She was the one woman, except for the ten-years-younger Anne Waldman, who was allowed to help Ginsberg institutionalize Beat literature in the writing program at the Naropa Institute in Boulder, Colorado. Naropa was a place for "work" to happen, and yet a place that remained notorious for its forms of play. When I was there for a conference in the 1980s, people reported being chased down the hall by the school's founder and guru, Trungpa Rinpoche, drunk and naked, a ribbon tied around his penis, announcing he had a gift for them. And such stories were standard lore of the place, ever since the opening fund-raising poetry reading, in 1974, when Gary Snyder and Robert Bly downed a bottle of bourbon onstage while Trungpa Rinpoche got trashed on sake.

Di Prima, who might lay claim to the title of first woman slacker, nonetheless edited magazines, wrote poetry, plays, and prose, took care of children, wrote for money, took care of rent and living space and bills, and made possible the life she and many of the people around her were living. She tried to live the dharma, but not the bum. She appreciated that for the men in the movement, play was the thing, and she worked to help them have the time and space to do so. She describes this as giving them the opportunity to "move toward the work they most wanted to do," not as allowing them to do nothing. Often she was disappointed, because the boys didn't want the sacred Work, they just wanted to play. As in the case of Samuel Johnson (and, at different times, Kerouac), di Prima was haunted by a sense that she needed to work. Doing nothing was important, but primarily because it made space for and provided material for work, for the work of writing. Di Prima and Joyce Johnson, like the feminists who would follow in the 1960s, valued work even if they agreed with the men around them that very little work was, in the end, worth doing.

∞

What the academic play theorists and many others assumed was that the reduction of work hours would continue, that the long-held, often-argued-for dream of the three- or four-hour wage-earning workday (if not di Prima's three- or four-hour workweek) would become a reality. In fact, however, the opposite, the slow creeping up of weekly work hours, had already begun. The suburban middle-level managers who stayed longer at work, and often brought work home with them, may have been the first to feel it, but the century-long reduction in the length of the workweek had stalled and had gone into reverse. Economic historian Juliet B. Schor, in *The Overworked American: The Unexpected Decline of Leisure* (1992), did the numbers: between 1850 and 1950 there had been a steady decline in the number of hours the average worker spent at work, but right after World War II that decline "abruptly ended," writes Schor. In the following fifty years, the number of hours has increased year by year. From 1948 to 1968 that increase was measurable but slight. After that, it increased more sharply, until the average employed person worked 305 more hours per year in 1987 than in 1969. By the late 1980s one-eighth of the labor force averaged fifty hours a week, and another eighth averaged sixty. In addition, paid leave was shrinking. By the end of the 1980s the average worker in America had three and a half fewer paid days off than a decade before, even as workers in many European countries had moved from a standard four to five weeks of paid vacation a year.

Part of this American increase in hours is due to the steady reduction in hourly rates of pay. Schor calculates that in order for the average nonsupervisory worker (that is for 80 percent of the workforce) to maintain a 1973 standard of living, he or she would have needed to work an extra 245 hours a year in 1990, or more than six extra weeks. This meant second jobs for many, or a second income in the household at least. The average workingman in this same period increased his paid labor by close to 100 hours a year, the average woman by a little more than 300 hours. Men had taken on slightly more of the unpaid labor of maintaining a household (although women still do twice as much of this work), so that for both men and women, the average increase of total labor, paid and unpaid, had increased by 160 hours a year.

But the real change was in the kind of work people were doing. The Beat outfit (and Mills's outfit) of workingmen's jeans and T-shirts was not simply an ironic statement about work, it was a protest against the gray flannel suit, the uniform of the new office worker. Images of standardized men in ties plugging away in faceless office buildings for enormous corporations already provoked alternating pride and horror in the 1920s, but it was not yet the norm. In the mid-1950s white-collar workers became the largest occupational group in the country (in 1900 the majority were still agricultural workers; from 1910 to

1955 it was blue-collar workers). By 2000, white-collar workers would grow to 60 percent of the workforce, and traditional blue-collar workers would shrink to 24 percent.

While unions helped maintain workweek levels for some blue-collar workers, many white-collar workers responded to subtle or not-so-subtle pressures to increase the hours spent in the office, especially those salaried workers who never punched a clock. As work hours increased, so did feelings of alienation, as analysts from Marx to Mills predicted, while at the same time the work these workers did became further and further abstracted from any particular product or result. "You talk about monotony on an assembly line," said one business magazine writer in 1956. "That's nothing compared with the stultifying effects of these big insurance offices." Mills argued that white-collar work brought the alienation Marx described in industrial labor "one step nearer to its Kafka-like completion." Like J. Pierpont Finch, the hero of *How to Succeed in Business Without Really Trying* (Broadway 1961–65, film 1967), white-collar workers seem to do things by a script they neither fully understand nor fully trust. Finch follows the advice of a "how to succeed" manual and rises comically quickly from window washer to mail-room clerk to "junior executive in plans and systems" to "head of plans and systems" to "vice president in charge of advertising" at the World-Wide Wicket Company. Finch never seems to actually do or accomplish anything; nor does it ever become clear what the World-Wide Wicket Company makes (presumably wickets—but sluice gates or croquet hoops?). The book and lyrics give no hint. Several years earlier Edward Albee in *The Zoo Story* (1959) had offered the tragic side of this critique: in it an alienated white-collar worker meets a "bum," a "permanent transient," and ends up having to face the worthlessness of his own life and its miserable side effects. Meanwhile, Douglas McGregor's very popular business text *The Human Side of Enterprise* (1960) made a plea for spontaneous creativity in the workplace rather than hierarchical conformism. And in *The Pyramid Climbers* (1962), Vance Packard took on white-collar anomie the way he had taken on advertising in *The Hidden Persuaders* (1957) and planned obsolescence in *The Waste Makers* (1960). As the 1960s dawned, the white-collar worker took center stage and declared the meaninglessness of his work.

John Kenneth Galbraith gave a partial explanation in his description of the "New Class" that, he argued, had replaced the leisure class. "To be idle," Galbraith explained, "is no longer considered rewarding or even entirely respectable." This new class, the managerial elite (which would come to be more commonly called the professional-managerial class), came to believe that their work, even though it caused no "pain, fatigue, or other mental or physical discomfort," was as arduous and taxing as manual labor. The belief that all work is essentially the same, Galbraith writes, is convenient for social scientists, justifies the wage and privilege differentials in both capitalist and Communist societies as based on intelligence and skill rather than social position, and thus "serves the democratic conscience," assuaging the "lurking sense of guilt" over this class's more "pleasant, agreeable, and remunerative life." Thus, compounding their sense of alienated purposelessness, the professionals and executives necessarily acquired a guilty conscience.

And along with these debilities, they were informed that they were giving themselves heart attacks as well. The type A personality, a.k.a. the successful Organization Man, was under cardiac strain day by day. The CEO in *The Man in the Gray Flannel Suit*, again, just to take one central example, is on the verge of a heart attack throughout the story, and the medical experts argued that his case was typical. The more women entered this class, the more they, too, suffered from heart disease. Like the physicians who treated neurasthenia almost a century before, the cardiologists suggested that the "wear and tear" of modern life, and in particular the modern tendency to overwork, caused the disease. Frenetic accumulation and overzealous grasping at material success were, as the Beats and the sociologists suggested, bad for people. The doctors argued that the nation's executives were working too hard, that they needed to take a rest to save their own lives. The sociologists argued that they needed to stop working so hard and play to save the social fabric. The Beats and Eisenhower argued that they needed to slow down to save the planet from nuclear-military-industrial destruction.

Like the slacker ethic and the work ethic, this argument coexisted with its opposite: that these managers were hardly working. In *The Apartment* (1960), C. C. "Bud" Baxter (Jack Lemmon) works as a "second administrative assistant" for a large insurance company. "I work on the nineteenth floor," he explains. "Ordinary Policy Depart-

ment, Premium Accounting Division, Section W, desk number 861."
He tries to get ahead by letting the higher-ups use his apartment for
clandestine meetings with their mistresses and/or secretaries, and he
spends large parts of every day organizing and running interference
for these trysts. It involves a lot of effort, but not what is usually called
work. In *How to Succeed in Business*, executives spend their time
avoiding responsibility: "I realize that I'm the president of this company, the man that's responsible for everything that goes on here," says
J. B. Biggely. "So, I want to state, right now, that anything that happened is not my fault." These comic exaggerations suggest not just a
C. Wright Mills–like level of white-collar alienation, but the idea that
nothing much is being accomplished, that jockeying for corporate position had replaced any other form of productive activity, and that
therefore, the higher up one went, the less work one did.

In 1969 Laurence J. Peter authored a new wrinkle in the theory of
executive alienation, *The Peter Principle: Why Things Always Go
Wrong*. Peter was a Canadian who began teaching school in 1941,
went on to get a doctorate in education, and became a professor at the
University of Southern California a few years before *The Peter Principle* was published. The principle is brilliantly simple and by now common knowledge: "In a hierarchy, every employee tends to rise to his
level of incompetence," Peter wrote in typically pithy fashion. Success
in one's assigned tasks led to promotion, and eventually, logically, one
would be promoted beyond one's abilities. The characters in film after
film, novel after novel, play after play, illustrated the point, and even
before Peter published his famous dictum, filmmakers and novelists
seemed to understand that alienation was born not just from guilt over
one's privileged class but also from guilt over one's own incompetence. The men in suits didn't know what they were doing, and they
didn't know who was directing them to do it or why they were doing it.
Barbara Ehrenreich is undoubtedly right in describing these years in
terms of a crisis of masculinity, but women in the corporation were
subject to the same alienating forces, although complicated by the
fact that they were left unfairly unpromoted more often than their
male counterparts.

During the 1960s, this kind of alienation did not affect the arguments being made about women's work. Betty Friedan, in *The Feminine Mystique* (1963), made the basic feminist case loud and clear.

Women who accept the ideal of feminine domesticity, women "stuck in the housewife trap," are pathologically over-adapted to their social role. To the extent that they become aware of their own unhappiness (and in Friedan's sample, most were), there is only one solution, just as there is only one solution to a man's identity crisis: "Work can now be seen as the key to the problem . . . The identity crisis of American women began a century ago, as more and more of the work important to the world, more and more of the work that used their human abilities and through which they were able to find self-realization, was taken from them." Women needed the same kinds of satisfying work men had, though as I've suggested, by most reports they had very very little.

This argument that women needed more work coexisted on the front lines of feminism with its opposite, the idea that women were overworked, a version of the time-honored notion that "a woman's work is never done." This was taken by some 1960s feminists to mean that the domestic labor of women should be rewarded on par with the work of men outside the home. Some—Selma James and Maria Rosa Dallacosta, for instance—argued that it should be directly compensated through "wages for housework." For Friedan, who called the middle-class home a "comfortable concentration camp," such wages were beside the point. Women didn't need to get paid for the dehumanizing work they were doing; they needed a "sex role revolution" that would allow them "real" work. What she had in mind was something similar to Hannah Arendt's notion of "action" rather than "labor," or, for that matter, what Diane di Prima called "the Work" or "the sacred task of pushing the container." Women were agitating for work, for equal pay, for opportunity, for advancement, as of course were many men. What women were not yet doing in any numbers was declaring themselves against the work ethic altogether.

As late as 1950, the number of women in the salaried workforce was still quite small: some 18 million women compared to 44 million men. In 2000, the numbers would become much closer (65 million women, 75 million men), and by then women would be proudly proclaiming themselves slackers as well. But until late in the century the only version of the female slacker was still the gold digger, the kind of character played by Marilyn Monroe in *Gentlemen Prefer Blondes* (1953), a remake of the 1920s original. The same year, Monroe, Betty

Grable, and Lauren Bacall all prefer to marry money rather than to try to make it themselves in *How to Marry a Millionaire* (later a TV sitcom for the last few years of the 1950s). The gold digger, in these satirical films, is being accused of a kind of slacking, a kind of bumming. But they don't claim that status for themselves. In *How to Marry a Millionaire* the women try hard to look as if they are better off than they in fact are, because they feel that rich men want to marry women of their own class. So they pretend to be successful career women. They don't want to work, but they certainly don't want to advertise the fact that they don't want to work.

Women had been accused just as men had through the years of malingering, laziness, and uselessness. In 1918, for instance, the *Taylor County* (Texas) *Times* took to task slackers of both sexes who refused to do their part in the war effort, pointing out that "the Red Cross sewing rooms are short on help, while healthy, strong girls and women are riding around in automobiles or playing bridge, whist, or coddling poodle dogs." Soon, as the cultural revolutions of the 1960s took hold, women would enter the workforce at rates almost equal to that of men, and then they would, like Diane di Prima, start to seek equity as slackers as well. The world of work was in the process of changing radically again, as Louis Levine, then the U.S. Department of Labor's chief analyst of "employment security," told Vance Packard in 1959: "The transformation we're now seeing will make the Industrial Revolution of the 18th Century look like a pink tea."

VIII

DRAFT DODGERS, SURFERS, TV BEATNIKS, AND HIPPIE COMMUNARDS

In which George W. Bush tries to go mano a mano *with Pappy—waves of new slacker types cycle through popular culture and hip subcultures—Maynard G. Krebs, Gidget, Abbie Hoffman, and Baba Ram Dass—dropping out—back to the farm—communal slacking—stealing books—and other ways to get money for nothing.*

Like many in his generation, George W. Bush had a problem with his father. In what is perhaps now the most famous story of his dissipated young adulthood, Bush drove home drunk one night, noisily crashing into the neighbor's garbage cans, and was summoned to his father's study. He weaved his way there and said, "I hear you're looking for me." In this charged moment—one might picture young George Washington about to confess the felling of the cherry tree—Bush fils asked his father, "You wanna go *mano a mano* right here?" His brother Jeb supposedly defused the situation by breaking the news to their father that George W. had been admitted to Harvard Business School. "But I'm not going," the younger George was quick to point out. "I just applied to prove to you I could get in."

Bush the elder is a classic overachiever, with perhaps the most impressive résumé ever assembled: successful oil company CEO, decorated combat pilot, twice elected to the U.S. House of Representatives, ambassador to the United Nations, chairman of the Republican National Committee, ambassador (or special envoy, as the post was called at the time) to China, director of the CIA, U.S. vice president and president. Bush the younger has a classic slacker biography. He was already noticed in grade school for lack of effort (except in baseball), and early childhood friends remember him as an impish prankster, not a kid who would excel at assigned tasks. His brother Jeb was the good student, George the fun guy. As one family friend put it, "W.'s kind of like the guy who spends the night before the test in his Corvette, running around with two cheerleaders, and drives by the brainiac's house and says, 'Jeb, can I have your notes?' The brainiac gets an A, but W. slides by with a B." When George left to go to Andover, his mother gave him a thesaurus, which he used so hurriedly in composing his first freshman English paper that the word "lacerates" seemed to him an apt improvement over "tears"—as in "the lacerates ran down my cheeks." His teacher called it "disgraceful," and George worried that he might not make it through his second week of school. "We were way behind the curve and at the bottom of the class," said Clay Johnson, his Texas friend, Andover classmate, and Yale roommate. "All of a sudden we were at the tail end."

Bush entered Yale in 1964 and pledged Delta Kappa Epsilon, a fraternity many later thought was the original for the beer-soaked frat house in *Animal House*. One DKE who pledged that same year claims that many thought that Bluto, the hard-drinking John Belushi character in that film, was based on George W. Others demurred. But there is wide agreement about the drinking, and some on drugs. "When I was young and irresponsible," Bush himself likes to say now with a classic slacker smirk, "I was young and irresponsible."

Graduating in 1968 meant that Bush was eligible for the draft at a time when 350 Americans were dying in combat each week. But he avoided the draft after a series of now-famous arm-twistings that resulted in his being admitted to the Texas Air National Guard ahead of 150 others on a waiting list. Just as famously, Bush was often missing in action during the six years he was in the Guard: the few members of his small unit that remember him at all recall a convertible-driving, hard-partying jokester. He spent three months here and six months there out of state, missed required physicals, and failed to be reassigned (as required) when he moved to Massachusetts for two years.

During this period, which Bush calls his "nomadic years," he lived in three states in seven different apartments—some offered for free by family friends—and held a few jobs between long periods of unemployment. "I had a taste of many different jobs," he wrote in his autobiography, A Charge to Keep (1999), adding in standard slacker style, "but none of them had ever seemed to fit."

At the age of twenty-six he went back to school somewhat reluctantly, enrolling at Harvard Business School after all. "I wasn't really that excited about going," he told reporters later. "I think if you look at my full life, I haven't had a game plan," and, he added, "it doesn't bother me." Professor Howard Stevenson remembers him as a student "who didn't bust his tail." Another professor, Michael Yoshino, who later developed a strategic plan for Texas when Bush was governor and who worked on Bush's 2000 campaign, remembers him more fondly as a "middle-of-the-road student." One of his economics professors, Yoshi Tsurumi, remembers him because, he said, professors always remember their best and worst students. Bush, he said, was "lazy. He didn't come to my class prepared. He did very badly." He was, according to Tsurumi, "totally devoid of . . . good study discipline." It was in Tsurumi's class that Bush declared to the class (somewhat ironically, given his wealth and lack of motivation) that poor people "are poor because they are lazy."

At the same time, Bush seemed to pride himself on not being one of the New England elite. Despite having spent a third of his life in high-priced, high-prestige New England schools, and despite his grandfather's eleven-year stint as U.S. senator from Connecticut, he played the good old boy from Texas, wearing cowboy boots, chewing tobacco, and spitting into a cup during class. One classmate, Mark Hopkinson, said, "I remember him making a comment about how he didn't think he'd ever see the need to wear a necktie." After Harvard, Bush returned to Texas and worked as a "landman," trying to secure rights to drill on other people's property, and he was noticed more for his frugality than his success. Doug Hannah, a friend at the time, described Bush's modus for Frontline:

> Never picked up a check, never spent his dollar when he could spend somebody else's dollar. If somebody else was treating, he was

there. Cheaper to go to somebody else's house for dinner than to go out to dinner. Cheaper to go to a deb party than to go out to dinner. Tight. Frugal. Cautious. I think tight's probably closest to the description.

After two years of little success, he formed an oil company in 1977, Arbusto, which did no drilling for another two years, allowing Bush the spare time to wage an unsuccessful campaign for the U.S. House of Representatives in 1978. He also got married and had twins.

Despite millions of dollars of investment that flowed to Bush's company after his father was elected vice president in 1980, Arbusto's fortunes went from bad to worse. As Michael Conaway, the chief financial officer, put it, "We didn't find much oil and gas." By the mid-1980s the outlook was bleak. "It got pretty thin," Conaway said. "We had to take, you know, salary cuts, compensation cuts, you know, do all kinds of things to reduce overhead to survive." In 1985 the company had a net loss of $1.6 million. In 1986, as Bush was turning forty, his company was $3.1 million in debt. "I'm all name and no money," Bush told a *New York Times* reporter. That was when Harken Energy stepped in and took over the debt, gave Bush and his partners $2.2 million in stock, and saved the enterprise from bankruptcy. While his investors received roughly twenty cents on the dollar for their trouble, Bush ended up with enough cash to fulfill a longtime dream: owning a baseball team, the Texas Rangers, which he bought a share of for $500,000. This investment would be much more profitable than his oil work; he sold his interest a decade later for $14.9 million.

The year Harken stepped in was also the year Bush stopped stepping out, and he quit drinking. He worked on his father's presidential campaign in 1988. He fought for a new stadium for the Texas Rangers, worked as one of two "general managing partners" of the team, and then, in 1994, won the governorship of Texas. It seemed that he had left his slacker days behind. The other general manager of the team at the time, a political supporter, has since praised Bush's work with the team:

> He was there every day . . . George chose to sit right next to the dugout, with the fans, every day. I mean, it's a hundred degrees down there. He's there from before the game, half an hour before

the game, didn't leave his seat except to go to the bathroom, cheering for the ball club, signing autographs, listening to hecklers, accepting well-wishes from season-ticket customers.

His diligence was such that he never stopped enjoying the game except to go to the bathroom: this almost sounds like one of Dennie's lounger parodies. Gail Sheehy's rendition of his workday as governor of Texas in the 1990s also has a bit of the sound of an eighteenth-century lounger's diary:

> Nothing engages Bush's attention for more than an hour, an hour max—more like 10 or 15 minutes. His workday as governor of Texas is "two hard half-days," as his chief of staff, Clay Johnson, describes it. He puts in the hours from 8 to 11:30 a.m., breaking it up with a series of 15-minute meetings, sometimes 10-minute meetings, but rarely is there a 30-minute meeting, says Johnson. At 11:30 he's "outtahere."

He then returned to the office, Sheehy wrote, at 1:30, where he would "play some video golf or computer solitaire until about three, and then it's back to the second 'hard half-day' until 5:30." When he launched his first presidential bid, he told a reporter, "I have no fear of failure in this venture. Nor do I fear success. If it works out, great. If it doesn't work out, hey, you know, come and see me. I'll be a retired governor living somewhere in Texas. Seriously."

Presidents Clinton and Carter each averaged less than three weeks a year away from the Oval Office; Bush has averaged nineteen. In 2001 *The Washington Post* calculated that Bush was off work 42 percent of the time since his inauguration. And even when he has been in the White House, his short workday has been the stuff of late-night comedy: he works "24/7—24 hours a week, 7 months a year" according to *Saturday Night Live*. Supporters have rushed to emphasize that these jokes are not fair, that all vacations, if one is president, are working vacations. As if defending himself from such charges, during one of the 2004 presidential debates Bush used the phrase "hard work" (and closely related terms) some twenty-three times. But no matter how often he says those words, George W. Bush will likely go down in history as our slacker president.

∞

And this seems, if nothing else, historically appropriate. The second half of the twentieth century has seen a quick succession of slacker types, from Beats to surf bums to hippies and yippies to punks to slackers proper. From Bob Dylan's "Maggie's Farm" ("I ain't gonna work on Maggie's farm no more") to Roger Miller's "I Ain't Gonna Work No More" to Lou Reed's "Don't Talk to Me About Work" to Johnny Paycheck's "Take This Job and Shove It" ("I ain't workin' here no more") to Joe Walsh's "Life's Been Good" ("They say I'm lazy, but I have a good time") to Tom Waits's "I Can't Wait to Get Off Work" ("It's nice work if you can get it") to Dire Straits's "Money for Nothing" ("Now that ain't workin', that's the way you do it / You play guitar on the MTV") to Bachman-Turner Overdrive's "Takin' Care of Business" ("I love to work at nothin' all day") to the Statler Brothers' "Flowers on the Wall" ("Smokin' cigarettes and watchin' 'Captain Kangaroo' / Now don't tell me, I've nothin' to do")—to take just a tiny sample—popular song has extolled the virtues of doing nothing and has found pleasure in reviling work. Television audiences, from the earliest sitcoms like *The Life of Riley* (1949–58) to Jerry Seinfeld's "show about nothing" (1990–98), have loved characters with a sketchy relation to work. Films—from *The Wild One* (1953) to *Easy Rider* (1969) to the film that renamed the phenomenon, *Slacker* (1991), to *Office Space* (1999)—have featured characters who avoid or drop out of the uncool nine-to-five world of work.

As in previous periods, though, it is often difficult to say what message any given viewer might take from these songs, stories, and characters. Maynard G. Krebs, TV's first sitcom beatnik, played the nonworking fool on *The Many Loves of Dobie Gillis* (1959–63). The character was performed by Bob Denver as even more of a lazy simpleton than his next (also lazy) incarnation as Gilligan on *Gilligan's Island* (1964–67). The main characteristic Maynard displayed, besides his beatnik slang—"cool, daddy-o," "like, what?"—was an aversion to work. He had just been kicked out of the army, and show after show he spent his time scat singing, with holes in his sweatshirt, listening to his transistor radio. Over and over the joke was Maynard's shocked horror at the idea that he might get a job: he would shudder and wail, "WORK!?!?!?" as if he had been stabbed through the heart. In this the show follows such critics of the Beat movement as Herb Caen, the columnist who nicknamed them beatniks and said, "They're only Beat, y'know, when it comes to work . . ." Krebs was in large part an object of ridicule, the laughs he drew often the result of his hyperstupidity. Maynard was the opposite of a cultural role model, a satire on the alternative argued by the actual Beats, without much actual relation between the two except hair and clothing styles.

The comedy of *The Life of Riley* in the early fifties was similarly based on Chester A. Riley's idiocy, although this time the dumb guy is a working-class slacker. A typical episode had Riley mistakenly believing that he was about to receive a new car (he takes the bus to work) in recognition of his fifteen years of work at the factory. Instead he receives a watch. The resulting disappointment is supposed to be funny, not infuriating, because the audience is in on the joke much earlier than Chester, and because Chester's fantasy, the show suggests, is just unreasonable wishful thinking on his part, given that the hallmark of his character is his laziness. The show opened with a stentorian voice-over as we see images of industrial parks, work whistles blowing, machinery turning, workers arriving at factory gates:

> America wakes to the sounds of her factories, the symphony of the whistle and whirl of the wheels which symbolize her greatness. America's heart is in her factories, the production lines are her life's blood, and each industry depends on the men and women who are cogs in the gigantic machine of progress. One of those cogs is Chester A. Riley, a man of action, a son of destiny, a cog whose soul is in his work, whose feet are firmly planted . . .

At that point the shot cuts to Riley's feet hanging out of his covers, still in bed, and a gale of canned laughter. His wife comes in to wake him and tell him he's late for work.

Riley deserves no better than he gets, the show always suggests, and maybe not even that. Chester has a standard factory worker's schedule, but his iconic pose is swinging in his hammock (which frequently manages to dump him on the ground). He would rather be resting, but for one reason or another—wife, boss, kids, neighbors—he never gets any rest. He comes up with schemes—"There's a fortune in this honey racket, Peg, and very little work attached to it, except the little that the bees do"—but they always implode. Chester, like Maynard, constantly gets the short end of the stick, and the laugh track lets us know that this is always funny. Both Chester and Maynard are hapless in the face of events, neither have the kind of work that Betty Friedan or Diane di Prima or Hannah Arendt thought people should have, and both exist at the parodic edges of the middle-class ideal.

Like Maynard, Chester occasionally performs a kind of idiot savant role, speaking the truth, however inadvertently. Maynard is a fool, but he is also the most up-to-date character, the one who knows about (that is, "digs") Dizzy Gillespie and Thelonious Monk. Riley may be an irascible numskull, but he is also the one person who is not duped by the pieties and proprieties of the middle-class, middle-century world. His incomprehension is critique, his anger funny but right-eous. Like Samuel Johnson's Idler, these slackers serve a kind of double function, ridiculing the culture's work pieties while making fun of the real or fictional people who, for one reason or another, have come to embody the leading edge of anti-work sentiment. Slackers always make fun not just of work, but of themselves, or perhaps it is bet-ter to say they make fun not just of themselves, but of work and its supporters.

Standing up for the work ethic in *Dobie Gillis* is Dobie's father, who runs a small grocery store and is constantly, and angrily, trying to get Dobie to take responsibility. His humorous inability to understand "kids these days" is just one sign he and his values are obsolete:

DOBIE'S FATHER

He doesn't know the meaning of the word work. Money, allowance, spending, these words he knows, so why can't he understand work?

DOBIE'S MOTHER

He's too busy discovering life. Put yourself in his place, he's young.

DOBIE'S FATHER

Let him put himself in my place.

But Dobie won't be in his father's place. Chester Riley and Mr. Gillis are already, in the 1950s, on the way out. Factory workers were being elbowed out of the center of the work world by mechanization, by professionals and service workers, and by the globalization of industry. Small shop owners were being pushed out of business by the supermarkets, department stores, and national chains. They were both on the verge of anachronism.

The culture was necessarily of two minds about all this, celebrating progress and bemoaning loss, the winners in these economic transformations obviously more happy with them than the losers. These characters and shows flamboyantly refuse to take sides. Maynard and Dobie are idiots, but they are also accidental geniuses—they are the very future, as surely as their parents represent the past. Yes, Riley is right to want to work as little as possible, and on the other hand, yes, his poor social status may not be entirely unrelated to his poor work ethic. Yes, Mr. Gillis is the voice of reason, and yes, he is well past his sell-by date. Dobie is hip and square. Maynard gets it and he doesn't. The anxieties about work in these shows, and in particular the double relation to throwing off the work ethic—to do so is comically infantile *and* it is the hippest and most honorable possibility—demonstrate not so much a culture coming to conclusions about work as one avoiding conclusions, embracing its own contradictions, bathing them in canned laughter.

∞

Other TV shows and films attempted to capture the changing work attitudes of young people: *Route 66* (1960–64), for instance, was inspired by *On the Road*, although little more than the testimony of the writers remains as evidence of it, and beatnik and proto-hippie characters started to appear in guest spots on many shows. Surfers were particularly well represented, for some of the same basic commercial reasons that explain *Baywatch*. *Gidget*, the 1959 Sandra Dee film, introduced a Hollywood version of surfer culture to audiences and was quickly followed by a series of sequels (*Gidget Goes Hawaiian*, *Gidget Goes to Rome*) and seemingly endless numbers of Frankie Avalon–Annette Funicello beach movies. Surfing, which has continued to be the subject of many books and documentary films in part because of its slacker quality, began growing noticeably in Hawaii again (it was widespread when Europeans first arrived, in 1778) in the first years of the twentieth century and started to sprout a noticeable subculture in California in the 1950s, growing in popularity through the 1960s.

Surfing is necessarily a slacker subculture because, as surfer after surfer testifies, it is addictive and incredibly time-consuming. According to surfing pioneer Fred Hemmings, "Surfing has no time restraints, no out of bounds, and other than commonsense safety practices and traditions, surfing has *NO RULES*." Surfing is for Hemmings everything that the white-collar world is not: "Surfing is creative and very individualistic. In a very regimented and regulated world surfing is an appealing outlet for self-expression." Stephen Wayne Hull, who grew up in the surf subculture of Santa Cruz, California, in the 1960s and went on to write a Ph.D. dissertation on the sociology of surfing, concluded that "a significant amount of downward intergenerational mobility occurs among surfers." In other words, surfers were earning a fraction of what their parents earned, and since many surfers had very little in the way of specific career goals beyond what they called "The Life," they were destined to remain downwardly mobile. More than 40 percent of the surfers Hull surveyed "did not have any idea what they wanted to do" for an occupation.

Surfers consider work, Hull writes, as a necessary evil that interferes with their real, surfing life. Tom Wolfe, who reported on surf culture in 1965 (reprinted 1968, in *The Pump House Gang*), suggests that surfers feel as if they "have this life all of their own; it's like a glass-bottom boat, and it floats over the 'real' world, or the square world or whatever one wants to call it. They are not exactly off in a world of their own, they are and they aren't. What it is, they float right through the real world, but it can't touch them." Like so many other slacker subcultures, surfers betray their mourning for a past way of life, and not just the standard postadolescent mourning for a world in which they don't have to worry about their income or future, but for a kind of primitive, natural, mythical past. Any devotee will tell you that the Hawaiians were surfing before the Europeans arrived and will find some way to suggest that surfing's allure has to do with a kind of premodern, elemental, unmediated relation between humans and nature, a primordial oneness with one's environment. Nature before culture, and therefore, in this Edenic understanding, before work. Jack London, who was introduced to surfing in 1907 in Hawaii, wrote that with its "ecstatic bliss," it was "a royal sport for the natural kings of the earth." Wolfe has one young surfer sum it up: "God, if only everybody could keep on living 'The Life' and not get sucked into the ticky-tacky life with some insurance salesman sitting forward in your stuffed chair on your wall-to-wall telling you that life is like a football game and you sit there and take that stuff. The hell with that."

Surf culture as a media phenomenon perhaps peaked with the "surf rock" of Jan and Dean, Dick Dale, the Surfaris, the Chantays, and the biggest surf band, the Beach Boys. The string of surf-related hit albums between 1962 and 1964 included *Surfin'*, *Surfing*, *Surfin' Safari*, *Surfin' U.S.A.*, *Surfin' Around*, *Surfin' Around the World*, *Surfer Girl*, *Surf City*, *Everybody's Surfin'*, *Surfin' Wild*, *Ride the Wild Surf*, *Surfer's Choice*, *Surfin' Bird*, *Wipe Out*, *Surf Stompin'*, *The Surf Family*, *Big Surf!*, *Pipeline*, *Surf Party*, *Summer Surf*, *Surf Rider!*, *Surf Rockin'*, and dozens more. Thomas Frank, in *The Conquest of Cool: Business Culture, Counterculture, and the Rise of Hip Consumerism* (1997), suggested that "business dogged the counterculture" of the 1960s "with a fake counterculture, a commercial replica that seemed to ape its every move for the titillation of the TV-watching millions and the nation's corporate sponsors." Most of the surf rock and surf films fit this model. In *Gidget*, for instance, Kahuna, the older surfer who "follows the sun" to Hawaii and Peru, explains the surfer work ethic to Gidget:

KAHUNA

I'm a surf bum, you know, ride the waves, eat, sleep, not a care in the world . . .

GIDGET

When do you work?

KAHUNA

Oh, yeah, well, I tried that once. But there were too many hours, and rules, and regulations . . .

GIDGET

But, what will happen to your future? I mean, doesn't everyone have to have a goal or something?

KAHUNA

Who said?

Moondoggie, Gidget's love interest, rips up the hefty allowance checks his father sends and has quit going to college, ready to follow the sun with Kahuna. The rest of the film is taken up with hamburgers, surfing lessons, romance, and a "wild" beach party where kids kiss each other, play bongos, and do backflips. Gidget even drinks half a beer. In the end, in the fall, Moondoggie, rechristened Jeffrey, reconciles with his father and decides to go back to school, and Kahuna, the kids discover, is not going to surf the Peruvian coast after all; he has taken a job as a pilot and has an employee identification badge, with all that implies. It was all just a youthful, rebellious pose.

The *Gidget* and *Beach Blanket* movies existed in the same tenuous relation to surfer culture that Maynard had to the Beats, flirting with the hip while washing it away in waves of ridicule and plot reversals. What Thomas Frank would call these "commercial replicas" of slacker subcultures often made such a weak and tepid set of references to the subcultures they mimicked that no one could possibly be taken in by the fraud. Between the film of *Gidget* and the TV show six years later came the whirl of events that defined the 1960s as a major historical turning point, very few of which were registered by this sitcom or any others. The Berkeley Free Speech Movement, student sit-ins, and the Port Huron Statement; Freedom Rides, the march on Washington, the Civil Rights Act, the marches in Selma, the burning of black churches, businesses, and homes, and the riots in Watts, New York, and Philadelphia; the Berlin wall, the Bay of Pigs, and the Cuban missile crisis; the assassinations of John F. Kennedy, Medgar Evers, and Malcolm X; Buddhist monks setting themselves on fire in the streets of Saigon, the doubling of the draft to 35,000 men a month as the American death toll topped 1,300 in Vietnam; Timothy Leary and Richard Alpert fired from Harvard for LSD experiments, the Beatles' arrival, Dylan going electric, and Ken Kesey and the Merry Pranksters taking their famous bus ride across America—all of this before 1965. TV and the large film studios barely, or only in the most superficial ways, registered these vast transformations, but they were being widely felt nonetheless. Reflecting on how these changes had made his life more difficult, Brian Wilson of the Beach Boys complained that songwriting had gotten too hard: in the early 1960s rock songs needed only a couple of rhymes and a youth-culture subject—surfboards, surf cars, surfer girls—but by the late 1960s even he felt that songs had to be about something more important, and when he couldn't figure out how to do it, he stopped being as "productive."

∞

As this familiar list of early 1960s events suggests, there was not "a counterculture" in the decade, but various subcultures that are often lumped together. Terry H. Anderson, in his history of the 1960s, estimates that perhaps three million people felt themselves part of "the counterculture" in 1970, but he considers them a "minority within another minority—the movement," by which he means the collection of political radicals from antiwar activists and old-school leftists to groups known as Black Power, El Movimiento, Gray Power, Women's Liberation, and the American Indian Movement (often themselves collections of subcultures with different agendas). Elsewhere, however, he estimates three million people living in urban and rural communes at around the same time, and communards would surely represent a small part of the total number of people who identified themselves as countercultural. Given the nomadic lifestyles of people in these subcultures and their disinclination to talk to investigators, as well as the spread of countercultural styles (hair, clothing, drug use, attitudes) through the dominant culture, estimates of the number of people involved are notoriously difficult. The baby boom demographic bulge was in the process of passing through college, making available an enormous number of possible recruits. From only three million students in 1960, the college population swelled to more than ten million by 1973. In 1930 only 12 percent of all people between the ages of eighteen and twenty-one were in school (and thus not in the full-time workforce), compared with 29 percent in 1950 and more than 50 percent by 1970. There were of course some pro–Vietnam War, anti-counterculture people on campuses in these years—George W. Bush, for instance, who identified with the silent majority of conservatives, as they began to call themselves—but they seemed to be in the minority on campuses across the country. Since some of them were also smoking pot, snorting cocaine, and getting into fights with their fathers, the groups could be hard to distinguish.

The various countercultural subcultures often advocated a weird mix of radical individualism and deep-seated communalism, and also, as I suggested in the introductory stories about my own communal days, they often espoused an odd mix of work and slacker ethics. Although these people were often called freaks, their complex, sometimes self-contradictory fantasies were becoming less and less freakish by the late 1960s, more and more mainstream. One 1970 survey found that roughly 35 percent of college students wanted to spend some time in a commune and fully a half wanted to try rural life. And if the more radical counterculturalists existed on the fringes of the society, their general sentiments about conformity and freedom were nonetheless widespread. Countercultural pop songs were big hits in all the genres, from country to soul. The *Whole Earth Catalog* (1968), which won the National Book Award, R. Buckminster Fuller's *Utopia or Oblivion* (1969), Charles Reich's *The Greening of America* (1970), Alicia Bay Laurel's *Living on the Earth* (1971), Baba Ram Dass's *Be Here Now* (1971), E. F. Schumaker's *Small Is Beautiful* (1973), and Carlos Castaneda's *Journey to Ixtlan* (1972) all made it to the bestseller lists, suggesting that the counterculture had mainstream appeal. Even management books, such as Robert Townsend's bestselling *Up the Organization* (1970), written by the president of Avis Rent-a-Car, included a thoroughgoing attack on the culture, as did Alvin Toffler's dystopic *Future Shock* (1970). Toffler, even though he complained of a "surfeit of subcults," was a proponent, like the hippies he ridiculed, of "a transcendence of technocracy and the substitution of a more humane, more far-sighted, more democratic" society. Townsend, in *Up the Organization*, offered a recapitulation of the 1920s hedonist ideal, giving his own version of what a more humane society would do for work: "To be satisfying a job should have variety, wholeness, autonomy, and feedback. In other words, no job description."

Some 1960s subcultures, like the hot-rodders, had a strong work ethic: *Hot Rod* magazine, for instance, clearly espouses work, skill, and competition. But a belief in play rather than work, in relaxing rather than striving, was the more common subcultural conviction. Tuli Kupferberg, who founded the performance group/rock band The Fugs with Ed Sanders (editor of *Fuck You: A Magazine of the Arts*), said in the late 1960s, "Play is as good as work. Work has been defined as something you *dislike* doing. Fuck that. Do the Beatles *work*? Who cares?" In this he was echoing the play ethic of the 1950s sociologists, which makes sense, given the fact that before being a Beat poet and a rock musician, Kupferberg was a sociology graduate student. The difference is in the diffidence. It is hard to imagine Riesman saying "fuck that" or Mills asking "Who cares?"

Many of the "subcults," like the surfers, had a dream that real life, a life of jobs and responsibilities, was something that couldn't "touch them," that they could float above it. Many replaced middle-class, industrial versions of the work ethic with older (although often called New Age) ethics of living off the land or wandering the globe in search of sustenance. Others called for an entire halt to the system, as in the case of Mario Savio, one of the leaders of the Free Speech Movement:

> There is a time when the operation of the machine becomes so odious, makes you so sick at heart, that you can't take part; you can't even tacitly take part, and you've got to put your bodies upon the levers, upon all the apparatus, and you've got to make it stop. And you've got to indicate to the people who own it, that unless you're free, the machine will be prevented from working at all.

Writing in the *Berkeley Barb* in 1968, Jerry Rubin claimed that what the counterculture wanted was to be "free from property hang-ups, free from success fixations, free from positions, titles, names, hierarchies, responsibilities, schedules, rules, routines, regular habits." Is that all? one is tempted to ask.

In *The Greening of America*, Charles Reich announced that a new consciousness was the cause and result of a peaceful revolution, and central to this new order was a new relation to work. "We have all been induced to give up our dreams of adventure and romance in favor of the escalator of success," Reich writes, but the new consciousness "says that the escalator is a sham and the dream is real." In the sham world, people work for the dubious benefit of more consumer products. "Why should we work 12 or 16 hours a day now when we don't have to?" one underground paper of the time asked. "For a color TV? For wall-to-wall carpeting? An automatic ice-cube maker?" One communard told a sociologist that he didn't need a job—precisely because he didn't want "things." He not only didn't want to buy more goods, he wanted to get rid of what he had. "It wasn't hard to drop out," he said. "I had lots of things to get rid of—a car, a hi-fi, a million useless things . . . I got rid of it all. It was like getting a good load off."

And it is no accident that his material disencumberment and his communal days coincided. Only one copy of *Be Here Now* is necessary in a group of twenty or fifty, and the communes tended toward the ascetic anyway. This was in part because the communal ideal was wrapped up with a desire to get by without jobs and without money. As Raymond Mungo, leftist turned communard turned back-to-the-lander, wrote, "Money's your problem? Move in with thirteen people, it's cheaper. And more interesting."

Communal life was seen, at the same time, as a better kind of social organization, one that avoided the antihuman traps of hierarchical groups. "Why did we start collectives?" the Canyon Collective asked rhetorically in their self-published manifesto. "Because we didn't dig being bossed around by bureaucrats whether on the job or in 'the movement.' We were tired of living and acting alone, and wanted to share more of our lives with each other." The communes, some urban, some rural, gave people a sense that they were founding a new way of being in the world: "The hippies have passed beyond American society," wrote Lawrence Lipton in the *Los Angeles Free Press* in 1968. "They're not really living in the same society. It's not so much that they're living on the leftovers, on the waste of American society, as that they just don't give a damn." One can agree with this last phrase, I suppose—that they didn't give a damn—without agreeing to the rest. One has to admit, for instance, that the hippies were in fact living in American society, and that they were living on its leftovers and waste. The *Whole Earth Catalog*, for instance, on a page that quotes someone named Fred Richardson saying "Workers of the world, disperse," also suggests that "Union Carbide can be scrounged for materials" and that a cardboard house for a family of four can be made for $35. The *Catalog* is a trove of ideas for putting the debris of the straight world to use, from scavenging food that grocery stores are about to throw away to dump-picking to procuring government cheese.

The classic of all guidebooks for living on the detritus of America was Abbie Hoffman's *Steal This Book* (1971), in which he claimed that he was not interested in the "greening of Amerika" except for "the grass that will cover its grave." He encouraged his readers to "make war on machines, and in particular the sterile machines of corporate death and the robots that guard them." In a dozen chapters, such as "Free Food," "Free Housing," "Free Medical Care," "Free Educa-

tion," and "Free Dope," he describes hundreds of forms of minor an-
ticapitalist sabotage, from eating happy-hour food—using someone
else's half-finished drink as a prop—to crashing bar mitzvahs, and
from switching price tags in stores to putting on matching coveralls
and renting a truck to look official while walking off with an apartment building's lobby furniture. He describes shoplifting and panhandling techniques and methods of burglary. These acts of civil
disobedience, he assures his readers, are not only morally defensible,
they are every person's moral responsibility:

> Whether the ways [this book] describes to rip-off shit are legal or il-
> legal is irrelevant. The dictionary of law is written by the bosses of
> order. Our moral dictionary says no heisting from each other. To
> steal from a brother or sister is evil. To *not* steal from the institutions
> that are the pillars of the Pig Empire is equally immoral.

He doesn't feel that people should work for the Pig Empire, either, although he does suggest that someone might want to take a job as a
cashier as part of pilfering and shoplifting schemes, or to take a job in
a shipping department to reroute goods to more deserving destina-
tions.

As Jackson Lears has pointed out in his 2003 book on gambling and
luck in America, the idea of getting "something for nothing" has long
been interwoven with the American dream. Hoffman's is as offbeat a
version of this utopian dream as any, but his argument is a common
one in this period: "the machine" needs to be broken before it can
be fixed, and the only way a new world can spring up is if the old is
demolished. "Our purpose is to abolish the system (call it the Greed
Machine, capitalism, the Great Hamburger Grinder, Babylon, Do-
Your-Job-ism)," wrote hippie journalist Marvin Garson in 1969, "and
learn to live cooperatively, intelligently, gracefully (call it the New
Awareness, anarchism, The Aquarian Age, communism, whatever you
wish)." Some believed that it was possible to destroy the system by
simply refusing to take part, that to "drop out," to simply resign from
the larger society, would, if enough people followed along, bring its
death.

Dropping out often involved some kind of self-sufficiency and thus
"living on the land." Here again, there was a raft of handbooks and

guides published in the late 1960s and early 1970s on everything from goat milking to seed storage to honey extraction. Books by Helen and Scott Nearing, the grandparents of the movement, were reissued; they had published *Living the Good Life: How to Live Sanely and Simply in a Troubled World* in 1954, which had all the basic ingredients— composting, organic gardening, building homes from local materi- als—of the later movement. An even earlier guide, *Five Acres and Independence*, published by M. G. Kains in 1935, was reissued in the late 1960s. *The Foxfire Book* (1972) and its numerous sequels were originally intended as a preservationist project, documenting the "folk arts" of the Appalachians. But as the subtitle suggests (the full title was *The Foxfire Book: Hog Dressing, Log Cabin Building, Mountain Crafts and Foods, Planting by the Signs, Snake Lore, Hunting Tales, Faith Healing, Moonshining*), they also served as guides for the new pio- neers. *The Mother Earth News* was launched in 1970 and became the semiofficial monthly magazine of the movement; it declared that any- one could make a perfectly good living on an eight-acre plot of land.

One of the most popular of these back-to-the-land guides was *Liv- ing on the Earth* (1971), which made the *New York Times* bestseller list in 1971 and gave advice on how to build a house, how to raise chickens, how to purify water, how to live "close to the land." Written by then twenty-year-old Alicia Bay Laurel, the book, in an anti- machine gesture, is not typeset: the text is handwritten in the author's loopy cursive, accompanied by her line drawings. Bay Laurel, she ex- plains in the book, is not her parents' surname, but it is one of her fa- vorite trees. In tune with this kind of self-invention, she managed to turn herself from a middle-class art student into a self-styled expert on farming and homesteading, and she did so in the short space of a year. At the age of nineteen she dropped out of an urban college and moved into the artist Bill Wheeler's commune in northern California, where she quickly realized that she wasn't alone in knowing nothing about how to live without electricity or supermarkets. She appointed herself the commune's information maven and started asking people what they knew how to do, collecting the available practical knowl- edge, and putting it together as an internal pamphlet for the com- mune, a kind of survivalist *Hints from Heloise*. One year later it had sold more than 350,000 copies and the author was flying to Japan and elsewhere promoting translations. The book captures the overweening arrogance of these new converts to rural living. The simple life in the countryside has enormous benefits, Bay Laurel writes: "We discover the serenity of living with the rhythms of the earth. We cease oppressing one another." Her small band of communards and single year may not seem to warrant such a strong conclusion, but it was an era of grand statements.

The book is written, it announces, "for people who would rather chop wood than sit behind a desk," and it is otherwise in line with the by now centuries-old slacker critique of industrial civilization. (It remains silent about people who would rather jet to Japan for promotional reasons.) "If you live on land that has been raped ('logged')," she writes, "you may find stumps that work as foundations for your house." This is remarkably bad advice, of course, since the stumps would rot long before anything one put on them, except perhaps a cardboard house. Not surprisingly, some of Bay Laurel's recipes are far from time-tested, and the back-to-the-land movement is full of stories of minor disasters based on improvised reinventions of agricultural and building techniques. Many who left communes have a "last straw" story, after years of winter outhouses and badly disguised soybean meals. Abbie Hoffman, in another common narrative, "resigned" from the counterculture after some of his radio and tape equipment was stolen. Reasons commonly given for the "death of the counterculture" include the Manson family murders, the Stones' Altamont concert, methamphetamine addiction, and other dystopian turns of the countercultural wheel. Others point to the lack of an actual program, as opposed to dreams and ideals; the globalization of capital markets; and a number of other factors. Often, too, the end of the draft and the war in Vietnam are cited as taking the wind out of the sails of the various movements, since it was the war that produced the majority of the active political involvement in these years.

But the contradictions within and among the movements can also be explanation enough. Many realized that their philosophical aversion to material things didn't change their enjoyment of them. Many who went back to the land found themselves, like Nathaniel Hawthorne before them, mired in labor from sunup to sundown, and they didn't like it. Wendell Berry, one of the Appalachian writers who helped inspire and guide the back-to-the-land movement, asked, in 1977, "Is work something we have a right to escape? And can we escape it with impunity? We are probably the first entire people to think so." He counsels a return to the "ancient wisdom" that tells us that our work is "our salvation and our joy." This may be bad cultural history, since most ancient wisdom suggested that labor was a curse, not a blessing, but it was the necessary flip side of the pastoral hippie dream. Other writers taken as important philosophers by the movement thought likewise. E. F. Schumacher, author of *Small Is Beautiful*, described work in a way any Zen-influenced hippie could embrace: "In the process of doing good work the ego of the worker disappears. He frees himself from his ego, so that the divine element in him can become active." And the *Whole Earth Catalog* was, more than anything else, a tool catalog, a place to find the implements (and machines) needed to do various kinds of work.

The film *Easy Rider* (1969) captures the conflicted images of the good life at the center of the counterculture, as Whitmanian loafing on the open road meets the twenty-four-hour party people. It is a film about, among other things, freedom from work. George, the alcoholic part-time lawyer played by Jack Nicholson, for instance, seems to find a new freedom when he throws off his small-town practice and hits the road with the drug-dealing antiheros Wyatt and Billy, played by Peter Fonda and Dennis Hopper. Wyatt and Billy have made a big score, and free to do whatever they want, they now have only one goal—getting to New Orleans for Mardi Gras. They are free from lovers and family, free from want, and, especially, free from labor. Wyatt starts their road trip by throwing away his watch, a kind of international symbol for sloughing off the industrial world of work, and George, in the famous campfire scene, declares, "It's real hard to be free when you're bought and sold in the marketplace."

But freedom doesn't work out that well for the characters. The lawyer, very soon into his experiment with free living on the road, gets bludgeoned to death, and our antiheroes, although we are supposed to accept them as liberating outlaws at the start, begin to doubt themselves and to question their own sense of freedom. They are awed by the farmer they meet who feeds himself and his very large family with his own produce (prompting Wyatt's astonishingly patronizing compliment: "It's not every man who can live off the land, you know. You can be proud."). Wyatt is also moved by seeing the hippie commune where people are working the land together. The drug dealers' own lives seem to hold less utopian allure after these meetings, especially to Wyatt. Sure enough, after their acid-fueled Mardi Gras, Wyatt declares, "We blew it, man." Film-minutes later, they end up dead as well.

Wyatt and Billy, as their different relations to fashion and hairstyle suggest (and their names, suggesting Wyatt Earp, the lawman, and Billy the Kid, the gunfighter), are already two very different versions of the hippie outlaw. Billy is a pot-addled, giggling, amoral freak, Wyatt the more thoughtful one who weeps when he does LSD. They sometimes seem heroic (or at least antiheroic) and sometimes stupid, abusive, and purposeless. The communards, too, look alternately silly and Edenic, or sometimes both, as when we see several of them stumble around a rocky, untilled patch of desert sowing seeds: the ground is so obviously barren and their lack of agricultural knowledge so apparent that the awed reaction from Wyatt and Billy simply increases our sense that the whole mess of them are touchingly deluded. The ending, in which they are killed by rednecks, is part of what Pauline Kael called the "sentimental paranoia" of the film: "In the late 1960s," she wrote, "it was cool to feel that you couldn't win, that everything was rigged and hopeless." These two equal parts of the countercultural view—the paranoid belief in ultimate impossibility and the utopian belief that seeds scattered on any barren ground will sprout and sustain—obviously could not coexist for very long.

The film was produced outside normal Hollywood channels, the financing supplied by maverick producer Bert Schneider from his own money, with no distributor lined up. The crew was a ragtag bunch, sometimes doing their jobs for the first time—actors turned soundmen, photographers turned lighting gaffers—and others were underground cameramen doing their first more or less regular feature. The making of the film has now entered Hollywood lore, with competing stories of who pulled knives on whom. The actor Rip Torn, who was originally signed to play the Nicholson part, for instance, won a $475,000 defamation suit against Hopper after Hopper claimed, on *The Tonight Show*, that Torn had assaulted him. By all accounts, the filming was a nightmare of extreme drug intake, incompetence, and violent disagreement. Like the period itself, we might say, the making of *Easy Rider* was a mixture of both utopian reinvention and dystopian, paranoid violence.

And like the counterculture it documented, *Easy Rider* managed to have some effect on the world of work. Its success helped open the American film industry to the new wave of directors—Martin Scorsese, George Lucas, Francis Ford Coppola, Robert Altman, Peter Bogdanovich, Terrence Malick, Steven Spielberg—who, in Peter Biskind's words, "saved Hollywood." Even if the studios reasserted their power eventually, independent directors and producers have ever since been an important part of the ways movies are made.

Likewise, the counterculture's interest in new ways of working, while never a match for corporate imperatives, nonetheless changed the way business did business. And the social revolutions of the late 1960s have had lasting impact on the way people think about work and the value of work—as well as freedom from work—ever since. This was perhaps most evident in the dot-com boom, with those companies' game rooms and de rigueur casual dress. But as we'll see, otherwise as well.

∞

Meanwhile, from the highest rungs of the culture ladder to the lowest, doing nothing was all the rage. In the elite art world, doing nothing was raised to, well, an art. Walter De Maria in the early 1960s suggested that artists should engage in "meaningless work":

> Meaningless work is obviously the most important and significant art form today. The aesthetic feeling given by meaningless work can not be described exactly because it varies with each individual doing the work. Meaningless work is honest.

His piece, *Boxes for Meaningless Work* (1961), has the instructions, "Transfer things from one box to the next box back and forth, back and forth, etc. Be aware that what you are doing is meaningless." Christian Boltanski, the French artist who began working in the 1960s, told *Tate Magazine* that "one of the beauties of my life is that I never work. I'm lazy and I have no other way to work." He was, he said, "a very traditional artist," which to him means he spends his time "making paintings and doing nothing." Ed Ruscha, another artist whose career took off in the 1960s, claims that "most artists are doing basically the same thing—staying off the streets." Artist and musician

Robert Fripp (whose band, King Crimson, recorded from 1969 to 1974) says it again: "Doing nothing is very hard: it is a form of radical neutrality, a determining feature of the accomplished artist."

Ray Johnson went perhaps as far as one can go with this idea. Johnson initiated the New York Correspondence School in the 1960s, an international network of artists who sent artwork to one another through the mail, thus short-circuiting the gallery system. Among other things, this was meant to be a criticism of the way commerce was corrupting art. This also made the job of being his art dealer tough. Frances Beatty spent fourteen years trying to get Johnson to do a regular show, i.e., one that would result in the sale of work, and finally one day on the phone he told her he might be ready. In the documentary film about Johnson, *How to Draw a Bunny* (2002), she tells the story of the show that almost was:

> I said, "Great, Ray, what's it going to be?" And he said, "We'll have *nothing* in the gallery." "Look, Ray," I said. "We could *do nothing* if we were *downtown*, but *uptown* I don't think we can do nothing." Now the thing is that you never knew whether Ray was really going to do *nothing*, or whether his nothing was one of his *nothings*, because he did these performances and they were called *nothings*. So maybe he meant that he was going to do *nothing* or did he mean that he was not going to do *anything*? You really didn't know.

The end result, from Beatty's perspective, was not good. Richard Feigen, through whose gallery Beatty worked, thought that Johnson "lived on another planet" and that he wouldn't help them help him make a living. "What you ended up with," Beatty said, "was nothing." Johnson's last artwork, as far as anyone could tell, was his suicide, which he committed on Friday the thirteenth, 1995, after staying in room 247 (equals 13) at a motel, off marker 13 on a Long Island beach. There was no suicide note, and so the question remains, Was he doing nothing? Can doing nothing leave an artist depressed enough to commit suicide?

On the opposite end of the cultural spectrum, skateboarders in the mid-1970s claimed that they were perfecting an art form, and they had some of the same arguments among themselves about their relation to the world of commerce. A series of recent films, the documentaries *Dogtown and Z-Boyz* (2001) and *Stoked: The Rise and Fall of Gator* (2002) and the feature *Lords of Dogtown* (2005), have been retelling the story of a group of teenage skateboarders in the mid-1970s who were at the center of an emerging industry—complete with national advertising campaigns and magazines—based on what had been their unsullied recreational life. In the course of the debates about the purity of the experience being diluted by commerce, in places like *Skateboarder* magazine in 1975, the "high state of the art" was a common motif, but so was the increasing downhill speed as wheel technology improved. *Skateboarder* writer Carlos Izan claimed that while 40 m.p.h. was the limit a year earlier, 50 m.p.h. was common in 1975. Physical injury is the center of skateboarder talk—"The thing is," skateboarding legend Tony Alva says, "if you really fall you really get hurt"—and speed and injury are intimately related. "It's at a different place and time for each rider, but after 45, it becomes increasingly apparent," Izan wrote. "An all-encompassing awareness of an impending bad situation. Something you pay no attention to, yet somehow can't ignore. An entity you don't want to look at, yet have the urge to see."

In 2003 these two worlds came together in an art exhibition called the PUSH Project, which originated in Seattle's Roq la Rue Gallery and traveled to New York and several other cities. Artists Charles Krafft, C. R. Steyck, Shawn Wolfe, Ries Niemi, Jim Woodring, Randy Wood, and Jeff Kleinsmith all produced, along with other works, a skateboard design as part of the exhibition. Krafft's was a porcelain skateboard (wheels and all) with a picture of Martha Stewart on it. Krafft had done a series of weapons in porcelain and what he calls Disasterware, a series of plates with images of, for instance, the fire-bombing of Dresden. His porcelain skateboard helps point out the fragility of skateboarders hurtling through space.

High art was keeping artists off the street, and skateboarding was putting them on it, but in both cases doing nothing was much more than a lack of activity. Doing nothing offered itself as a deep basis for identity. Doing nothing, purposely meaningless work, unsullied play, meaningless movement—in a culture obsessed with purpose, pragmatism, and productivity, to do nothing is not a neutral act. To conspicuously do nothing is to assert and insist upon a countercultural identity. Artists and quasi-delinquent teens, however much their identities otherwise might not overlap, find in slackerhood the seemingly firm ground of their difference from the rest of their society.

∞

One of the most profound changes in the world of work was the doubling and then almost tripling of women's participation in the workforce. From 1900 to 1947, women increased from 18 percent to 28 percent of workers. By 1980 they accounted for 42.5 percent, and by 1990 they would be 50 percent. In 1950 only 12 percent of married women with children worked for pay; forty-five years later, 70 percent did. A series of studies in the 1970s and 1980s found that women were bringing new attitudes, concerns, and practices into the workplace. Women were significantly more likely than men, researchers found, to value creativity, freedom, cooperation, enjoyment, fulfillment, and personal challenge than men. Some of these studies, with their rosy predictions of a more humane and fulfilling workplace when women were in charge, were obviously wishful thinking rather than sound research—one flashes to Leona Helmsley, "the Queen of Mean," for instance. And none of these researchers corrected for the fact that men, too, might be becoming more interested in these same aspects of work for their own reasons.

In the late 1950s and early 1960s, management theories had already been revised along these lines, offering what came to be called the "enrichment" school of business administration. Douglas McGregor separated management styles into the old-fashioned authoritarian Theory X and the participatory, nonhierarchical Theory Y— Theory X the appropriate style for the standardized, segmented, formalized work patterns of the factory; Theory Y for the more discretionary, open-ended tasks of information, service, and professional jobs. Other management theorists (like Herzberg, Mausner, and Snyderman) were arguing along with McGregor that feelings of achievement and personal growth were the most important motivating factors in workers' lives. Rather than any internal, inculcated work ethic, the possibility of fulfillment and satisfaction were assumed to motivate work, and worker discretion and autonomy bred that satisfaction. As the number of factory workers continued to shrink and the composition of the American workforce became increasingly white-collar, many economists, sociologists, and industrial engineers assumed that there would necessarily be a general increase in workers' control of their own time, and therefore an increased level of satisfaction.

But at least one official study of the quickly changing workplace noticed the opposite trend, despite agreeing about what made work worthwhile. *Work in America*, a 1973 report from a special task force set up by Secretary of Health, Education, and Welfare Elliott Richardson, argued that the work ethic was declining, evidenced by the proliferation of panhandlers, increased early retirement and absenteeism, the move toward four-day weeks, growing welfare rolls, and, somewhat oddly, union strikes and the growth of the commune movement. This decline was less cause than effect, according to the report. The prime reason people were uninterested in work was that it was unsatisfying, they said, and this "diminishing job satisfaction" was due to diminishing opportunities to be one's own boss. The highest level of work satisfaction was among university professors, who had control over the majority of their time, and the lowest was among blue-collar workers with little control over their daily schedules. Virtually all the professors (93 percent) reported that yes, they gained satisfaction from their work. But white-collar workers said yes only 43 percent of the time, and blue-collar workers only 24 percent. These very low numbers, the report suggested, portended huge problems in the future and helped explain the declining work ethic. Harry Braverman's *Labor and Monopoly Capital* (1974), an academic bestseller the following year, also found "labor degradation" across the economy, a dilution of workers' autonomy, and a downgrading of skills and discretion in white-collar as well as blue-collar jobs.

The HEW report also noted that *talk* about the work ethic was increasing dramatically. They found an average of seven articles a year in major mass-market magazines on the topic from 1970 to 1975, compared with just one article a year on the topic in the 1960s. In the spirit of the time, much of this mass-market talk was involved with challenges to traditional understanding; it is no accident, for instance, that the term "workaholic" was coined in the same years that spawned the hippie work ethic. Studs Terkel's bestseller *Working: People Talk About What They Do All Day and How They Feel About What They Do* (1974) documents some of this talk. As his subtitle suggests, Terkel accepted the idea that what was important was not the ethics of working, but how work made workers feel. The 125 people who described their work lives to Terkel came down on both sides of the central issues, some feeling alienated by their lack of control, some not, some finding satisfaction in the most rote tasks. A bookbinder simply loved working on books; a gravedigger was proud of how straight and clean his cuts into the earth were. Workers found pleasure and meaning in various ways, some more or less illicit—like switchboard operators eavesdropping or meter readers indulging sexual fantasies—and some based on a reasonable if somewhat imaginary upgrading of the work itself. A waitress, for instance, describes feeling that she is onstage, that laying down a fork without making a noise and gracefully bending to pick things up approaches ballet. Terkel's book was popular not just because it exposed worker alienation but because it had such unexpected inspirational stories of fulfillment as well.

A few years later Daniel Yankelovich and John Immerwahr calculated the amount of effort people put into their jobs, especially "discretionary effort"—the amount of effort beyond the minimum necessary to avoid being fired or penalized—and they argued that discretionary effort was increasing. As people move from assembly lines to service jobs, they necessarily have more control over their own level of effort, if nothing else. By the late 1970s, these authors noted, public school teachers outnumbered the combined production workers in the chemical, oil, rubber, plastic, paper, and steel industries, and this is one of many figures showing that discretionary workers were the norm. Yankelovich and Immerwahr also found that all the talk about a deteriorating work ethic was "badly off-target; the American work ethic is strong and healthy, and may be growing stronger."

Yankelovich argued that roughly 50 percent of high school graduates and 63 percent of college graduates had a strong work ethic, and that the rate was even higher for countercultural types: fully 72 percent of those who subscribed to "the new cultural values" had top scores on his work ethic scale. Still, Yankelovich and Immerwahr found, most workers felt that there was not enough relation between effort and pay, and three-quarters of them did not feel that they were working at their full potential. The authors blame managers for not reinforcing what they claim is a healthy preexisting work ethic. Interestingly enough, the managers, Yankelovich found in another study, blame the workers. Roughly 80 percent of managers he surveyed in 1976 believed that their workers' work ethic had eroded.

Like most people writing in these decades, Yankelovich and Immerwahr assume that work is a prime arena of satisfaction and gratification, either granted or denied, not a duty in the Weberian sense. John Paul II, in his encyclical letter *Laborem Exercens* (*On Human Work*, 1981) also took the "work as benefit" approach. "Work is a good thing for man—a good thing for his humanity—because through work man not only transforms nature, adapting it to his own needs, but he also achieves fulfillment as a human being and indeed in a sense becomes 'more a human being.' " This is a somewhat tautological argument, but it does replace older notions of duty with a somewhat diffuse sense of betterment. At the same time, the old exhortations to work as a moral imperative continued to be made. Edward Banfield, for instance, sounds exactly like a Victorian moralist when he says, in *The Unheavenly City: The Nature and Future of Our Urban Crisis* (1970):

> The lower class individual lives from moment to moment . . . Impulse governs his behavior, either because he cannot discipline himself to sacrifice a present for a future satisfaction or because he has no sense of the future. He is therefore radically improvident.

The bad work ethic causes the dissatisfaction, not the other way around, Banfield wrote, just like his forbears a hundred and two hundred years earlier.

Into this whirl of contradictory opinions and attitudes—some tasting of the latest styles of thought, some hoary with age—sociologists and other researchers, editorialists and essayists threw themselves, attempting to sort out what exactly was the spirit of the times. Many of the young people of these decades, whatever their relation to the counterculture, watched the debates from the sidelines as the rate of youth unemployment continued to grow, reaching rates of 30 percent and more in some communities in the United States and many other developed countries. Young people started to hear, for the first time in American history, that chances were that they would not earn as much money as their fathers had, that the jobs they may have hoped to get would be too few and growing scarcer, that perhaps progress, as measured by the improvement of the next generation's standard of living, may have come to an end. The generations to follow would hear this as well; for the slackers of Generation X, it would be a major theme.

∞

Despite the pervasive dread of "underwork," people still worried about overwork. Wayne Oates introduced the term "workaholic" in an obscure article in a pastoral care journal in 1968, but after his *Confessions of a Workaholic* became a bestseller in 1971, the word immediately entered common usage. Born into a poor South Carolina family in 1917, abandoned by his father at birth, Oates was determined to get ahead, and after putting himself through college and then a master's and a Ph.D. program, he managed to publish some forty-seven books before he died, all the while working as a pastor and a full-time faculty member, first at a seminary and then at the University of Louisville Medical School. Oates wrote that a workaholic (and he admitted it took one to know one) was someone who cannot stop working, who needs larger and larger doses to get by. They have "forced themselves into exhaustion, depression, cardiovascular disorders, excessive eating in order to maintain energy, and all manner of imbalances of the human life."

Later researchers would distinguish between types of workaholics—in one case between the "enthusiastic" and "unenthusiastic," or those who are driven and happy and those who are driven and unhappy about it. But for Oates they were all diseased, and he prescribed vacations, even if the workaholic could stand only a five-minute one to start. At the same time, he castigated "the gold-brickers, free-loaders, rip-off artists, and lead butts of society" and warned that "the hazards of addiction to laziness are as great as the hazards of addiction to work." The workaholic needs to slow down, according to Oates, but not slow down so much as to become an idler. The workaholic and the slacker are the poles, work satisfaction and fulfillment the center. Oates may seem mealymouthed or trite in this, but he was far from alone. The dissection and castigation of the type A personality continued apace in the psychological and medical journals and the popular press.

In fiction and film, however, the type A personality went on worrying more about his (still usually "his") chances for promotion than about any actual work. The joke of Joseph Heller's title *Something*

Happened (1974), for instance, is that nothing happens. And Heller's book points out the other pertinent fact: the large corporation, which more and more people were working for, was the elephant in this theoretical room—it was the large corporation that was shaping people's work lives. The executive protagonist lives in a work world of endless corridors and organizational charts. He describes his boss as a "small-minded oblivious prick, a self-satisfied simpleton" who buys puzzles, perpetual-motion toys, and other novelties and has his secretary send for the narrator and other employees to show them off:

> "Look at this," he will command, beaming, as though he had just chanced upon something of vast benefit to all mankind. "Isn't it something? Just stand still there and look at it. It will never stop as long as you keep doing this. Each one is always different."
>
> "That's really something," I have to respond, and have to remain standing there until he grows tired of having me in his office and sends me back.
>
> I hate to have to stand still.

But when the narrator goes back to his office, he does stand still, performing little actual work, just a smidge more than his bosses but less than his underlings. The twelve men at the top of the company do the least. They hold meetings (as Galbraith said, "meetings are indispensable when you don't want to do anything") and make promotion decisions, but mostly they just sign memos prepared and sent by someone else. "Nobody is sure anymore," he says, "who really runs the company." And he admits that "most of the work we do in my department is, in the long run, trivial." He tries to succeed without really trying. Between martinis at lunch, flirting with secretaries in the afternoon, whispering fearfully in the hallways, feigning interest in those above him in the hierarchy, and feigning indifference to those below, he never seems to do much of anything. Nothing happens. He is alienated from everyone.

Aside from the still-new corporate slackers, the culture kept producing young, unemployed slackers, too, as hippies became replaced in the media's attention by "punks." Some punks took hippie slackerdom an extra yard by declaring that their protest had no real object, that they were uninterested in any program for the future. As one punk said, "We did it because we had to; we were genetically programmed to be adolescent and, anyway, there wasn't anything else to do on Friday night." Johnny Rotten of the Sex Pistols asked, "When did being an adolescent ever mean anything? It's all about being yourself. Be a fucking individual." Rock critic Simon Frith would eventually reduce the movement to a "spectacle of middle-class children dressing up in a fantasy of proletarian aggression and lying desperately about their backgrounds." It was, one British punk later said, simply his generation's "fumbled attempts to get drunk, listen to the band, get laid and get the last bus home."

Paul Corrigan, in his study of youth in mid-1970s London, writes that "the main action of British subculture is, in fact, 'doing nothing.'" Here is a segment of an interview that is part of his study:

CORRIGAN
What sort of thing do you do with your mates?

DUNCAN
Just stand around talking about footy. About things.

CORRIGAN
Do you do anything else?

DUNCAN
Joke, lark about, carry on. Just what we feel like really.

CORRIGAN
What's that?

DUNCAN
Just doing things. Last Saturday someone started throwing bottles and we all got in.

CORRIGAN
What happened?

DUNCAN
Nothing really.

The kids are bored, Corrigan writes, and they turn to the street not because it is a "wonderfully lively place," but because it is simply more
likely that something will happen there than at home or at some
youth club. For these British youths, "doing nothing" on the street is
an alternative to having nothing to do *and* no hope that anything exciting will ever happen.

Americans continued to glorify and condemn idlers like *Easy
Rider's* Billy and Wyatt and soon would produce an entire new wave
of countercultural slackers. In the meantime, though, the antiauthori-
tarian and pro-work strains of countercultural thinking met their
match in the anti-entitlement politics of the right. Charles Murray,
whose writings on welfare were important to the Reagan administration and the conservative movement, wrote *Losing Ground* (1984), in
which he claimed that the federal programs devised to help poor people in the 1960s and 1970s actually hurt them, that giving money to
poor people destroyed their work ethic and made them and their children congenital wards of the state. The solution to poverty was to reduce the government's role in people's lives as much as possible. The
cure for slackers was to get the government out of the business of supporting them. Himself supported by the American Enterprise Institute
and the Manhattan Institute, Murray became one of the main spokes-
men for the dismantling of the welfare state, one of the main framers
of the debate through the 1980s and 1990s—the debate that led, finally, to the welfare legislation of the mid-1990s.

During the Reagan, Bush, and Clinton administrations, various arguments were accreted to Murray's original one, which is that the system breeds dependency. Murray himself added the idea that the
welfare system decreases the IQ of recipients and increases illegiti-
macy. The idea that poor women have babies to increase their pay-
ments was perennial. But the other idea that keeps returning is that
welfare programs do their most societal damage by destroying the
work ethic. The doomsday scenario suggested that eventually America
would be swamped by dependent, lazy spongers and lose its competitive edge in the world altogether. Without the work ethic, the United
States would sink to the productivity level of the U.S.S.R. This argument was so politically salient that Democrats joined Republicans in
declaiming it. Mickey Kaus, senior editor at *The New Republic*, who
otherwise was arguing classic new-leftie style that the state needed to

intercede to keep the gap between rich and poor from becoming too wide, bought Murray's line wholesale in "The Work Ethic State: The Only Way to Break the Culture of Poverty" in 1986: "The point is to enforce the work ethic. This is a long-term cultural offensive, not a budget-control program or an expression of compassion." Bill Clinton said the welfare system "defies our values as a nation. If we value work, we can't justify a system that makes welfare more attractive than work."

At the same time, studies were being done that suggested that the work ethic as it had always been understood was not particularly important to any society's success. Richard Lynn, in one of the largest cross-cultural studies ever done, surveyed attitudes toward work among university students in forty-three countries in the late 1980s. He reviewed the major theories for why some capitalist economies are more successful than others, and found that the only thing the successful societies had in common was pure competitiveness. He found no correlation between the strength of the work ethic and the relative incomes of developed and developing nations, no correlation between the work ethic and per capita GNP or other economic measures. From a very different perspective, Edmund F. Byrne, in *Work, Inc: A Philosophical Inquiry* (1990), argued that the work ethic might be a bit of a phantom issue. The only real evidence we can have for a work ethic is that someone works hard, and therefore all we know about them is that they are working hard: "We assume that the work ethic is internalized by workers, that those who work hard do so because they have a strong work ethic, and those that don't, don't. But this is tautological." Perhaps the work ethic never really existed. More importantly, Byrne wrote, all of our talk about work at a philosophical level misses the point, because the basic social contract between workers and those they work for has broken down. "Corporations are becoming the world's most powerful de facto bearers of sovereignty" and thus have complete control over their workers' lives. In a world in which individual autonomy at this most fundamental level is undermined by corporate requisites, work styles and ethics have little real power.

And indeed, in the 1980s, citing increased overseas competition, economic recessions, and dwindling profits, corporations turned their backs on Theory Y and the various attempts they had been making toward "job enrichment," and once again they accelerated moves toward mechanization and routinization. The computerization of many production processes spelled the end of what little worker control had been reintroduced to factory floors and in many service jobs. Think of McDonald's automated French fryers, for instance, or accounting programs that require only simple data entry. According to James Rinehart, who has studied "lean production" and other innovations in these decades, corporations were much less likely than in the past to justify these changes as improvements in the quality of work life—the fact that a job remains at all after restructuring was taken to be benefit enough.

From the yuppies on Wall Street to the autoworkers in Detroit, work seemed to be returning from its countercultural detour. The deinstitutionalization of the mentally ill, along with other widening holes in the safety net, accelerated by cuts in federal funding during the Reagan administration, helped make homelessness epidemic in the 1980s, and thus a new image of the nonworking American was in the media. The homeless became walking icons of alienation in American cities. Thousands of what looked like ruthless, soulless stock and bond traders got rich and gave making money a worse name than ever, while thousands of beggars watched them get into their taxis and limousines. It was a propitious moment for the postmodern slacker to arrive.

IX

SLACKERS

In which slackers finally get their proper name — the game room rules the workplace — kids make movies instead of working — the Church of the SubGenius reinvents the lounger — the slacker novel has yet another renaissance — we visit the slackers of Japan and find that globalization in fact has made us all kin — the poor stay poor — the Internet and Anna Nicole Smith show us the Way of the Slacker — and the author reports that his son, Cody, has left the couch.

"Repent! Quit your job!! REPENT!" the photocopied pamphlet declares. A crazy hodgepodge of typefaces, graphics, sidebars, inserts, and boxes, the flyer looks like the back pages of a comic book from the 1950s. "Are you abnormal?" it asks. "THEN YOU ARE PROBABLY BETTER THAN MOST PEOPLE." Something called the Church of the SubGenius seems to be the author, and whoever they are, they would like your money. As far as one can make out, the Church's belief system boils down to this schematic:

> The Goal: SLACK
> The Method: The Casting Out of False Prophets
> The Weapon: Time Control
> The Motto: Fuck Them If They Can't Take a Joke

Satire, hoax, Dada-esque art project, science fiction, and parody religious cult, the Church published its first scripture (this pamphlet) in 1980. It and subsequent pamphlets were a hit on the underground comics circuit and were then expanded into *The Book of the Sub-Genius*, published by McGraw Hill in 1983. The Church continues to run its Web site, selling mugs, T-shirts, and ordinations. It is also at the center of several very active Usenet groups and radio programs, and it sponsors live shows, although, like most slacker events, these are somewhat sparsely attended.

Slack, *The Book of the SubGenius* declares, is both the natural state of human beings and the highest attainable state of enlightenment, like nirvana. "For Slack *comprises the Universe*. It is the Logos, the Tao, the *Wor*, the *Ain Soph* of the Qabbala." Mere physical slack, the scripture warns, can be dangerous, leading to impotence. True slack, on the contrary, "somehow manages to be a great Motive without slapping the speed-limit of Death on the Road." It is "a surge of gumption, an explosion of the 'self'—not obliterating it, but *bloating* it." Very much like the eighteenth-century lounger, then, the SubGenius is someone who is both completely absolved of worldly success, ironically aloof from all bourgeois desires, and clearly protesting too much his own superiority. And taking the lounger's wink one step further, the SubGenius announces his own auto-befuddlement through the scripture's self-help slogans: "Relax in the safety of your own delusions," the scriptures exhort. "Pull the wool over your own eyes." The fact that the pose has a commercial motive is alluded to regularly as well: a graphic, for instance, shows a left-wing ranter and a right-wing ranter having their wallets plucked simultaneously by a SubGenius. "There's a whole market, a type of person there's no word for. I want 'SubGenius' to be that word," says "Bob," the Church's deity. Elsewhere he says, "I don't practice what I preach because I'm not the kind of person I'm preaching *to*." Perhaps more than any other proponent of slackerism before or since, the Church of the SubGenius recognizes its own complicity in suspect commerce—recognizes and admits, winking all the while, that it is, in fact, primarily selling a fantasy, and one that it doesn't itself believe.

Meanwhile, more mainstream popular culture continued to produce slacker characters for fun and profit through the 1980s, such as Sean Penn's memorable portrayal of surfer dude/high school student

Jeff Spicoli in *Fast Times at Ridgemont High* (1982). "Why don't you get a job, Spicoli?" a classmate with a McJob asks. "What for?" he answers. "You need money," the classmate says. Spicoli disagrees: "All I need are some tasty waves, a cool buzz, and I'm fine." This is not, as written, particularly funny; what makes it so is Sean Penn's performance, from the moment he arrives on-screen, tumbling out of a pot-smoke–filled VW van onto the asphalt of the school's parking lot, through his quasi-transformation into a reasonable, although still semiliterate surfer dude: "So what Jefferson was saying was, 'Hey! You know, we left this England place because it was bogus. So if we don't get some cool rules ourselves, pronto, we'll just be bogus too.' Yeah?" The other kids work at fast-food franchises or other shops in the mall, but Spicoli gets high and goes to classes late, when he goes at all, without the assignment done. He lives his slacker life with real glee and unconcern.

Ferris Bueller is ostensibly a more respectable citizen than Spicoli, but in *Ferris Bueller's Day Off* he explains, facing the camera, the various ways in which one can, while in high school, avoid all responsibility without getting caught. He and his classmates have no idea what their future holds and no interest in the past. Their economics professor gives them a lecture on the relation of the Great Depression, the Hawley-Smoot Tariff Act, and the Laffer curve, but they couldn't be less engaged. Because Ferris lives entirely in the present and very near future, because he can so successfully do nothing, he is the school's and the film's unrivaled hero.

Somewhat higher up the cultural food chain, the slacker ethos remains central to novels like Jay McInerney's *Bright Lights, Big City* (1984, film 1988), Bret Easton Ellis's *Less Than Zero* (1985, film 1987), Tama Janowitz's *Slaves of New York* (1986, film 1989), and Michael Chabon's *Mysteries of Pittsburgh* (1988). In a typical interchange from *Less Than Zero*, a character asks the narrator, "What have you been doing, dude?" He replies, "Oh, not too much . . . There's not a whole lot to do anymore." These 1980s slackers were the idling mirror images of high-flying traders like arbitrageur Ivan Boesky and junk bond king Michael Milken, who made hundreds of millions of dollars on Wall Street and set the tone for the decade's "greed is good" ethos. That phrase, from Oliver Stone's *Wall Street* (1987), was a paraphrase of Ivan Boesky's speech at UC Berkeley in

1986 in which he declared that "Greed is healthy." Boesky's speech was to a class of graduating M.B.A.s, and M.B.A. programs themselves were a growth industry in the decade, performing the newly requisite credentialing of happily greedy, hyper-achieving yuppies. The underground press subgeniuses and movie truants were their slacker opposite numbers.

Slackers are noticeably absent from the proceedings of the American Sociological Association's 1985 meeting, which is especially odd given that the theme was "Working and Not Working." Kai Erikson, who edited a volume of papers from the conference, found that the one thing all participants agreed on was that "the nature of work in America is being transformed in important ways." Factory jobs were migrating to the third world, information and service jobs were the new "industrial center of gravity," and the "meaning of work" was under revision. Cynthia Fuchs Epstein, a sociologist at the CUNY Graduate Center, noted that groups from the fundamentalist right to the nostalgic left were mourning the passing of a traditional relation to work, the kind of Marlboro man, blue-collar family breadwinner in Bruce Springsteen's rust-belt anthems. Epstein knew that this image of the American worker was already a myth, that even in Springsteen's songs the heroic laborer is ruefully aware that change is at hand and that it is leaving him behind. In place of the older division between white-collar and blue-collar workers, both groups of which could purchase their house-and-car American dreams, there was a new "split society," as other sociologists called the contemporary labor market: "a set of good jobs that pay relatively well, are secure, and afford opportunities for advancement and a second group that are relatively poorly paid, dead-end jobs." The chasm between these two groups yawned before young moviegoers eager to believe in the alternative offered by Bueller and Spicoli, or at least to enjoy it as fantasy.

While Hollywood honed its formulas and the sociologists were reading papers to one another, the young men who more than any others would become associated with slackers in the 1990s, Douglas Coupland and Richard Linklater, were preparing their debuts. The not-yet-a-writer Coupland was in Japan, at the Hokkaido College of Art and Design. He was in postgraduate art school, a classic venue for slackers, and he thought of himself as a sculptor and designer, not a writer. A series of quasi-accidental encounters with editors later, however, Coupland published *Generation X*, which forever after stuck as the name for his cohort. Coupland's novel offered a kind of alternative sociology, coming furnished with a statistical appendix: the items include the number of people in the workforce per Social Security beneficiary in 1949, 1990, and 2030, for instance, and the number of people aged twenty-five to twenty-nine owning homes in 1973 and 1987. The last item in the appendix is a *Time*/CNN poll. The poll found that 65 percent of eighteen- to twenty-nine-year-old Americans agreed that it was much harder for their generation to live as comfortably as previous generations had, and that nonetheless 58 percent agreed "there is no point in staying at a job unless you are completely satisfied." One of Coupland's characters explains, "You really have to wonder why we even bother to get *up* in the morning. I mean, really: *Why work*? Simply to buy more *stuff*? That's just not enough . . ." But since the characters have to meet basic needs, they have McJobs (Coupland's coinage) even though, given their aptitudes and educations, the jobs represent "occupational slumming." These characters have jobs; they just don't have *good* jobs.

The characters used to have better jobs, in offices, but at some point preferred not to have them, in a late-1980s version of dropping out. Ever since "Bartleby," and certainly since *Metropolis* and *The Crowd* in the 1920s, the specter of a ghoulish standardization has hovered over the American workplace, and in the 1980s and 1990s the image of that standardization was the cubicle and its computer monitor. The characters of *Generation X* reject life in cubicles, which the narrator dubs "veal-fattening pens." (A marginal note explains: "Small, cramped office workstation built of fabric-covered disassembleable wall partitions and inhabited by junior staff members. Named after the small preslaughter cubicles used by the cattle industry.") This image of the cubicled office became, sometime in the late 1980s, the dominant image of work, the picture of what the average workspace was like, just as Riley's factory and Mr. Gillis's shop had been images of former workspaces. While Melville imagined the office as the incubator of absurdity and tragedy, Generations X and Y were much more likely to see the problems of such work in terms of boredom and irony. Without a viable alternative vision—such as adventure on the high seas or a cabin on Walden Pond—these slacker generations saw their choice as acceptance or rejection. To reject the office, however, meant working at the convenience store or the construction site or bartending. Even Peter, the hero of *Office Space*, only manages his blithe disregard for the world of employment very briefly; then he joins his neighbor at manual labor.

Coupland was immediately recognized as the "spokesperson" for Generation X. The *Boston Globe* called him "the nonvoice for a nongeneration." *Newsweek* called the book the "defining document for people with too many TVs and too few job opportunities." And Coupland was quickly proved right about the relation between history and marketing—the speed with which Generation X went from being a report from the front lines of youth culture to being a marketing strategy was breathtaking. The *Atlanta Journal-Constitution* mentioned Coupland's novel in June of 1991 in a piece that discussed the twentysomethings in terms of their films, television shows, and movies, but also in terms of the marketing problem they represented. This was two weeks before the paper reviewed the novel. "I Am Not a Target Market" is the title of the fourth chapter of *Generation X*, and marketers quickly understood that the postmodern ironic distance this generation had on themselves and their cynical relation to advertising made them a new kind of problem. Articles about the generation as a market segment for consumer products and TV shows, music, and film appeared in magazines like *Business Week* and *Advertising Age* as well as in general magazines and newspapers. The consensus was, in the words of a *Marketing News* piece, "The twentysomethings are a marketer's worst nightmare. They could very well be the demographic group from hell."

Richard Linklater, whose film *Slacker* (1991) gave the generation its other enduring nickname, also saw the success of *Slacker* and *Generation* X in terms of market demographics:

> Out of nowhere there were these two things addressing a market that people didn't really know existed or had any unifying element. So by default we got linked and Douglas Coupland and I ended up doing interviews and talk shows together. In America, once they sense a new target-market they can sell to, they go into a little feeding frenzy—even though we don't have as much cash, so whatever you're gonna sell to us, it'd better be cheap.

Like the characters in his films, Linklater is hyperaware of the media landscape in which he lives and works. He is simultaneously absolutely cynical about it and in love with it. Unlike those loafers and loungers who refused to admit their relation to commercial culture or who preached against it, bewailing the evils of the market, the slackers of the 1980s and 1990s accepted it as a given, as the necessary if tawdry context for their own activity. Kerouac rarely admitted to a desire for consumer products except wine and jazz, and the hippies claimed to hate them all. These new slackers admitted to loving the spending; they just argued against the getting.

The characters in *Slacker* have rejected work, and they spend entire days wandering around spouting monologues, usually with a philosophical tinge. Only rarely do they come out and mention work, and then only when asked. "What do you do to earn a living?" one character is asked. "You mean work? To hell with the kind of work you have to do to earn a living. All it does is fill the bellies of the pigs who exploit us. Look at me, I'm making it. I live badly, but at least I don't have to work to do it." When the film came out, it was seen, perhaps simply because of the title, as primarily a rejection of the work ethic. In a *Boston Globe* review of *Slacker*, for instance, the reviewer wrote that the characters are

> ironic, sardonic, in some cases narcoleptic; they won't ally themselves to anything, have written everything off, except maybe staying cool. Cut off from upward mobility, nowhere close to a replication of the exploding economy of the '80s, feeling tapped out for life by our huge national deficit, there's hardly anything left for them, as they see it, but to zone out. This they do with spacey dedication in Linklater's comedy of withdrawal that definitively nails down in pseudodocumentary style the New Enervation.

But most of the characters are far from enervated. In fact, the characters are almost all quite energetic, anxious to bloviate at great length with manic emphasis on their pet topics, like the sexuality of the Smurfs, the aliens who brought us here, the class system, or the Kennedy assassination. They are not working at jobs or looking for them, as far as we can see, but they are not exhausted or listless.

As in the past, what enervation exists is part pose, part guilty conscience, part the wear and tear of bucking one's own cultural prescriptions, and part simply the misapprehension of people outside the subculture—that is, what looks like exhaustion to an outsider may just be a pose of disdainful disinterest. Linklater said in interviews after the film was released that it was not about a generation, but about an ageless rejection of the societal pressure to work in traditional ways. He himself had spent years in which people berated him for "doing nothing," when he was in fact shooting film, editing film, watching films, exhibiting films, and talking film day and night; he just had no "product" to show for it. He thought of the title *Slacker* as akin to the gay community taking the social condemnation "queer" and proudly appropriating it, and this makes sense given his own hardworking relation to the slacker ethos. Some of his characters, too, are working at things, playing in bands or taking photographs or painting. But others are simple provocateurs like the many we have seen over the last hundreds of years:

PHOTOGRAPHER

So, what? Do you fancy yourself as some sort of artist or what?

ANTI-ARTIST

No, I'm an anti-artist.

PHOTOGRAPHER

Oooooh, one of those neo-poseur types that hangs out in coffee shops, and doesn't do much of anything. Yeah.

Another character asks, "Who's ever written the great work about the immense effort required not to create?" These, of course, are meant to be funny, but they also pointedly reject the utopian "new economy" dreams of an ever-widening creative class. Not only are software programmers not artists, these scenes suggest, artists are not even really artists anymore.

Coupland and Linklater brought this new generation's anti–work-ethic beliefs, feelings, and ideas to a culture disgusted with its own 1980s excesses and worried about its own millennial future. Like many of the loafers and loungers before them, they offered less a coherent plan than a satisfying plaint, couched, as usual, in depressive comedy. What they added was a new level of knowingness, an increased sense of their own instant marginalization and co-optation. Unlike the utopian slackers of the past, they were aware of their own disposability.

∞

Several researchers and pundits in the 1980s and 1990s argued that Information Age jobs, with the high level of discretion and decision making they required, meant that work would no longer be associated with self-sacrifice, pain, drudgery, and subservience. Instead, they decided quite rosily, the new work ethic now stressed self-expression, self-fulfillment, dignity, and autonomy. Others embraced the new workplace as more humane, as integrating workers' lifestyles and natural work rhythms into a corporate setting, melding work with what British writer and musician Pat Kane calls the Play Ethic. Kane foresees a world in which the proletariat is replaced by a souletariat, a workforce dedicated to its own creativity and fulfillment, thereby putting the soulfulness lost to industrial and postindustrial engineering back into the working day. Richard Florida, of Carnegie Mellon University and the Brookings Institution, sees these developments as the natural outcome of the rise of "the creative class," itself related to the integration of countercultural ideas into the mainstream. Such changes began in media and high-tech firms, but once these creative, counterculture-flavored companies started stealing valued employees from more staid, rigidly hierarchical organizations, even law firms and accounting firms began adopting "new economy" office styles. This new workplace, epitomized by the dot-com office with its foosball table and no dress code, was to be the wave of the future.

This "new office utopia," as scholar Andrew Ross calls it, embodied what many pundits have been arguing were the attitudes and temperament of the generations born after 1960. According to business consultant and writer Michael Maccoby in *Why Work?: Leading the New Generation* (1988), workers in Generation X and beyond look at their jobs as arenas for personal growth, self-knowledge, and empowerment. In a series of books beginning with *Generations* (1991), William Strauss, Neil Howe, and their colleagues have been at work describing the nature of the different generations in the workforce, suggesting that Gen Xers are stuck in impotent, furious reaction to their elders, while what they call the "millennial generation," born after 1982, are very different. "They will rebel against the culture by cleaning it up, rebel against political cynicism by touting trust, rebel against individualism by stressing teamwork, rebel against adult pessimism by being upbeat, and rebel against social ennui by actually going out and getting a few things done," they write in *Millennials Rising: The Next Great Generation* (2000). This new generation will have very few slackers, and it sounds, in fact, like Maccoby's and Bruce Tulgan's version of Generation X. Tulgan, in *Managing Generation X: How to Bring Out the Best in Young Talent* (1995, rev. ed. 2000), writes that Gen Xers are "flexible, technoliterate, information-savvy, entrepreneurial, and perfectly adaptable to the new just-in-time workplace."

In other words, it's not that Gen Xers are rebellious and sullen; they're just clear about what they want. Like the Generation Yers, they have a free-agent mind-set, Tulgan says, so managers have to keep them happy or they will leave: "GenXers' willingness to walk away from any unsatisfactory employment relationship launched the staffing crisis that plagues employers today and has allowed them to become the most entrepreneurial generation in history." Barbara Schneider and David Stevenson, in *The Ambitious Generation: America's Teenagers, Motivated but Directionless* (1999), analyzed studies done in 1972, 1982, and 1992 and concluded that there had been "a significant rise in the ambitions of American adolescents." Based on the number of students in the class of 1992 that expected to earn undergraduate and graduate degrees and wanted to go to graduate and professional schools, Schneider and Stevenson say, these Gen Xers are "America's most ambitious teenage generation ever." Ron Zemke, Claire Raines, and Bob Filipczak analyze all the generational work ethics in *Generations at Work: Managing the Clash of Veterans, Boomers, Xers, and Nexters in Your Workplace* (2000). They argue that Xers thrive on change while the Nexters will reprise the pre-boomer work ethic and its desire for stability. Carolyn Martin writes, in *Managing Generation Y* (2001), that the "global citizens" born in the late 1970s and early 1980s have been unfairly maligned in the press for being pampered and lazy. She also cites survey data showing this generation to be the most optimistic and hopeful in history.

One problem with all of these generational characterizations, beyond their contradicting one another, is that they cannot correct for even the most obvious life-cycle differences. For instance, Lynne Lancaster and David Stillman, in *When Generations Collide* (2002), claim that my parents and their pre-boomer generation were primarily interested in a job well done, boomers like myself in financial success and the corner office, and Generation X in their own freedom. But twenty years ago, my generation and many pundits of the time were clear that *we* were interested in freedom, our parents in the corner office, and the generation before them in the job well done. One suspects that twenty years down the road a similar shift in the pattern will be seen.

The data supporting these generalizations is also suspect, as the same person might answer questions about the future in very different ways on different days. In many of the slacker books and films of the 1990s, earlier generations are sometimes cast as the enemy, the people who have sucked the world dry of resources and jobs, leaving nothing for the "baby busters" in their wake: "I have to endure pinheads like you rusting above me for the rest of my life," a character in *Generation X* says to his boomer boss. "Always grabbing the best piece of cake first and then putting a barbed wire fence around the rest." But at other times current conditions seem to be the problem instead. "I don't know," a slacker ponders, "whether I feel more that I want to punish some aging crock for frittering away my world, or whether I'm just upset that the world has gotten too big—way beyond our capacity to tell stories about it, and so all we're stuck with are those blips and chunks and snippets on bumpers." In *Shampoo Planet*, the millennial protagonist, Tyler, pities his hippie mother for her lack of pragmatism, for her inability to grab her piece of cake. "I know what I want from life," he says. "I have ambition." He is confounded, in fact, by his elders' poor work ethic, asking, "Whatever happened to work?" But at another point Tyler has his own doubts: "Work and money; money and work," he muses. "Strange but true. Fifty years of the stuff ahead of me—it's a wonder I don't just hurl myself off the bridge in the center of town right away." His ambition, like that of Coupland's Gen Xers, waxes and wanes, his relation to work changing with circumstance and opportunity.

Schneider and Stevenson point to another factor. A generation may be more or less ambitious, but that does not mean anything about their actual prospects. Many young people have what the authors call "misaligned ambitions," or a poor estimate of their own abilities. Justin Kruger and David Dunning addressed this issue in a 1999 article in the *Journal of Personality and Social Psychology*, "Unskilled and Unaware of It: How Difficulties in Recognizing One's Own Incompetence Lead to Inflated Self-Assessments." Many young people hold overly favorable views of their abilities. This overestimation occurs, in part, because unskilled people "not only . . . reach erroneous conclusions and make unfortunate choices, but their incompetence robs them of the metacognitive ability to realize it." People whose scores on tests of humor, grammar, and logic were in the bottom 25 percent of their study grossly overestimated how well they had done on the tests. Their test scores put them in the 12th percentile, while they estimated themselves to be in the 62nd. The authors link this miscalibration to "deficits in metacognitive skill, or the capacity to distinguish accuracy from error." Bad thinking, in other words. The increased ambition and decreased level of skill lead to what Schneider and Stevenson call the "ambition paradox" faced by this generation. And this ambition paradox can only be further fueled by the utopian talk of management writers like Michael Hammer, who gushes, "It is thrilling to be part of a revolution that replaces meaningless work, petty bureaucracy and dead-end jobs with a workplace to which people enjoy coming, knowing they will be challenged and appreciated." Tell this to the assistant shift manager at a Home Depot.

The comic slacker figure is often a dreamer who suffers from exactly this kind of miscalibration and inflated sense of opportunity. Wayne, a slacker character created by Mike Myers for *Saturday Night Live* in the 1980s, introduces himself in *Wayne's World* (1992) as a slacker with a dream:

WAYNE

Let me bring you up to speed. My name is Wayne Campbell. I live in Aurora, Illinois, which is a suburb of Chicago—excellent. I've had plenty of joe-jobs, nothing I'd call a career. Let me put it this way: I have an extensive collection of nametags and hairnets. OK, so I still live with my parents, which I admit is bogus and sad. However I do have a cable access show—and I still know how to party. But what I'd really like is to do *Wayne's World* for a living.

The film follows his attempts at (and fears of) moving his public access TV show to commercial television. The improbability of his basement interview show becoming a hot commercial property is overridden by his cheerful, enthusiastic self-confidence. The character is fun precisely because he so blithely expects the best even as he understands that from another perspective everything about his life is bogus and sad. He has great expectations, always.

Even in Kevin Smith's *Clerks* (1994), the film that more than any other stayed focused on twenty-something slackers in unrelenting McJobs, the question of ambition hovers. Randall, a video store clerk, appears to be a lifer, having acquired an entirely negative relation to work. He closes his store several times a day just to sit in the convenience store next door and jaw with Dante, the clerk there. Dante, however, is somewhat less confirmed in this attitude, and prodded by a girlfriend, he considers making something of his life. Along the way, we get a number of other comic takes on the work ethic. A customer tells the young men, "It's important to have a job that makes a difference, boys. That's why I manually masturbate caged animals for artificial insemination." When one obsessive-compulsive convenience store customer takes an hour to pick out a perfectly matched dozen eggs, the clerks speculate that he is damaged by his "meaningless job." Randall bets Dante a million dollars that the man is a guidance counselor.

This kind of sardonic distance on conventional career planning is extremely important to independent film in this era. The Coen brothers, Ethan and Joel, for instance, have made an art of the slacker comedy, from *Raising Arizona* (1987) to *Fargo* (1996), *The Big Lebowski* (1998), and beyond; Lebowski, the narrator says, was "quite possibly the laziest [man] in all of Los Angeles County. Which would place him high in the runnin' for laziest worldwide." In Jim Jarmusch's *Down by Law* (1986), *Night on Earth* (1991), and *Ghost Dog* (1999), slacker characters are given a fuller range of socioeconomic backgrounds and a wider set of emotional registers to work with, while Gus Van Sant specializes in more dramatic and tragic tales of slacker life, as in his tale of street hustlers, *My Own Private Idaho* (1991). Mainstream films were also treating slacker life dramatically, from Cameron Crowe's *Singles* (1992), set against a background of the Seattle grunge scene, itself a slacker mecca, and Ben Stiller's *Reality*

Bites (1994), through mindless comedies like *Slackers* (2002). In all of these and dozens and dozens of other films, the comedy and the tragedy spring at least in part from this same source: the characters overestimate their opportunities for achievement, wealth, and happiness. They have no idea how ill-equipped they are.

This avalanche of slacker films suggests a central cultural preoccupation with the changing nature and value of work, and therefore it is no surprise to find slacker concerns running through other genres, forms, and forums as well. Slacker guides and handbooks and other novelty books hit the shelves. Playwright Eric Bogosian's *subUrbia* (1994) includes a number of idle characters, as does Marc Meyers's play *Whywork.com* (2000). From comic-strip slackers like *Doonesbury*'s Zonker and Duke (not to mention a continued stream of books by slacker gadflies like Duke's model Hunter Thompson) to Bart "Underachiever and Proud" Simpson, his barely working father, Homer, and Beavis and Butthead, the slacker themes of Beetle Bailey and Dagwood took updated form. Even the most mainstream television shows, such as *Friends* (a horrified "Job?" is a common punch line, as it was for Maynard), featured an array of layabouts and couch potatoes, and MTV's *The Real World* and its spin-offs displayed the "reality" version. Bestselling memoirs like Elizabeth Wurtzel's *Prozac Nation* (1994) and bestselling novels like Nick Hornby's *About a Boy* (1998), with its protagonist at thirty-six still living off his dead father's novelty-song royalties, were part of a veritable literary movement. Arthur Nersesian's *The Fuck-Up* (1991) follows the trials and tribulations of a late-twenties slacker; when he is prodded by a girlfriend to ask for a raise, his boss says, "A raise? You mean a monetary raise?" "Sure." "I've never given a raise before. This isn't that kind of job, kid. It's minimum wage; the President gives you a raise here." Slacker novels have been coming so fast and furious I'll just mention some of them: Denis Johnson's *Jesus' Son* (1992), Russell Smith's *How Insensitive* (1994), Michael Chabon's *Wonder Boys* (1995), Michael Hornburg's *Bongwater* (1996), Blake Nelson's *Exile* (1997), Joy Nicholson's *The Tribes of Palos Verdes* (1997), Jonathan Lethem's *Motherless Brooklyn* (1999), Rachel Resnick's *Go West Young Fucked-Up Chick* (1999), Gary Shteyngart's *The Russian Debutante's Handbook* (2002), Dave Eggers's *You Shall Know Our Velocity* (2002), T. C. Boyle's *Drop City* (2003), Sam Lipsyte's *Home Land* (2004), Benjamin

Kunkel's *Indecision* (2005), and Paul Mandelbaum's *Adriane on the Edge* (2005) all worry the same basic themes from their various angles, as did many, many more, including at least a half dozen with the word "slacker" in the title, scores by genre writers like Elmore Leonard, Carl Hiaasen, and Kinky Friedman that focus on low-life loafers, and dozens of Hollywood novels and academic novels that focus on prime professional slacker careers. David Gilbert's first novel, *The Normals* (2004), has been called the ultimate slacker novel, since the protagonist is so uninterested in getting ahead that he basically sells his body to science while he is alive, becoming a paid subject in drug trials. Again, this is a tiny fraction of any complete list. We have been experiencing the golden age of the slacker narrative.

As always, the authors and makers of these slacker characters tend to be workaholics. In his mid-thirties, Dave Eggers has published four books, edited four more, started and edited a couple of magazines and numerous collections, founded a publishing company, written introductions to editions of classic works, created a multicity charity that offers free writing classes and tutoring to underprivileged kids, written regularly about art and music in periodicals, and done graphic design for his own publications and elsewhere. But Eggers, being interviewed by David Amsden in *Salon.com*, claimed that he has trouble working, that he can get caught in bouts of "unproductivity" unless he has real deadlines imposed from outside, and that the only way he can feel productive is if he feels as though he is procrastinating:

> You only want to work on the stuff you're not supposed to be working on. That's how it always is. I'll always be working on five things at once, usually with those documents open at the same time because if I get stuck somewhere I'll jump over to something else. That's how my head has always worked. I don't know if it's 'cause I watched too much TV as a kid or what. It really could be that.

Kevin Smith, also in his mid-thirties, has already produced eighteen films, written, directed, and acted in twelve of them, and edited eight. Coupland has published eleven novels and six volumes of nonfiction since 1991, or a bit more than a book a year, and has remained active as an artist; his sculpture, photographs, and installations appear in numerous exhibitions and gallery shows every year: "I can't wait to get back in there and work," he says. These slacker-creators work all the time, and they are aware that they are addressing people who—however much each of them may be working—are caught in the same conceptual binds and battered by the same cultural double-talk, an audience that will continue to find the slacker compelling and repellent in equal measure.

The avalanche of slacker narratives suggests that we are as confused and conflicted as we have ever been about work and what it should mean. The various generations may have slightly different relations to their jobs and aspirations, but they are all in the same basic boat. Hours are going up; income is going down. Job security is a thing of the past. Welfare is disappearing. Work is changing more rapidly than ever. And as a result, slacker characters are everywhere, voicing and relieving their audiences' ever-increasing anxiety about the world of getting and spending, fueling and ridiculing their desire to find meaningful work and their desire to escape the workaday grind, finding tragicomic resolution on page and screen.

∞

Nothing represented the change and lack of change in working life more than the dot-com office. The dot-com boom in the 1990s brought the "new economy" and the "new workplace" into the news, even if the actual numbers of workers in these firms represented a minuscule portion of the workforce. Doing away with cubicles and replacing them with game rooms, "the no-collar workplace" encouraged informal, unstructured interaction, and people sitting diligently at desks was taken as a sign that things were not going well, since creativity is "fundamentally social." The dot-coms pioneered the pool table and Ping-Pong table in the public areas of the company offices, and the public areas tended to be the majority of the space. Some offices had separate game rooms complete with basketball hoops and foosball tables; some had nap rooms, or conference rooms with 100 percent beanbag seating for lounging. The workplace seemed to be meeting the slacker halfway.

Coupland's 1995 novel, *Microserfs*, was written at the height of the boom, and it ends with the characters forming their own Silicon Valley firm. Early in the novel the programmers are under the sway of a Bill Gates–like mogul and are in it for the money, with no misapprehension about their own autonomy—they know they don't really have any—and no illusions about the economic basis or benefit of their labor. But then the characters quit their jobs and start a company to develop a computer game, not for the money, but for all the unalienated reasons: they want to work with one another; they want to make something from scratch and see it to a conclusion; they want to use their talents to the fullest. A character named Bug says, late in the novel, "I would have come here for *nothing*. I never *had* to get paid . . . It's not the money. It's *never* been the money. It rarely ever *is*." This novel begins by outlining a dystopian vision of monster corporations sapping the vital energies and creativity of the best minds of a generation, but it ends by celebrating the total absorption in work for the sake of the work itself, lauding its pleasures. Unlike *Generation X*'s bartenders, they love what they do. They want to write elegant code—that is, they are not alienated from their product, but have real desires for what Veblen called "workmanship." And they are the farthest possible from slackers: they want to fall, regularly, back into the pure flow of work. The characters feel that their work has given them a kind of pleasant autism: in the flow of it they can shut out everything and everyone. At the end of an exhausting day, they lay back, have a drink, and fall asleep, getting up like addicts only to dive into it again. They are hooked on free, creative, nonhierarchical work, and the workplace they have created for themselves is an unalloyed ideal. Andrew Ross, who observed two New York high-tech firms in the late 1990s, wrote in *No-Collar: The Humane Workplace and Its Hidden Costs* (2003) that it "seemed their intent was to squeeze every drop of white-collar alienation out of the workplace."

Ross is one of many who applaud the more humane workplace, although as his subtitle suggests, he has his criticisms. One is that, as in *Microserfs*, the environment that is most free from coercion "often results in the deepest sacrifice of time and vitality"—that in making work play, work tends to encroach on the worker's off time until it virtually disappears. Also, the humane workplace is not the same as a just workplace: there may have been lots of creative freedom, unstructured time, and games to play, but there was no job security at these firms, no economic equality, no real control over the enterprise. Some go further and find in these new office arrangements simply a newer, shinier form of oppression. A performance-art group named ®™ark (pronounced "art-mark") takes this negative view. ®™ark is a kind of corporate-sabotage guerrilla cell: they organize national "call in sick" days, for instance, and offer money to lacrosse teams and jai alai players who will toss tear gas back at police at anti–World Trade Organization demonstrations. ®™ark calls the various perks of the no-collar workplace so many "carefully placed peanuts." The peanuts, the group argues, function as they do for circus elephants, keeping workers lumbering around in circles more effectively than cracking the whip.

Nonetheless, say some business writers, the humane New Economy workplace has had a perceivable and good effect on how workers are treated across the economy. Just as the early industrial engineers created public space for employee interaction during breaks, the new workplace encourages workers to interact, and thus, necessarily, there is a slight slackening of work-time discipline. On the other hand, the opposite tendency is afoot: at the same time that casual dress has become more common and break-room amenities have been augmented, surveillance of workers has undeniably and dramatically increased. Between 1997 and 2001, the number of companies performing routine electronic monitoring of their employees doubled, to 78 percent—monitoring that included, for instance, the length of time between keystrokes. Although writers like Ross see the handful of dot-com veterans carrying their dream of a playful workplace into the future, the number of people working in such places is even less than it was ten years ago, and the countertendencies are perhaps even greater.

And laid-off dot-commers are not sure even they would like to return to the utopian workrooms. Janelle Brown and Katharine Mieszkowski interviewed a number of such workers for *Salon* in 2001. They found a group of "recovering workaholics" who "are now rediscovering the joys of life beyond the monitor: the wonders of *Magnum P.I.* reruns, the thrill of going dancing on school nights, the restorative luxury of spending half the day in bed." Instead of scrambling for their next job, these dot-commers, Brown and Mieszkowski find, are "just reveling in doing nothing." The authors note that it was the same kids criticized for being slackers in the early 1990s who staffed the dot-com boom in the late 1990s, and when it caused the stock market bubble and crash, they were again objects of scorn. Since the culture hated them when they *weren't* working and then hated them when they *were* working, suggest Brown and Mieszkowski, they thought to themselves, Why work? "I think my time is better wasted when I am the one wasting it," said one. Although most assume they will need eventually to get a job, many said their time doing nothing would have a lasting effect: they plan to keep smelling the roses and vow to avoid returning to sixty- to ninety-hour workweeks, no matter how many Ping-Pong tables they are offered next to their desks.

The explosion of slacker figures in film, fiction, advertising, and other forums over the next decade showed that people were far from snowed by the glowing visions they were being offered of work in the near future. Spicoli, Bueller, the SubGenius, and the slackers who followed in their wake incarnated the culture's distrust of and distaste for these new advertisements for work. Unlike the slackers of the 1950s and 1960s, these rebels did not feel they were moving history forward; in fact, history, they felt, had stopped. The Vietnam War was the last world historical event in "genuine capital *H* history times," thinks one character in Coupland's *Generation X*, "before *history* was turned into a press release, a marketing strategy, and a cynical campaign tool." Unlike the 1960s counterculturalists, many of the slackers of the 1990s and beyond have not felt much power to change the world. The only thing that ever changes, many of them have suggested, is style.

Of course the sixties generation, as I suggested in the first section of this book, is still very much with us, and the progressive, utopian slacker thus still makes an appearance. Wendy Wasserstein's *Sloth* (2005), for instance, is a parodic self-help manual in which she counsels inactivity as the royal road to happiness. "With sloth you will live a longer, happier, and more rewarding life," she writes. Sloth provides comfort by removing "the nagging tug of passion, creativity, and individual desire," and comfort, she notes, "is *much* more important than any achievement or social contract." A classic slacker discourse, the book laughs at hypertense, ulcerated workaholics and at its own remedy. "It's all downhill from here," she writes on the last page. "And nothing *really* matters." For Wasserstein, things did matter, and the slacker is a conceit, finally, whose rhetorical effect is a call to action. For many slackers from the last decade and a half, the only action suggested is a rubbing of the eyes and a look around.

∞

Not surprisingly, the Web is a natural home for today's slacker, and Googling that word, one is treated to endless sites that outline, in time-honored fashion, an ironic aversion to work. The individuals who mount slacker Web pages sound very much like Joseph Dennie, Jerome K. Jerome, or Paul Lafargue. *"The sooner you fall behind, the more time you have to get caught up"* was the quote of the week on angelfire.com/ct/SlackersDomain in November of 2003, and true to the slacker ethos, in April of 2005 it was still the quote of the month. The site is best viewed in "3-B," it says—that is, after three beers—and the home page welcomes slackers: "PULL UP A COUCH AND DO NOTHING." The site offers a list of aphorisms, including "Never put off until tomorrow what can be put off until the day after tomorrow" and "Hard work has a future. Laziness pays off now." These witticisms may not be as elegant as Oscar Wilde's, but the joke remains the same. The Flash introduction to www.slackersinc.com begins: "Remember: Motivation *can* be overcome." It is appropriate, we are told on the home page of slacker.com, that the site "neither aspires to nor manages to provide any useful content or features." The Web site hellyeah.com has a list of the contributing "slackers," including Mark Schebel, who describes himself as "support specialist for a synthetic DNA manufacturer by day. Slacker and all-around good-for-nothing by night." Heidi Ziegler somewhat more straightforwardly, we guess, "calls herself a slacker extraordinaire, but is really a full time law student with several jobs." Bryan Boyer's profile says, in toto: "I'm a lazy fuck." The adoption of such "lazy fuck" personae remains, as it always has, a kind of paper identity, one that has no necessary relation to the actual life of the Web slacker, which may include, for instance, being a support specialist for a DNA manufacturer—something that has required, we can safely assume, a little effort somewhere along the way.

Sometimes it isn't clear how intentional all the humor is. One site, www.slackers.meetup.com, is a bulletin board for local slacker groups that meet once a week in cities around the country. There are eighteen groups, seven of which have only one member, six of which have two, and the biggest of which, in New York, has six. "I went to the International Slackers Meetup Day website," one slacker posted. "But I was told that not enough slackers in Los Angeles had signed up, so that the meetup day was cancelled for this month." (The real do-nothing slackers, we might say, are not those launching slacker meet-up day Web sites, but the ones not showing up at the events.) The home page of the Canadian Slackers Association (www .angelfire.com/ct/CanadianSlackers/) asks, rhetorically, "By making this page am I still a slacker?" And the answer, of course, is yes: "Just because you're a slacker doesn't mean you put in no effort, it means you are unmotivated and don't put in full effort. I've had this page in my mind for months before I actually created it and i [the author was not, apparently, willing to put out the necessary effort to use the shift key this last time] most likely will only update it every few months." Thus, in the tradition as old as Johnson's and MacKenzie's Idlers, the Canadian slacker justifies the work of presenting himself as a slacker and performs his laziness with words.

And in a tradition just as long, the anti-welfare right fights to preserve the American work ethic against the entitlement-addicted liberals and the poor who are debilitated by state charity—and again, much of this conflict plays out on the Web. As one "former Democrat" put it on his Web site, "I'm mad as hell. I don't want to pay for welfare anymore, because it doesn't work, it just invites people to watch Jerry Springer all day." Like this work proponent, his counterparts in the anti-welfare party are an angry lot. One says he has

> no sympathy at all for these people. They . . . pop out kid after kid they can't afford and then expect taxpayers to support them in perpetuity . . . My youngest brother and his new wife would love to have kids, but they are waiting and trying to save money until they can afford them. Meanwhile, their hard-earned dollars are being stolen by the government and given to these parasites. Really makes me angry.

Another wants to be clear that it is equal opportunity anger:

> My gripe is with ALL the loafers and freeloaders and sorry, lazy noaccounts. It angers me just as much to see a white man draw welfare and sit on his lazy rear end drinking beer as it does to watch black teenage girls produce baby after baby so they can get AFDC and other federal welfare benefits.

The political right harnessed this anger, adding their defenses of the classical work ethic. In the early 1990s, with the Gingrich revolution and its Contract with America, they were in the policy driving seat and helped make the 1996 welfare reform act what it was. The Capitalist Conservative home page praises the 1996 act thusly:

> Before this bill a person could be born on welfare, raised on welfare, live their life on welfare, and have children on welfare while not having to work 1 single hour. A PERSON COULD LIVE THEIR WHOLE LIFE SITTING AROUND WHILE THE GOVERN-MENT GAVE THEM HARD EARNED TAX DOLLARS IN PAY-MENTS. A person would do this because it is certainly easier to sit around watching TV all day waiting for FREE MONEY to arrive than it is to work for a living. Now people are encouraged to get a job.

Again, this is perhaps less elegant than Franklin's description of the work ethic, and therefore it is even easier to see that the veneer of moral outrage is barely covering these writers' fantasies of the work-free life. Ah, to sit and watch TV and get free money! That, my friends, is the American dream. The anti-welfare advocates and the slackers seem to be in full agreement at least here.

∞

A study published in 2000 by the Committee for Economic Development, a group made up of corporation presidents and chairmen along with a couple of academics, concluded that "the central premises" of the "workfare" legislation of 1996 were sound and that the act was a success: "as a matter of simple equity, able-bodied recipients should work; and as a matter of simple economics, only employment, with public support and encouragement where necessary, offers a permanent path out of poverty." Welfare reform cannot help everyone, they conceded, but "our more realistic goal here is to present a balanced and achievable agenda for moving our society more effectively from welfare to work, and eventually to the highly productive and rewarding work to which all Americans aspire."

Between 1994 and 1999, welfare caseloads fell 50 percent, a number often quoted as proof of the act's success. But the average wage of people who moved from welfare to work under the new program was $6.61 an hour, or $13,750 for full-time, full-year employment, well below the poverty rate. Only 23 percent of the new workers had insurance; even fewer had any chance of advancement. And this was during the boom of the 1990s, when the United States had the lowest unemployment rate since 1970. Aaron Bernstein, reporting in *BusinessWeek*, told a typical story: Semicoe Glover had spent fourteen years on welfare before getting her high school equivalency degree and a job at a Salem, Massachusetts, day-care center. Two years later she took home $353 every two weeks, instead of the $417 she got from AFDC. She had to get a car and pay $86 a month for her children's after-school care. She supplemented her income with food from local charities. "I got this job because I knew I would be cut off from welfare," she told Bernstein. "But I don't know how I'd make it without the milk and bread I get." The number of children living below *half* the poverty rate increased in the five years since the bill went into effect, and the poorest 10 percent of the population overall saw a 14 percent drop in their income. Cashiers, waitstaff, janitors, and sales clerks all earned less, on average, than the poverty level.

These figures are readily available, but Barbara Ehrenreich's experiment in participant observation, *Nickel and Dimed* (2001), helped give the working poor, however briefly, a higher visibility and a larger part in the national conversation. Ehrenreich wondered how the four million women "about to be booted into the labor market by welfare reform" would get by on $6-an-hour jobs. In order to write the book, she took unskilled jobs—as a waitress in Florida, as a maid in Maine, as a "Wal-Martian" in Minnesota—and tried to make ends meet. She rented the cheapest available apartments at $500 to $600 a month and found that she could not stay solvent with only one forty-hour job in any of these places. As she admits in her introduction, the experiment was not entirely necessary; various institutes had already set the "livable wage"—a wage at which people can pay for minimum food, clothing, and shelter—at $8.89 an hour. Her Wal-Mart job paid $7, and anyone can do this simple math. In Portland, with two jobs, working seven days a week, she made enough to pay her rent and basic expenses. In the other two places she ended her monthlong experiments with less in her pocket than she started with, even when she received some free groceries from a food bank. Even so, as she admits, she had many advantages going in—she was white and a native English speaker, she had no children to support, and she had an ATM card to rely on until she got situated or if she got into trouble. She had it easy.

Many young people facing this low-wage crunch decide to enter the military. The military has long been the choice of people unsure about their futures or unable to see any other path, which may be why Jack Kerouac drunkenly signed up for the navy, the coast guard, and the merchant marine all on the same day. When a reporter asked one nineteen-year-old why he had enlisted, he explained, "I'm an unmotivated slacker . . . My slacker attitude had closed so many doors. I needed someone to yell at me." Michael Moore, who represents the plight of working-class people in his films, interviews two Marine recruiters in *Fahrenheit 911* and follows them on their daily rounds in Flint, Michigan. He suggests that recruiters mill about low-end malls targeting poor minority kids who have no other options, conning them into risking their lives in wars undertaken to benefit the rich. His left-wing bias and class analysis of the war led to the predictable Web responses. One is from author and blogger Jim Kunstler, whose bow tie serves as a badge of his political ideology in much the same way that Moore's baggy getup does his. Kunstler takes issue with Moore's depiction of the poverty in Flint:

> The Flint that Moore revisits is a slum partly self-made, full of people too busy watching $50-a-month cable television to paint their houses or even clean up their yards. Moore is angry that the great paternalistic institutions of American life have stopped being good Daddies, and so his ire and paranoia eventually fasten on the chief big daddy of all, the President.

Moore does in fact show a brief clip of George W. Bush giving him fatherly career advice: "Behave yourself, will ya?" Bush says to Moore. "Go find real work." Moore, who has a knack for marketing, plays up this accusation of slackering. He called his last speaking and promotional tour (in 2004) "The Slacker Uprising Tour," and in his standard speech he said of the Republicans, "They are relentless, dedicated, without shame, well-funded and like sharks. . . . They're up early figuring out which minority group shouldn't be allowed to marry. They're up at the crack of dawn. We slackers only see the sun if we've been up all night partying." Here "slacker" is offered as a pretend group identity, one that he assumes his audience of progressive young people will find appealing, though few will actually find it a compelling way of life for any length of time. Moore himself, of course, is no more a slacker than the majority of the ambitious college students who come see him speak.

College is the other main avenue out of the McJob world, and the percentage of people opting in continues to climb, with more and more students taking on more and more debt in a gamble at the better life. The students in colleges and universities around the country—I can testify from my own experience, and the survey data backs it up—are petrified about what the job market might hold for them. The college degree is seen as necessary to any decent job, but the value of the diploma has steadily eroded the more common it has become. Two-thirds of graduating high school seniors now go on to higher education, while the "creative class" of professionals and managers they want to join accounts for less than a third of all jobs in the United States.

And the middle option, skilled industrial labor, has been moving out of the country for decades. Part of the problem in Flint, Michigan, is that the auto industry jobs that used to sustain the place have disappeared. Jeremy Rifkin, in *The End of Work* (1995), suggests that we just have to adjust to the fact that "human work is being systematically eliminated from the production process." The dream that utopian thinkers have always had, that technology will lessen the workload of human beings, is happening, and quickly. He gives a series of policy suggestions having to do with taxation and guaranteed living wages, but he admits that the future is far from clear. "The end of work could spell a death sentence for civilization as we have come to know it," he writes. "The end of work could also signal the beginning of a great social transformation, a rebirth of the human spirit. The future lies in our hands."

Well, yes, I suppose it could be a death and could be a rebirth. But in either case, neither the work ethic nor the slacker ethic can save us from our fate. Together, however, these two opposed ethics create the context within which we meet that future. The fact that the 1990s slacker subculture came to prominence at the same time that the welfare state was being dismantled is simply another example of the way in which slacker subcultures arise and flourish alongside newly heated pro-work rhetoric. The two ways of understanding may goad each other into more extreme positions, but the two together form, through their opposing pressures, the way we feel about work. They do so in part by deflating two of our culture's prime motivating fantasies: the dreams of a perfectly realized calling on the one hand and of a life of guilt-free leisure on the other. By challenging such fantasies, the work and slacker ethics can help us revise our understanding of our own work lives, a process that, as those lives continuously change, is repeatedly necessary.

∞

The other prime site for today's slackers, appropriate given its creation of a nation of couch potatoes, is television. One recent TV slacker, Anna Nicole Smith, a Gen Xer born in Houston, Texas, in 1967, is, among other things, exactly the kind of person, socioeconomically, that the anti-welfare folks are talking about. She was abandoned by her father as an infant, and by her husband, a seventeen-year-old fry cook, when she gave birth to an infant herself at seventeen. Instead of relying on welfare, though, she went to work as a stripper. A couple of breast implants (on each side) later, she posed for *Playboy*, eventually becoming Playmate of the Year in 1993. In the year that followed, she appeared in small parts in a couple of films, modeled for Guess Jeans, and married J. Howard Marshall II, an oil billionaire who was born sixty years before Smith, in 1907, and who met his bride-to-be when he bought a lap dance from her. He was confined to a wheelchair and died a year after their nuptials. After years of legal wrangling—complicated by a suit for sexual harassment brought against Smith by a former female assistant (the assistant was granted $850,000, after which Smith declared bankruptcy)—Smith was awarded $475 million dollars from the estate. Then a higher court voided the award, another gave her $88 million, and the latest decision has erased that. To date, all she has from the marriage is some $6 million dollars' worth of "gifts."

If this were the whole story, as in the case of Lorelei Lee or the women in *How to Marry a Millionaire*, it would not make much of a slacker narrative. But in 2002 Smith launched *The Anna Nicole Show*, a reality show that ran for three seasons on the E! network. Made from footage of Smith's everyday life, spliced together into the semblance of a story, one show chronicles the blowsy blonde's driving lessons; another follows her on a Las Vegas gambling junket. We watch her choose fabrics with her decorator and limp through various stunts concocted by the producers—a series of blind dates, a contest to pick a new cook, a guest spot on *Texas Justice*, in which she tries her hand at being Judge Judy. But such events are not the essence of the show. Audiences tune in to watch Smith laze about. While hunting for a new house on the premiere episode of the first season, she announces that she needs to stop: "I didn't get to masturbate this morning, and I've been dying to, so I've gotta go." On the way home from a Vegas trip on another episode, the camera lingers on Smith, slumped in the backseat, passed out, a bag of Cheetos open on her chest. She often derails the proceedings by whining that she's hungry.

The show regularly has fun with Smith's relation to work. When she complains about her life one day in a diner, her lawyer suggests that she trade places with the waitress. Smith does (the waitress has clearly already signed a release), becomes a hilariously incompetent server for a day and an even worse caretaker for the waitress's children. The waitress has a crisis of conscience thinking of Smith caring for her children and rushes home, at which point Smith is more than happy to return to her idle splendor. She halfheartedly considers offers for appearances and endorsements, always choosing to pass unless her lawyer browbeats her into accepting. Much of the humor is based on Smith's brattiness at moments like this, her pure and unthinking sense of entitlement. She acts like a spoiled empress, forcing a Los Angeles sushi chef to go out and get A.1. sauce for her Kobe steak and treating her "best friend" and lawyer like a slave ("Get me a [bleep]ing soda, Howard!").

Even in her pursuit of an entertainment career she continues to be a slacker. According to *FHM*, the men's magazine, she canceled an interview appointment four times before their reporter got to talk to her. But she has promised to "work really hard" on her new column for *The National Enquirer*, which debuted April 17, 2005. She will be getting someone else to do the spelling, she says.

Smith's reality show is the flip side of *The Apprentice*, the show in which candidates vie for a job as Donald Trump's assistant. In Trump's "unscripted" reality show, The Donald plays at hiring people who play at wanting to work for him. His refrain, "You're fired!" seems to be endlessly pleasurable to an audience schooled in the theater of mortification by *Survivor*, *Fear Factor*, and *Jerry Springer*, and like those shows, the opportunities for schadenfreude abound even before the final humiliation. Oddly, the jobs the apprentices are asked to do are extremely trivial—selling lemonade, renting bicycle cabs—keeping the sense of what work means at its most basic rather than asking them to do depreciation analyses and futures projections: the kinds of things, one assumes, that Trump actually hires people to do for $250,000 a year. These furiously ambitious aspirants live on the opposite end of the work ethic scale from Anna Nicole Smith, but their filmed antics provide a similar kind of viewing pleasure. The slacker and the suck-up, the lounger and the knee-pumper, the tortoise and the hare: how we love to watch the endless drama of success and failure, these images of perfect, lazy serenity and encompassing, grasping angst. Our own work lives, we must happily admit, exist somewhere in between, and these characters help remind us why. We may not have endless leisure, and we may not have the money we'd like to have, but we have avoided some extreme forms of degradation. We are spared that, at least. Anna Nicole reminds us that we don't want to be *that* inert; the grasping, disgraced apprentices remind us that we don't want to be rich and successful enough to behave *that* badly.

Psychologists have in recent years suggested a couple of other ways of looking at people's working lives that help explain the pleasure we take in watching someone like Smith. Psychologist Howard Gardner, writing in *The Chronicle of Higher Education* in 2002, bewailed the "strange neglect" that the experience of working had received in academic circles. There are studies of motivation, studies of the relation of rewards to performance, studies of efficiency, but no studies of the place of work in the overall life experience of the individual. Gardner, Mihaly Csikszentmihalyi, and William Damon have tried to fill that gap and have come up with two factors they consider essential to "good work." One is that the work involves high levels of expertise—whatever the work, from plasma physics to grave digging, people want to feel that they are exercising an expert skill, ideally to the best of their ability. And the other is a sense that their work "entails regular concern with the implications and applications of [their] work for the wider world." At the center of all slacker resistance to the work ethic, from the eighteenth century to the present, has been exactly this. The question slackers posed was not only Why should I work? but What is work good for? What good does the work that people do serve? Wouldn't the world be a better place if we all slowed down and were more reflective? At the same time, the slacker can absolve us of this larger ethical question if it bothers us: Certainly we are serving the wider world better than someone who does nothing, aren't we?

"Everybody yearns to be productive," claims Mel Levine, a professor of pediatrics at University of North Carolina Medical School. He has been studying children labeled lazy and argues that schoolchild laziness is a "myth." Some children just suffer from "output failure" because of "developmental weaknesses." This may just be a fancy way to say "lazy," but Levine's studies suggest that many of the weaknesses—like poor writing skills or poor oral expression—can be solved. Students take on the lazy identity and thus compound their problems rather than fixing them. What's needed is not attitude adjustment (as in the case of the Protestant work ethic), but skills adjustment. One obvious extrapolation is that the slackers are who they are in part because they're called slackers. What slackers need, Levine and Gardner suggest, are skills they can enjoy exercising. Levine calls it "cultivating and restoring output." It used to be called finding work one loves.

Anna Nicole Smith is a classic lazy kid who never learned to spell, and watching her lie about in her mansion, whining while her assistants hover, waiting on her latest whim, plays into our fantasies of unjust reward, of luck winning out over hard work, a kind of reductio ad absurdum of the American dream. The Horatio Alger myth, the idea that with "luck and pluck" anyone can rise from the bottom of society to moneyed success, is embodied, in a perverse way, by her plus-size, junk-food-scarfing life of lounging about on beds, couches, and limousine backseats. On the other hand, every week she is absolutely humiliated. She is tacky, she is bratty, she is overweight, she is friendless, she is pathetic, and perhaps more important than any of these, she has no expertise, no skills to exercise, no work to pursue, no reason for being. Her "larger purpose" in Gardner's terms seems only to demonstrate what life is like without that purpose. Like the idler, loafer, and lounger, she offers in one and the same package both a fantasy life and a cautionary tale.

The latest, and perhaps TV's most inadvertently ironic, entry is ABC's *Kicked Out*, a reality show in which a twenty-something jobless moocher is booted from his (or her) parents' house and followed by a camera crew as he tries to live for ten days on his own. For the crime of lying around watching television, these kids are forced to be on television for ten days so that other couch potatoes can enjoy their humiliations from the comfort of their sofas. Since moving into an apartment doesn't guarantee a show's worth of mortification in the space of ten days, the parents (with the help of the producers) concoct some extra "challenges" for their overgrown fledglings. The show dares the slackers to "grow up already!" and stop sitting around watching TV shows like the one they are now, however briefly, on.

∞

Loafing, lounging, sponging-off-their-parents children are everywhere. The Golden Gai, a cobweb of alleys in the Shinjuku section of Tokyo, was for decades Japan's slacker mecca. An area of three or four city blocks, its dozen alleys, too narrow for cars, are wallpapered with one- and two-story ramshackle buildings that house as many as two hundred tiny bars, each with five or six stools and maybe a table or two. One of the oldest neighborhoods in the city, it hasn't been rebuilt since it was haphazardly thrown up in the 1950s, and everything about it is low-tech and cobbled together, with a spaghetti of wires here and there and a general look of dilapidated impermanence. By the 1960s, because rents were low, it had attracted the mixed population of prostitutes, artists, intellectuals, and other fringe types that such neighborhoods do, and it became the center of Tokyo's social, political, and artistic radicalism, and, therefore, Japan's slacker central. A real estate developer scared the Bohemian enclave's enthusiasts by buying up parcels of the land in the late 1980s and early 1990s with plans to raze it and build a shopping center, but then the economy tanked, and the Golden Gai continues in its quiet, laid-back way to house countercultural types and serve drinks to locals.

A few blocks to the west is the neon extravaganza of ultramodern shopping that is Shinjuku proper, a neighborhood that practically screams out its dedication to the work ethic. The Golden Gai, in contrast, can look almost quaint in the daytime and slightly menacing at night. Guidebooks warn tourists that these are neighborhood bars with regular local clienteles, and not particularly welcoming to westerners, and indeed it is rare to find a tourist anywhere in the warren after dark. There is a noir feel to the place at night as one glimpses, through half-curtained doorways, small, smoky, badly lit conclaves that would turn immediately to silent, unwelcoming stares if a gaijin walked in the door. But there is also something about the place that resembles a slightly tacky Japanese beatnik museum: the cutesy bar names in English (I finally went into one called Orange), the basic cleanliness, the absence of crowds and engine noise, and the feeling of time standing still all give a sense that the neighborhood honors its own past more than it has confidence in its own present. I tried Orange because it was empty, just a woman behind the bar reading a paper, although a couple of men came in later. She was, it turned out, an aspiring actor (she was about to open in a play at one of Tokyo's major theaters for innovative new work), and she had a fair amount of English; the friend of a friend I was with was fluent in Japanese.

I asked the bartender-actor about *freeters* or *freetahs*, the young, mostly male members of Japan's loose slacker subculture. *"Freeter"* is said to be a contraction of the German words *frei* and *arbeiter*, "free" and "to work": this is a chilling contraction because of its perhaps unintended reference to the iron scrollwork reading *"Arbeit Macht Frei"* over the entrance to Auschwitz (not to mention the importance of unemployed German youth to the rise of Hitler in the 1920s and the much more recent spate of immigrant beatings by unemployed skinheads in Europe). *Freetahs* have been the subject of countless Japanese journalistic and academic accounts bemoaning the degeneration of values, social bonds, filial piety, and duty. Most agree that the causes, as in the American case, are popular culture, affluence, and rebelliousness. Bad parenting is cited less frequently in Japan, bad economic conditions more. For many editorialists in Japan, the problem is severe: "There are negative consequences for a society whose young people refuse to work full time even as the overall number of young people continues to decline," one points out. Many simply call the *freetahs* "parasites."

The bartender thought about the question for a minute and then said, "There is not one *freetah*. There are three." She pulled a napkin off a stack and drew a pie chart with three roughly equal slices. "One," she said, pointing to the top slice, "is just the lazy person"—someone, she explained, who would be lazy in any time or place, subculture or not. "The other is *hikikomori*," which, with the help of my Japanese-speaking friend, I learned was the name given to post-adolescents who live too long with their parents, still accepting free rent, food, and laundry services long after school, sometimes into their thirties. (*Hikikomori*, I have come to learn, is more often used to describe someone who has become agoraphobic. "*Parasaito shingulu*" — literally, parasitic single — is the more common term for what the bartender meant.) And the third, she said, and here she smiled, is a person with "the Dream."

"The Dream" was different for everyone, she thought, but most often it had to do with artistic accomplishment. Some are waiting to become novelists or filmmakers or dancers. "And you?" I asked. "Are you a *freetah*?" She shook her head and laughed, her hand over her mouth. "No! I work, here, other places. I do not live with my parents!" "But you have the Dream, right?" Yes, she said, her dream is to be a film actor in Japan, maybe even in America, but in the meantime, she said, quite seriously, she works hard to support herself.

Although this woman did not consider herself a *freetah*, the economists do. A white paper issued by the Japan Institute of Labor (JIL) defines *freetahs* as workers between eighteen and thirty-five who have only part-time or side jobs (*arubaito*) for up to five years; in 1997 they totaled 1.5 million workers, twice as many as a decade before (other estimates run as high as 12 million). The JIL conducted a small study in which they interviewed about 100 *freetahs* whose average age was twenty-three. Just under half were high school graduates, an eighth were college graduates, and an eighth college dropouts. The average number of working days per week for these *freetahs* was 4.9 (or almost identical to full-time workers), and their monthly income averaged ¥139,000, or at that time roughly $15,000 a year, considerably below average. The JIL also came up with three types of *freetahs*, which almost but not entirely overlapped the bartender's three: "dead-end *freeters*" who stay underemployed because they have tried and failed to get regular work; "moratorium types" who have no immediate future vision; and "*freeters* with a dream" who want to work in show business or other professions. Slightly more than two-thirds of all the interviewees lived with their parents. The bartender and the bureau agree that there is a difference between the dreamers and the rest, but the bartender divides the non-dreamers into the craven and the lazy, or those who have no motivation and those who have no motivation *and* no parental support. The JIL finds parental support across the types, but assumes motivation in all three classes, some frustrated by temporary indecision, some frustrated by lack of opportunity.

There is a sense of crisis surrounding the *freetahs* that is not based on the economic facts. The *freetahs* are not, given their 4.9-day work-week, ending up "on the street" or otherwise disrupting anything except the Japanese sense of the value of work. The "salaryman" has gone from being a cultural ideal to something like the man in the gray flannel suit, a figure that represents what is wrong rather than what is right. And the *freetahs*, like the loafers, loungers, and slackers, function as a rejection of the received work ethic, a rejection of the salaryman ideal.

The Japanese Ministry of Education, Science, Sports and Culture conducted a much larger survey of students who graduated from high school between 1996 and 1998. Twenty-seven percent said that they were *freetahs* "because they did not know what they really wanted to do," 21 percent "did not regret their employment status because there was something they wanted to do (apart from getting regular work)," 16 percent thought that "they should have thought more seriously (about their future)," and 14 percent "were glad that they did not get a regular job because they were now free to do what they liked." These distinctions are finer, but basically about half hadn't figured out their own futures, and half wanted to do something else.

Japanese sociologist Sengoku Tomatsu has argued that the concept of Bushido (the way of the samurai) is a close cousin to Weber's notion of the Protestant "calling" to work; that is, Bushido is a semireligious dictate about how one should spend one's life. The popularity in Japan of Samuel Smiles's *Self-Help*, a book on work and success that was a bestseller in both England and America, attests to that similarity; it sold more than a million copies when translated into Japanese soon after its original publication in 1859. And the *freetahs*, as it turns out, are also similar to American slackers in that they are longer on the slacker pose than on slacker reality. The *freetahs* in these surveys may not have found their life's work, but they work quite a lot. Yoshinori Ogawa is a bassist in a rock group, and he works in a laundry from ten to six, five days a week, just barely under a forty-hour week. His status as a temporary worker is fine with him because, although he graduated from a technical college seven years ago, he is still on his father's health plan. Since it means that he doesn't get paid holidays either, he ends up working about as much as permanent employees, for much less money. But he likes the freedom to take time off for gigs and recording, and he likes not feeling any career pressure or anxiety, except in relation to his music career. His freedom from work, in other words, is largely illusory. Still, it helps create a sense of opportunity for him and those like him, even as it creates a sense of cultural crisis among his generation's parents, labor officials, and editorialists.

One thing they worry about is the loss of traditional values. A cross-cultural survey in 1972 asked students what their goal in life was; only 9 percent of American and French students answered "rewarding work," compared with 13 percent in Britain and 28 percent in Japan. Another survey in 1975 asked students in Japan and the United States, "Would you rather work or idle away the time?" Three times as many American high school and college students as Japanese said they would prefer to idle; 90 percent of the Japanese students said they would prefer to work. But by the late 1980s, further surveys show, those national differences had already been erased.

At the same time that this slacker crisis impends, following the same pattern as in the United States, there is renewed concern about overwork. *Karoshi*, a medical term for death from overwork, is thought by some to be epidemic. The first case of *karoshi*, so declared, was the 1969 death of a twenty-nine-year-old married man working in the shipping department of a large newspaper. A number of other cases were reported in the 1970s, but only in the 1980s did the phenomenon become well-known. In response to the death of a thirty-nine-year-old police sergeant who had worked double shifts for a month, a *karoshi* hotline was started in 1989 by a group of lawyers and doctors led by Hiroshi Kawahito, and 135 people called on the first day. That same year a poll of 500 Tokyo white-collar workers found that 46 percent were afraid they might die from overwork. In 1989 the average Japanese worked 2,150 hours, compared with 1,924 hours for Americans and 1,643 hours for the French, but *karoshi* victims typically work more than 3,000 hours a year. While the Ministry of Labor claims that there are only 30 to 40 deaths a year from *karoshi*, another government agency suggests 1,000, and Kawahito and some physicians argue that the real number is closer to 10,000 deaths a year (the actual cause of death in all these cases is heart attack or stroke). Dr. Yoshinori Hasegawa, one of the leading researchers on *karoshi*, claims that most of the victims did not receive any overtime pay for what sometimes came to 100 hours of extra labor per week, but were salaried managers who worked constantly "out of a samurai-like pride." In Korea, the same phenomenon is known as *kwarosa*, and there the common assumption is that it is related not to samurai culture but to a Confucian work ethic.

The concern about *karoshi*, however, produces much less press and cultural comment than the concern about *freeters*. Japan has long been noted for the strength of its work ethic, said to be responsible not just for the rash of *karoshi* deaths but for the "economic miracle" that took the country from the rubble of World War II to one of the largest, most productive economies in the world in a matter of decades. Loyalty, diligence, cooperation, and perseverance are all highly valued, and workers are famous for working long hours with few breaks and few vacations. And so it comes as no surprise that the *freetah* is such a powerful cultural figure. Every work ethic needs a slacker, so he appears everywhere that the industrial work does. The stronger the work ethic, the more vibrant the slacker culture. Japan, like the West, excels at both.

∞

At a family party recently I had a chat with a man of my parents' generation, a man who had had a fairly successful professional career. He is old-school charming, boisterous in an engaging way, conscious of himself as a bit of a character, a fun guy. After retiring, he moved back to his childhood hometown, and there he got a civil service job. It was a great job, he told me, good pay and very easy. Everything he needed to do for his job, he assured me, could be done in roughly an hour and a half. "I get in around ten or so, take care of business, and I'm done for the day in time to have lunch with my wife! It's great!" For this eight-hour week he gets a full-time salary. A great arrangement, he felt. "What about you?" he asked. I told him I was writing a history of slackers, loafers, loungers, and bums. "Interesting. Listen"—he looked around to make sure our conversation was private—"I know it's not right to say this, but I'm a southerner." Okay. "You're going to write something about the blacks, right?" he asked. "About the blacks?" I asked. "You know, they're lazy! You've got to write about that, right?"

Ah, the perennialness of it all! A man proud of getting a full-time salary for seven and a half hours of work a week straight-facedly complaining about the poor work ethic of others! On the one hand, this could simply be racism, but racism isn't necessary to explain it. It is simply the way the work ethic operates. Its loudest champions are often its most reckless violators. Sociological research lends no support to racial stereotypes about the work ethic—a review of twenty-one major surveys of worker attitudes over the last thirty years showed no significant difference among African Americans', European Americans', and Asian Americans' belief in the need to work hard to get ahead. An analysis of those same and additional studies found Mexican Americans to have a strong work ethic and strong work satisfaction, despite the fact that as a group, they were on the lower end of the scale in terms of education level, occupational status, and age, all of which are otherwise correlated with negative work attitudes. A 2000 study of Asian, European, and American managers of a multinational corporation found no significant difference in systemic work values based on gender or national origin.

The work ethic, finally, has little to do with reality. It's simply an attitude or feeling about how we and others spend our days the way we do. It all depends on who is looking at whom, at what moment. Freud wrote in *Civilization and Its Discontents* (1930) that once "man discovered that it lay in his own hands, literally, to improve his lot on earth by working, it cannot have been a matter of indifference to him whether another man worked with or against him." Freud understood that the eye we cast on our neighbor's labor is the origin of what we call the work ethic, not some internalized form of self-understanding. We know how we really feel about work when the person we are counting on fails to come through, when *someone else* is lying on the couch. Back in my commune days, we came up with a basic mathematical formula, finding that if two people were each doing 50 percent of the dishes or the woodchopping or any other chore, chances were that they both thought they were doing two-thirds of the work themselves. This meant, naturally, that they also assumed that the other person was slacking off with only a third. Perhaps we would by now actually be living in some Aquarian Age if this weren't the way we are as a species, or at least as a culture.

One's own slacking can cause guilt or pleasure over the idea of getting something for nothing, while the slacking of others can excite laughter, envy, or rage. And as I've tried to point out throughout, we all tend to embody a bit of both ends of the spectrum: like Samuel Johnson and Benjamin Franklin, like Oscar Wilde and Jack Kerouac, most of us contain both self-images. Most of us tend to believe both that others work harder than we do *and* that we work harder than others. The history of slackers is the history not just of our distaste for work and our fantasies of escaping it (*as well as* the history of our vilification of those who *do* escape it) but also a history of complexly distorted perceptions. One man's welfare queen is another man's struggling mother. One man's slacker son may be preparing his arrival as an artist, and another may simply be, as Chris Davis's father said, "a useless article." But the father in either case is probably not in the best position to judge, and usually neither is the slacker. They may hold up a mirror to us all, but often slackers can't see themselves in it very well.

In that mirror, are we not clearly a nation of slackers, plopped down in front of our TV sets for umpteen hours a day, the actual figure always shockingly large and growing larger? The idea that we are a nation of couch potatoes, in what is gradually becoming a world of couch potatoes, has been around since TV arrived in the 1950s, and before that the same arguments were made about radio: from the 1920s on, people worried that young people would glue themselves to the speaker and never again go outside and be active. Even earlier, when novels became popular in the eighteenth century, the moralists worried that striving had been replaced by the vegetative consumption of fictional pap. And in each of these periods, not surprisingly, we can find the opposite arguments—that we are too busy and need to slow down; that we devote too much time, worry, and energy to work; that we have never been so ridiculously busy, our weekly hours creeping up faster than our paychecks. Now, some say, we spend the time when we should be relaxing furiously working out in gyms, turning our sports into forms of achievement and effort, never slowing down.

(One researcher has shown that "vacation illness"—the tendency to get sick when granted vacation time—is also on the rise, as if we are incapable of enjoying even our minimal sanctioned free time.)

How can we be both of these things? How can we be the laziest and the most driven people in history at the same time? The slacker as a figure exists smack in the middle of these questions. People have asked me as I worked on this book to tell them what slacking *means*, as if it were possible to decode the phenomenon—as we might perhaps say that our culture's obsession with female beauty is a form of oppression or that the popularity of hip-hop exposes a white suburban desire for authenticity. Many of my academic colleagues want me to say that it is "just the economy, stupid," that the slacker is a class phenomenon, but it is not that easy. I have often found that the dominant explanations in academic cultural studies—"capitalism" and "consumerism" among them—since they explain everything, end by explaining nothing in particular. But beyond this, the slacker, I hope I have shown, cannot be reduced to a simple idea or a simple set of causes and effects. The figure of the slacker needs to mean different things to different people at different times in order to serve its complex function as a goad to examining our relation to work, as a role to adopt while finding our relation to work, as a critique of our culture's twisty relation to work and to leisure, and as a celebration of the same.

I should confess as well that I had a very difficult time sitting down and writing this book. The research, as always, I found fun, but the hard part, the writing, I just kept deferring. It was almost as if slackerism was contagious and I had come down with a bad case of it myself. Just ask my editor, my agent, my wife. They were afraid I had died, or at least the first two were; my wife thought maybe I was in a persistent vegetative state. For months on end I could make no progress, and I alternated obvious procrastinations with time-consuming, useless projects, all to avoid putting the proverbial pen to paper, finger to key.

I found, though, that I couldn't enjoy this time when I wasn't writing, couldn't exult in it, couldn't, as Whitman might suggest, invite my soul to a good loafe. I simply couldn't see any humor or feel any pleasure in the role. Too old, I guess. Or too disillusioned. When I wrote a book about tears, I stopped crying for a while, and perhaps this was the same thing. I had spent too much time examining, and therefore could no longer enjoy, my own idleness. At any rate, the pressure built and built until finally I just had to write or go completely crazy.

But I could always enjoy a good slacker story. In 2002, for instance, a thirty-year-old man in Naples, Italy, sued his parents for not supporting him, even though he owned his own apartment, had a sizable trust fund of his own and a law degree, and had turned down several job offers. His father, Giuseppe Andreoli, a wealthy former member of the Italian parliament, said he just wanted his son to grow up, and so cut off his allowance. A lower court ruled in the son's favor, ordering his parents to give him 750 euros a month. His father appealed, and Italy's highest court, the Corte di Cassazione, ruled again in favor of the son. "You cannot blame a young person, particularly from a well-off family," the judge said, "who refuses a job that does not fit his aspirations." The parents were ordered to continue the support until he reached "economic autonomy." This story was picked up by several news services and printed in newspapers all over the world, and for me, and for many of those not involved directly in the case, it was a comic story, a bit of fun.

Just like ABC's *Kicked Out*. The slacker son is always a comic figure. Unless, of course, he is your own son and ABC hasn't come calling.

My son, Cody, it turned out, was quickly off my couch and into the world of Hollywood, where he ended up working fourteen-hour days, and longer sometimes, as a production assistant, then on the writing team for a major Hollywood comedian, and now as an aspiring screenwriter who gets by doing various production jobs. He fast became ensconced in the hectic, intermittent schedule of the film world, which oddly resembles the work life of the medieval peasant, with bouts of sunup-to-sundown (or its equivalent) labor alternating with periods of absolute inactivity. Since he has now become a writer, too, he likes having his periods of unemployment to work on spec scripts, even if, frankly, he likes being unemployed anyway. As a writer, he faces the dilemma that all writers seem to, which is that we can't stop working even when we're supposed to be relaxing, and that often it is when we get a block of free time we have the most difficulty hunkering down. He and I have even written one screenplay together and put together a couple of other treatments. Like Hirschel Marx and his son Karl, we have learned to weather whatever storms come our way. We have developed, I'm glad to report, a very good working relationship (although it seems to me, as I suppose it has to, that I do a little bit more of the heavy lifting . . .).

My own workaholic father? And his father, who died trying to get to his railroad job in the middle of a blizzard? Well, those are other stories. Perhaps I'll write them someday, if I can find the energy and perseverance.

Right now, I'd rather stop and rest. Do nothing for a while. I know that people have said doing nothing is the hardest thing in the world to do, but I feel that now, after the work of making this book, I'm ready for the challenge. I'm ready to get off the treadmill, to face the slow, beautiful emptiness and say, Yes, this too is good.

BIBLIOGRAPHY

Abbott, Charles Conrad. *The Rambles of an Idler*. Philadelphia: G. W. Jacobs, 1906.

Adorno, Theodor. "Free Time." In *The Culture Industry: Selected Essays on Mass Culture*, edited by J. M. Bernstein. New York: Routledge, 1991.

A. K. H. B. "Concerning Hurry and Leisure." *Living Age* 66.852 (September 29, 1860): 787.

Akhtar, Syed. "Influences of Cultural Origin and Sex on Work Values." *Psychological Reports*, 86.3 (June 2000): 1037.

Albee, Edward. *The Zoo Story* [1959]. In *The Plays*. New York: Coward, McCann, 1981.

Algren, Nelson. *Nonconformity* [1953]. New York: Seven Stories Press, 1998.

Allmendinger, Blake. *The Cowboy: Representations of Labor in an American Work Culture*. New York: Oxford University Press, 1992.

Amburn, Ellis. *Subterranean Kerouac: The Hidden Life of Jack Kerouac*. New York: St. Martin's, 1998.

American Slacker Association. http://members.xoom.com/temas/about.html.

Amis, Kingsley. *Lucky Jim* [1954]. New York: Viking, 1958.

Amsden, David. "The Believer: Dave Eggers Talks about Production by Procrastination." *Salon* (March 9, 2005). www.salon.com.

Anderson, Nels. *The Hobo*. Chicago: University of Chicago Press, 1923.

———. *On Hobos and Homelessness*. Edited by Raffaele Rauty. Chicago: University of Chicago Press, 1998.

Anderson, Sherwood. *Dark Laughter* [1925]. New York: Liveright, 1960.

———. *Poor White*. New York: Huebsch, 1920.

Anderson, Terry H. *The Movement and the Sixties*. New York: Oxford University Press, 1995.

Andrew, Ed. *Closing the Iron Cage: The Scientific Management of Work and Leisure*. Montreal: Black Rose, 1981.

Andrisani, Paul J., et al. *The Work Ethic: A Critical Analysis*. Madison, WI: Industrial Relations Research Association, 1983.

Anon [Boyd, Nellie]. *Vagabond Rhymes, by an Idler*. Boston: J. G. Cupples, 1892.

Anon. *Letters to Friends at Home from June 1843, to May 1844: By an Idler*. Calcutta: Star Press, 1844.

Anon. "A Lift to the Lazy." *United States Democratic Review* 25.134 (August 1849): 190.

Anon. "Make Your Leisure Work for You." *House and Garden* (August 1942): 43.

Anon. "The Menace of the Slacker." *Month* 126.616 (October 1915): 405.

Anon. "The New Eight-Hour Law." *Manufacturer and Builder* 24.8 (August 1892): 185.

Anon. *The Tibetan Book of the Dead*. Translated by Robert Thurman. New York: Bantam, 1993.

Anon. "To Get the Alien Slacker." *Literary Digest* 55.5 (August 4, 1917): 22.

Anon. "To Make the Slacker Vote or Pay." *Literary Digest* 92.5 (January 29, 1927): 13.

Anon. "The Vote-Slacker Peril." *Literary Digest* 89.5 (May 1, 1926): 12.

Anon. "Where Is the Slacker?" *Nation* 18.15 (January 8, 1916): 529.

Anthony, Peter D. *The Ideology of Work*. Great Britain: Tavistock, 1977.

Aoi, Yasue. "Japanese-style Slackers Work, but Get a Life." *Christian Science Monitor* (April 20, 2000): 1.

Applebaum, Herbert A. *The American Work Ethic and the Changing Work Force: An Historical Perspective*. Westport, CT: Greenwood, 1998.

Appleby, Joyce. *Materialism and Morality in the American Past: Themes and Sources, 1600–1860*. Reading, MA: Addison-Wellesley, 1974.

Arendt, Hannah. *The Human Condition*. Chicago: University of Chicago Press, 1958.

———. "Labor, Work, Action" [1969]. In *The Portable Hannah Arendt*. New York: Penguin, 2000.

Aristotle. *The Politics*. Translated by Trevor J. Saunders and T. A. Sinclair. New York: Penguin, 1981.

Ashcroft, John. "Which Will Survive: The Welfare State or the Republican Revolution?" [1995]. http: www.heritage.org/Research/Welfare/HL539.cfm.

Atherton, Gertrude. *The Splendid Idle Forties: Stories of Old California*. New York: Grosset and Dunlap, 1902.

Augst, Thomas. *The Clerk's Tale: Young Men and Moral Life in Nineteenth-century America*. Chicago: University of Chicago Press, 2003.

Baldoz, Rick, Charles Kroeber, and Philip Kraft. *The Critical Study of Work: Labor, Technology, and Global Production*. Philadelphia: Temple, 2001.

Ballin, Hugo. *Dolce Far Niente*. 2nd ed. Los Angeles: Suttonhouse, 1933.

Banfield, Edward C. *The Unheavenly City: The Nature and Future of Our Urban Crisis*. Boston: Little, Brown, 1970.

Barbash, J., R. J. Lampman, S. A. Levitan, and G. Tyler, eds. *The Work Ethic: A Critical Analysis*. Madison, WI: Industrial Relations Research Association, 1983.

Baritz, Loren. *The Servants of Power: A History of the Use of Social Science in American Industry*. Middletown, CT: Wesleyan University Press, 1960.

Barker, Gerard A. *Henry Mackenzie*. Boston: Twayne Publishers, 1975.

Barlowe, Arthur. *The First Voyage to Roanoke 1584*. www.docsouth.unc.edu/nc/barlowe/barlowe.html.

Barnard, C. I. *The Functions of the Executive*. Cambridge, MA: Harvard University Press, 1938.

Barthes, Roland. "Osons Etre Paresseux." *Le Monde Dimanche* (September 16, 1979). In *Roland Barthes: Œuvres Complètes, Tome 3*. Paris: Seuil, 2002.

Baudelaire, Charles. *Arts in Paris, 1845–1862: Salons and Other Exhibitions Reviewed by Charles Baudelaire*. London: Phaidon, 1965.

——. *The Painter of Modern Life and Other Essays*. New York: Da Capo, 1964.

Bay Laurel, Alicia. *Living on the Earth: Celebrations, Storm Warnings, Formulas, Recipes, Rumors, and Country Dances Harvested*. New York: Random House, 1971.

Beard, George M., M.D. *American Nervousness: Its Causes and Consequences*. New York: G. P. Putnam, 1881.

Beder, Sharon. *Selling the Work Ethic: From Puritan Pulpit to Corporate PR*. New York: Zed Books, 2000.

Bell, Daniel. *The End of Ideology: On the Exhaustion of Political Ideas in the Fifties*. New York: Free Press, 1960.

——. *Work and Its Discontents*. Boston: Beacon Press, 1956.

Bellamy, Edward. *Looking Backward: 2000–1887* [1888]. Cambridge, MA: Harvard University Press, 1967.

Benjamin, Walter. *The Arcades Project*. Cambridge, MA, and London: Harvard University Press, 1999.

Bentham, Jeremy. *A Table of the Springs of Action*. London: R. Hunter, 1817.

Berkowitz, Edward D. *The "Safety Net" After Three Years: Income Maintenance and Redistribution Programs in the Reagan Administration*. Washington, D.C.: American Enterprise Institute, 1983.

Bernstein, Aaron. "Commentary: Off Welfare—and Worse Off." *Business Week* (Dec. 11, 1997). http://www.businessweek.com/1997/51/b3558082.htm.

Bernstein, Paul. *American Work Values: Their Origin and Development*. Albany, NY: SUNY Press, 1997.

——. "The Work Ethic: Economics, Not Religion." *Business Horizons* 31.3 (1988): 8–11.

Berry, Wendell. *The Unsettling of America: Culture and Agriculture*. New York: Avon, 1977.

Besharov, Douglas J. "Welfare As We Don't Know It." *Washington Post* (July 4, 1993). http://www.welfareacademy.org/pubs/welfare/welfare0793 .shtml.

Best, Fred, ed. *The Future of Work*. Englewood Cliffs, NJ: Prentice-Hall, 1973.

Bestor, Arthur Eugene. *Backwoods Utopias: The Sectarian and Owenite Phases of Communitarian Socialism in America, 1663–1829*. Philadelphia: University of Pennsylvania Press, 1950.

Bindman, David. *Hogarth*. New York: Thames and Hudson, 1981.

Biskind, Peter. *Easy Riders, Raging Bulls: How the Sex-Drugs-Rock'n'Roll Generation Saved Hollywood*. New York: Simon and Schuster, 1998.

Bleakley, David. *Work: Shadow and Substance*. London: SCM Press, 1983.

Blessington, Marguerite. *The Idler in France*. London: H. Colburn, 1841.

——. *The Idler in Italy*. London: H. Colburn, 1839.

Blythe, Samuel G. "Tapering Off on Work." *Saturday Evening Post* (August 8, 1925): 198.

Bogosian, Eric. *subUrbia* [1994]. New York: Theater Communication Group, 1995.

Boltanski, Christian. "Studio Visit." *Tate Magazine* 2. http://www.tate.org.uk/ magazine/issue2/boltanski.htm.

Bonebright, Cynthia A., Daniel L. Clay, and Robert D. Ankenmann. "The relationship of Workaholism with Work-life Conflict, Life Satisfaction, and Purpose in Life." *Journal of Counseling Psychology* 47.4 (October 2000): 469.

Boorstin, Daniel J. *The Americans: The Democratic Experience*. New York: Vintage, 1973.

Borne, Etienne, and François Henry. *A Philosophy of Work*. Translated by Francis Jackson. New York: Sheed and Ward, 1938.

Bosch, Gerhard, Peter Dawkings, and François Michon, eds. *Times Are Changing: Working Time in 14 Industrialised Countries*. Geneva: International Institute for Labour Studies, 1994.

Boswell, James. *Life of Samuel Johnson*. [1791]. New York: Everyman, 1993.

Bowe, John, Marissa Bowe, and Sabin Streeter. *Gig: Americans Talk About Their Jobs at the Turn of the Millennium*. New York: Crown, 2000.

Boyle, T. C. *Drop City*. New York: Viking, 2003.

Brand, Stewart, ed. *The Last Whole Earth Catalog*. New York: Random House, 1971.

Braude, Lee. *Work and Workers: A Sociological Analysis*. New York: Praeger, 1975.

Braudy, Leo. *From Chivalry to Terrorism: War and the Changing Nature of Masculinity*. New York: Knopf, 2003.

Braverman, Harry. *Labor and Monopoly Capital: The Degradation of Work in the Twentieth Century*. New York: Monthly Review Press, 1974.

Breines, Wini. *Young, Female and White: Growing Up Female in the Fifties*. Chicago: University of Chicago Press, 1992.

Brewer, William H. "What Shall We Do with the Tramps?" *New Englander* 37 (1878): 521.

Bridenbaugh, Carl. *Cities in the Wilderness: The First Century of Urban Life in America, 1625–1742*. New York: Oxford University Press, 1971.

Bridges, J. S. "Sex Differences in Occupational Values." *Sex-Roles: A Journal of Research* 20 (1989): 205–11.

Bromell, Nicholas K. *By the Sweat of the Brow: Literature and Labor in Antebellum America*. Chicago: University of Chicago Press, 1993.

Brooks, David. *Bobos in Paradise: The New Upper Class and How They Got There*. New York: Simon and Schuster, 2000.

Brown, Janelle, and Katharine Mieszkowski. "The New Slackers." http://www.salon.com/tech/feature/2001/02/26/new_slackers/index.html.

Brown, L. Ames. "A New Phase of the Menace of the Slacker." *Journal of the American Bankers Association* 9 (July 1916): 730.

Brown, Lewis P. "The Jew Is Not a Slacker." *North American Review* 207 (January 1918): 857.

Bruni, Frank. *Ambling into History: The Unlikely Odyssey of George W. Bush*. New York: HarperCollins, 2002.

Buck-Morss, Susan. "The *Flâneur*, the Sandwichman and the Whore: The Politics of Loitering." *New German Critique* 39 (1986): 99.

Bunting, Madeleine. *Willing Slaves: How the Overwork Culture Is Ruling Our Lives*. London: HarperCollins, 2004.

Burg, Dale. *Sloth: Ode to Disarray and Delay*. New York: Red Rock, 2001.

Burnett, John. *Idle Hands: The Experience of Unemployment, 1790–1990*. New York: Routledge, 1994.

Burnett, John, ed. *Useful Toil: Autobiographies of Working People from 1820s to 1920s*. [1971]. New York: Routledge, 1994.

Burns, C. Delisle. *Leisure in the Modern World*. Boston: Stratford, 1932.

Burroughs, John. *Notes on Walt Whitman as Poet and Person*. [1867]. http://www.whitmanarchive.org/disciples/burroughs_files/NotesOnWalt Whitman.html.

Burton, Robert. *Anatomy of Melancholy* [1624]. New York: Oxford University Press, 1989.

Bush, George W. *A Charge to Keep*. New York: William Morrow, 1999.

Bushmiller, Ernie. *Bums, Beatniks and Hippies*. Princeton, WI: Kitchen Sink Press, 1991.

Byrne, Edmund F. *Work, Inc.: A Philosophical Inquiry*. Philadelphia: Temple University Press, 1990.

Byron, George Gordon. *Don Juan*. [1819]. New York: Penguin, 1987.

———. *Hours of Idleness* [1807]. In *The Poems and Plays of Lord Byron*. New York: Dutton, 1915.

Cain, James M. *Mildred Pierce*. New York: Knopf, 1941.

Call, Annie Payson. *Power Through Repose* [1891]. http://www.gutenberg.org/etext/4337.

Campbell, Tommy. *The Slacker Confessions: True Stories from a Decade of Jobs*. Toronto: Hideen Brook, 2002.

CanadianSlackers.com. http://www.angelfire.com/ct/ CanadianSlackers.

Capitalist Conservative. http://members.tripod.com/~GOPcapitalist/republican1.html.

Capra, Fritjof. *The Tao of Physics*. Berkeley: Shambhala, 1975.

Carr, Jay. " 'Slacker': A Wry Look at Baby Busters." *Boston Globe* (October 4, 1991): 47.

Carter, John F. " 'These Wild Young People' by One of Them." *Atlantic Monthly* 126 (September 1920): 301.

Caruthers, William. *Loafing Along Death Valley Trails: A Personal Narrative of People and Places*. Ontario, CA: Death Valley, 1951.

Castaneda, Carlos. *Journey to Ixtlan: The Lessons of Don Juan*. New York: Simon and Schuster, 1972.

Chabon, Michael. *Mysteries of Pittsburgh*. New York: Morrow, 1988.

———. *Wonder Boys*. New York: Villard, 1995.

Chakrabarty, Dipesh. "Universalism and Belonging in the Logic of Capitalism." *Public Culture* 12.3 (Fall 2000): 653.

Chamberlain, Bryn. "The Quintessential Punk." http://www.film.queensu.ca/Critical/Chamberlain4.html.

Chambers, Ross. *Loiterature*. Lincoln: University of Nebraska Press, 1999.

Chan, David. "Method Effects of Positive Affectivity, Negative Affectivity, and Impression Management in Self-Reports of Work Attitudes." *Human Performance* 14.1 (2001): 77.

Chaplin, Charlie. *My Autobiography* [1964]. New York: Penguin, 2003.

Charters, Ann, ed. *The Portable Sixties Reader*. New York: Penguin, 2003.

Chase, Stuart. *Idle Money, Idle Men*. New York: Harcourt, Brace, 1940.

———. *Men and Machines*. New York: Macmillan, 1929.

Cheever, John. *The Stories of John Cheever*. New York: Knopf, 1978.

Cherrington, D. J. *The Work Ethic: Working Values and Values that Work*. New York: AMACOM, 1980.

Chmielewski, Philip J. *Bettering Our Condition: Work, Workers, and Ethics in British and German Economic Thought*. New York: P. Lang, 1992.

Chopra, Deepak. *The Seven Spiritual Laws of Success: A Practical Guide to the Fulfillment of Your Dreams*. Novato, CA: New World Library, 1995.

Churchill, Allen. *The Improper Bohemians*. New York: Dutton, 1959.

Ciscell, Jim. *American Slacker*. New York: Writers Club, 2002.

Ciulla, Joanne B. *The Working Life: The Promise and Betrayal of Modern Work*. New York: Times Books, 2000.

Clarke, Dudley. "The Gentle Slacker." *Punch* 149 (July 1915): 108.

Clayre, Alasdair. *Work and Play: Ideas and Experience of Work and Leisure*. London: Weidenfeld and Nicolson, 1974.

Collier, John. "The Red Atlantis." *Survey Graphic* (October 1922): 16.

Colson, Charles W. *Why America Doesn't Work*. Dallas: Word, 1991.

Committee for Economic Development. *Welfare Reform and Beyond: Making Work Work: A Policy Statement*. New York: Committee for Economic Development, 2000.

Commons, John R., et al. *History of Labor in the United States*, 4 vols. New York: Macmillan, 1918–35.

Connell, Ryann. "'Free' Lifestyle Lures Job-hoppers into Dim Future." *Mainichi Daily News* (June 14, 2001). http://www12.mainichi.co.jp/waiwai/0106/010614freeter.html.

Cook, John D., et al. *The Experience of Work: A Compendium and Review of 249 Measures and Their Use*. New York: Academic Press, 1981.

Cooley, Charles Horton. *Social Organization*. New York: Charles Scribner's Sons, 1909.

Corrigan, Paul. "Doing Nothing." In Stuart Hall and Tony Jefferson, eds., *Resistance Through Rituals: Youth Subcultures in Post-War Britain*. London: Hutchinson, 1976.

Coupland, Douglas. *Generation X*. New York: St. Martin's, 1991.

——. *Microserfs*. New York: ReganBooks, 1995.

——. *Shampoo Planet*. New York: Pocket Books, 1993.

Crane, Frank. "The Greatest Delusion in the World." *American Magazine* (August 1920): 59.

Creative Loafing.com.http://atlanta.creativeloafing.com/apps/pbcs.dll/section?category=ATL.

Cresswell, Tim. *The Tramp in America*. London: Reaktion, 2001.

Csikszentmihalyi, Mihaly. *Becoming Adult: How Teenagers Prepare for the World of Work*. New York: Basic Books, 2000.

——. *Flow: The Psychology of Optimal Experience*. New York: Harper and Row, 1990.

Cumbler, John T. *Working Class Community in Industrial America: Work, Leisure, and Struggle in Two Industrial Cities, 1870–1920*. Westport, CT: Greenwood, 1983.

Cutten, G. B. *The Threat of Leisure*. New Haven: Yale University Press, 1926.

Daft, Richard L., and Richard M. Steers. *Organizations: A Micro/Macro Approach*. Glenview, IL: Scott, Foresman, 1986.

Dana, Richard Henry. *Two Years Before the Mast* [1840]. New York: Modern Library, 2001.

Dawley, Alan. *Class and Community: The Industrial Revolution in Lynn*. Cambridge, MA: Harvard University Press, 1976.

Dawson, William Harbutt. *The Vagrancy Problem: The Case for Measures of Restraint for Tramps, Loafers, and Unemployables, with a Study of Continental Detention Colonies and Labour Houses*. London: P. S. King, 1910.

Deans, R. C. "Productivity and the New Work Ethic." In *Editorial Research Reports on the American Work Ethic*, edited by W. B. Dickenson Jr. Washington, D.C.: *Congressional Quarterly*, 1972.

De Grazia, Sebastian. *Of Time, Work, and Leisure*. New York: Random House, 1962.

De Lacroix, Auguste. "Le Flâneur." In *Les Français peints par eux-mêmes*. Paris: L. Curmer, 1841.

Dell, Floyd. *Love in Greenwich Village*. New York: George H. Doran, 1926.

De Maria, Walter. *Boxes for Meaningless Work* [1961]. http://www.artnotart .com/fluxus/wdemaria-meaninglesswork.html.

Dennie, Joseph. *A Collection of Essays, on a Variety of Subjects*. Newark, NJ: John Woods, 1797.

——. *The Farrago*. Edited by Bruce Granger. Delmar, NY: Scholars' Facsimiles, 1985.

——. *The Lay Preacher, or Short Sermons, for Idle Readers*. Edited by Milton Ellis. Delmar, NY: Scholars' Facsimiles, 1943.

——. *The Letters of Joseph Dennie, 1768–1812*. Edited by Laura Green Petter. Orono, ME: University of Maine Press, 1936.

Denning, Michael. *Mechanic Accents: Dime Novels and Working-Class Culture in America*. New York: Verso, 1987.

Denver, Bob. *Gilligan, Maynard & Me*. Secaucus, NJ: Carol, 1993.

Depastino, Todd. *Citizen Hobo: How a Century of Homelessness Shaped America*. Chicago: University of Chicago Press, 2003.

Dery, Mark. "Church of SubGenius Spoofs Cult Mentality." *New York Times* (December 26, 1985): B18.

——. "The Merry Pranksters and the Art of the Hoax." *New York Times* (December 23, 1990): B1.

Di Prima, Diane. *Memoirs of a Beatnik* [1969]. New York: Penguin, 1998.

——. *Recollections of My Life as a Woman: The New York Years*. New York: Penguin, 2001.

Dorfman, Joseph. *The Economic Mind in American Civilization, 1606–1685*, 5 vols. New York: A. M. Kelly, 1966–69.

Dowing, William C. *Literary Federalism in the Age of Jefferson: Joseph Dennie and the Port Folio, 1801–1812*. Columbia, SC: University of South Carolina Press, 1999.

Dowson, Martin, and Dennis M. McInerney. "Psychological Parameters of Students' Social and Work Avoidance Goals: A Qualitative Investigation." *Journal of Educational Psychology* 93.1 (March 2001): 35.

Dreiser, Theodore. *An Amateur Laborer* [1903]. Philadelphia: University of Pennsylvania Press, 1983.

——. *Sister Carrie* [1900]. New York: Signet, 2000.

Drew, Elizabeth. *Fear and Loathing in George W. Bush's Washington.* New York: New York Review Books, 2004.

Dublin, Thomas. *Women at Work: The Transformation of Work and Community in Lowell, Massachusetts, 1826–1860.* New York: Columbia University Press, 1993.

Dunn, Sarah. *The Official Slacker Handbook.* New York: Warner, 1994.

Durkheim, Emile. *The Division of Labor in Society* [1893]. Translated by George Simpson. New York: Free Press, 1964.

eFilmCritic.com.http://www.eFilmCritic.com.

Eggers, Dave. *You Shall Know Our Velocity.* San Francisco: McSweeney's, 2002.

Ehrenreich, Barbara. *The Hearts of Men: American Dreams and the Flight from Commitment.* New York: Anchor, 1983.

——. *Nickel and Dimed: On (Not) Getting By in America.* New York: Metropolitan Books, 2001.

Eisenberger, Robert. *Blue Monday: The Loss of the Work Ethic in America.* New York: Paragon House, 1989.

Eisenhower, Dwight. "Farewell Address." January 17, 1961. http://www.eisenhower.utexas.edu/farewell.htm.

Ellberg, John. *Tales of a Rambler.* New York: Macaulay, 1938.

Ellis, Bret Easton. *Less Than Zero.* New York: Simon and Schuster, 1985.

Ellis, Havelock. *Sexual Inversion* [1897]. In *Studies in the Psychology of Sex.* New York: Random House, 1936.

Ellis, Joseph. *Joseph Dennie and His Circle: A Study in American Literature from 1792 to 1812* [1915]. New York: AMS Press, 1971.

Ellison, Ralph. *Invisible Man* [1952]. New York: Vintage, 1995.

Ellmann, Richard. *Oscar Wilde.* New York: Knopf, 1988.

Engels, Friedrich. *The Condition of the Working Class in England* [1845]. Translated by W. O. Henderson and W. H. Chaloner. London: Blackwell, 1971.

——. *The Part Played by Labour in the Transition from Ape to Man* [1896]. Moscow: Foreign Languages Publishing House, 1949.

Epstein, Cynthia Fuchs. "The Cultural Perspective and the Study of Work." In *The Nature of Work: Sociological Perspectives,* edited by Kai Erikson and Steven Peter Vallas. New Haven: Yale University Press, 1990.

Erez, Miriam and P. Christopher Earley. *Culture, Self-Identity, and Work.* New York: Oxford University Press, 1993.

Erikson, Kai, and Steven Peter Vallas, eds. *The Nature of Work: Sociological Perspectives.* New Haven: Yale University Press, 1990.

Fabian, Johannes. *Time and the Other: How Anthropology Makes Its Object.* New York: Columbia University Press, 1983.

Faler, Paul G. *Mechanics and Manufacturers in the Early Industrial Revolution: Lynn, Massachusetts, 1780–1860.* Albany: SUNY Press, 1981.

Faulkner, William. *Mosquitoes* [1927]. New York: Liveright, 1955.

Fay, Doris, and Michael Frese. "Conservatives' Approach to Work: Less Prepared for Future Work Demands?" *Journal of Applied Social Psychology* 30.1 (January 2000): 171.

Fisher, Cynthia D., and Neal M. Ashkanasy. "The Emerging Role of Emotions in Work Life: An Introduction." *Journal of Organizational Behavior* 21 (March 2000): 123.

Fitzgerald, F. Scott. *The Beautiful and the Damned* [1922]. New York: Scribner, 1995.

———. *The Great Gatsby* [1925]. New York: Scribner, 2004.

———. *The Pat Hobby Stories.* New York: Scribner, 1995.

Fliegelman, Jay. *Prodigals and Pilgrims: The American Revolution Against Patriarchal Authority, 1750–1800.* New York: Cambridge University Press, 1982.

Florida, Richard. *The Rise of the Creative Class: And How It's Transforming Work, Leisure, Community, and Everyday Life.* New York: Basic Books, 2002.

Flynt, Josiah. "The Tramp at Home." *Century* 47.4 (February 1894): 517.

———. "Tramping with Tramps." *Century* 47.1 (1893): 99.

Folsom, Ed. *Walt Whitman's Native Representations.* New York: Cambridge University Press, 1994.

Folsom, Ed, and Kenneth M. Price. "Biography." *The Walt Whitman Archive.* http://www.iath.virginia.edu/whitman.

Ford Foundation. *Not Working: Unskilled Youth and Displaced Adults.* New York: Ford Foundation, 1983.

Fourier, Charles. *The Social Destiny of Man.* Translated by Henry Clapp. New York: Robert M. Dewitt, 1857.

Frank, Thomas. *The Conquest of Cool: Business Culture, Counterculture, and the Rise of Hip Consumerism.* Chicago: University of Chicago Press, 1997.

Franklin, Benjamin. *Advice to a Young Tradesman* [1748]. In *Benjamin Franklin: Writings.* New York: Library of America, 1987.

———. *Autobiography* [1793]. Ibid.

———. *Experiments and Observations on Electricity* [1751]. Ibid.

———. *The Way to Wealth* [1758]. Ibid.

Free Republic. http://209.157.64.200/focus/f-news/814412/posts.

Freidson, Eliot. "Labors of Love in Theory and Practice." In *The Nature of Work: Sociological Perspectives*, edited by Kai Erikson and Steven Peter Vallas. New Haven: Yale University Press, 1990.

Freud, Sigmund. *Civilization and Its Discontents* [1930]. Translated by James Strachey. New York: Norton, 1962.

———. "A Reply to Criticisms of Anxiety Neurosis." In *A General Selection from the Works of Sigmund Freud*, edited by John Rickman and Charles Brenner. New York: Doubleday, 1975.

Friedan, Betty. *The Feminine Mystique*. New York: Norton, 1963.

Friedman, Kinky. *The Love Song of J. Edgar Hoover*. New York: Simon and Schuster, 1996.

———. *Spanking Watson*. New York: Pocket Books, 2000.

Friedmann, Georges. *The Anatomy of Work: Labor, Leisure, and the Implications of Automation*. New York: Free Press, 1962.

Frith, Simon, ed. *Facing the Music*. New York: Pantheon, 1988.

Fuller, R. Buckminster. *Utopia or Oblivion: The Prospects for Humanity*. New York: Bantam, 1969.

Furnham, Adrian. *The Protestant Work Ethic*. Oxford, UK: Pergamon Press, 1990.

Fussell, Paul. *Class: A Guide Through the American Status System*. New York: Summit Books, 1983.

Galbraith, John Kenneth. *The Affluent Society*. Boston: Houghton Mifflin, 1958.

Gamst, Frederick C., ed. *Meanings of Work: Considerations for the Twenty-first Century*. Albany: SUNY Press, 1995.

Garson, Marvin. Quoted in Terry H. Anderson, op. cit.

Gary, Romain. *The Ski Bum*. New York: Harper and Row, 1965.

Gault, William Campbell. *Don't Cry for Me*. New York: Dell, 1952.

George, Henry. *Social Problems*. Chicago: Belford, Clarke, 1883.

Getzels, J. W., J. M. Lipham, and R. F. Campbell. *Educational Administration as a Social Process*. New York: Harper and Row, 1968.

Gibbons, Euell. *Stalking the Wild Asparagus*. New York: D. McKay, 1962.

Gibbons, Judith L., Deborah A. Stiles, Jo D. Schnellmann, and Italo Morales-Hidalgo. "Images of Work, Gender, and Social Commitment among Guatemalan Adolescents." *Journal of Early Adolescence* 10.1 (February 1990): 89.

Gibson, Arell. *Santa Fe and Taos Colonies: Age of the Muses, 1900–1942*. Norman: University of Oklahoma Press, 1983.

Gilbert, David. *The Normals*. New York: Bloomsbury USA, 2004.

Gilbert, James B. *Work Without Salvation*. Baltimore: Johns Hopkins University Press, 1977.

Gilbert, Matthew. "Richard Linklater defines 'Slacker,'" *Boston Globe* (September 29, 1991): A9.

Gilens, Martin. *Why Americans Hate Welfare: Race, Media, and the Politics of Antipoverty Policy*. Chicago: University of Chicago Press, 1999.

Gill, Eric. *A Holy Tradition of Working*. Ipswich, UK: Golgonooza, 1983.

Gill, Flora. "The Meaning of Work: Lessons from Sociology, Psychology and Political Theory." *Journal of Socio-Economics* 28.6 (1999): 725.

Gilman, Charlotte Perkins. *The Living of Charlotte Perkins Gilman*. New York: Appleton-Century, 1935.

Gimlin, Hoyt, ed. *Editorial Research Reports on Work Life in the 1980s*. Washington, D.C.: *Congressional Quarterly*, 1981.

Gini, Al. *The Importance of Being Lazy: In Praise of Play, Leisure, and Vacations.* New York: Routledge, 2003.

Gini, A. R., and T. J. Sullivan. "A Critical Overview." In *It Comes with the Territory: An Inquiry Concerning Work and the Person,* edited by A. R. Gini and T. J. Sullivan. New York: Random House, 1989.

Ginsberg, Allen. *Howl.* San Francisco: City Lights, 1956.

Gitlin, Todd. *The Sixties: Years of Hope, Days of Rage.* Revised edition. New York: Bantam Books, 1993.

Givhan, Robin D. "TV Target: The Post-Boomers." *San Francisco Chronicle* (September 24, 1992): D3.

Gleason, William A. *The Leisure Ethic: Work and Play in American Literature, 1840–1940.* Stanford, CA: Stanford University Press, 1999.

Gluck, Mary. "The Flâneur and the Aesthetic Appropriation of Urban Culture in Mid-19th-Century Paris." *Theory, Culture & Society* 20.5 (2003): 53.

Godelier, Maurice. "Work and Its Representations: A Research Proposal." *History Workshop Journal* 10 (Autumn 1980): 164.

Goffman, Ken, and Dan Joy. *Counterculture Through the Ages: From Abraham to Acid House.* New York: Villard, 2004.

Goodman, Paul. *Growing Up Absurd: Problems of Youth in the Organized System.* New York: Random House, 1960.

Goodwin, Leonard. *Do the Poor Want to Work? A Social-Psychological Study of Work Orientations.* Washington: Brookings Institution, 1972.

Gouk, Penelope, ed. *Wellsprings of Achievement: Cultural and Economic Dynamics in Early Modern England and Japan.* Brookfield, VT: Variorum, 1995.

Gratzon, Fred. *The Lazy Way to Success: How to Do Nothing and Accomplish Everything.* Fairfield, IA: Soma, 2003.

Gregory, Eliot. *Worldly Ways and Byways, by "An Idler."* New York: Charles Scribner's Sons, 1899.

Gregson, J. A. "Work Values and Attitudes Instruction as Viewed by Secondary Trade and Industrial Education Instructors." *Journal of Industrial Teacher Education* 28.4 (1991): 34.

Gudeman, Stephen. *Economics as Culture: Models and Metaphors of Livelihood.* London: Routledge, 1986.

Gueron, Judith M. "The MDRC Work/Welfare Project." *Policy Studies Review* 4.3 (1985): 417.

——. "Reforming Welfare with Work." *Public Welfare* 45.4 (1987): 13.

Guthmann, Edward. "Dropouts of the '90s Find a Voice in 'Slacker.'" *San Francisco Chronicle* (August 9, 1991): F3.

Gutman, Herbert G. *Work, Culture and Society in Industrializing America.* New York: Knopf, 1976.

Halberstam, David. *The Fifties.* New York: Fawcett, 1993.

Hall, Stephen J. G., and Juliet Clutton-Brock. *Two Hundred Years of British Farm Livestock*. London: British Museum, 1989.

Harris, Lee O. *The Man Who Tramps: A Story of To-day*. Indianapolis: Douglass and Carlson, 1878.

Hammer, Michael. *Reengineering the Corporation: A Manifesto for Business Revolution*. New York: HarperBusiness, 2001.

Harding, Walter. *Thoreau as Seen by His Contemporaries*. New York: Dover, 1989.

Hardwick, Elizabeth. *Bartleby in Manhattan and Other Essays*. New York: Vintage, 1984.

Harkin, Maureen. "Mackenzie's Man of Feeling: Embalming Sensibility." *English Literary History* 61.2 (Summer 1994): 317.

Harrison, Steven. *Doing Nothing: Coming to the End of the Spiritual Search*. New York: Putnam, 1997.

Hawthorne, Julian. *Nathaniel Hawthorne and His Wife: A Biography*. Boston: Ticknor, 1884.

Hawthorne, Nathaniel. *The Blithedale Romance* [1852]. In *The Complete Novels and Selected Tales of Nathaniel Hawthorne*, edited by Norman Holmes Pearson. New York: Modern Library, 1937.

———. *The House of the Seven Gables* [1851]. Ibid.

Hay, J. R. *The Development of the British Welfare State, 1880–1975*. London: Edward Arnold, 1978.

Haywood, Bill, and Frank Bohn. *Industrial Socialism*. Chicago: Charles H. Kerr, 1911.

Heilbroner, Robert L. *The Act of Work*. Washington: Library of Congress, 1985.

Heineman, Ben W., Jr., et al. *Work and Welfare: The Case for New Directions in National Policy*. Washington, D.C.: Center for National Policy, 1987.

Heller, Joseph. *Something Happened*. New York: Knopf, 1974.

hellyeah.com. http://hellyeah.com.

Hemingway, Ernest. *A Farewell to Arms* [1932]. New York: Scribner, 1995.

———. "American Bohemians in Paris." In *Byline: Ernest Hemingway*, edited by William White. New York: Scribner, 1967.

———. *A Moveable Feast*. New York: Scribner, 1964.

———. *The Green Hills of Africa* [1935]. New York: Scribner, 1996.

———. *The Sun Also Rises* [1926]. New York: Scribner, 1995.

Hemmings, Fred. *The Soul of Surfing Is Hawaiian*. Honolulu: Sports Enterprises, 1997.

Henderson, Helen Weston. *A Loiterer in London*. New York: Doran, 1924.

———. *A Loiterer in New England*. New York: Doran, 1929.

———. *A Loiterer in New York: Discoveries Made by a Rambler Through Obvious Yet Unsought Highways and Byways*. New York: Doran, 1917.

———. *A Loiterer in Paris*. New York: Doran, 1921.

Henry, J. W. *"Dolce Far Niente": The Compositions of My School Days.* Washington, D.C.: Rufus H. Darby, 1881.

Heron, Alexander Richard. *Why Men Work* [1948]. New York: Arno Press, 1977.

Herreshoff, David Sprague. *Labor into Art: The Theme of Work in Nineteenth-Century American Literature.* Detroit: Wayne State University Press, 1991.

Herschlag, Rich, and Brian Harris. *Lay Low and Don't Make the Big Mistake: The Lazy Person's Guide to Success on the Job.* New York: Fireside, 1997.

Hersey, Rexford Brammer. *Workers' Emotions in Shop and Home: A Study of Individual Workers from the Psychological and Physiological Standpoint.* Philadelphia: University of Pennsylvania Press, 1932.

Herzberg, Frederick, Bernard Mausner, and Barbara Bloch Snyderman. *The Motivation to Work.* New York: John Wiley, 1959.

Hesiod. *Theogony, Works and Days.* Translated by M. L. West. New York: Oxford University Press, 1988.

Hiaasen, Carl. *Lucky You.* New York: Warner, 1998.

Hill, Roger B. "A New Look At Selected Employability Skills: A Factor Analysis of the Occupational Work Ethic." *Journal of Vocational Education Research* 20.4 (1995).

———. "The Work Ethic Site." http://www.coe.uga.edu/workethic/index.html.

Hine, Thomas. *The Rise and Fall of the American Teenager.* New York: Perennial, 1999.

Hinrichs, Karl, William Roche, and Carmen Sirianni, eds. *Working Time in Transition: The Political Economy of Working Hours in Industrial Nations.* Philadelphia: Temple University Press, 1991.

Hirschfeld, Robert R., and Hubert S. Field. "Work Centrality and Work Alienation: Distinct Aspects of a General Commitment to Work." *Journal of Organizational Behavior* 21.7 (November 2000): 789.

Hobsbawm, Eric. *Labouring Men: Studies in the History of Labour.* London: Weidenfeld and Nicolson, 1968.

———. *Worlds of Labour: Further Studies in the History of Labour.* London: Weidenfeld and Nicolson, 1984.

Hochschild, Arlie Russell. *The Time Bind: When Work Becomes Home and Home Becomes Work.* New York: Henry Holt, 1997.

Hodgkinson, Tom. *How to Be Idle.* London: Hamish Hamilton, 2005.

Hodgkinson, Tom, and Matthew De Abaitua. *The Idler's Companion: An Anthology of Lazy Literature.* Hopewell, NJ: Ecco Press, 1997.

Hoffman, Abbie. *Steal This Book* [1971]. New York: Four Walls Eight Windows, 1996.

Hofstede, Geert H. *Culture's Consequences: International Differences in Work-Related Values.* Beverly Hills: Sage Publications, 1984.

Honoré, Carl. *In Praise of Slowness*. New York: HarperSanFrancisco, 2004.

Hopkins, Tighe. *An Idler in Old France*. London: Hurst and Blackett, 1899.

Hornburg, Michael. *Bongwater*. New York: Grove, 1996.

Hornby, Nick. *About a Boy*. New York: Riverhead, 1998.

Horton, Robert. "Meet Richard Linklater—No Slacker He." *Film Comment* 26:4 (July/August 1990): 77.

Howe, Neil, William Strauss, and R. J. Matson. *Millennials Rising: The Next Great Generation*. New York: Vintage, 2000.

Howells, William Dean. *A Traveler from Altruria* [1894]. New York: Hill and Wang, 1957.

Huart, Louis. *Physiologie du flâneur*. Paris: Aubert et Lavigne, 1841.

Hughes, Thomas. *Tom Brown's Schooldays* [1857]. New York: Oxford University Press, 1999.

Huizinga, Johan. *Homo Ludens: A Study of the Play Element in Culture* [1938]. Boston: Beacon, 1957.

Humphrey, Seth King. *Loafing Through Africa*. Philadelphia: Penn Publishing, 1929.

——. *Loafing Through the Pacific*. Garden City, NY: Doubleday, Page, 1927.

Hunnicutt, Benjamin Kline. *Kellogg's Six-Hour Day*. Philadelphia: Temple University Press, 1996.

——. *Work Without End: Abandoning Shorter Hours for the Right to Work*. Philadelphia: Temple University Press, 1988.

Hunt, Leigh. *A Saunter Through the West End*. London: Hurst and Blackett, 1861.

Inaba, Yasuo. "Part-Time Workers Top 1.5 Million Mark." *Mainichi Shimbun* (June 28, 2000). http://mdn.mainichi-msn.co.jp/.

Indik, Bernard P. *The Motivation to Work*. New Brunswick, NJ: Institute of Management and Labor Relations, 1966.

Inge, M. Thomas, ed. *Bartleby the Inscrutable: A Collection of Commentary on Herman Melville's Tale "Bartleby the Scrivener."* Hamden, CT.: Archon Books, 1979.

Irving, Washington. *History, Tales and Sketches*. Edited by James W. Tuttleton. New York: Library of America, 1983.

——. *Letters of Jonathan Oldstyle, Gent. Salmagundi; Or the Whim-Whams and Opinions of Launcelot Langstaff, Esq. & Others*. Edited by Bruce I. Granger and Martha Hartzog. Vol. 6 of *The Complete Works of Washington Irving*. Boston: Twayne, 1977.

——. *Selected Writings of Washington Irving*. New York: Modern Library, 1984.

Isaacson, Walter. *Benjamin Franklin: An American Life*. New York: Simon and Schuster, 2003.

Isaksen, Jesper. "Constructing Meaning Despite the Drudgery of Repetitive Work." *Journal of Humanistic Psychology* 40.3 (Summer 2000): 84.

Izzo, John B., and Pam Withers. *Values Shift: The New Work Ethic and What It Means for Business.* Vancouver: Fairwinds, 2001.

James, Henry. *The American* [1877]. New York: Penguin, 1981.

James, William. "The Gospel of Relaxation" [1899]. In *Talks to Teachers on Psychology.* New York: Norton, 1958.

——. *Varieties of Religious Experience* [1902]. New York: Penguin, 1982.

Janis, Elsie. "The Slacker." *Theatre* 26 (July/Dec. 1917): 210.

Janowitz, Tama. *Slaves of New York.* New York: Crown, 1986.

Japan Institute of Labor. "Working Conditions and the Labor Market." *Japan Labor Bulletin* 39 (1 November 2000): 11.

Jarrett, Derek. *England in the Age of Hogarth.* New York: Viking, 1974.

Jerome, Jerome K. *Idle Ideas in 1905* [1905]. McLean, VA: IndyPublish, 2002.

——. *The Idle Thoughts of an Idle Fellow* [1886]. Ibid.

——. *The Second Thoughts of an Idle Fellow* [1898]. Ibid.

——. *Three Men in a Boat* [1889]. New York: Penguin, 2000.

Joe, Tom, and Cheryl Rogers. *By the Few, For the Few: The Reagan Welfare Legacy.* Lexington, MA: Lexington Books, 1985.

John Paul II. *Laborem Exercens: Encyclical Letter of Pope John Paul II on Human Work* [1981]. Translated by Joseph Kirwan. London: Catholic Truth Society, 1981.

Johnson, Alvin. "To a Slacker." *New Republic* 15.183 (May 4, 1918): 18.

Johnson, Denis. *Jesus' Son.* New York: Perennial, 1992.

Johnson, Joyce. *Minor Characters: The Romantic Odyssey of a Woman in the Beat Generation.* New York: Washington Square, 1983.

Johnson, Rossiter. *Idler and Poet.* Boston: J. R. Osgood, 1883.

Johnson, Samuel. *Dictionary of the English Language* [1755]. London: Times Books, 1983.

——. *The History of Rasselas, Prince of Abissinia.* Edited by J. P. Hardy. New York: Oxford University Press, 1999.

——. *Johnson's Lives of the Poets: A Selection.* Edited by J. P. Hardy. Oxford, UK: Clarendon, 1971.

——. *The Letters of Samuel Johnson.* 3 vols. Edited by Bruce Redford. Princeton, NJ: Princeton University Press, 1992–94.

——. *Selected Essays.* Edited by David Womersley. New York: Penguin, 2003.

Johnston, Sheila. "The Blank Generation." *Independent* (November 20, 1992): 23.

Jordan, Sarah. "Samuel Johnson and Idleness." *The Age of Johnson* 11 (2000): 145.

Jubera, Drew. "Twentysomething: No Image in the Mirror." *Atlanta Journal and Constitution* (June 10, 1991): E1.

Jurca, Catherine. *White Diaspora: The Suburb and the Twentieth-Century American Novel.* Princeton: Princeton University Press, 2001.

Kains, M. G. *Five Acres and Independence* [1935]. New York: Dover, 1973.

Kane, Pat. *The Play Ethic: A Manifesto for a Different Way of Living*. London: Macmillan, 2004.

Kaplan, Justin. *Walt Whitman: A Life*. New York: Simon and Schuster, 1980.

Katz, Michael B. *In the Shadow of the Poor House: A Social History of Welfare in America*. New York: Basic Books, 1986.

Katz, Richard. *Loafing Round the Globe: A Two Years' Tour Through Africa, Asia, Australia, New Zealand, Polynesia and America*. Translated by Gerald Griffin. London: Hutchinson, 1935.

Katzell, Raymond, and David Yankelovich. *Work, Productivity and Job Satisfaction*. New York: Psychological Corp., 1976.

Kaus, Mickey. "TANF and 'Welfare': Further Steps Toward the Work Ethic State." *Brookings Review* 19.3 (Summer 2001): 43.

———. "The Work Ethic State: The Only Way to Break the Culture of Poverty." *New Republic* (July 7, 1986): 26.

Keats, John. "Ode on Indolence." In *John Keats: The Major Works*, edited by Elizabeth Cook. New York: Oxford University Press, 2001.

———. *Selected Letters: John Keats*. Edited by Robert Gittings. New York: Oxford University Press, 2002.

Keats, John. *The Crack in the Picture Window*. New York: Ballentine, 1956.

Keeler, Bob. "Was Jesus a Slacker?" *U.S. Catholic* 63.9 (September 1998): 17.

Kelly, Fred C. *The Wisdom of Laziness*. Garden City, NY: Doubleday, Page, 1924.

Kelly, Kitty. *The Family: The Real Story of the Bush Dynasty*. New York: Doubleday, 2004.

Kennedy, Walker. "Walt Whitman." *North American Review* 138.331 (June 1884), 591.

Kerouac, Jack. *The Dharma Bums* [1958]. New York: Penguin, 1971.

———. "Essentials of Spontaneous Prose." *Good Blonde and Others*. San Francisco: Grey Fox Press, 1993.

———. *On the Road* [1957]. New York: Penguin, 1991.

———. *Selected Letters, 1940–1956*. Edited by Ann Charters. New York: Penguin, 1996.

———. *Selected Letters, 1957–1969*. Ibid.

———. *The Town and the City* [1950]. New York: Harvest, 1970.

———. *Vanity of Duluoz* [1968]. New York: Penguin, 1994.

Kicked Out. Homepage. http://abcfamily.go.com/kickedout/.

Kim, Kwang Chung, and Shin Kim. "Family and Work Roles of Korean Immigrants in the United States." In *Resiliency in Native American and Immigrant Families*, edited by Hamilton I. McCubbin, Elizabeth A. Thompson, et al. Thousand Oaks, CA: Sage, 1988.

Kinsey, Alfred. *Sexual Behavior in the Human Female*. Philadelphia: Saunders, 1953.

Koditschek, Theodore. *Class Formation and Urban-industrial Society: Brad-ford, 1750–1850*. New York: Cambridge University Press, 1990.

Konieczny, Leon. http://www.leonkonieczny.com/politics.htm.

Kruger, Justin, and David Dunning. "Unskilled and Unaware of It: How Difficulties in Recognizing One's Own Incompetence Lead to Inflated Self-Assessments." *Journal of Personality and Social Psychology* 77.6 (December 1999): 1121.

Kulik, Liat. "Impact of Gender and Age on Attitudes and Reactions to Un-employment: The Israeli Case." *Sex Roles* 43.1–2 (July 2000): 85.

——. "Impact of Length of Unemployment and Age on Jobless Men and Women: A Comparative Analysis." *Journal of Employment Counseling* 38.1 (March 2001): 15.

Kunkel, Benjamin. *Indecision*. New York: Random House, 2005.

Kunstler, James Howard. http://jameshowardkunstler.typepad.com/ clusterfuck_nation/2004/07 /farenheit_911.html.

Kusmer, Kenneth L. *Down and Out, On the Road: The Homeless in Ameri-can History*. New York: Oxford University Press, 2002.

La Bossière, Camille R. *The Progress of Indolence: Readings in (Neo)Augus-tan Literary Culture*. Toronto: York, 1997.

Lafargue, Paul. "Reminiscences of Marx." http://www.marxists.org/archive/ lafargue/1890/xx/marx.htm.

——. *The Right to Be Lazy* [1883]. Translated by Len Bracken. Ardmore, PA: Fifth Season, 1999.

Lancaster, Lynne, and David Stillman. *When Generations Collide: Who They Are, Why They Clash, How to Solve the Generational Puzzle at Work*. New York: HarperCollins, 2002.

Lane, Peter. *The Industrial Revolution: The Birth of the Modern Age*. New York: Harper and Row, 1978.

Latham, Rob. *Consuming Youth: Vampires, Cyborgs, and the Culture of Con-sumption*. Chicago: University of Chicago Press, 2002.

Laurence, John. *A New System of Agriculture*. London: T. Edward, 1726.

Lears, Jackson. *Something for Nothing: Luck in America*. New York: Viking, 2003.

Lee, Agnes. "Pictures of Women: The Slacker." *Poetry* 13 (October 1918): 200.

Lee, Gerald Stanley. *Rest Working: A Study in Relaxed Concentration*. New York: J. J. Little and Ives, 1925.

Leech, Harry Harewood. *Letters of a Sentimental Idler, from Greece, Turkey, Egypt, Nubia, and the Holy Land*. New York: D. Appleton, 1869.

Leff, Walli F., and Marilyn G. Haft. *Time Without Work: People Who Are Not Working Tell Their Stories, How They Feel, What They Do, How They Survive*. Boston: South End Press, 1983.

LeGoff, Jacques. *Time, Work, and Culture in the Middle Ages*. Translated by Arthur Goldhammer. Chicago: University of Chicago Press, 1980.

Leland, Charles Godfrey. *The English Gipsies and Their Language*. London: Trubner, 1873.

Leonard, Elmore. *Mr. Paradise*. New York: Morrow, 2004.

———. *Pagan Babies*. New York: Delacorte, 2000.

Lethem, Jonathan. *Motherless Brooklyn*. New York: Doubleday, 1999.

Levine, Mel. *The Myth of Laziness*. New York: Simon and Schuster, 2003.

Lewis, Sinclair. *Arrowsmith* [1925]. New York: Harcourt, Brace, 1952.

———. *Babbitt*. New York: Harcourt, Brace, 1922.

———. *Dodsworth*. New York: Harcourt, Brace, 1929.

———. *Main Street* [1920]. New York: Library of America, 1992.

Lipking, Lawrence I. *Samuel Johnson: The Life of an Author*. Cambridge, MA: Harvard University Press, 1998.

Lippmann, Walter. *A Preface to Morals*. New York: Macmillan, 1929.

Lipset, Seymour M. "The Work Ethic—Then and Now." *Public Interest* (Winter 1990): 61.

Lipsyte, Sam. *Home Land* [2004]. New York: Picador, 2005.

Littrell, Jill, and Elizabeth Beck. "Do Inner-City, African-American Males Exhibit 'Bad Attitudes' Toward Work?" *Journal of Sociology and Social Welfare* 27.2 (June 2000): 3.

Lloyd, Nelson. *The Chronic Loafer*. New York: J. F. Taylor, 1900.

Loeb, Paul Rogat. "Greeks and Granolas and Steeps and Slackers." *Mother Jones* 19.5 (September/October 1994): 56.

Logan, Gertrude Moore. *The Rambler*. Cedar Rapids, IA: Torch Press, 1947.

London, Jack. *Martin Eden* [1909]. New York: Holt, Rinehart, Winston, 1956.

———. *The Road*. New York: Macmillan, 1907.

Loos, Anita. *Gentlemen Prefer Blondes: The Illuminating Diary of a Professional Lady* [1925]. New York: Liveright, 1963.

Loprest, Pamela J. "Disconnected Welfare Leavers Face Serious Risks." August 21, 2003. http://www.urban.org/url.cfm?ID=310839.

———. "Fewer Welfare Leavers Employed in Weak Economy." August 21, 2003. http://www.urban.org/url.cfm?ID=310837.

Luskin, Fred, and Kenneth Pelletier. *Stress Free for Good: 10 Scientifically Proven Life Skills for Health and Happiness*. New York: HarperSanFrancisco, 2005.

Lutz, Tom. *American Nervousness, 1903: An Anecdotal History*. Ithaca: Cornell University Press, 1991.

———. "The Cultural History of Neurasthenia." In *A History of Clinical Psychiatry*, edited by German Barrios and Roy Porter. London: Wellcome Institute for the History of Medicine and Athlone Press, 1995.

———. "Spending Time." In *Consumption in an Age of Information*, edited by Sande Cohen and R. L. Rutsky. New York: Peter Berg, 2005.

———. " 'Sweat or Die': The Hedonization of the Work Ethic in the 1920s." *American Literary History* 8.2 (1996): 259.

——. "Varieties of Medical Experience: Doctors and Patients, Psyche and Soma in America." In *Cultures of Neurasthenia From Beard to the First World War*, edited by Roy Porter and Marijke Gijswijt. Amsterdam: Wellcome Institute/Rodolpi, 2001.

Lynd, Robert. "The Slacker." *New Statesman* 29 (April 16, 1927): 615.

Lynd, Robert S., and Helen Merrill Lynd. *Middletown: A Study in Contemporary American Culture*. New York: Harcourt, Brace, 1929.

Lynn, Kenneth. *A Divided People*. Westport, CT: Greenwood, 1977.

Lynn, Richard. *The Secret of the Miracle Economy: Different National Attitudes to Competitiveness and Money*. London: Social Affairs Unit, 1991.

Maccoby, Michael. *Why Work?: Leading the New Generation*. New York: Simon and Schuster, 1988.

Mackenzie, Henry. *The Lounger: A Periodical Paper Published at Edinburgh in the Years 1785 and 1786*. New York: Samuel Campbell, 1789.

——. *The Man of Feeling* [1771]. In *The Works of Henry Mackenzie*. Edinburgh: A. Constable, 1808.

Mailer, Norman. "The White Negro." In *The Beat Generation and the Angry Young Men*, edited by Gene Feldman and Max Gartenberg. New York: Dell, 1958.

Maier, Corinne. *Bonjour Paresse: De l'art et la nécessité d'en faire le moins possible en enterprise*. Paris: Michalon, 2004.

Mandelbaum, Paul. *Adriane on the Edge*. New York: Berkley, 2005.

Marcuse, Herbert. *Eros and Civilization: A Philosophical Inquiry into Freud* [1955]. Boston: Beacon, 1966.

Marquand, J. P. *Sincerely, Willis Wayde*. Boston: Little, Brown, 1955.

Marrs, William Taylor. *Confessions of a Neurasthenic*. Philadelphia: F. A. Davis, 1908.

Martin, Carolyn. *Managing Generation Y*. Amherst, MA: HRD Press, 2001.

Marx, Karl. *The Eighteenth Brumaire of Louis Bonaparte*. New York: International Publishers, 1964.

——. *The German Ideology*. In *The Marx-Engels Reader*, edited by Robert C. Tucker. New York: Norton, 1972.

——. *The Marx-Engels Reader*, 2nd ed. Edited by Robert C. Tucker. New York: Norton, 1978.

——. *Portable Karl Marx*. Translated by Eugene Kamenka. New York: Viking, 1983.

——. "Reflections of a Young Man on the Choice of a Profession" [1835]. http://www.marxists.org/archive/marx/works/1837-pre/marx/1835-ref.htm.

Matherly, Walter J. "The Industrial Slacker." *Industrial Management* 61.3 (February 1, 1921): 146.

Matthiessen, F. O. *American Renaissance: Art and Expression in the Age of Emerson and Whitman*. New York: Oxford University Press, 1941.

Maurer, Harry. *Not Working: An Oral History of the Unemployed*. New York: Holt, Rinehart and Winston, 1979.

Mayo, Elton. *The Human Problems of an Industrial Civilization*. Cambridge, MA: Harvard Business School, 1946.

Maywood, A. G. "Vocational Education and the Work Ethic." *Canadian Vocational Journal* 18.3 (1982): 7.

McClelland, David. *The Achieving Society*. New York: Free Press, 1961.

McCormick, Charles H. *Seeing Reds: Federal Surveillance of Radicals in the Pittsburgh Mill District, 1917–1921*. Pittsburgh: University of Pittsburgh Press, 1997.

McGregor, Douglas. *The Human Side of Enterprise*. New York: McGraw-Hill, 1960.

McInerney, Jay. *Bright Lights, Big City*. New York: Vintage, 1984.

McMahon, John R. *Toilers and Idlers: A Novel*. New York: Wilshire, 1907.

Mehring, Franz. *Karl Marx: The Story of His Life* [1918]. http://www.marxists.org/archive/mehring/1918/marx/ch01.htm.

Meilaender, Gilbert C., ed. *Working: Its Meaning and Its Limits*. Notre Dame, IN: University of Notre Dame Press, 2000.

Melville, Herman. "Bartleby, the Scrivener" [1853]. In *Pierre, Israel Potter, The Piazza Tales, Uncollected Prose, Billy Budd*, edited by Harrison Hayford. New York: Library of America, 1984.

——. "Hawthorne and His Mosses." In *Moby-Dick, Billy Budd, and Other Writings*. New York: Library of America, 2000.

——. *Moby-Dick* [1851]. Ibid.

——. *Omoo: A Narrative of Adventures in the South Seas* [1847]. In *Typee, Omoo, Mardi*, edited by G. Thomas Tanselle. New York: Library of America, 1982.

——. *Pierre, or, The Ambiguities* [1852]. In *Pierre, Israel Potter, The Piazza Tales, Uncollected Prose, Billy Budd*, edited by Harrison Hayford. New York: Library of America, 1984.

——. *Typee: A Peep at Polynesian Life* [1846]. In *Typee, Omoo, Mardi*, edited by G. Thomas Tanselle. New York: Library of America, 1982.

Mergendahl, Charles. *It's Only Temporary*. New York: Doubleday, 1950.

Meyer, Marc. *Whywork.com*. Harry de Jur Playhouse, New York. August 18–27, 2000.

Mill, John Stuart. *Principles of Political Economy, with Some of Their Applications to Philosophy* [1848]. New York: A. M. Kelly, 1965.

Miller, Cyndee. "Marketing to the Disillusioned: Twentysomethings Aren't for Things, They're Against Them." *Marketing News* (July 6, 1992): 6.

Miller, Edwin Haviland. *Salem Is My Dwelling Place: A Life of Nathaniel Hawthorne*. Iowa City: University of Iowa Press, 1991.

Miller, John. *Alexander Hamilton: Portrait in Paradox*. New York: Harper and Row, 1959.

Miller, M. David. *Principles and a Philosophy for Vocational Education.* Columbus, OH: Ohio State University Press, 1985.

Miller, W. F. "Emerging Technologies and Their Implications for America." *USA Today* 115 (November 1986): 60.

Mills, C. Wright. *White Collar: The American Middle Classes.* New York: Oxford University Press, 1951.

Mitchell, Langdon. *Understanding America.* New York: Doran, 1927.

Mitchell, S. Weir. *Doctor and Patient.* Philadelphia: Lippincott, 1888.

———. *Fat and Blood and How to Make Them.* Philadelphia: Lippincott, 1878.

Moffitt, Robert A., and Michele Ver Ploeg, eds. *Evaluating Welfare Reform in an Era of Transition.* Washington, D.C.: National Academy Press, 2001.

Montgomery, Maureen E. *Displaying Women: Spectacles of Leisure in Edith Wharton's New York.* New York: Routledge, 1998.

Moore, Tim. *Frost on My Moustache: The Arctic Exploits of a Lord and a Loafer.* New York: St. Martin's, 2001.

Moravsky, M. "Learn While Loafing." *Education Review* 69 (May 1925): 240.

More, Thomas. *Utopia* [1516]. New York: Penguin, 2003.

Morehouse, H. F. "The 'Work Ethic' and 'Leisure' Activity: The Hot Rod in Post-War America." In *The Historical Meanings of Work,* edited by Patrick Joyce. New York: Cambridge University Press, 1987.

Morgan, Edmund S. "The Labor Problem at Jamestown, 1607–1618." *American Historical Review* 76.3 (June 1971): 595.

Morris, Richard Brandon. *Government and Labor in Early America.* New York: Columbia University Press, 1946.

Muir, John. *Our National Parks.* Boston: Houghton Mifflin, 1901.

Mungo, Raymond. *Total Loss Farm: A Year in the Life.* New York: Dutton, 1970.

Munro, William B. "Is the Slacker Vote a Menace?" *National Municipal Review* 17.2 (February 1928): 80.

Muro, Mark. "Complaints of a New Generation; 'Baby Busters' Resent Life in Boomers' Debris." *Boston Globe* (November 10, 1991): 1.

———. "The Nonvoice of a Nongeneration." *Boston Globe* (August 12, 1992): 39.

Murolo, Priscilla, and A. B. Chitty. *From the Folks That Brought You the Weekend: A Short Illustrated History of Labor in the United States.* New York: New Press, 2001.

Murphy, James Bernard. *The Moral Economy of Labor: Aristotelian Themes in Economic Theory.* New Haven: Yale University Press, 1993.

Murphy, Joseph. "The Loafer and the Loaf-Buyer: Whitman, Franklin, and Urban Space." *Modern Language Studies* 28.2 (1998): 41.

Murray, Charles. *Losing Ground: American Social Policy.* New York: Basic Books, 1984.

Myerson, Abraham. *The Nervous Housewife.* Boston: Little, Brown, 1920.

Nabokov, Vladimir. *Lolita* [1955]. In *Novels, 1955–1962*. New York: Library of America, 1996.

———. *Pnin* [1957]. Ibid.

Naisbitt, John. *Megatrends: Ten New Directions Transforming Our Lives*. New York: Warner, 1984.

Naisbitt, John, and Patricia Aburdene. *Megatrends 2000*. New York: Morrow, 1990.

Naito, Yuko. "Part-Timers Reshaping Japan's Work Ethic: When Are You Going to Get a Real Job and Settle Down?" *Japan Times* (September 14, 2000). http://www.japantimes.co.jp.

National Defence Council for Victims of Karoshi. *Karoshi: When the Corporate Warrior Dies*. Tokyo: Mado Sha, 1991.

Neal, Joseph C. "Street Corner Loungers." *United States Democratic Review* 13.62 (August 1843): 113.

Nearing, Helen, and Scott Nearing. *Living the Good Life: How to Live Sanely and Simply in a Troubled World* [1954]. New York: Schocken Books, 1970.

Nelson, Blake. *Exile*. New York: Scribner, 1997.

Nersesian, Arthur. *The Fuck-Up* [1991]. New York: MTV, 1999.

Niall, Ian. *The Idler's Companion*. London: Heinemann, 1978.

Nicholson, Joy. *The Tribes of Palos Verdes*. New York: St. Martin's, 1997.

Nishiyama, Katsuo, and Jeffrey V. Johnson. "Karoshi—Death from Overwork." http://www.workhealth.org/whatsnews/lpkarosh.html.

Novak, Michael. *Business as a Calling: Work and the Examined Life*. New York: Free Press, 1996.

Oates, Wayne. *Confessions of a Workaholic*. New York: World Publishing, 1971.

———. *Workaholics, Make Laziness Work for You*. Garden City, NY: Doubleday, 1978.

Oestreicher, Richard. "The Two Souls of American Democracy." In *The Social Construction of Democracy, 1870–1990*, edited by George R. Andrews and Herrick Chapman. New York: New York University Press, 1995.

O'Toole, James, ed. *Work and the Quality of Life*. Cambridge, MA: MIT Press, 1974.

Overstreet, H. A. *A Guide to Civilized Loafing*. New York: Norton, 1934.

Overton, Mark. *Agricultural Revolution in England: The Transformation of the Agrarian Economy, 1500–1850*. New York: Cambridge University Press, 1996.

Packard, Vance. *The Hidden Persuaders*. New York: D. McKay, 1957.

———. *The Pyramid Climbers*. New York: McGraw-Hill 1962.

———. *The Status Seekers: An Exploration of Class Behavior in America and the Hidden Barriers that Affect You, Your Community, Your Future*. New York: D. McKay, 1959.

——. *The Waste Makers*. New York: D. McKay, 1960.

Page, Ellen Welles. "A Flapper's Appeal to Parents." *Outlook* (December 6, 1922): 607.

Pahl, R. E., ed. *On Work: Historical, Comparative and Theoretical Approaches*. New York: Blackwell, 1988.

Parker, Carleton. *The Casual Laborer and Other Essays*. New York: Harcourt, Brace and Howe, 1920.

Parker, Dorothy. *The Portable Dorothy Parker*. Edited by Brendan Gill. New York: Penguin, 1976.

Parker, Stanley. *The Future of Work and Leisure*. London: MacGibbon and Kee, 1977.

Parry, Albert. *Garrets and Pretenders: A History of Bohemianism*. New York: Covici Friede, 1933.

Pascarella, Perry. *The New Achievers: Creating a Modern Work Ethic*. New York: Free Press, 1984.

Pemberton, Max. *The Footsteps of a Throne; Being the Story of an Idler, and of His Work; and of What He Did in Moscow in the House of Exile*. New York: D. Appleton, 1900.

Percival, Olive. *Mexico City: An Idler's Note-book*. Chicago: H. S. Stone, 1901.

Perls, Fritz, and Ralph Hefferline. *Gestalt Therapy: Excitement and Growth in the Human Personality*. New York: Julian, 1951.

Peter, Laurence J. *The Peter Principle: Why Things Always Go Wrong*. New York: William Morrow, 1969.

Pfister, Joel. *Individualism Incorporated: Indians and the Multicultural Modern*. Durham: Duke University Press, 2004.

Phillips, Kevin P. *American Dynasty: Aristocracy, Fortune, and the Politics of Deceit in the House of Bush*. New York: Viking, 2004.

Philonous [pseud.], "A Slacker's Apology." *New Republic* 21.261 (December 3, 1919): 19.

Pierson, John. *Spike, Mike, Slackers and Dykes: A Guided Tour Across a Decade of American Independent Cinema*. New York: Miramax Books/ Hyperion, 1995.

Piven, Frances Fox, Joan Acker, Margaret Hallock, and Sandra Morgen, eds. *Work, Welfare and Politics: Confronting Poverty in the Wake of Welfare Reform*. Eugene, OR: University of Oregon Press, 2002.

Plato. *The Republic of Plato*. Translated by Allan Bloom. New York: Basic Books, 1991.

Pollard, Sidney. *Typology of Industrialization Processes in the Nineteenth Century*. New York: Harwood, 1990.

Porat, M. U. *The Information Economy: Definition and Measurement*. Washington, D.C.: U.S. Department of Commerce, 1977.

Pound, Ezra. *Poems and Translations*. New York: Library of America, 2003.

Procter, Ian, and Maureen Padfield. "Work Orientations and Women's Work: A Critique of Hakim's Theory of the Heterogeneity of Women." *Gender, Work and Organization* 6.3 (July 1999): 152.

Proudhon, Pierre-Joseph. *The Utility of the Celebration of Sunday* [1839]. In *Selected Writings*, edited by Stewart Edwards. Translated by Elizabeth Fraser. Garden City, NY: Anchor, 1969.

——. *What Is Property?* [1840]. Translated by Benjamin R. Tucker. http://www.marxists.org/reference/subject/economics/proudhon/property/index.htm.

Pryor, Frederic L., and David L. Schaffer. *Who's Not Working and Why: Employment, Cognitive Skills, Wages, and the Changing U.S. Labor Market.* New York: Cambridge University Press, 1999.

Quintanilla, S., Antonio Ruiz, and George W. England. *How Working Is Defined: Structure and Stability.* Ithaca, NY: Center for Advanced Human Resource Studies, 1994.

Rabinbach, Anson. *The Human Motor: Energy, Fatigue, and the Origins of Modernity.* New York: Basic Books, 1990.

Ram Dass, Baba. *Be Here Now.* New York: Crown, 1971.

Rand, Ayn. *The Fountainhead* [1943]. New York: New American Library, 1971.

ReclaimingtheSouth.com. http://www.mindspring.com/~dennisw/debates/sldebate/part4.htm.

Rector, Robert. "Welfare Critics Were Wrong." *National Review* (March 10, 2003). http://www.nationalreview.com/comment/comment-rector031003.asp.

Reich, Charles. *The Greening of America: How the Youth Revolution Is Trying to Make America Livable.* New York: Random House, 1970.

Reich, Robert B. *The Future of Success.* New York: Knopf, 2001.

Reitman, Ben. *Sister of the Road: The Autobiography of Box-car Bertha as Told to Dr. Ben L. Reitman.* New York: Macaulay, 1937.

Reitz, John. "Walter Whitman, Sr." In *Walt Whitman: An Encyclopedia*, edited by J. R. LeMaster and Donald D. Kummings. New York: Garland, 1998.

Resnick, Rachel. *Go West Young Fucked-Up Chick.* New York: St. Martin's, 1999.

Reynolds, David S. *Beneath the American Renaissance: The Subversive Imagination in the Age of Emerson and Melville.* Cambridge, MA: Harvard University Press, 1989.

——. *Walt Whitman's America: A Cultural Biography.* New York: Vintage, 1996.

Richardson, Elliott, et al. *Work in America: Report of a Special Task Force to the Secretary of Health, Education, and Welfare.* Cambridge, MA: MIT Press, 1973.

Richardson, Joanna. *The Bohemians.* London: Macmillan, 1969.

Riesman, David, et al. [1950]. *The Lonely Crowd: A Study of the Changing American Character*. New Haven: Yale University Press, 1961.

Rifkin, Jeremy. "After Work." *Utne Reader*. http://hometown.aol.com/genxcoal/info-20.htm.

——. *The End of Work: The Decline of the Global Labor Force and the Dawn of the Post-Market Era*. New York: G. P. Putnam's Sons, 1995.

Rigal, Laura. *The American Manufactory: Art Labor, and the World of Things in the Early Republic*. Princeton, NJ: Princeton University Press, 1998.

Riis, Jacob A. *How the Other Half Lives: Studies Among the Tenements of New York* [1890]. New York: Dover, 1971.

——. *The Making of an American*. New York: Macmillan, 1901.

Rimer, Sara. "A Self-Described Slacker Decides He's Ready to Be a Soldier." *New York Times* (November 12, 2001): A8.

Rinehart, James. *Just Another Car Factory? Lean Production and Its Discontents*. Ithaca, NY: ILR Press, 1997.

Roberts, Bryan, Ruth Finnegan, and Duncan Gallie, eds. *New Approaches to Economic Life: Economic Restructuring, Unemployment and the Social Division of Labour*. Manchester, UK: Manchester University Press, 1984.

Roberts, Kenneth Lewis. *Florida Loafing: An Investigation into the Peculiar State of Affairs Which Leads Residents of 47 States to Encourage Spanish Architecture in the 48th*. Indianapolis: Bobbs-Merrill, 1925.

Roberts, Morley. *The Idlers*. Boston: L. C. Page, 1905.

Robins, Stephen. *The Importance of Being Idle*. London: Prion, 2000.

Robinson, Bryan E. "A Typology of Workaholics with Implications for Counselors." *Journal of Addictions and Offender Counseling* 21.1 (October 2000): 34.

Robinson, Joe. *Work to Live: The Guide to Getting a Life*. New York: Perigee, 2003.

Rockman, Seth, ed. *Welfare Reform in the Early Republic: A Brief Documentary History*. New York: Bedford/St. Martin's, 2003.

Rodgers, Daniel T. *The Work Ethic in Industrial America, 1850–1920*. Chicago: University of Chicago Press, 1978.

Roediger, David. " 'Not Only the Ruling Classes to Overcome, but Also the So-Called Mob': Class, Skill and Community in the St. Louis General Strike of 1877." *Journal of Social History* 19 (1985–86): 214.

Rogers, Cameron. *The Magnificent Idler: The Story of Walt Whitman*. Garden City, NY: Doubleday, Page, 1926.

Rose, Michael. *Reworking the Work Ethic: Economic Values and Social-Cultural Politics*. New York: Schocken Books, 1985.

Rosenzweig, Roy. *Eight Hours for What We Will*. New York: Cambridge University Press, 1983.

Ross, Andrew. *No-Collar: The Humane Workplace and Its Hidden Costs*. New York: Basic Books, 2003.

Ross, Marilyn Heimberg. *Creative Loafing: A Shoestring Guide to New Leisure Fun*. San Diego: Communication Creativity, 1978.

Ross, Steven J. *Workers on the Edge: Work, Leisure, and Politics in Industrializing Cincinnati, 1830–1890*. New York: Columbia University Press, 1985.

Rothman, Robert A. *Working: Sociological Perspectives*. Upper Saddle River, NJ: Prentice Hall, 1998.

Rulli, Jamie. "Former Slacker Explains the Art of Loafing." http://home town.aol.com/genxcoal/info-04.htm.

Russell, Bertrand. *Collected Papers*. 34 vols. Various publishers and editors.

——. "In Praise of Idleness." *Harper's Magazine* 165 (October 1932): 552.

Sachs, William, and Ari Hoogenboom. *The Enterprising Colonials: Society on the Eve of the Revolution*. Chicago: Argonaut, 1965.

Saint Benedict. *Rule of St. Benedict* [530]. New York: Vintage, 1998.

Salinger, J. D. *The Catcher in the Rye* [1951]. Boston: Little, Brown, 1991.

Salmansohn, Karen. *How to Change Your Entire Life by Doing Absolutely Nothing: 10 Do-Nothing Relaxation Exercises to Calm You Down Quickly So You Can Speed Forward Faster*. New York: Simon and Schuster, 2003.

Saltus, Edgar. *Oscar Wilde: An Idler's Impression*. Chicago: Brothers of the Book, 1917.

——. *The Pace that Kills*. Chicago: Belford, Clarke, 1889.

——. *The Philosophy of Disenchantment*. Boston: Houghton Mifflin, 1885.

Sandburg, Carl. *The American Songbag*. New York: Harcourt, Brace, 1927.

Santayana, George. *Character and Opinion in the United States*. New York: Scribner, 1920.

——. *The Idler and His Works, and Other Essays*. New York: G. Braziller, 1957.

Sayers, Dorothy L. "Why Work?" In *Creed or Chaos?* London: Methuen, 1942.

Scherer, John. *Work and the Human Spirit*. Spokane, WA: JS&A, 1993.

Schesser, Roy. *Loafing with the Earth*. Siloam Springs, AR: Bar D Press, 1940.

Schleuning, Neala. *Idle Hands and Empty Hearts: Work and Freedom in the United States*. New York: Bergin and Garvey, 1990.

Schneider, Barbara, and David Stevenson. *The Ambitious Generation: America's Teenagers, Motivated but Directionless*. New Haven: Yale University Press, 1999.

Schor, Juliet. *The Overworked American: The Unexpected Decline of Leisure*. New York: Basic Books, 1992.

Schorr, Alvin Louis. *Welfare Reform: Failure and Remedies*. Westport, CT: Praeger, 2001.

Schroeder, Doris. *Work Incentives and Welfare Provision: The 'Pathological' Theory of Unemployment*. Brookfield, VT: Ashgate, 2000.

Schumaker, E. F. *Small Is Beautiful: Economics As If People Mattered*. New York: Harper and Row, 1973.

Scott, Walter. *Waverly* [1814]. New York: Penguin, 1981.

Segalen, Martine. *Love and Power in the Peasant Family: Rural France in the Nineteenth Century*. Oxford: Blackwell, 1983.

Seigel, Jerrold. *Bohemian Paris*. New York: Viking, 1986.

Sengoku, Tamotsu. *Willing Workers: The Work Ethics in Japan, England, and the United States*. Translated by Koichi Ezaki and Yuko Ezaki. Westport, CT: Quorum Books, 1985.

Sheehy, Gail "The Accidental Candidate." *Vanity Fair* (October 2000), http://gailsheehy.com/Politics/polimain_bush3.html.

Sheehy, J. W. "New Work Ethic is Frightening." *Personnel Journal* 69.6 (1990): 28.

Shore, Carrie L. *A Caustic Review of Familiar Characters, including the Flirt . . . the Gent . . . the Idler . . . the Humbug . . .* Chicago: Rhodes and McClure, 1882.

Shteyngart, Gary. *The Russian Debutante's Handbook*. New York: Riverhead, 2002.

Sidani, Yusuf Munir, and William L. Gardner. "Work Values Among Lebanese Workers." *Journal of Social Psychology* 140.5 (October 2000): 597.

Sinclair, Andrew. *The Hallelujah Bum*. London: Faber and Faber, 1963. Reprinted as *The Paradise Bum*. New York: Atheneum, 1963.

Sinclair, Upton. *The Jungle* [1906]. New York: Signet, 1960.

Sircello, Guy. *Mind and Art: An Essay on the Varieties of Expression*. Princeton: Princeton University Press, 1972.

Slacker's Creed. http://www.arkay.net/dcm/slacker.html.

SlackersDomain. http://angelfire.com/ct/SlackersDomain.

Slackers, Inc. http://www.slackersinc.com.

SlackersMeetup.com.http://www.slackers.meetup.com.

Slater, Philip. *The Pursuit of Loneliness*. Boston: Beacon, 1970.

Slocum, Chuck. "A Talk with Chuck Slocum." www.screenwriter.com/insider/CSlocum.html.

Smiles, Samuel. *Self-Help* [1859]. New York: Oxford University Press, 2002.

Smith, Albert Richard. *The Natural History of the Idler upon Town*. London: D. Bogue, 1848.

Smith, Aron. "Ah, to Be Young, Japanese and a Schnorrer." *Japan Times* (May 28, 2001). http://user.ecc.u-tokyo.ac.jp/~g040794/thesis.html.

Smith, Russell. *How Insensitive* [1994]. Toronto: Anchor Canada, 2002.

Smithson, Janet, and Suzan Lewis. "Is Job Insecurity Changing the Psychological Contract?" *Personnel Review* 29.5–6 (2000): 680.

Spiegelman, Willard. *Majestic Indolence: English Romantic Poetry and the Work of Art*. New York: Oxford University Press, 1995.

Stang, Ivan. *The Book of the SubGenius*. New York: McGraw-Hill, 1983.

Stearns, Peter N. *The Industrial Revolution in World History*. 2nd ed. Boulder, CO: Westview, 1998.

Steinbeck, John. *The Grapes of Wrath* [1939]. New York: Penguin, 2002.

Stephens, Carlene E. *On Time: How Americans Learned to Live by the Clock*. Boston: Bulfinch, 2002.

Stevenson, Robert Louis. "An Apology for Idlers" [1877]. In *Virginibus Puerisque and Other Papers*. McLean, VA: IndyPublish.com, 2002.

——. *The Black Arrow* [1888]. In *Novels*. New York: Barnes and Noble, 1992.

——. *An Inland Voyage* [1878]. New York: AMS, 1974.

——. *Kidnapped* [1886]. New York: Penguin, 1995.

——. *The Silverado Squatters* [1883]. San Francisco: Arion, 1996.

——. *The Strange Case of Dr. Jekyll and Mr. Hyde* [1886]. In *Novels*. New York: Barnes and Noble, 1992.

——. *Travels with a Donkey in the Cévennes* [1879]. New York: AMS, 1974.

——. *Treasure Island* [1883]. In *Novels*. New York: Barnes and Noble, 1992.

Stoddard, Charles Coleman. *Kimono Ballades; Some Cheerful Rhymes for Loafing Times*. New York: Calkins, 1908.

Stowe, Harriet Beecher. *Uncle Tom's Cabin* [1852]. New York: Oxford University Press, 2002.

Strauss, William, and Neil Howe. *Generations* [1991]. New York: Perennial, 1992.

Strahorn, Robert E. *To the Rockies and Beyond, or, A Summer on the Union Pacific Railroad and Branches: Saunterings in the Popular Health, Pleasure, and Hunting Resorts of Nebraska, Dakota, Wyoming, Colorado, Utah, Idaho, Oregon, Washington, and Montana*. Omaha: New West Publishing Company, 1879.

Super, D. E. "The Relative Importance of Work: Models and Measures for Meaningful Data." *Counseling Psychologist* 10.4 (1982): 95.

Swados, Harvey. "The Myth of the Happy Worker." In *A Radical's America*. Boston: Atlantic-Little, Brown, 1962.

——. "A Note on the Worker's Cultural Degradation" [1958]. *American Socialist*. http://www.marxists.org/history/etol/newspape/amersocialist/amersoc_5807.htm.

Swanberg, W. A. *Theodore Dreiser*. New York: Scribner, 1965.

Szanto, George H. *Not Working*. New York: St. Martin's, 1982.

Taft, Philip A. "The Federal Trials of the IWW." *Labor History* 3 (Winter 1962): 42.

Tait, John Robinson. *Dolce Far Niente*. Philadelphia: Parry and McMillan, 1859.

Takahashi, Hiroyuki, and Jeanette Voss. " 'Parasite Singles': A Uniquely Japanese Phenomenon?" *Japan Economic Report* 31 (August 11, 2000).

Taylor, Jeremy. *The Rule and Exercise of Holy Living*. London: Bell and Daldy, 1857.

Terkel, Studs. *Working: People Talk About What They Do All Day and How They Feel About What They Do*. New York: Pantheon, 1974.

Tester, Keith, ed. *The Flâneur*. London and New York: Routledge, 1994.

Thirsk, Joan, et al., eds. *The Agrarian History of England and Wales*. New York: Cambridge University Press, 1967–91.

Thomas, Keith, ed. *The Oxford Book of Work*. New York: Oxford University Press, 1999.

Thompson, E. P. "Time, Work-Discipline and Industrial Capitalism." *Past and Present* 38 (1967): 56.

Thompson, Harold William. *A Scottish Man of Feeling: Some Account of Henry Mackenzie, Esq., of Edinburgh, and of the Golden Age of Burns and Scott*. New York: Oxford University Press, 1931.

Thompson, Hunter. *Fear and Loathing in Las Vegas: A Savage Journey into the Heart of the American Dream*. New York: Random House, 1971.

Thompson, Paul. *The Nature of Work: An Introduction to Debates on the Labour Process*. London: Macmillan, 1983.

Thomson, James. *The Castle of Indolence* [1748]. New York: Oxford University Press, 1986.

Thoreau, Henry David. "Life Without Principle" [1863]. In *The Portable Thoreau*, edited by Carl Bode. New York: Penguin, 1977.

——. *Walden* [1854]. Ibid.

Tilgher, Adriano. *Homo Faber: Work Through the Ages*. Translated by D. C. Fisher. New York: Harcourt Brace, 1930.

Tocqueville, Alexis de. *Democracy in America* [1835]. New York: Signet, 2001.

Toffler, Alvin. *Future Shock*. New York: Random House, 1970.

——. *The Third Wave*. New York: Bantam, 1980.

Tomc, Sandra. "An Idle Industry: Nathaniel Parker Willis and the Workings of Literary Leisure." *American Quarterly* 49.4 (December 1997): 780.

Towne, Charles Hanson. *Loafing Down Long Island*. New York: Century, 1921.

Townsend, Robert. *Up the Organization: How to Stop the Corporation from Stifling People and Strangling Profits*. New York: Knopf, 1970.

Tulgan, Bruce. *Managing Generation X: How to Bring Out the Best in Young Talent* [1995]. New York: Norton, 2000.

Tull, Jethro. *The New Horse Houghing Husbandry: or, an Essay on the Principles of Tillage and Vegetation* [1731]. London: W. Cobbett, 1829.

Turner, Michael E., J. V. Beckett, and Bethanie Afton. *Farm Production in England, 1700–1914*. Oxford University Press, 2001.

Twain, Mark. *The Adventures of Tom Sawyer* [1876]. Berkeley: University of California Press, 2001.

——. *The Celebrated Jumping Frog of Calaveras County, and Other Sketches* [1867]. New York: Oxford University Press, 1996.

——. *A Connecticut Yankee in King Arthur's Court* [1889]. Berkeley: University of California Press, 1979.

——. *Huckleberry Finn* [1885]. Berkeley: University of California Press, 2001.

——. *The Prince and the Pauper* [1882]. Berkeley: University of California Press, 1979.

——. *The Tragedy of Pudd'nhead Wilson* [1894]. New York: Pocket, 2004.

——, and Charles Dudley Warner. *The Gilded Age: A Tale of Today* [1873]. New York: Oxford University Press, 1996.

Twelve Southerners. *I'll Take My Stand: The South and the Agrarian Tradition*. New York: Harper, 1930.

Tyler, Royall. *The Contrast* [1787]. McLean, VA: IndyPublish.com, 2003.

United Nations Universal Declaration of Human Rights. http://www.un.org/overview/rights.html.

Updike, John. *The Poorhouse Fair* [1959]. New York: Ballantine, 2004.

——. *Rabbit, Run* [1960]. New York: Ballantine, 1996.

U.S. Congress. *Personal Responsibility and Work Opportunity Reconciliation Act of 1996*. www.access.gpo.gov/congress/wm015.txt.

Van Vechten, Carl. *Spider Boy: A Scenario for a Moving Picture*. New York: Knopf, 1928.

Veblen, Thorstein. *The Instinct of Workmanship: And the State of Industrial Arts*. New York: Macmillan, 1914.

——. *The Theory of the Leisure Class* [1899]. New York: Penguin, 1979.

Vienne, Véronique. *The Art of Doing Nothing*. New York: Potter, 1998.

Viereck, Peter. "The Slacker Apologizes." *Horizon* (London) 19:112 (April 1949): 234.

Vingerhoets, Ad J.J.M.; Maaike Van Huijgevoort; and Guus L. Van Heck. "'Leisure Sickness': A Pilot-Study on its Prevalence, Phenomenology, and Background." *Psychotherapy and Psychosomatics* 71 (2002): 311.

Wagner, Gillian. *Children of the Empire*. London: Weidenfield and Nicolson, 1982.

Wallman, Sandra, ed. *Social Anthropology of Work*. New York: Academic Press, 1979.

Walt Whitman Archive. http://www.iath.virginia.edu/whitman.

Wang, Gabe T. *A Comparative Study of Extrinsic and Intrinsic Work Values of Employees in the United States and Japan*. Lewiston, NY: Edwin Mellen, 1996.

Warner, Charles Dudley. *Saunterings*. Boston: Houghton Mifflin, 1872.

Wasserstein, Wendy. *Sloth*. New York: Oxford University Press, 2005.

Wattenberg, B. J. *The Good News Is the Bad News Is Wrong*. New York: Simon and Schuster, 1984.

Weaver, Charles N. "Work Attitudes of Asian Americans." *North American Journal of Psychology* 2.2 (2000): 209.

———. "Work Attitudes of Mexican Americans." *Hispanic Journal of Behavioral Sciences* 22.3 (August 2000): 275.

Weber, Max. *The Protestant Ethic and the Spirit of Capitalism*. Translated by Talcott Parsons [1905]. New York: Scribner, 1958.

Weil, Alan, and Kenneth Finegold, eds. *Welfare Reform: The Next Act*. Washington, D.C.: Urban Institute, 2002.

Weinberg, Meyer. *A Short History of American Capitalism*. Gloucester, MA: New History Press, 2002.

Wells, H. G. *The History of Mr. Polly*. New York: Duffield, 1909.

Wertham, Fredric. *Seduction of the Innocent*. New York: Rinehart, 1954.

Wharton, Amy S. *Working in America: Continuity, Conflict, and Change*. Boston: McGraw-Hill, 2002.

Wharton, Edith. *The Age of Innocence* [1920]. New York: Modern Library, 1999.

Wheen, Francis. *Karl Marx: A Life*. New York: Norton, 2001.

Whipp, Richard. " 'A Time to Every Purpose': An Essay on Time and Work." In *The Historical Meanings of Work*, edited by Patrick Joyce. New York: Cambridge University Press, 1987.

Whipple, Edwin P. "Loafing and Laboring." *North American Review* 153.416 (July 1861): 32.

White, Michael Reginald Maurice. *Working Hours: Assessing the Potential for Reduction*. Geneva: International Labour Office, 1987.

Whitman, Walt. Review of *Omoo*. *Brooklyn Daily Eagle*. http://www .melville.org/hmomoo.htm.

———. "Song of Myself" [1850]. In *The Portable Walt Whitman*, edited by Michael Warner. New York: Penguin, 2003.

———. "A Song for Occupations" [1855]. Ibid.

———. *Specimen Days* [1882]. In *The Portable Walt Whitman*, edited by Mark Van Doren and Malcolm Cowley. Harmondsworth, NY: Penguin, 1977.

Whyte, William H. *The Organization Man*. New York: Simon and Schuster, 1956.

Wiener, Martin J. *English Culture and the Decline of the Industrial Spirit, 1850–1980*. New York: Cambridge University Press, 2004.

Wigginton, Elliot, ed. *The Foxfire Book: Hog Dressing, Log Cabin Building, Mountain Crafts and Foods, Planting by the Signs, Snake Lore, Hunting Tales, Faith Healing, Moonshining*. Garden City, NY: Doubleday, 1972.

Wikoff, Henry. *The Reminiscences of an Idler*. New York: Fords, Howard, and Hulbert, 1880.

Wilde, Oscar. *The Critic as Artist* [1891]. In *The Portable Oscar Wilde*, edited by Stanley Weintraub and Richard Aldington. New York: Viking, 1981.

———. *An Ideal Husband* [1895]. In *Lady Windermere's Fan; Salome; A Woman of No Importance; An Ideal Husband; The Importance of Being Earnest*, edited by Peter Raby. New York: Oxford, 1995.

———. *Lady Windermere's Fan* [1891]. Ibid.

———. *The Picture of Dorian Gray* [1891]. New York: Modern Library, 1998.

———. *Salome* [1894]. In *Lady Windermere's Fan; Salome; A Woman of No Importance; An Ideal Husband; The Importance of Being Earnest*, edited by Peter Raby. New York: Oxford, 1995.

———. "The Soul of Man Under Socialism" [1891]. In *The Portable Oscar Wilde*, edited by Stanley Weintraub and Richard Aldington. New York, Viking, 1981.

———. "The True Function and Value of Criticism: With Some Remarks on the Importance of Doing Nothing" [1890]. Ibid.

Wiley, Hugh. "Sweat or Die!" *Saturday Evening Post* (April 10, 1920): 31.

Willard, Josiah Flynt. *My Life*. New York: The Outing Publishing Company, 1908.

———. *Tramping with Tramps: Stories and Studies of the Vagabond Life*. New York: The Century Company, 1899.

Williamson, Tom. *The Transformation of Rural England: Farming and the Landscape, 1700–1870*. Exeter, UK: Exeter University Press, 2002.

Willis, Paul E. *Learning to Labour: How Working Class Kids Get Working Class Jobs*. Farnborough, UK: Saxon House, 1978.

Wilson, Sloan. *The Man in the Gray Flannel Suit*. New York: Simon and Schuster, 1955.

Wilson, William Julius. *When Work Disappears: The World of the New Urban Poor*. New York: Knopf, 1999.

Wolfe, Tom. *The Electric Kool-Aid Acid Test*. New York: Farrar, Straus and Giroux, 1968.

———. *The Pump House Gang*. New York: Farrar, Straus and Giroux, 1968.

Wood, Gordon S. *The Americanization of Benjamin Franklin*. New York: Penguin, 2004.

Wordsworth, William. *The Prelude* [1799, 1805, 1850]. New York: Norton, 1978.

Wurtzel, Elizabeth. *Prozac Nation: Young and Depressed in America*. Boston: Houghton Mifflin, 1994.

Wylie, Elinor. *Jennifer Lorn* [1923]. In *Collected Prose of Elinor Wylie*. New York: Knopf, 1933.

Yankelovich, Daniel. *New Rules: Searching for Self-fulfillment in a World Turned Upside Down*. New York: Random House, 1981.

Yankelovich, Daniel, and Sidney Harman. *Starting with the People*. Boston: Houghton Mifflin, 1988.

Yankelovich, Daniel, and John Immerwahr. *Putting the Work Ethic to Work: A Public Agenda Report on Restoring America's Competitive Vitality*. New York: Public Agenda Foundation, 1983.

Yezierska, Anzia. *Bread Givers* [1925]. New York: Persea, 2003.

Yogananda, Paramajansa. *Autobiography of a Yogi*. New York: Philosophical Library, 1951.

Young, Arthur. *A Course of Experimental Agriculture* [1770]. Dublin: J. Ek-
    shaw, 1771.
Yousef, Darwish A. "Organizational Commitment as a Mediator of the Rela-
    tionship between Islamic Work Ethic and Attitudes toward Organiza-
    tional Change." *Human Relations* 53.4 (April 2000): 513.
Zelinski, Ernest J. *The Joy of Not Working: A Book for the Retired, Unem-
    ployed, and Overworked*. Berkeley, CA: Ten Speed Press, 1997.
Zemke, Ron, Claire Raines, and Bob Filipczak. *Generations at Work: Man-
    aging the Clash of Veterans, Boomers, Xers, and Nexters in Your Work-
    place*. New York: American Management Association, 2000.
Zimpel, Lloyd, ed. *Man Against Work*. Grand Rapids, MI: Eerdmans, 1974.

INDEX

Portland Community College